POLICY CHOICES FOR THE 1990s

Policy Choices for the 1990s

Bela Balassa
Professor Emeritus, Political Economy
The Johns Hopkins University, Baltimore

Foreword by W. Max Corden
Professor of International Economics
The Johns Hopkins University, Baltimore
School of Advanced International
Studies, Washington

A Personal Tribute by Sir Alan Walters

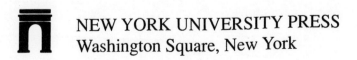

NEW YORK UNIVERSITY PRESS
Washington Square, New York

First published in the U.S.A. in 1993 by
NEW YORK UNIVERSITY PRESS
Washington Square,
New York, N. Y. 10003

Library of Congress Cataloging-in-Publication Data
Balassa, Bela A.
Policy choices for the 1990s / Bela Balassa.
p.   cm.
Includes bibliographical references and index.
ISBN 0–8147–1201–0 (cloth)
1. International economic relations.   2. Economic development.
3. International economic integration.   I. Title.
HF1359.B35   1993
337'.09'049—dc20   92–25487
                                             CIP

Printed in Hong Kong

In memoriam
Bela Balassa
(1928–91)

In memoriam
Bela Balassa
(1928–91)

Contents

Acknowledgements

Soon after Bela's death, I found the table of contents and outline of the present volume among his papers, most of which had been written during Stanley Fischer's Vice-Presidency at the World Bank. From among the many devoted friends and colleagues who had generously offered support and encouragement throughout his illness, I turned to a small group to help carry out Bela's final plans.

Jaime de Melo, who, along with André Sapir, was responsible for the Festschrift volume that gave Bela so much pleasure, was a constant source of guidance and support in arranging the many details of publication. Professor Max Corden graciously found time in his own busy schedule to write the professional overview to the volume. Sir Alan Walters, who earlier had written a spontaneous tribute to Bela, allowed his statement to serve as a personal overview. Professors Carl Christ and Bruce Hamilton provided ongoing counsel, reflecting the devotion of Bela's colleagues and students at the Department of Political Economy of Johns Hopkins University. The unswerving friendship of the late Professor Jean Bénard of the University of Paris I (Panthéon-Sorbonne) will not be forgotten. Meta de Coquereaumont lent her editorial expertise, Rebecca Sugui provided logistic support, and Gabor Balassa carefully checked out final editorial questions.

Acknowledgements for this volume would be incomplete without special mention of Bela's outstanding medical team – Doctors John C. Price, Benjamin S. Carson, and Ding-Jen Lee of Johns Hopkins Hospital in Baltimore, and Dr Louis Balla in Washington. Their medical skills, combined with wise and compassionate counsel, permitted Bela to continue his beloved work until the final day of his life. That was his ultimate wish.

Washington, DC   CAROL BALASSA

The following have kindly granted permission to reproduce copyright material appearing in this book:

Chad Evans Wyatt of Washington, DC, for the *frontispiece* photograph.

Elsevier Science Publishing Company, Inc., Amsterdam, The Netherlands, for Chapter 1 (H. Chenery and T.N. Srinivasan, editors, *Handbook of Development Economics*, volume II, 1989; pp. 1646–1689).

Westview Press, Boulder, Colorado, for Chapter 2 (P. Marer and A. Koves, editors, *Foreign Economic Liberalization: Transformations in Socialist and Market Economies*, 1991, pp. 71–80).

World Bank, Washington, DC

– for Chapter 3 (paper prepared as the background for Adjustment Lending: An Evaluation of Ten Years of Experience, Policy and Research Report no. 1, Country Economics Department, 1988)

– for Chapter 6 (Policy, Planning and Research Working Paper, no. 31, August 1988)

– for Chapter 9 (Policy, Research and External Affairs Working Paper, no. 439, May 1990)

– for Chapter 12 (Policy, Research and External Affairs Working Paper, no. 636, March 1991)

– for Chapter 14 (P.A. Messerlin and K.P. Sauvant, editors, *Uruguay Round: Services in the World Economy*, 1990).

Pakistan Development Review for Chapter 4 (Summer, 1989; 28; pp. 73–94).

Wayne University Press, Detroit, for Chapter 5 (M. Neumann and K.W. Roskamp, editors, *Public Finance and Performance of Enterprises*, 1989; pp. 417–33).

Transaction Publishers, New Jersey, for Chapter 7 (*Studies in Comparative International Development*, Winter 1990/91, 25, no. 4; pp. 56–70).

Banco Nazionale del Lavoro Quarterly Review, for Chapter 8 (March 1990; no. 172; pp. 101–18).

Geonomics Institute for International Economic Advancement, Middlebury, for Chapter 10 (M. Kraus and R.D. Leibowtiz, editors, *Perestroika and East-West Economic Relations: Prospects for the 1990s*, New York University Press, New York, 1990; pp. 105–21).

Journal of World Trade for Chapter 13 (April, 1989, vol. 23, no. 3; pp. 63–79).

Institute for International Economics, Washington, DC, for Chapter 15 (J.J. Schott, editor, *Free Trade Areas and US Trade Policy*, 1989; pp. 293–312).

Economia for Chapter 16 (January 1990; pp. 89–122).

Tocqueville Review for Chapter 17 (1988/89; pp. 191–203).

Commentaire for Chapter 18 (Summer 1991, no. 54; pp. 307–14).

American Economist for "My Life Philosophy" (Summer 1989; pp. 16–23).

Note: The reprinted materials appear as in the original publications except that minor alterations have been made to the style and presentation for the purpose of publishing this collection of readings in book form.

Foreword

Bela Balassa continued to have tremendous vitality to the end of his life. As he wrote himself in his life philosophy, he had the feeling of living on borrowed time during his last three years, 1988 to 1991, which is when he wrote the essays in this volume. Many of them have not been published before. They deal with some of the most important economic policy issues of that period and each one continues to be highly relevant. This is true even of Chapter 11, which analyzes *perestroika* and was presented at a conference in Budapest in November 1989. It is worth reading with hindsight: 1989 was already rather late, but if Mr Gorbachev and his fluctuating team had understood its arguments and acted upon them, history might have been rather different. A common theme runs right through most of the papers, namely, the virtues of the free market and the costs of distortions. There is also a common method, a highlight of which is the comprehensive presentation of the empirical material relevant to each issue. Bela Balassa did not believe in making judgments purely on the basis of abstract arguments.

In this collection, in my view, two papers stand out. The first is the survey from the *Handbook of Development Economics* of "Outward Orientation" (Chapter 1). For many years of his life Bela Balassa has been an analyst of the consequences of inward and outward orientation of developing countries, and on the basis of his work, indeed, an advocate. Perhaps this has been the single most prominent theme in his writings for 20 years. This is an impressive survey which reviews all the issues and digests a massive literature. It should really be a basic reference for all students of developing countries. The other outstanding paper is "A Quantitative Appraisal of Adjustment Lending" (Chapter 4), written for the World Bank in 1988 as a basis for its systematic assessments of structural adjustment lending.[1] This was a very influential paper; it shows how skillfully Bela Balassa could handle a difficult problem empirically.

To give a brief overview of the book, the first nine chapters all deal with policy issues for developing countries.

Chapter 1 is the *Handbook* chapter which gives strong support to the view that an outward orientation has yielded superior results for developing countries, leading to higher rates of growth than an inward-oriented development strategy. Among other things, this chapter reviews the complex issue of the relationship between export growth and the overall growth of economies. Chapter 2 follows up by comparing the policies applied and the effects of these policies in the Far Eastern and the Latin American newly-industrializing countries. The message that emerges is straightforward: outward-oriented policies have turned out to be superior. Chapter 3 is a brief and neat essay written for the World Bank that provides a conceptual framework for adjustment policies. Chapter 4 is the important paper on the quantitative appraisal of adjustment lending to which I have already referred.

Then follow four chapters that provide overviews of a number of important issues and give the reader valuable surveys of the relevant literature. Chapter 5 reviews the role of public enterprises in developing countries and issues of privatization. Chapter 6 deals with public finance: the effects of the budget deficit, the size of the public sector and public investment on economic development. Chapter 7 deals with financial liberalization, and Chapter 8 provides evidence on the effects of interest rates on savings. These four chapters together really make up a short introductory textbook on public finance and financial policy in developing countries.

Chapter 9 is a short, highly critical paper on indicative planning, something that was once very fashionable in developing countries – and earlier in Europe – but that has turned out to be pretty pointless, and done harm by diverting attention and human resources from more important matters.

Chapter 10 was written in 1988 and deals with the foreign economic ties of the former Soviet Union. It makes various proposals for improving Soviet trade, stressing the crucial need for domestic policies to change in order for foreign trade to be optimized. By now these ideas are familiar, but Bela Balassa was one of the first to write systematically along these lines, and these few pages are still useful as setting out the issues clearly. Chapter 11 is the critical evaluation of *perestroika* written in 1989 to which I have already referred, and Chapter 12 inquires into the possible future relationships of the economies of the reforming socialist countries.

Next we come to several chapters on international trade issues. Chapters 13 and 14 deal with the GATT multilateral trade negotiations, Chapter 13 with the negotiations on subsidies and countervailing action, and Chapter 14 with the effects that liberalization of trade in services may have on the United States. The European

Community enlargement progresses parallel with the GATT negotiations, and Chapter 15 considers its effects on nonmember countries and Chapter 16 its effects on the North African–Southern European region.

The final chapters deal with France. Chapter 17 considers the implications for France of the "1992" completion of the internal market. Chapter 18 reviews the economic policies of the Rocard Government. In Bela Balassa's judgment the record has been pretty good, though there is a particular need to reduce the budget deficit and generally raise national savings.

As a final reflection, certain features stand out in Bela Balassa's writings and his style.

The theory is implicit. He does not start off papers by laying out models, mathematical equations, and so on, and then proceed to empirical testing or policy discussion. This is a common approach these days, but gets rather boring to read when the models are obvious, at least to reasonably educated economists. His method presents no difficulties in these papers because the implicit models are quite orthodox and thus well-known. Most of the papers can be easily read by non-economists, though they will not usually be made aware of all the implicit assumptions.

The style is straightforward and unfussy, indeed low-key. The main facts and arguments are there, nothing is obscure, and there is no varnish. These papers are written for busy people. They want relevant facts, the main results from the literature, especially econometric evidence, and the main issues and arguments neatly laid out. Having read, or felt obliged to read, much that is varnished, fussy, pretentious, and sometimes obscure, this is all a relief. Of course, there is often a need for explicit theorizing when dealing with policy-relevant issues, particularly when the theory is new or in doubt. In certain papers, particularly the *Handbook* chapter (Chapter 1), I would have preferred to see some of it. But the Balassa style – so easy to read and yet hard to emulate – filled a great need, and one hopes that young economists, tempted by modern fashions, will recognize that this is the style that is often appropriate. For policy-oriented economists the world over, and especially for those concerned with developing countries, not least the staff of the World Bank, the sad passing away of this remarkable man is a great loss.

W. MAX CORDEN

Note

1. See Country Economics Department, the World Bank, *Adjustment Lending: An Evaluation of Ten Years of Experience*, Washington, DC, 1989; and Country Economics Department, the World Bank, *Adjustment Lending Policies for Sustainable Growth*, Washington, DC, 1990.

Bela Balassa's own paper was written in advance of the first of these two papers, soon after the decision to make an appraisal was made.

Bela Balassa: A Personal Tribute

In the 25 years or so that I have known Bela he continued to astonish me – right to the courageous end. There will never be another like him. God broke that mould 63 years ago.

I first heard of Bela in the mid-1960s when he produced his great paper on bias in national income comparisons. In 1966 we were both consultants at the World Bank, I a rather casual one but Bela was a resident economist. I was trying to sell my theories of pricing policies, while Bela had begun that long conversion of the Bank towards the great classical precepts of free trade and outward-oriented policies.

Bela reviewed my manuscripts on pricing policy with shrewdness and generosity. But through all his comments and conversations there was an abiding theme – Bela was a liberal in the grand European tradition from Adam Smith to Fritz Hayek. His teacher at Yale was the incomparable William Fellner, surely the most cultivated and subtle liberal economist of the postwar era.

But Bela's appreciation of a free and open society was no mere academic exercise. He had not only witnessed but had resisted the Russian invasion of Hungary in 1956 and, as one of the freedom fighters, he had fled for his life as well as his liberty. He knew firsthand the miseries of socialism and communism.

Through the 1960s and early 1970s, when the vicious cycle (of poverty), central planning, the promotion of state-owned heavy industry, and trade restrictions through high tariffs and low quotas were such fashionable concepts, Bela was never diverted from his vision of an open liberal society. Trade and commerce and all contacts with other nations were the only way in which Western civilization and material advance were spread to benefit all. Coming from a small country like Hungary, Bela was more subtly attuned to the liberating forces of international trade, commercial and cultural contacts.

Professionally Bela eschewed the massive complex modelling of economics that was then so fashionable and that then addled many an able brain. He forged his chain of argument in short sharp links. And while all the large complex models were suffocated by their pseudo sophistication, Bela's propositions on trade and development stand more firmly today than they ever did.

Whatever task Bela undertook, he discharged it with a determination and thoroughness that I could only admire – even envy. He was the terror of lazy-minded administrators. I recall when, elected to the Academic Council of Hopkins, he became convinced that tuition at Hopkins was far too low relative to alternative schools. For its own reasons the administration was opposed to a tuition hike. Bela advanced his case with a massive statistical analysis and a thoroughly argued and documented brief. Of course, he won the argument.

Nor was it only his work that brought forth this astonishing energy and organization. Bela and I shared a love for opera which we used to discuss on the frequent occasions that he accompanied me on the journey from Hopkins to Washington. Both of us collected opera videos with equal enthusiasm. But compared with my haphazard inventory Bela's collection was well-recorded and superbly organized. For the most part I, with only the tiniest twinge of conscience for being a free rider, was content to accept Bela's enthusiastic offer to lend me any items I wanted.

But Bela's generosity to me extended far beyond opera. He had the model life, I thought, for a policy economist – one foot in academe and one foot on the quarter-deck of the Bank. He encouraged me to join him at Hopkins and the Bank. Eventually in 1976 I did. That was an important turning-point in my life for various reasons. But Bela had an even bigger influence on me later. In early 1980 I was dithering over an invitation to return to London, from my agreeable Hopkins/Bank position, to become the economic adviser to Mrs Thatcher. I had all sorts of reservations which I aired to Bela. But with that magnificent finality of judgment Bela said: "Of course you must take it. It is your great opportunity." He was right. I realized this when I could collect my thoughts. All the niggling doubts and uncertainties were trivial compared with the opportunities. Bela's view had a profound effect on my decision. I told him later – indeed much later in 1989 – of the importance I placed on his advice. I believe he was pleased – truly he had every reason to be. He said that he knew I would go to London, but he had doubted whether I would return to Hopkins/Washington. Again, although I did return, Bela was nearer to the truth in his prediction.

Stories of Bela's fabulous ability to do three things at the same time abound. In a seminar he would simultaneously listen to the speaker and write a paper – and even, on occasion, engage in an intermittent *sotto voce* conversation (often with me). The really extraordinary thing was that he did all very well. His seminar comments and papers were all pithy and to the point. No one has really explained to me how Bela managed to do so many things so well at the same time. I think it was part of his genius which we, who lack such astonishing abilities, can only admire and never seek to emulate. The 27 books and 270 articles speak volumes! But Bela detested any waste of his time. He regarded his time as a precious wasting asset. How right he was! We had all hoped he would be with us for two or three more decades.

The loss is all the more poignant because, just as cancer struck, his beloved Hungary and all central Europe shook off the yoke of totalitarianism. Who better prepared and worthy to advise on this grand transition than Bela Balassa? He had the knowledge, the intellectual agility and the surety of fundamentals which can be gained only from long reflection and scholarship. Bela knew what would work and what would not – and indeed what was right and what was wrong. Although he made signal contributions (to the Hungarian Blue Ribbon Commission for example), the damned malignancy took its toll. His return to Budapest to receive all honours was a rare celebration of his incomparable will. Through all the pain and suffering he saw his ideas triumph. That is a lot.

Finally, in this immensely productive life as a professional economist *par excellence*, Bela also cherished a close and affectionate family. He always had time for Mara, Gabor and for Carol. When we talked about his children, a soft tenderness suffused those large brown eyes. He understood.

SIR ALAN WALTERS

Part I

Development Strategies

1 Outward Orientation*

INTRODUCTION

In the early postwar period, pessimistic predictions were made as to the prospects for the transmission of economic growth from developed to developing countries. These predictions were translated into policy recommendations for import protection and the recommendations were followed by a number of developing countries during the period.

The experience of subsequent years provided evidence on the inappropriateness of the predictions that represented a form of historical determinism as far as the exports of the developing countries are concerned. Rather, it became apparent that the country's own policies play a crucial role in affecting export expansion and the prospects for economic growth.

Broadly speaking, one may distinguish between outward-oriented and inward-oriented strategies, when the former provides similar incentives to sales in domestic and in foreign markets and the latter discriminates in favor of import substitution and against exports. With the manufacturing sector being protected, inward orientation also involves a bias against primary production that is not found under outward orientation.

The first section of this chapter examines the propositions that have been put forward in regard to the role of external conditions in regard to export expansion and economic growth in developing countries. The first part analyzes the trade–growth nexus; the next part reviews empirical evidence on trends in the terms of trade; and the final part provides an appraisal of proposals made for joint action on the part of the developing countries.

The second section of the chapter focuses on individual country experiences. It examines the effects of alternative policies on exports

* Originally published in the *Handbook of Development Economics*, volume II, edited by H. Chenery and T.N. Srinivasan, Elsevier Science Publishers B.V., 1989.

The author is indebted for valuable comments to Hollis Chenery, Stephen Lewis and T.N. Srinivasan. He alone is responsible for the contents of the chapter that should not be considered to reflect the views of the World Bank.

3

and economic growth, with further consideration given to their impact on employment and income distribution. The first part concerns the early postwar period (1945–60), the second part the period of rapid world economic growth (1960–73), and the third part the decade of external shocks (1973–83).

The topics covered in this chapter represent various facets of the outward orientation–inward orientation controversy. At the same time, it has been attempted to minimize overlapping with Ronald Findlay's "Growth and Development in Trade Models" and Anne Krueger's "Trade Policies in Developing Countries," both of which appeared in the *Handbook of International Economics*, Volume I (1984), and with Henry Bruton's "Import Substitution," Chapter 30 in the *Handbook of Development Economics*, Volume II (1989).

INTERNATIONAL TRADE AND ECONOMIC GROWTH

The export–growth nexus

Predictions on developing country exports

In borrowing an expression introduced by Sir Dennis Robertson, Ragnar Nurkse suggested that trade was the engine of growth during the nineteenth century as economic expansion from Western Europe, in particular the United Kingdom, was transmitted to countries on other continents through international exchange. He cited as evidence the fact that trade was increasing at a rate exceeding the growth of world production by a considerable margin.

Nurkse added that in the twentieth century, and especially after 1928, a marked slackening occurred in the expansion of world trade, with its growth rate falling behind that of world production. Thus, in the first Wicksell lecture, delivered in Stockholm in April 1959, he expressed the view that the "center [the industrial countries], in terms of real income per head, is advancing vigorously, but is not transmitting its own rate of growth to the rest of the world through a proportional increase in its demand for primary products" (Nurkse, 1961, p. 294).

The discussion was conducted in terms of demand for primary products; Nurkse tended to dismiss the possibilities for the developing countries to export manufactured goods by reference to an alleged discontinuity in the comparative cost scale, lack of skills in the developing countries, as well as the danger of protection in the industrial countries. Rather, he called for the parallel expansion of industries to provide for increases in domestic demand in the developing countries.

But, apart from temporary protection on infant industry grounds, Nurkse did not endorse industrial protection or other forms of interference with the process of international trade. In his view, "output expansion for domestic consumption can go ahead side by side with international specialization. It need not be a substitute for international specialization. It is a substitute rather for the growth transmission mechanism which for reasons indicated may not be as powerful today as it was in the nineteenth century" (1961, p. 257).

The alleged slow growth of demand for the developing countries' (the "periphery") primary exports on the part of the industrial countries (the "center") was also given emphasis in early work by Prebisch (1950), who applied to the developing countries the dollar shortage hypothesis that found its full expression in Hicks (1953). While the dollar shortage explanation was subsequently dropped and the thesis of the secular deterioration of the terms of trade (see later) assumed importance in Prebisch's writings, he formulated the view that, at identical rates of economic growth, the periphery would develop a balance-of-payments deficit *vis-à-vis* the center, because its income elasticity of import demand is lower than that of the center (Prebisch, 1959).

As noted by Flanders (1964), Prebisch considered the policy choice for the developing countries to be growing less rapidly than the developed countries or taking measures to improve their balance of payments. Among possible measures, Prebisch rejected a devaluation on the grounds that foreign demand for the periphery's exports is price-inelastic and recommended import protection (export taxes) instead.[1] The call for protection was also echoed by Myrdal (1957), in whose view the income elasticity of import demand in the developing countries is further increased by the "demonstration effect" on their pattern of consumption emanating from the developed countries.

The role of policies in export growth

Under the assumption of complete specialization, with the developing countries exporting primary products and importing manufactured goods, Prebisch expected the export earnings of these countries to increase as their import protection drew away resources from the primary sector whose exports were said to face price-inelastic demand. Yet, Prebisch's own country, Argentina, is a *par excellence* case where a reduction in export volume led to losses in export market shares rather than to an increase in export earnings. Thus, as Nurkse (1966, p. 256) noted somewhat facetiously, "we are all indebted to Colonel Perón for an excellent demonstration of the loss which a country can suffer by sacrificing its traditional exports and hence its import capacity also."

As indicated in the final part of this section, with the principal exception of tropical beverages, this conclusion applies generally to primary commodities, exported by the developing countries, which compete with production in the developed countries and face price-elastic rather than price-inelastic demand. Yet, models of complete specialization are again in vogue as evidenced by the work of Bacha (1978), Findlay (1980), Chichilnisky (1981), Taylor (1981), and Vines (1984).

The policies advocated by Prebisch and Myrdal came to be widely applied by developing countries in the early postwar period, through the imposition of import protection on manufactured goods and export taxes on primary products. The adverse effects of these measures on the export performance of the developing countries are indicated by aggregated as well as by disaggregated estimates.

Kravis (1970) showed that, after gaining export market shares in previous periods, developing countries lost market shares in both primary and in manufactured exports between 1953 and 1966. The losses were particularly large in primary exports that suffered the largest discrimination under the policies applied. Excluding fuels, the primary exports of the developing countries increased by 1.8 percent a year as against a rise of 5.7 percent a year for the developed countries during the period.

Among primary products, the losses in market shares were the largest in agricultural exports (cereals, meat, and oilseeds) between 1934–8 and 1959–60 (Porter, 1970). These losses continued between 1959–61 and 1967–8, while developing countries achieved gains in nonagricultural raw materials, where domestic supply limitations led to a divergence between the growth of domestic demand and that of import demand in the developed countries, as well as in manufactured goods, where the adoption of outward-oriented policies in several developing countries led to increases in export market shares (Cohen and Sisler, 1971).

Kravis (1970) added that differential export performance among developing countries was linked to their success in increasing export market shares and diversifying exports which, in turn, were explained by the policies followed. Adams (1973), however, claimed that the intercountry pattern of changes in export market shares was due to differences in initial market shares, the commodity concentration of exports, their geographical concentration, and the rate of inflation, which are structurally given in the short-to-medium term rather than to differences in policies. Crafts (1973) also asserted that initial trade position importantly affects changes in export market shares and emphasized the role of foreign demand – as against domestic supply – in determining export performance.

In his reply, Kravis noted that none of the above variables is structurally given. He further showed that, in the first half of the 1960s, the introduction of initial trade position and export concentration variables does not add to the explanatory power of the regressions, which include the growth of external markets, changes in export market shares, and export diversification as variables explaining intercountry differences in export and GNP growth rates (Kravis, 1973a, 1973b). His conclusion that the countries' own policies, rather than external factors, determine intercountry differences in export and economic performance was reconfirmed by subsequent work.

Thus, time series analysis of data for 27 developing countries in the period led to the conclusion that the country's own policies, rather than external factors, dominated export growth in the developing countries. In particular, "the results are consistent with [the] hypothesis that export success is related to favorable internal factors influencing countries' abilities to compete and diversify" (Love, 1984, p. 289). Further evidence on the issue is provided by data on individual countries reported in the second part of the final section.

Prospects for the future

In examining the prospects of the developing countries for the future, in his Nobel Prize lecture Sir Arthur Lewis (1980) restated the pessimistic predictions put forward in the early postwar period. He suggested that while a 6 percent rate of economic growth in the developing countries would require a 6 percent rate of export growth, the imports of the developed countries would rise only 4 percent a year. Apart from the slowdown of economic growth in the developed countries after 1973, Lewis attributed the latter result to the historical relationship he claimed to have established between the growth of industrial production in the developed countries and world exports of primary products, in the form of an elasticity of 0.87.

Lewis further suggested that price-inelastic demand on the part of the developed countries would lead to declines in the export earnings of the developing countries in the event of increases in export volumes. However, as Riedel (1984) noted, this assumption applies best to traditional noncompeting tropical commodities (largely tropical beverages) that constitute a relatively small and declining share of developing country exports. For all other primary commodities, the developing countries are competing with the developed countries and, rather than there being a strict relationship between exports and developed country output, the outcome will depend on their own policies.

Riedel further considered the possibilities for expanding manufactured exports. This contrasts with Lewis's view, according to whom the main link between the two groups of countries has been through trade in primary products and, with a slowdown of industrial growth, the developed countries are more likely to take less rather than more manufactured goods from the developing countries.

A pessimistic view about the prospects for the exports of manufactured goods was also expressed by Cline (1982) in a paper with the provocative title: "Can the East Asian export model be generalized?". Cline gave a negative answer to the question he posed on the grounds that the corresponding expansion of manufactured exports would not be acceptable to the developed countries. According to his estimates, based on earlier analysis by Chenery and Syrquin, the manufactured exports of all other developing countries would have to increase sevenfold in order to match the East Asian ratio of manufactured exports to GNP, with allowance made for differences in population size and per capita incomes. Attaining this ratio, in turn, would necessitate raising the share of the developing countries in the manufactured imports of the seven major developed countries from 17 to 61 percent.

The prospects are less forbidding if one considers instead the share of the developing countries in the developed countries' consumption of manufactured goods. This share was approximately 1.3 percent in 1976, the year Cline's estimate refers to, in the developed countries, on the average (Balassa, 1985b). The assumed increase in the manufactured exports of the developing countries would raise the ratio to 9.1 percent on the assumption that the consumption of manufactured goods in the developed countries remained unchanged. Yet, the introduction of lower-priced goods imported from the developing countries would tend to increase manufacturing consumption.

Rather than considering changes in market penetration ratios for all of manufacturing, Cline presents results for four-digit sectors established according to the International Standard Industrial Classification in cases when the developing countries would provide more than 15 percent of domestic consumption in the developed countries under the assumptions made. This calculation, however, neglects the fact that differences in factor endowments among developing countries lead to differences in the composition of their manufactured exports.

Nor can it be assumed that countries at varying levels of development, ranging from Mali to Israel, would attain the manufactured export norm of the four East Asian countries within a time period that has practical relevance for the problem at hand. Cline himself makes calculations for a limited group of seven countries (Argentina, Brazil, Colombia, Mexico, Indonesia, Israel, and Malaysia) he calls newly-industrializing, and obtains a fourfold increase in manufactured exports from the developing countries.

But the group includes Indonesia, which cannot be considered a newly-industrializing country, and whose petroleum and other natural resources should not lead to manufacturing export ratios even remotely resembling those of East Asian economies should it in fact reach such a status. More generally, there is no reason to assume that the adoption of outward-oriented policies would lead to identical shares of manufactured exports in all developing countries, for a given population size and per capita incomes. Thus, the East Asian economies are poor in natural resources and one can expect them to have a higher ratio of exports, in particular manufactured exports, to GNP than most other newly-industrializing developing countries.

An alternative approach involves considering the import requirements of economic growth in the developing countries. Following Lewis, assume for these countries a 6 percent target growth rate, an income elasticity of import demand of 1, and a 4 percent growth rate of primary exports to developed countries. Limiting attention to the non-OPEC developing countries, in whose exports manufactured goods had a share of 40 percent in 1983, a simple calculation will show that the import requirements of these countries postulated by Lewis will be met if their manufactured exports were to rise 9 percent a year.

This figure is substantially below the 13 percent rate of growth of manufactured exports from the developing to the developed countries during the 1973–83 period that was characterized by low growth in the latter group of countries. It would also give rise to much lower market penetration ratios than implied by Cline's estimate. Assuming that the consumption of manufactured goods in the developed countries grew at an average annual rate of 4 percent over a ten-year period, the market shares of the developing economies in their manufacturing consumption would increase from 2.3 percent in 1983 to 3.7 percent in 1993. And, even if the exports of manufactured goods from the developing countries to the developed countries rose by 12 percent a year, their market share in the latter's consumption of manufactured goods would not reach 5 percent after a decade.

At the same time, developing countries would use the additional foreign exchange generated through exports to increase their imports, thereby creating demand for the manufactured exports of the developed countries. If the balance of trade in manufactured goods did not change, industrial activity in the developed countries would not be affected in toto, while a reallocation would occur from relatively low-skill to high-skill industries where their comparative advantage lies.

Such a reallocation would take place over a long period, since policy changes in the developing countries, which are a precondition for the acceleration of their economic growth, would have an impact over time. Also, experience indicates that a growing part of the expansion of trade in manufactured goods between the developed countries and the newly-industrializing developing countries involves intra-industry rather than inter-industry specialization, in which case changes will occur in the product composition of the firm rather than in the industrial structure of the economy. This tendency is expected to accelerate in the future as developing countries attain higher levels of industrialization.

Cline's estimates further assume that developing countries would increase their exports of manufactured goods to other developing countries at the same rate as to the developed countries. But, apart from the period immediately following the Mexican financial crisis of August 1982, developing country exports of manufactured goods to developing country markets have been rising more rapidly than to the developed countries. The continuation of this trend may be expected in the future. For one thing, higher economic growth rates in the developing countries will lead to more rapid increases in their demand for manufactured imports than in the developed countries. For another thing, with their increased degree of economic sophistication, the newly-industrializing countries can supply the needs of countries at lower levels of development in an increasing array of commodities.

The terms-of-trade issue

The secular deterioration of the terms-of-trade thesis

Prebisch (1950) and Singer (1950) simultaneously put forward the view that the (commodity) terms of trade of the developing countries have the tendency to deteriorate over time.[2] This secular deterioration was attributed to differences in the process of adjustment to technical progress. While in the developed countries productivity improvements were said to be translated into higher wages, in the developing countries labor supply pressure was said to keep wages unchanged, thus leading to lower prices. Correspondingly, Prebisch claimed that "the great industrial centers not only kept for themselves the benefit of the use of new techniques in their own economy, but are in a favorable position to obtain a share of that deriving from the technical progress of the periphery" (1950, p. 14).

In support of this proposition, Prebisch (1950) presented calculations on the British terms of trade for the 1876–80 to 1946–7 period. He interpreted the apparent improvement in the terms of trade of the United Kingdom, an exporter of manufactured goods and importer of primary products, as implying the secular deterioration of the terms of trade of the developing countries.

In a retrospective evaluation, Singer asserted that "treated as a projection, one can certainly claim that [the secular deterioration of the terms of trade thesis] has passed the test better than most other economic projections" (Singer, 1984, p. 282). In support of this proposition, Singer cited data for the post-1950 period, with the exclusion of petroleum after 1973.

The results for a relatively short period are, however, affected to a considerable extent by the choice of the initial and the terminal years. Thus, the results cited by Singer were much affected by the fact that 1950 was a year of very high primary product prices following the onset of the Korean war[3] while increases in petroleum prices in 1973–4 contributed to the decline in the prices of nonfuel primary products through their adverse effects on world economic activity.

At any rate, just as Prebisch had done, in his 1950 paper Singer considered long-term tendencies; hence, in judging the validity of his and Prebisch's proposition, data for a longer period are needed. In the 1984 paper, Singer cited estimates made by Spraos (1980) for the 1900–70 period.[4] He claimed that, "even if the individual trends [Spraos] calculates are statistically insignificant when taken one by one, the fact that they all point in the same direction surely adds significance" (Singer, 1984, p. 291).

However, the individual results do not point in the same direction. The trend coefficient derived by the use of the UN index is positive, representing a terms of trade improvement for the developing countries; a negative result is obtained only if the UN index is spliced to the World Bank's index for the postwar period. We thus have a positive and a negative result, neither of them statistically significant, which hardly establishes a trend.[5]

Spraos further presented estimates on the terms of trade of primary products *vis-à-vis* manufactured goods for the 1871–1938 period. These estimates show a deterioration in the terms of trade for primary products, albeit the extent of the deterioration is only about one-half of that shown by the terms-of-trade index Prebisch utilized. And, the extent of the deterioration decreases again by nearly one-half if 1929 is taken as the terminal year, with an average annual rate of decline of 0.3 percent estimated by Sir Arthur Lewis (1952) whose results Spraos considers more reliable than competing estimates.

The results indicate the importance of the choice of the benchmark years. The extent of deterioration is smaller if 1929 rather than 1938 is taken as the terminal year since, due to the world depression, primary product prices were particularly low in the latter year. In turn, the early 1870s represented a relatively favorable stage of the business cycle. At the same time, apart from the choice of the benchmark years, several questions arise with regard to the validity of the estimates for judging trends in the terms of trade of the developing countries.

The terms-of-trade controversy

All the reported estimates pertain to the terms of trade of primary commodities vs manufactured goods. The question has been raised if these calculations are indicative of the terms of trade of the developing vs the developed countries, when both countries export primary as well as manufactured products.

Spraos (1980) cited calculations made by Lipsey (1963) on improvements in the US terms of trade and by Kindleberger (1956) on the relative decline of the prices of primary products imported by European countries as indirect evidence of adverse changes in the terms of trade of the developing countries, adding however that the estimates are subject to considerable error. He also cited Maizels'

(1963) results, according to which trends in primary product prices had been practically identical for the exports of both developing and developed countries in the 1899–1937 period.

The next subsection presents more recent estimates which also include manufactured goods that were neglected in earlier work. Prior to that, two too much-debated issues require attention: the implications for the results of changes in transportation costs and in the quality and composition of manufactured exports.

The estimate cited by Presbisch utilized the UK import unit value index to represent the prices of primary products and the UK export index to represent the prices of manufactured goods. This procedure has been criticized on the grounds that it fails to consider decreases in transportation costs. Thus, with the terms of trade being measured as the ratio of fob export unit values to cif import unit values, reductions in the cost of transportation may lead to improvements in the so measured terms of trade of all the trading partners. In fact, Ellsworth (1956) provided evidence that the entire improvement in the terms of trade of the United Kingdom between 1876 and 1905 is explained by the decline in the transportation costs of primary products, and the terms of trade of primary producing countries may have even slightly improved during this period. At the same time, improvements in the productivity of transportation services originated in the developed countries.

These observations also apply to the estimates of other authors who relied on fob export and cif import unit value indices. Spraos, however, argued that the resulting bias in the results might have been cancelled by subsequent increases in transportation costs. But while Isserlis's (1938) estimates of tramp shipping freight support Spraos's contention. Kindleberger's (1956) freight index, constructed subsequently and representing more reliable estimates, show that increases in transportation costs in the later period made up only one-half of the earlier decline.

Subsequently, Bairoch (1975) suggested that the decline in the difference between the cif value of the world imports of primary products and the fob value of the world exports of these products from 23 percent in 1976–80 to 10 percent in 1926–9 indicates the existence of a valuation bias in the terms-of-trade indices due to decreases in transportation costs. The conclusion was queried by Spraos on the grounds that the cif–fob differential covers also factors other than freight and insurance costs, in particular the underestimation of exports. But, this point would be relevant only if it could be established that the underestimation of exports declined over time, an issue Spraos failed to consider.

Data on transport costs for a longer period are available for pig iron. It has been estimated that while in the second half of the eighteenth century the cost of transporting pig iron across the Atlantic was 18–29 percent of the fob export price in New York, the ratio declined to 11 percent by the mid-1970s (Balassa, 1977). These comparisons are of particular interest as they relate to a standardized commodity, and hence are not affected by changes in the composition of trade. And, although transportation costs may vary to a considerable extent, depending on the direction of trade, this will not affect the conclusion as to the decline in transportation costs over time.

The view has further been expressed that quality improvements and the introduction of new products result in an upward bias of the unit value index for manufactured goods, which does not exist in regard to primary commodities. As Haberler (1961, p. 282) put it: "copper remains copper, cotton remains cotton, and wheat remains wheat, while an automobile, a rubber tire, a radio, an antibiotic, either did not exist at all or was entirely different, less durable, and infinitely less serviceable commodity in earlier periods."

While accepting the view that improvements in quality rarely occur in the case of primary products, Spraos suggested that their export composition will change over time, with higher-quality varieties replacing the lower-quality ones. "Perhaps more important [he added] than any of these is the processing of primary products before shipment (for instance, cocoa beans turned into cocoa butter and cocoa paste) which has been increasing all the time, though in developing countries it had gained great momentum only in the last twenty years" (Spraos, 1980, pp. 117–18).

Spraos further suggested that quality deterioration may occur in manufactured goods and that quality improvements in these products may be related to improvements in their primary inputs. He also cited evidence from German and US studies as to the lack of differences between unit value and genuine price indices for manufactured goods in the 1968–74 and 1965–70 periods, respectively.

All in all, Spraos reached the agnostic conclusion that "if quality improvements are liable to be under-allowed on both sides, no presumption can be established in the abstract regarding a systematic bias in terms of trade from this source" (1980, p. 118). Subsequently, Singer claimed that Spraos "has shown convincingly that these difficulties of measurement do not go to the heart of the matter, even empirically" (Singer, 1984, p. 286).

However, the processing of primary commodities is irrelevant for the problem at hand, since unit value indices of primary commodities include unprocessed but not processed goods. At any rate, as Spraos himself noted, the exportation of processed commodities by developing countries is a recent phenomenon. The same comment applies to the upgrading of primary commodities; in fact, all Spraos's examples pertain to the post-Second World War period. At the same time, as noted in the next subsection, for this period a genuine price index for primary products is available that has been constructed by using prices for specific grades of commodities.

In turn, the unit value index for manufactured goods is customarily derived as a ratio of value to weight. Now, apart from quality improvements and changes in product composition referred to earlier, a bias is introduced due to the shift over time from heavier to lighter materials. This shift is unrelated to changes in the quality of primary inputs since it is due to substitution among such inputs.

These considerations are particularly relevant to machinery and transport equipment where increased sophistication as well as the shift from steel to aluminum and, again, to plastics raised the ratio of value to weight. Confirmation of this tendency was provided by Kravis and Lipsey (1971) whose monumental work was overlooked by Singer. Supplementing data for Germany and the United States referred to above by data for the United Kingdom and Japan, Kravis and Lipsey established that the average price index for machinery and equipment exported by these countries increased by 13 percent between 1953 and 1964, compared with a 24 percent rise in the UN unit value index for these commodities indicating the upward bias of the unit value indices.

Recent evidence on the terms of trade

Kravis and Lipsey subsequently extended the country, commodity, and time coverage of their earlier investigation and estimated a price index for manufactured goods exported by the developed countries to the developing countries. The index shows a 127 percent increase between 1953 and 1977, the time period covered by the estimates, compared with a rise of 162 percent in the UN unit value index for these exports. Deflating by the UN price index for the world exports of primary products other than petroleum, the authors found that the terms of trade of manufactured goods exported by the developed to the developing countries, relative to the prices of nonfuel primary products, declined by 6 percent during the period. This contrasts with an increase of 13 percent estimated from the UN unit value indices for manufactured goods and for food and raw materials.

Balassa (1984c) adjusted the Kravis–Lipsey estimates by replacing the UN price index for the world exports of primary commodities other than petroleum by the price index estimated by the World Bank for 33 nonfuel primary commodities, weighted by the exports of the developing countries. The index shows an average price increase of 154 percent for these primary products between 1953 and 1977, compared with an increase of 145 percent in the UN index.

Utilizing the World Bank's index, we observe a decline of 10 percent in the terms of trade of the developed countries in their exchange of manufactured goods for primary products other than fuels with the developing countries during the 1953–77 period. An even larger decline is shown if adjustment is made for quality changes that are not reflected in the cited price index. In the case of the United States, for which Kravis and Lipsey made such estimates, a 105 percent rise in the unadjusted price index for machinery and transport equipment in 1953–77 gives place to a 77 percent increase in the adjusted index. If this result applied to all manufactured goods exported by the developed countries the decline in their terms of trade would be 22 rather than 10 percent.

Changes in relative prices between 1977 and 1985 may have offset the improvements in the terms of trade of the developing countries that occurred during the previous quarter of a century.[6] But, the results are again affected by the choice of the terminal years.

The comparison of the UN and the World Bank indices points to the conclusion that the prices of nonfuel primary products exported by the developing countries rose more rapidly than average world primary product prices during the period under consideration. This conclusion was confirmed by Michaely's (1985) estimates that showed unit value indices for primary products exported by low-income countries to have risen by 27 percent between 1952 and 1970, compared with an increase of 10 percent for primary products exported by high-income countries. Michaely's results further showed a 27 percent improvement in the terms of trade for primary products in the case of low-income countries, compared with a 23 percent deterioration for high-income countries, during this period.[7]

The unit values of manufactured goods exported by low-income countries also increased more rapidly (45 percent) than those exported by high-income countries (19 percent) between 1952 and 1970. In the same period, the terms of trade for manufactured goods improved by 14 percent in low-income countries and deteriorated by 12 percent in high-income countries.

For all merchandise trade, taken together, Michaely observed an improvement of 19 percent in the terms of trade for the low-income countries, and a deterioration of 15 percent for the high-income countries, during the 1952–70 period. He further established that terms-of-trade changes were negatively correlated with income levels in a fivefold classification scheme; the changes between 1952 and 1970 were −26, −11, −8, +11, and +47 percent as one moves from the top to the bottom quintile.

Michaely's results thus reinforce the findings of Kravis and Lipsey, indicating that the developing countries improved their terms of trade relative to the developed countries in the post-Korean war period. It is further observed that primary and manufactured commodities exported by the developing countries increased more in price than goods in the same categories exported by the developed countries and that improvements in the terms of trade were inversely correlated with the level of economic development.

These results pertain to the post-Korean war period, which begins with high primary product prices as noted above. Kravis and Lipsey (1984) further calculated changes in the terms of trade between "Industrial Europe" and the developing countries for the 1872–1953 period, by replacing the world export unit value indices of the United Nations with unit value indices for the manufactured exports of Industrial Europe to the developing countries. The results show no change in the terms of trade of Industrial Europe relative to the developing countries between 1872 and 1953. In view of the upward bias of the unit value for manufactured goods, it follows that the use of price indices would show a deterioration in the terms of trade of Industrial Europe, and an improvement in the terms of trade of the developing countries, during this period.

The reported findings disprove the contentions of Prebisch and Singer as to the alleged secular deterioration of the terms of trade of the developing countries. This conclusion is strengthened if account is taken of the growth of manufactured exports by the developing countries and of primary exports by the developed countries that is neglected in conventional calculations of the terms of trade between the two groups of countries. At the same time, the terms of trade may fluctuate to a considerable extent in shorter periods, reflecting the effects of changes in business cycles and other influences, such as major wars.

The developing countries in the world economy

Possibilities for joint action

Prebisch and Singer used the alleged tendency for the secular deterioration of the terms of trade of the developing countries as an argument for monopolistic action by these countries. The lack of such a tendency does not exclude, however, the exploitation of the monopoly power developing countries may possess in regard to particular commodities which face inelastic demand in the developed countries.

Following the quadrupling of petroleum prices by OPEC, Bergsten (1974) expressed the view that this should not represent a unique case, and that developing countries could form cartels in regard to other commodities as well. Apart from a number of minor commodities, he considered copper, tin, bauxite, phosphates, rubber, tropical timber, coffee, tea, cocoa, and bananas as prime candidates for cartellization. Mikesell (1974), however, raised doubts about the possibilities for developing countries to establish effective cartels for metals, with the conceivable exception of bauxite.

According to Johnson (1968), developing countries that have monopoly power in particular export markets may pursue the following objectives: maximizing export revenue, maximizing profits, maximizing national gain, and maximizing consumption. The first two of these objectives were considered by Radetzki (1975) in the case of copper.

On the bias of assumptions made in regard to demand and supply elasticities in developing and in developed countries, Radetzki concluded that in raising prices by 10 percent through joint production cuts, developing countries would find their combined export revenue lowered by ever-increasing amounts while the rise of profit rates in the first three years would be offset by subsequent losses. These conclusions are said to follow because of the importance of scrap and the availability of highly-competitive substitutes for copper.

Correspondingly, according to Radetzki (1975, p. 53): "the best longer-term policy for copper exporting developing countries would be to accept lower prices and to increase their market share through an aggressive policy of capacity expansion, which would push high cost producers out of business." He subsequently confirmed this conclusion by showing that, during the 1960–74 period, the profits accruing to developing-country copper producers would have increased substantially if these countries doubled the rate of growth of output (Radetzki, 1977).

Radetski's estimate did not allow for the depletion of an exhaustible resource. This was introduced by Pindyck (1978) who estimated that, acting as a collective monopoly, the copper-exporting developing countries could increase the discounted value of their profits by 8 or 30 percent, depending on the discount rate used. However, this outcome would require large fluctuations in the monopolistically-determined price that consuming countries could anticipate and counteract through stockpiling. Pindyck accordingly concluded that there was little incentive for the copper-exporting developing countries to follow a unified policy of pricing and production.

The negative conclusions reached by Pindyck on the desirability of monopolistic action on the part of the copper-exporting developing countries are strengthened if we consider that he only took account of proven reserves while new reserves are continuously being found. Also, Pindyck appears to have underestimated the possibilities for expansion by competing suppliers and the substitution of other materials for copper.

In the case of bauxite, too, Pindyck used proven rather than potential reserves in his calculations. At the same time, it is of interest to observe that the actual price of bauxite differs little from the estimated monopoly price. Yet, despite Pindyck's reference to cartel-type action, there is no evidence of the operation of a bauxite cartel.

Pindyck further estimated that monopolistic action by OPEC may raise the discounted value of profits by 50–100 percent. For various reasons, this estimate is subject to a serious upward bias. It is again based on estimates of proven rather than potential reserves; it assumes long-term price elasticities of 0.35 under the competitive price of $6 per barrel in constant 1975 dollars and 0.52 if the price is doubled, which are much lower than estimate elasticities for the post-1973 period; and it does not sufficiently allow for the emergence of new suppliers.

In fact, OPEC's share in world petroleum production declined from 68 percent in 1973 to 40 percent in 1985. Also, the price per barrel fell from its peak of $34 in 1980 to $13 in February 1986 under the pressure of competition from other suppliers and the desire on the part of each OPEC country to increase its petroleum earnings with only a small increase to $15 per barrel by the end of the year.

The last point leads to the conditions that need to be fulfilled for collusive behavior to be effective. According to Stern and Tims (1975), the principal such conditions include the domination of the markets by a small number of suppliers, the existence of common interest among them, the essentiality of the commodity, the lack of competing suppliers in the developed countries, and limited possibilities for substitution.

Essentiality is an important characteristic of strategic metals, including chromium, cobalt, manganese, niobium, tungsten, and vanadium, all of which face inelastic demand when taken individually and whose output is dominated by a few producers. However, there is substitution among these metals and the benefits of a cartel encompassing all of them would be small while the problems of coordination would be considerable since 12 countries would need to participate (Radetzki, 1984).

Among the commodities listed by Bergsten, which were not considered so far, tin and rubber have good substitutes and phosphates are produced in the developed countries as well. There remain coffee, tea, and cocoa, tropical timber, and bananas, where developing-country producers are the only suppliers. And while coffee and tea face very low demand elasticities, cocoa has substitutes in chocolate manufacturing, bananas compete with other fruits, and tropical timber competes with timber from temperate zone forests.

Thus far, there have been no successful cartels in these commodities although the International Coffee Agreement, designed to stabilize coffee prices, may have raised prices somewhat as the two largest producers, Brazil and Colombia, were willing to reduce their output share. Such reductions were not accepted by India and Sri Lanka, the two largest producers of tea, where six producers account for 70 percent of world exports. Nor has agreement on production quotas been reached in the case of cocoa, bananas, and tropical timber where 4, 9, and 6 developing-country producers account for 70 percent of world exports, respectively.

Delinking

The discussion in the previous subsection indicated the limitations of monopolistic action on the part of developing countries. At the same time, in cases when the conditions for cartellization are fulfilled, developing countries may increase welfare by imposing optimal export taxes to limit production and exports without otherwise interfering with the system of incentives (Balassa, 1978a).

While monopolistic action represents the exploitation of possibilities offered by the world trading system, delinking means reducing or, in an extreme case, severing links with this system. The idea of delinking first gained currency in the Soviet Union, where it was considered to be a condition for full independence and for eliminating the repercussions of business cycles emanating from the capitalist countries.

In fact, complete delinking was never attained by the Soviet Union which wished to exploit the benefits of trade with the developed capitalist countries. Also, having reduced to a considerable extent trade with the West in the years immediately following the Second World War, the countries of Eastern Europe have since endeavored again to increase such ties. In particular, the Minister of Planning and Deputy Prime Minister of Hungary indicated that increasing exports to the developed capitalist countries is the principal objective of medium-term economic policy (Faluvégi, 1984).

In the literature on developing countries, the advocates of complete delinking considered this to be the logical conclusion of the alleged impossibility of economic development in the capitalist world-system and suggest it as a permanent (Amin, 1977) or a temporary (Senghaas, 1980) solution. Others advocated partial delinking through the imposition of extensive import controls.

In searching for actual cases of delinking, the proponents of such a policy tend to refer to China, Cambodia, Cuba, North Vietnam, and Tanzania. But the experience of these countries hardly supports a policy of delinking. To begin with, its high economic costs have led the Chinese government to reject this policy and importantly to increase international exchange. And, while the consequences of delinking and of political oppression are difficult to separate in the case of Cambodia, political oppression is a pre-condition for making delinking effective. Also, exchanging links with capitalist countries for links with socialist countries has meant that Cuba has been unable to exploit the advantages offered by its educated labor force (Balassa, 1986b).

Virtual delinking from developed capitalist countries appears to have been largely responsible for North Korea increasingly losing ground in competition with South Korea. Thus, while in 1960 per capita incomes in the North were one-half higher than in the South, two decades later South Korea surpassed North Korea's income level by a considerable margin (World Bank, 1981).

Finally, Tanzania has practiced selective delinking through import controls, with unfavorable economic results (Balassa, 1985b). More generally, socialist countries in sub-Saharan Africa that have, to a greater or lesser extent, engaged in selective delinking had greatly inferior performance than countries of the area that continued to participate in the international division of labor (Balassa, 1984b).

Trade among developing countries

On the whole, one may agree with Diaz-Alejandro (1978, p. 88) that "the case for delinking is primarily political and sociological rather than economic." The statement made by the same author that "a global international economic order allowing for selective delinking should reduce friction between South and North" (1978, p. 158), in turn, leads to the question of preferential trade among developing countries.

One form of preferential trade arrangements, sanctioned by GATT, is the establishment of regional common markets and free trade areas. While such arrangements have been successful in the developed countries, this has not been the case in the developing countries. Lewis (1980) gives several reasons for this outcome.

First, the region is not a homogeneous area and there may be considerable differences in the level of industrial development among the countries concerned. Countries at higher levels of development may then attract more industries than less advanced countries that feel exploited by the former. Such differences have largely been responsible for the demise of the East African Common Market, and real or assumed disparities in the allocation of benefits from integration have also contributed to the regression of the Central American Common Market.

Second, countries objected competition from partner countries in the fear that this may adversely affect their own industries. Such may be the case, in particular, for relatively simple industries that each developing country wishes to retain. Third, decreases in transportation costs have reduced the attractiveness of trading with neighboring countries.

The above considerations have led Lewis to advocate trade among developing countries in a world-wide context. The question is, then, as to how such trade may be promoted. Under the heading of collective self-reliance, proposals have been made for the developing countries to extend mutual preferences among themselves.

One may consider the delinking of developing countries from the developed economies as an extreme form of collective self-reliance. In fact, Amin suggested the need for the developing countries to establish a new world system, independent from the capitalist one. He further claimed that such a new world system cannot be based on the market, but would rather require planning (Amin, 1974, p. 33).

As it is difficult to imagine planning on the world level, the proponents of collective self-reliance generally posited the need for a scheme of preferences among developing countries (Haq, 1976). However, for various reasons, these propositions have not been followed up in practice.

To begin with, a world-wide preference scheme among developing countries would bring together countries whose level of industrialization varies greatly. Correspondingly, the fears as to the consequences of economic disparities among the partner countries may be even greater than in the regional context.

The lack of information on faraway countries adds to these fears. Thus, while countries will have information on the economic potential of their neighbors, they will rarely possess such information on countries in other regions, thereby augmenting uncertainty as to possible adverse effects for their industries.

Finally, developing countries are reluctant to offer preferences to other developing countries that would involve buying commodities at higher prices than the prices of commodities imported from the developed countries. At the same time, in view of the relatively small markets of the developing countries, the preferences received may be considered to have less value to them than exporting to the larger markets of the developed countries.

These considerations support Lewis's proposition that the route towards increased trade among the developing countries is through offering goods to each other on a competitive basis. This recommendation, in turn, leads to the choice of appropriate policies in a national context that is the subject of the next section of this chapter.

COUNTRY EXPERIENCES WITH OUTWARD
ORIENTATION

The experience of the early postwar period (1945–60)

*From the staple theory of export-led growth to the exportable
surplus approach*

As cited earlier, Nurkse considered the nineteenth century to have
been a period of export-led growth in the newly-developing areas.
This explanation was questioned by Kravis (1970) who found little
evidence for the existence of a positive relationship between exports
and economic growth in the United States. However, Kravis's data
begin in 1834 and, for earlier periods, North (1961) provided evidence on the importance of exports for US economic growth.

Also, Caves (1965, p. 426) concluded that "statistical and descrip-
tive analysis of several 'regions of recent settlement' such as Canada,
Australia, New Zealand, and South Africa make it clear that through
much of their history the export sector has provided the primary
source of disturbances to the economy." Economic growth, in turn,
was much affected by the magnitude and the direction of the
"disturbances."

Although Nurkse reached similar conclusions as far as these
temperate zone areas are concerned, he expressed the view that the
tropical countries remained outsiders, "being relatively neglected in
the process of transmission of economic growth" (Nurkse, 1961,
p. 289). Arthur Lewis, however, suggested that, through growing
trade, "the tropics were transformed during the period 1880 to 1913"
(Lewis, 1969, p. 12). This conclusion is supported by Leff's (1973)
analysis of the experience of Brazil, one of the largest tropical countries, which had earlier been cited as a classic instance of the failure of
export expansion to lead to economic development (Kindleberger,
1953, p. 375).

Leff noted that the growth in export receipts "was perhaps the
major source of income growth in an otherwise relatively stagnant
economy" (Leff, 1973, p. 691). Increases in exports raised incomes
directly as well as indirectly, with incomes generated in the export
sector creating demand for domestically-produced manufactured
goods and primary products. Also, railway construction associated
with export expansion stimulated growth in the domestic agricultural
sector. However, the size of the overall benefits to the Brazilian

economy was limited by the relatively low share of exports in domestic output, characteristic of large countries and by the relatively slow growth of exports, owing to the emergence of new competitors in cotton and sugar.

In Brazil, a land-abundant country, immigration contributed to the growth of exports. In India, another large tropical country, abundant labor supplies became an important source of exports. The latter case was generalized by Myint (1955) in an application of the vent-for-surplus theory, which puts emphasis on the utilization of a country's labor surplus through exports, and its contribution to economic growth.

The growth effects of primary exports were categorized by Watkins (1963), who applied Hirschman's (1958) terminology to the "staple theory" of economic growth initiated by Innis (1957), when staples refer to resource-intensive exports. First, export expansion engenders backward linkages by creating demand for transportation facilities and for domestically-produced inputs. Second, an impetus is provided for the establishment of processing activities. Third, there is a final demand linkage as increased incomes in the export sector create demand for domestically-produced consumer goods.

The extent of the transmission of economic growth from the export sector to the rest of the economy will vary positively with size of the export sector and the rate of growth of exports and negatively with the relative importance of foreign ownership in production for export. Other factors that bear on this relationship include the use of skilled vs unskilled labor, the capital intensity of the production process, and economies of scale in export production; the transportation requirements of exports; the availability of underutilized factors in the rest of the economy; the level of entrepreneurial skills; and the distribution of incomes (Caves, 1965, pp. 433–7).

While students of nineteenth-century economic history have come to emphasize the effects of exports on economic growth, in earlier periods exports had often been considered undesirable on account of the ensuing decline in the availability of goods for domestic consumption (Schumpeter, 1954, pp. 369–74). This idea rarely made its appearance in subsequent periods in the present-day developed countries, except in war-time and in cases of short-term shortages (e.g. the limitations imposed on soybean exports by the United States in the mid-1970s). It was, however, espoused in several developing countries during the early postwar years.

According to Leff, in the years following the Second World War, the Brazilian government applied the "exportable surplus" approach to international trade, under which "a country exports only the 'surplus' which is 'left over' after the domestic market has been 'adequately' supplied" (Leff, 1967, p. 289). This approach is also said to have been utilized in India (Cohen, 1964) and, for particular commodities, such as rice, in Egypt and Thailand (Leff, 1969, pp. 346–7).

The exportable surplus approach neglects the adverse effects of export limitations on import capacity and fails to consider the advantages a country can derive from resource allocation according to comparative advantage. It reflects the assumption that the supply of exportable products is price-inelastic, so that increases in exports would reduce the availability, and increase the price, of products for domestic use.

While starting out from different premises, this approach rejoins that of Prebisch and Myrdal on the desirability of limiting exports in developing countries. But, whereas Prebisch and Myrdal focused on the case when the commodity is exported but it is not consumed domestically, the exportable surplus theory pertains to the case of commodities that are both exported and consumed domestically.

Interpreted in a more general sense, the "exportable surplus" theory also includes the case when countries keep prices low in order to benefit consumers, thereby discouraging domestic production and encouraging the shift of resources from export activities to production for domestic needs. In recent years, several developing countries have taken such action.

These policies may be considered as part of an inward-oriented development strategy that discriminates in favor of import substitution and against export industries and, within individual industries, in favor of import substitution and against exports (in short, an anti-export bias). In Balassa and Associates (1971), this bias was interpreted to mean negative effective protection of value added in export activities. In turn, outward orientation was defined as neutrality in the system of incentives, with effective rates of protection being, on the average, approximately equal in import substituting and in export activities. The asymmetry in the definition corresponds to a real life situation as a considerable number of developing countries bias their system of incentives against exports whereas others tend to approximate neutrality without there being cases of the opposite bias.

Policies in free market and socialist economies[8]

Responding to the ideas of Prebisch and Myrdal, an inward-oriented development strategy found application in several developing countries during the early postwar period. Such a strategy was also applied in socialist countries in Central and Eastern Europe that followed the example of the Soviet Union in attempting to reduce reliance on the outside world. Although the measures applied may have differed between the two groups of countries, their overall policy orientation was similar; they contrast with the case of several Northern European countries that adopted an outward-oriented development strategy at the time.

To begin with, inward-oriented countries protected their industries against foreign competition. In market economies, this was done by using a mixture of tariffs and import controls, whereas socialist countries relied on import prohibitions. At the same time, while the infant industry argument calls for temporary protection until industries become internationally competitive, in both groups of countries protection was regarded as permanent and there was a tendency towards what has been described as "import substitution at any cost" by Prebisch.

Furthermore, in all the countries concerned, there were considerable variations in rates of explicit and implicit protection among industrial activities. This was the case, first of all, as continued import substitution involved undertaking activities with increasingly high domestic resource costs per unit of foreign exchange saved. In market economies, the generally uncritical acceptance of demands for protection contributed to this result and, in the absence of international price comparisons, the protective effects of quantitative restrictions could not even be established. In socialist countries the aim was to limit imports to commodities that could not be produced domestically, or were not available in sufficient quantities, and no attempt was made to gauge the extent and the cost of protection the pursuit of this objective entailed.

In both groups of countries the neglect of inter-industry relationships further increased the dispersion of protection rates on value added in processing, or effective protection, with adverse effects on economic efficiency. In Argentina, for example, high tariffs imposed on caustic soda at the request of a would-be producer made the theretofore thriving soap exports unprofitable. In Hungary, the high cost of domestic steel, produced largely from imported iron ore and coking coal, raised costs for steel-using industries while the large investments made in the steel industry delayed the substitution of aluminum for steel, although Hungary possesses considerable bauxite reserves.

Countries applying inward-oriented development strategies were further characterized by the prevalence of sellers' markets. In market economies, the size of national markets limited the possibilities for domestic competition while import competition was virtually excluded by high protection. In socialist countries, the system of central planning applied did not permit competition among domestic firms, or from imports, and buyers had no choice among domestic producers, or access to imported commodities.

The existence of sellers' markets provided little incentive for catering to the users' needs. In the case of industrial users, it led to backward integration as producers undertook the manufacture of parts, components, and accessories in order to minimize supply difficulties. This outcome, observed in market as well as in socialist economies, increased production costs, since economies of scale in the production of these inputs were foregone.

Also, in sellers' markets, firms had little incentive to improve productivity. In market economies, monopolies and oligopolies assumed importance, and the oligopolists often aimed at maintaining market shares while refraining from actions that would invoke retaliation. In socialist countries, the existence of assured outlets and the emphasis on short-term objectives on the part of managers discouraged technological change.

The managers' emphasis on short-term objectives in socialist countries had to do with uncertainty as to the planners' future intentions and the length of their own tenure. In market economies, fluctuations in real exchange rates (nominal exchange rates, adjusted for changes in inflation rates at home and abroad) increased uncertainty for business decisions. These fluctuations, resulting from intermittent devaluations in the face of domestic inflation, reinforced the adverse effects of the bias against exports as the domestic currency equivalent of export earnings varied with the devaluations, the timing of which was uncertain.

In inward-oriented countries, distortions were often apparent in the valuation of time. In market economies, negative real interest rates adversely affected domestic savings, encouraged self-investment, including inventory accumulation, at low returns, and provided inducements for the transfer of funds abroad (McKinnon).

Negative real interest rates also led to credit rationing that generally favored import-substituting investments, irrespective of whether rationing was done by the banks or by the government. In the first case, the lower risk of investments in production for domestic, as compared to export, markets gave rise to such a result; in the second case, it reflected government priorities. In turn, in socialist countries, ideological considerations led to the exclusion of interest rates as a charge for capital and as an element in the evaluation of investment projects.

There was also a tendency to underprice public utilities in countries following an inward-oriented strategy, either because of low interest charges in these capital-intensive activities or as a result of conscious decisions. The underpricing of utilities benefited especially energy-intensive industries and promoted the use of capital.

In general, countries applying inward-oriented development strategies de-emphasized the role of prices in the allocation process. In socialist countries, resources were in large part allocated centrally in physical terms; in market economies, output and input prices were distorted and reliance was placed on nonprice measures of import restrictions and credit allocation. A possible explanation is that while price distortions would interfere with the exploitation of the possibilities available in international markets if an outward-oriented strategy is applied, such is not the case under inward orientation.

The described policies were exemplified by the experience of Argentina and Chile among market economies and that of Czecho-slovakia and Hungary among socialist countries. In turn, Denmark and Norway provided examples of outward orientation in the early postwar period. The latter two countries not only eliminated quantitative import restrictions but reduced tariffs below the levels observed in the developed countries, with little inter-industry differences in tariff rates. They also adopted realistic exchange rates and interest rates.

Effects on exports and economic growth

Discrimination against exports did not permit the development of manufactured exports in countries that adopted an inward-oriented development strategy. There were also adverse developments in primary exports as low prices for producers and consumers reduced the exportable surplus by discouraging production and encouraging consumption.

In fact, rather than improvements in the external terms of trade as assumed by Prebisch and Myrdal, turning the internal terms of trade against primary activities led to declines in export market shares in the countries concerned. Losses in market shares were especially pronounced in temperate zone agricultural products and metals, benefiting developed countries, in particular the United States, Canada, and Australia.

Among the countries under consideration, the volume of Argentina's principal primary exports, beef and wheat, remained, on the average, unchanged between the mid-1930s and the early 1960s, while the world exports of these commodities doubled. In the same period, Chile's share fell from 28 to 22 percent in the world exports of copper, which accounted for three-fifths of the country's export earnings. Notwithstanding its climatic advantages, the economic policies followed also forestalled the development of Chilean agriculture, thereby impeding the expansion of exports and contributing to increased food imports.

Similar developments occurred in socialist countries. In Hungary, for example, the exports of several agricultural commodities, such as goose liver, fodder seeds, and beans, declined in absolute terms and slow increases in production necessitated the importation of cereals and meat that had earlier been major export products.

In the same period, Denmark nearly doubled its market shares in major agricultural exports and Norway also experienced increases in market shares. And whereas countries following an inward-oriented development strategy failed to expand industrial exports, manufacturing industries in Denmark and Norway became increasingly export-oriented, with the share of manufactured goods in total exports increasing to a considerable extent.

The conclusions obtained for the six countries under consideration were confirmed in a study of 29 developing countries by De Vries (1967). The study showed that outward-oriented countries were much more successful in maintaining and improving their market position in primary exports, and developing manufactured exports, than inward-oriented countries.

The slowdown in the growth of primary exports and the lack of emergence of manufactured exports did not provide the foreign exchange necessary for rapid economic growth in countries pursuing inward-oriented development strategies. The situation was aggravated as net import savings declined because of the increased need for foreign materials, machinery, and technological know-how (Bruton, 1970). Correspondingly, economic growth was increasingly constrained by limitations in the availability of foreign exchange, and intermittent foreign exchange crises occurred as attempts were made to expand the economy at rates exceeding that permitted by the growth of export earnings (Berlinski and Schydlowsky, 1982).

Also, high-cost, capital-intensive production raised incremental capital–output ratios under continuing import substitution, requiring ever-increasing savings ratios to maintain rates of economic growth at earlier levels. At the same time, the loss of incomes due to the high cost of protection reduced the volume of available savings, resulting in a decline in GNP growth rates.

In several developing countries pursuing an inward-oriented development strategy, the cost of protection is estimated to have exceeded 5 percent of the gross national product (Balassa and Associates, 1971). And while it had been suggested that the high cost of inward-oriented policies will remain temporary (De Vries, 1967, pp. 62–9), this did not prove the case.

Thus, in the highly protected Latin American countries productivity growth slowed down once the first stage of import substitution, involving the replacement by domestic production of the importation of nondurable consumer goods and their inputs, had been completed (Bruton, 1967; Elias, 1978). And, according to a summary of the findings of studies on a number of developing countries, "the misallocation produced by conventional IS [import substituting] policies not only reduces total output below the level that it might have otherwise reached, but it also reduces the growth rate, principally through its effect on productivity growth and the flexibility of the economy" (Bruton, 1970, p. 140).

These results may be explained by reference to changes in product requirements as a country undertakes the production of intermediate commodities and durable goods in proceeding to the second stage of import substitution. Whereas the production of nondurable consumer goods and their inputs requires mainly unskilled labor, uses relatively simple technology, and the efficient scale of production is low, with costs rising little at lower levels of output, at the second stage of import substitution production tends to be capital- and/or skill-intensive, requires sophisticated technology, as well as large-scale production for efficient operation, with costs rising rapidly at lower output levels (Balassa, 1980).

Thus, at a higher stage of import substitution, developing countries increasingly embarked on the production of commodities, which did

not correspond to their production conditions. This, in turn, necessitated high protection in order to establish the industries in question.
Yet, as Johnson (1967) showed, in a country that faces world market
prices and protects its capital-intensive sector, increases in the capital
stock may lead to a fall in real incomes, measured in world market
prices, owing to the transfer of labor from the labor-intensive to the
capital-intensive sector. Subsequently, Martin (1977) demonstrated
that this will be the case if one plus the rate of protection of the
capital-intensive sector exceeds the ratio of labor's share in the labor-
intensive sector to that in the capital-intensive sector.

While these models are based on restrictive assumptions since they
assume factor-price equalization in a two-sector economy, the
observed results indicate the potential adverse effects of protection
on the long-term growth of the economy. This is confirmed by the
cited evidence, which points to the conclusion that, rather than
reducing the economic distance *vis-à-vis* the industrial countries infant industry protection was supposed to achieve, in highly protected
developing countries there was a tendency for this lag to increase
over time.

Similar developments were observed in Czechoslovakia and Hungary, where the slowdown of export growth and increases in incremental capital–output ratios led to declines in the rate of economic
growth. By contrast, the rapid expansion of exports provided the
foreign exchange necessary for economic growth in Denmark and
Norway, and resource allocation according to comparative advantage
permitted reducing incremental capital–output ratios, resulting in the
acceleration of economic growth.

The period of rapid world economic growth (1960–73)

Alternative policy choices[9]

The slowdown in economic growth that eventually resulted from the
continued pursuit of an inward-oriented development strategy led to
policy reforms in several of the countries applying such a strategy.
Among market economies, policy reforms were undertaken in the
mid-1960s in Brazil and, to a lesser extent, in Argentina and Mexico.
The reforms generally involved providing subsidies to manufactured
exports, reducing import protection, applying a system of crawling
peg, adopting positive real interest rates, and introducing greater
realism in the pricing of public utilities.

Among socialist countries, central resource allocation and price determination gave place to the decentralization of decision-making in Hungary. This involved introducing market relations among firms and increasingly linking domestic prices to world market prices through the exchange rate, with adjustment made for import tariffs and for export subsidies.

The policy reforms undertaken by countries that engaged in second-stage import substitution thus involved making increased use of the price mechanism and reducing price distortions, in particular in foreign trade. The incentive systems that emerged as a result of the reforms in the period preceding the 1973 oil crisis may be compared with the incentive systems applied in countries that adopted an outward-oriented industrial development strategy in the early 1960s, immediately following the completion of first-stage import substitution. The countries in question are Korea, Singapore, and Taiwan.

In comparing the incentive systems applied by the three Far Eastern countries and those adopted in the three Latin American countries following second-stage import substitution, several features deserve attention. These relate to the treatment of the export sector, relative incentives to exports and to import substitution, the variability of incentive rates among particular activities, relative incentives to manufacturing and to primary production, and the automaticity and stability of the incentive system.

In the three Far Eastern countries, a free trade regime was applied to exports. Exporters were free to choose between domestic and imported inputs; they were exempted from indirect taxes on their output and inputs; and they paid no duty on imported inputs. The same privileges were extended to the producers of domestic inputs used in export production.

The application of these procedures provided virtually equal treatment to all exports. And while some additional export incentives were granted, they did not introduce much differentiation among individual export commodities. At the same time, these incentives ensured that in the manufacturing sector, on average, exports received similar treatment as import substitution. Furthermore, there was little discrimination against primary exports and against primary activities in general; incentives were on the whole provided automatically; and the incentive system underwent few modifications over time.

The three Latin American countries that reformed their incentive system after engaging in second-stage import substitution granted subsidies to their nontraditional exports and reduced the extent of import protection. These countries did not, however, provide exporters with a free choice between domestic and imported inputs. Rather, in order to safeguard existing industries, exporters were required to use domestic inputs produced under protection. To compensate exporters for the resulting excess cost, as well as for the effects of import protection on the exchange rate, the countries in question granted explicit export subsidies.

These subsidies did not suffice, however, to provide exporters with incentives comparable to the protection of domestic markets. Thus, there continued to be a bias in favor of import substitution and against exports, albeit at a reduced rate. The extent of discrimination was especially pronounced against traditional primary exports that did not receive export subsidies and, in some instances, continued to be subject to export taxes.

Furthermore, with export subsidies and the protection of inputs used in export industries differing among industries, there was considerable variation in the extent of export subsidies to value added in the production process. Considerable inter-commodity variations were observed also in regard to effective rates of protection on sales in domestic markets. At the same time, some of the incentives were subject to discretionary decision-making.

Nevertheless, with the adoption of the crawling peg, the policy reforms undertaken in the three Latin American countries imparted considerable stability to the incentive system. Also, discrimination against exports and against primary activities was reduced while such discrimination persisted in countries that continued to apply policies of import substitution during the period. Such was the case in India, Chile, and Uruguay during the 1960–73 period.

In India, the introduction of selected export subsidies in the mid-1960s was far overshadowed by the continued use of import prohibitions and the controls imposed on investment; subsidies were also subject to complex regulations and discretionary decision-making. Chile traditionally had the highest level of import protection in Latin America and, after brief experimentation with import liberalization, import restrictions were reimposed in the early 1970s. Protection levels were also high in Uruguay and little effort was made to promote exports.

Incentives and export performance

The incentives applied greatly influenced export performance in the three groups of countries. This may be indicated by reference to the rate of growth of exports and changes in export–output ratios. While export growth rates are affected by a country's initial position, the use of the two measures gave broadly similar results in the present case. Increases in manufactured exports and in export–output ratios during the 1960–6 period were the most rapid in the three Far Eastern countries, which adopted an outward-oriented strategy in the early 1960s. These countries further improved their export performance in the 1966–73 period, when they intensified their export promotion efforts. As a result, the share of exports in manufactured output rose from 1 percent in 1960 to 14 percent in 1966 and to 41 percent in 1973 in Korea; from 11 percent to 20 percent and to 43 percent in Singapore; and from 9 percent to 19 percent and to 50 percent in Taiwan. Notwithstanding their poor natural resource endowment, the three countries also had the highest growth rates of primary exports, and hence of total exports, among the nine countries under consideration (Balassa, 1978a).

Between 1966 and 1973, the growth of manufactured exports accelerated in the three Latin American countries that reformed their system of incentives during this period. As a result, the share of exports in manufactured output rose from 1 percent in 1966 to 4 percent in 1973 in both Argentina and Brazil. Still, this share remained much lower than in the Far East and the Latin American countries experienced a continued erosion in their traditional primary exports, although they made gains in nontraditional primary exports that received subsidies. Correspondingly, while the countries in question experienced an acceleration in the rate of growth of their total exports, they were far surpassed by the three Far Eastern countries.

India, Chile, and Uruguay, which continued with an inward-looking development strategy, did poorly in primary as well as in manufactured exports and showed a decline in the share of exports in manufactured output between 1960 and 1973. India lost ground in textiles, its traditional export, and was slow to develop new manufactured exports. As a result, its share in the combined exports of manufactured goods of the nine countries declined from 70 percent in 1960 to 13 percent in 1973. In the same period, Chile's share fell from 3 percent to below 1 percent and Uruguay's share from 1 percent to practically zero.

These results relate export incentives to export performance in a comparative framework. In turn, several authors estimated for individual countries the effects on manufactured exports of changes in domestic relative prices, which are affected by changes in export incentives. A review of estimates showed that the price elasticities of export supply, which were statistically significant at least at the 5 percent level, ranged from 0.3 in Pakistan to 3.0 in Egypt, with a median of 0.6–0.7 (Donges and Riedel, 1977).

The estimates were obtained by utilizing the ordinary least squares (OLS) method that is known to have a downward bias. Evidence of this bias is provided in a study of Greek and Korean exports, in a simultaneous equation framework. In the case of Greece, the price elasticity of supply of total exports was estimated at 1.2 by ordinary least squares and 1.6 utilizing two-stage least squares (TSLS); both estimates are statistically significant at the 1 percent level. For the same country, the price elasticity of supply of manufactured exports was estimated at 1.3 using OLS and 2.1 using TSLS; the former is significant at the 5 percent, the latter at the 1 percent level. In turn, the estimated price elasticity of supply of total exports for Korea was 1.5 under OLS and 1.9–2.4 under TSLS estimation, depending on the relative price variable employed. All the elasticities are statistically significant at the 1 percent level (Balassa, Voloudakis, Fylaktos and Suh, 1986).

Yet, the econometric results show the short-term effects of changes in relative prices. The long-term effects may be substantially greater, in part because adjustment takes time and in part because producers and consumers may not react to changes they consider temporary. The latter point is supported by the export supply equations estimated for Korea, where the exchange rate cum export incentives variable was separated from the domestic and foreign price variables. While the elasticity of export supply ranges between 1.9 and 2.5 in regard to the former, it is between 1.0 and 1.5 for the latter, conforming to expectations that businessmen consider changes in the exchange rate and in export incentives as permanent and changes in domestic and foreign prices as temporary.

As far as the effects of exchange rate changes are concerned, the *locus classicus* is "Currency devaluation in developing countries" (Cooper, 1971). Having reviewed some three dozen devaluations occurring over the 1953–66 period, Cooper concluded that devaluation appears to improve both the trade balance and the balance of payments after the first year. Subsequently, in a study of 12 developing countries, which adopted stabilization programs in the 1970–6 period, Donovan (1981) concluded that export performance exhibited a striking improvement following the devaluation of the currency. Thus, while exports in these countries declined on the average by

1.3 percent in the year prior to the depreciation, they increased by 9.2 percent in the first post-depreciation year, although the rate of expansion of world exports hardly changed.

The effects of exchange rate changes on exports were examined by Balassa (1986c), utilizing an econometric model that combined time series data for 52 developing countries. The author found that a 1 percent change in the real exchange rate was accompanied by a 0.5 percentage point change in the ratio of exports to output. The corresponding result for agricultural exports alone was 0.6.

Effects on economic growth, employment, and income distribution

Continued import substitution behind high protection in narrow domestic markets involves "travelling up the staircase" by undertaking the production of commodities that involve increasingly higher domestic costs per unit of foreign exchange saved. By contrast, exporting involves "extending a lower step on the staircase" by increasing the production of commodities in which the country has a comparative advantage, with low domestic resource costs per unit of foreign exchange. Exporting further permits full use of capacity and allows reductions in unit costs through the exploitation of economies of scale, contributing thereby to efficient import substitution. Finally, exposure to foreign competition provides stimulus for technological change.

Resource allocation according to comparative advantage, higher capacity utilization, and the exploitation of economies of scale under an outward-oriented development strategy improve investment efficiency, when the resulting savings in capital may be used to increase output and employment elsewhere in the economy in countries where labor is not fully employed. This will occur through the indirect effects of export expansion that create demand for domestic inputs and generate higher incomes which are in part spent on domestic goods.

Data on the three groups of countries analyzed in the previous subsection show considerable differences in regard to the efficiency of investment. For the 1960–73 period as a whole, incremental capital–output ratios were 1.8 in Singapore, 2.1 in Korea, and 2.4 in Taiwan. At the other extreme, these ratios were 5.5 in Chile, 9.1 in Uruguay, and 5.7 in India. Incremental capital–output ratios fell in the three Latin American countries that undertook policy reforms in the mid-1960s, the decline being the largest in Brazil (from 3.8 in 1960–6 to

2.1 in 1966–73), where the policy changes were the most pronounced and excess capacity could be utilized in exporting (Balassa, 1978a).

At the same time, domestic savings will rise as higher incomes are attained under outward orientation. Domestic savings would increase further if a higher than average share of incomes generated by exports were saved. This proposition received support from a cross-section study of 14 developing economies by Weisskopf (1972), who found a positive correlation between exports and domestic savings. Weisskopf's results were confirmed by Papanek (1973) in a cross-sectional analysis of 34 developing economies for the 1950s, and 51 developing countries for the 1960s.

A positive correlation between exports and domestic savings has also been found in a time series analysis of four developed and eight developing economies by Maizels (1968, ch. 4) for the early post-Second World War period extending to 1962. Maizels' sample includes India; for the same country Bhagwati and Srinivasan (1975, ch. 16) obtained inconclusive results in a comparative study of ten industries for the 1950s and 1960s. Given India's orientation toward import substitution during the entire period, however, the lack of clear-cut results in an inter-industry framework may not modify the cross-sectional and time series results obtained for the developing economies cited above.[10]

Lower incremental capital–output ratios and higher investment shares resulting from increased domestic and foreign savings contribute to economic growth under outward orientation as compared to inward orientation. This is shown by observed differences in rates of economic growth, ranging from 9–10 percent in Korea, Singapore, and Taiwan, to 2–3 percent in India, Chile, and Uruguay, with Argentina, Brazil, and Mexico occupying the middle ground following the acceleration of their economic growth in the wake of the reforms introduced in the mid-1960s.[11]

One may further examine the relationship between alternative policy choices and economic growth by establishing a correlation between the rate of growth of exports and that of output, when export expansion is taken to reflect the extent of outward orientation. Michaely (1977) suggested, however, that this correlation does not provide an appropriate test for the above hypothesis, since exports are part of output and hence multicollinearity is present. In turn, Heller and Porter (1978) noted that Michaely's own procedure of correlating the growth rate of the export share of output with the output growth rate is subject to the same criticism, and they proposed replacing the latter variable by the growth of output net of exports. The authors obtained a high positive correlation between the two variables in a cross-section investigation of 41 developing countries. Their result was reconfirmed by Balassa (1978b) who correlated export growth with the growth of output net of exports by combining data for the 1960–6 and 1966–73 periods for the nine countries referred to above.

These procedures abstract from the fact that exports and output are affected simultaneously by other variables, such as increases in the capital stock and in the labor force. Michalopoulos and Jay (1973) attempted to remedy this deficiency by introducing domestic and foreign investment and labor as explanatory variables, together with exports, to explain inter-country differences in GNP growth rates for 39 developing countries in the 1960–6 period. The inclusion of exports in a production function-type relationship was designed to test for the favorable effect of export expansion on output growth.

While inter-country differences in domestic and foreign investment and in the growth of the labor force explained 53 percent of the inter-country variation in GNP growth rates, adding the export variable raised the coefficient of determination to 0.71. Applying the same procedure to pooled data of nine semi-industrial countries for the 1960–6 and 1966–73 periods, Balassa (1978b) found that adding the export variable increased the explanatory power of the regression equation from 58 to 77 percent. Subsequently, Feder (1983) separated the effects of exports on economic growth into two parts, productivity differentials between export and nonexport activities and externalities generated by exports; he obtained highly significant results in regard to both variables for broadly as well as for narrowly defined semi-industrial countries for the 1964–77 period.

As long as labor is not fully employed, the rapid growth of output under an outward-oriented strategy benefits employment, when additional gains are obtained to the extent that exports are more labor-intensive than import substitution. However, these gains are reduced in the event that outward orientation leads to more rapid increases in labor productivity than would otherwise be the case.

Banerji and Riedel (1980) analyzed the effects of these factors on industrial employment in India and in Taiwan. Their results indicate that the favorable effects of rapid output growth on employment were enhanced by the shift towards labor-intensive export activities in Taiwan while output grew at a slower rate and a shift occurred towards relatively capital-intensive import-substituting activities in

India. With higher productivity growth in Taiwan than in India, industrial employment grew at an average annual rate of 10 percent in the first case and 3 percent in the second during the 1960s.

Furthermore, in a comparative study of eight developing countries, Krueger (1983) found that considerable employment gains may be obtained through a shift from import substitution to export orientation. These gains, calculated by the use of labor input coefficients for individual sectors, varied between 21 and 107 percent, with results for Indonesia and Thailand exceeding 100 percent.[12]

Fields (1984) examined the employment effects of outward orientation in Far Eastern countries. He found that between the early 1960s and the early 1970s unemployment rates declined from 8 to 4 percent in Korea, from 9 to 7 percent in Singapore, and from 6 to 2 percent in Taiwan. Also, Carvalho and Haddad (1981, Table 2.15) showed that greater outward orientation in Brazil after the mid-1960s led to a 27 percent increase in the labor-intensity of exports relative to import substitution in Brazil.

Apart from its impact on economic growth and on the inter-industry allocation of the factors of production, trade orientation will affect employment through changes in factor prices. Under inward orientation capital goods are underpriced, both because the exchange rate is overvalued and because tariffs on capital goods tend to be low or nonexistent.

Among countries for which estimates have been made in the framework of the Krueger study, the elimination of protection would involve reducing capital costs by 30–40 percent in Chile, Pakistan, and Turkey and by 8 percent in Argentina (Krueger, 1983, Table 7.1). Since a 1 percent change in the relative prices of capital and labor has been shown to be associated with a 1 percent change in the use of labor relative to capital (Behrman, 1982, p. 186), eliminating this distortion would lead to increases in employment commensurate with the rise in the relative cost of capital.

With the growth of employment, real wages increased considerably in outward-oriented economies where exports expanded rapidly. This increase reflects the fact that the rate of growth of the demand for labor on the part of the manufacturing sector exceeded the rate of growth of the supply of labor to this sector. As a result, between 1966 and 1973, real wages in manufacturing doubled in Korea and increased by nearly three-fifths in Taiwan. Also, real wages in manufacturing rose by three-tenths in Brazil after its shift towards increased outward orientation. In turn, real wages decline by one-tenth in India between 1966 and 1973, which continued with inward-oriented policies during this period.

Fields (1984) compared the experience of the three Far Eastern countries with that of three Caribbean countries (Barbados, Jamaica, and Trinidad and Tobago) he considered as open economies albeit, given their high level of protection, they may better be classified as inward-oriented. And whereas he attributed the high level of unemployment in these countries to the application of a "lenient" wage policy as against the "strict" wage policies allegedly followed by the Far Eastern countries, this assertion conflicts with the fact that real wages rose much more rapidly in the Far East than in the Caribbean countries, with an absolute decline observed in Jamaica. These differences may be explained by reference to the fact that rapid export expansion "pulled up" wages in the Far Eastern countries that did not occur in the Caribbean where raising wages above productivity levels through labor legislation discouraged exports, thereby adding to unemployment.

Finally, a survey of countries following an inward-oriented strategy showed that this policy produces low employment growth and inequality of incomes (Bruton, 1974). The results reflect slow growth of employment and wages in the manufacturing sector as well as the deterioration of the domestic terms of trade through agricultural protection. Subsequently, in an econometric study of developing countries for the postwar period, Morrison (1985) found that the expansion of the exports of manufactured goods and exports derived from small-scale agriculture tended to substantially improve the distribution of incomes while exports originating in mines and latifundia had the opposite effect.

The decade of external shocks (1973–83)

Alternative adjustment policies

Developing countries experienced substantial external shocks between 1973 and 1983. In the first half of the period, the quadrupling of oil prices was accompanied by a world recession, followed by a slow recovery; in the second half, oil prices increased two-and-a-half times, the developed countries again experienced a recession, and interest rates rose to a considerable extent. At the same time, policy responses to these shocks varied greatly. This is discussed in the following in regard to 12 newly-industrializing and 12 less-developed countries, drawing on estimates for the periods 1974–8 and 1978–83, reported in Balassa (1984a, 1986a).

Among newly-industrializing developing economies, defined as having per capita incomes between $1100 and $3500 in 1978 and a manufacturing share in GDP of 20 percent in 1977, Korea, Singapore, and Taiwan continued with their outward-oriented development strategy and were joined by Chile and Uruguay. In turn, after earlier efforts to reduce the bias of the incentive system against exports, Argentina, Israel, Mexico, Portugal, Turkey, and Yugoslavia again increased the degree of inward orientation.

Less-developed countries span the range between newly-industrializing developing economies and the least-developed countries. Within this group, Kenya, Mauritius, Thailand, and Tunisia applied relatively outward-oriented strategies. Conversely, inward orientation predominated in Egypt, India, Jamaica, Morocco, Peru, the Philippines, Tanzania, and Zambia.

The classification scheme has been established on the basis of the policies applied in the 1974–8 period. Policy charges have occurred in several countries since. Among newly-industrializing economies, Portugal applied a stabilization programme in 1978, followed by reductions in import protection. Turkey undertook a far-reaching policy reform in January 1980, while Chile and Uruguay introduced considerable distortions in the system of incentives by fixing their exchange rates in 1980–1. Among less-developed countries, Kenya and Tunisia moved in the direction of inward orientation while Jamaica carried out partial reforms. Nevertheless, in order to ensure comparability in the results, the same classification scheme has been used for the second period as well.

In the process of estimation, external shocks have been defined to include terms-of-trade effects, associated in large part with increases in oil prices; export volume effects, resulting from the recession-induced slowdown in world trade; and, in the second period, interest rate effects, due to the rise of interest rates in world financial markets. In turn, policy responses to external shocks have included additional net external financing, defined as increased reliance on foreign capital compared to past trends; export promotion, reflected by increases in export market shares; import substitution, measured as decreases in the income elasticity of import demand; and deflationary macroeconomic policies, expressed by decreases in economic growth rates.

Effects on foreign trade and economic growth

In the 1974–8 period, outward-oriented developing countries suffered considerably larger external shocks than inward-oriented countries (7.5 vs 3.9 percent of GNP), owing to the fact that they had a much larger export share. However, differences in economic growth rates increased over time and offset differences in the size of external shocks several times. Thus, while outward-oriented countries maintained their rate of economic growth between 1963–73 and 1973–9 at 7.1 percent, on the average, average growth rates declined from 5.7 to 5.0 percent in inward-oriented countries. Differences in economic growth rates, in turn, find their origin in differences in the policies applied that affected investment efficiency as well as domestic savings rates.

Following the quadrupling of oil prices of 1973–4 and the world recession of 1974–5, outward-oriented countries adopted output-increasing policies of export expansion and import substitution that fully offset the adverse balance-of-payments effects of external shocks during the 1974–8 period. By contrast, inward-oriented countries lost export market shares, experienced little import substitution, and financed the balance-of-payments effects of external shocks almost entirely by borrowing abroad.

Apart from the development strategies applied, differences in export performance are explained by the fact that outward-oriented economies maintained realistic exchange rates while inward-oriented countries supported overvalued exchange rates by foreign borrowing. At the same time, a variety of factors contributed to the result that outward-oriented economies experienced substantially more import substitution than their inward-oriented counterparts.

To begin with, the maintenance of realistic exchange rates furthered import substitution in outward-oriented as compared to inward-oriented countries. Furthermore, the lack of discrimination against primary activities and the adoption of realistic energy prices gave rise to import substitution in foodstuffs and petroleum in the first group of countries. Finally, cost reductions through the exploitation of economies of scale in exporting contributed to import substitution in manufactured goods in outward-oriented economies, whereas increasing costs were incurred behind high protective barriers and net foreign exchange savings declined under inward orientation.

At the same time, high and rising protection adversely affected investment efficiency in inward-oriented countries, and the situation was aggravated by the lack of sufficient attention given to economic considerations in their large public investment programs. In turn, apart from the neutrality of the system of incentives, outward-oriented countries had smaller public investment programs and gave greater attention to economic factors in carrying out these programs.

Higher levels of investment efficiency in outward-oriented countries were accompanied by superior savings performance, with average domestic savings ratios rising from 18.0 percent in 1963–73 to 24.4 percent in 1973–9. For one thing, private savings were encouraged through the adoption of realistic interest rates; for another thing, public dissavings were limited through reductions in government budget deficits. In turn, domestic savings ratios rose only from 19.3 to 21.0 percent in inward-oriented countries that generally maintained negative real interest rates and high budget deficits.

As noted above, inward-oriented countries relied to a considerable extent on foreign borrowing. As a result, the debt-service ratios of these countries nearly doubled between 1973 and 1978, reaching 43 percent of export value, while the ratio remained at 12 percent in outward-oriented countries.

Their high indebtedness did not permit inward-oriented countries to continue relying exclusively on foreign borrowing to finance the balance-of-payments effects of external shocks in the 1978–83 period. Nor did they adopt output-increasing policies of export promotion and import substitution. Thus, apart from external borrowing, the countries in question applied deflationary measures to offset the effects of external shocks.

Outward-oriented countries, too, had to rely in part on deflationary policies to cope with the external shocks they suffered during the period. Nevertheless, output-increasing policies remained their principal policy response to external shocks as they continued to gain export market shares and to replace imports by domestic production.

Correspondingly, outward-oriented countries maintained higher economic growth rates than their inward-oriented counterparts between 1979 and 1982. At the same time, the slowdown owing to the imposition of deflationary measures remained temporary, and outward-oriented countries averaged GNP growth rates of 5 percent in 1983. By contrast, inward-oriented countries had to reinforce the application of deflationary measures as interest rates rose on their large external debt, leading to the stagnation of their national economies in 1983.

Policies and performance in a cross-section framework

The above results have been obtained by classifying developing countries as outward-oriented and inward-oriented. While such a binary classification necessarily involves a certain degree of arbitrariness, the results have been reconfirmed in an econometric study of 43 developing countries, in which initial trade orientation and policy responses to external shocks have been separately introduced (Balassa, 1985a).

The extent of trade orientation has been estimated as deviations of actual from hypothetical values of per capita exports, the latter having been derived in a regression equation that includes the ratio of mineral exports to the gross national product in addition to per capita incomes and population, first used by Chenery (1960) as explanatory variables. In turn, alternative policy responses have been represented by relating the balance-of-payments effects of export promotion, import substitution, and additional net external financing to the balance-of-payments effects of external shocks.

The impact of trade orientation on economic growth has been indicated by estimating differences in GNP growth rates between a country in the upper quartile of the distribution in terms of trade orientation, representing the median among outward-oriented countries, and the neutral case where the trade orientation variable takes a zero value. The results show a gain of 0.5 of a percentage point for the country concerned. In turn, a country in the lower quartile of the distribution, representing the median among inward-oriented countries, is shown to experience a shortfall of 0.5 of a percentage point in its GNP growth rate. *Ceteris paribus*, there is thus a difference in GNP growth rates of 1.0 percentage point between the median outward-oriented and the median inward-oriented country.

In turn, the regression coefficient of the export promotion variable exceeds that of the import substitution and the additional net external financing variables two to two-and-a-half times, indicating that greater reliance on export promotion in response to external shocks permits reaching higher GNP growth rates. Correspondingly, increasing export promotion by 10 percentage points at the expense of import substitution and additional net external financing would add

0.3 of a percentage point to the rate of economic growth. The gain is 0.7 of a percentage point if comparison is made between the upper quartile and the median in terms of reliance on export promotion, and a loss of 0.4 of a percentage point in GNP growth is shown if a country at the lower quartile of the distribution is compared to the median. Comparing the two quartiles, then, a gain of 1.2 percentage points is obtained.

The results are cumulative, indicating that both initial trade orientation and the choice of adjustment policies in response to external shocks importantly contributed to economic growth during the period under review. In fact, these factors explain a large proportion of inter-country differences in GNP growth rates that averaged 5.0 percent in the 43 developing countries under consideration during the 1973–9 period, with an upper quartile of 6.5 percent and a lower quartile of 3.3 percent.

CONCLUSIONS

Following a review of the world environment in which these policies operate, the present chapter examined the experience of developing countries with outward- and inward-oriented development strategies. While under outward orientation similar incentives are provided to exports and to import substitution, inward orientation involves biasing the system of incentives in favor of import substitution and against exports. With agriculture being the principal export sector in most developing countries, inward orientation also entails discriminating against primary, in particular agricultural, products, whereas agriculture and industry receive similar incentives under outward orientation.

This chapter has provided evidence on the adverse effects of continued inward orientation in developing countries. Such a policy may initially permit rapid economic expansion, but it will eventually run into difficulties as the limitation of domestic markets leads to shifts into new activities that do not conform to the country's resource endowment and circumscribe the possibilities for the exploitation of economies of scale, and do not provide scope for sufficient competition.

In fact, while according to the infant industry argument the short-run costs of import protection would be eventually offset by long-term benefits through increased productivity, available evidence indicates a decline in productivity growth under continued inward orientation.[13] Thus, the growth of total factor productivity, derived as a ratio of the growth of output to that of factor inputs combined, turned negative in India which long persisted in pursuing an inward-oriented development strategy (Ahluwalia, 1986) as well as in Mexico which turned increasingly inward (Balassa, 1986c).

Also, a survey of estimates for 20 developing countries showed that total factor productivity increased at annual rates of over 3 percent in outward-oriented economies[14] while increases were less than 1 percent or even negative in countries with an especially pronounced inward orientation (Chenery, 1986, Table 2–2).[15] These results may be explained by reference to the fact that outward orientation leads to the efficient use not only of existing resources but also of increments in resources, permits the exploitation of economies of scale, and provides the stick and carrot of competition that gives inducement for technological change.

It has been suggested, however, that foreign market limitations would not permit the adoption of outward-oriented policies by an increasing number of developing countries. The proponents of this view neglect the possibilities existing in developed-country markets for the manufactured products of the developing countries that still have a small share in these markets; disregard the fact that increased exports by the developing countries lead to their increased imports from the developed countries, in particular of manufactured goods; and fail to recognize the potential for trade among developing countries.

Also, outward orientation should not be confused with export promotion. The adoption of a neutral incentive scheme will promote efficient import substitution in industries that are discriminated against under inward orientation. Apart from primary products, in most developing countries this is the case for capital goods that enter duty-free or are subject to low tariffs.

It should further be emphasized that the success of outward orientation will depend on the removal of policy-imposed distortions on capital and in labor markets. Such distortions tend to raise the price of labor relative to the price of capital (Krueger, 1983), thereby hindering the exploitation of comparative advantage. Also, the availability of financial resources is necessary to undertake investments that permit the practical implementation of a strategy of outward orientation.

This chapter has emphasized differences between two archetypes of development strategies: outward and inward orientation. A more complete treatment would also consider intermediate cases that may combine the characteristics of the two. And, very importantly, consideration would need to be given to problems of transition: the path of reform that may lead from inward to outward orientation.

Notes

1. This argumentation neglects the elasticity of demand for the products of the center in the periphery. For a formalization of the argument in a model of complete specialization, see Johnson (1954).
2. From the welfare point of view, it is double-factoral terms of trade (i.e. the commodity terms of trade adjusted for changes in productivity in the production of traded goods) rather than the commodity terms of trade that is relevant. However, in keeping with the Prebisch–Singer analysis, this chapter will not consider the double-factoral terms of trade for which statistical information is not available in any case.
3. In an earlier defense of the secular deterioration of the terms-of–trade thesis, Baer (1962) provided data on changes in the terms of trade of primary products until 1947–8 and from 1950 onwards without, however, taking note of the rapid rise of primary product prices that occurred between the two dates.
4. Apart from adding a reference to Kravis and Lipsey (1971), the article was reproduced in a virtually unchanged form in Spraos's later book (1983).
5. Spraos noted that combining the UN index with the one constructed by Yates (1959) for the 1913–53 period would give rise to an upward adjustment in the prices of manufactured goods. He added, however, that Yates considered his unit value index for manufactured goods to be of low reliability and that utilizing the index developed by Maizels (1963) would involve an adjustment of identical magnitude in the opposite direction.
6. Between 1977 and 1985, the UN unit value index for manufactured goods exported by the developed countries increased by 23 percent. Assuming that the extent of the bias in the unit value index was the same as in the 1953–77 period, the increase in the prices of manufactured goods exported by the developed countries would be estimated at 11 percent, with a further downward adjustment needed for quality changes. In turn, the World Bank's price index for the nonfuel primary exports of developing countries declined by 12 percent. At the same time, the UN unit value index of manufactured goods exported by the developing countries, which came to exceed their nonfuel exports, rose by 22 percent.
7. More exactly, the calculations pertain to price changes for goods classified by income level, when the income level of exports (imports) is derived as an income-weighted average of exports by individual countries. The cited results refer to data for the lower half and the upper half of the distribution. The relevant formulas are provided in Michaely (1985).

8. This section draws on Balassa (1970), where appropriate references are provided.
9. This section relies on Balassa (1980), where appropriate references are provided.
10. At the same time, one may agree with Bhagwati (1978, p. 147) that "while there is much empirical evidence in support of a statistical association between exports and saving, there is little evidence so far for some of the hypotheses that could provide a *rationale* for such an association implying a causal relationship running from exports to savings."
11. This is not to imply that economic growth rates provide an appropriate success indicator. A more appropriate choice is the rise of factor productivity, to be discussed below.
12. An apparent exception is Chile but this was due to the capital-intensity of its intra-Latin American exports under the policies applied; the labor-intensity of exports in trade with developed countries much exceeded that for import substitution (Krueger, 1983, Table 6.2).
13. It should be noted, however, that infant-industry objectives can be more efficiently pursued by production subsidies than by import protection.
14. Hong Kong, Korea, and Taiwan, in earlier periods; Israel, Spain, and Singapore, however, provide an exception.
15. Argentina, Chile (prior to 1974), India, and Venezuela.

References

Adams, N.A., "A note on 'Trade as a handmaiden of growth'," *Economic Journal*, 83, 1973, pp. 210–12.

Ahluwalia, I.S., "Industrial growth in India: Performance and prospects," *Journal of Development Economics*, 23, 1986, pp. 1–18.

Amin, J., *Accumulation on a World Scale: A Critique of the Theory of Underdevelopment*, Vol. 1. New York, Monthly Review Press, 1974.

Amin, J., "Self-reliance and the new international economic order," *Monthly Review*, 29, 1977, pp. 1–21.

Bacha, E., "An interpretation of unequal exchange from Prebisch–Singer to Emmanuel," *Journal of Development Economics*, 5, 1978, pp. 319–30.

Baer, W., "The economics of Prebisch and ECLA," *Economic Development and Cultural Change*, 10, 1962, pp. 169–82.

Bairoch, P., *The Economic Development of the Third World Since 1900*, London, Methuen, 1975.

Balassa, B., "Growth strategies in semi-industrial countries," *Quarterly Journal of Economics*, 84, 1970, pp. 24–47.

Balassa, B., "The effects of commercial policy on international trade, the location of production, and factor movements," in B. Ohlin, P.-O. Hesselborn, and P.M. Wijkman, eds, *The International Allocation of Economic Activity*, London, Macmillan, 1977.

Balassa, B., "Export incentives and export performance in developing countries: A comparative analysis," *Weltwirtschaftliches Archiv*, 114, 1978a, pp. 24–61.

Balassa, B., "Exports and economic growth: Further evidence," *Journal of Development Economics*, 5, 1978b, pp. 181–9.

Balassa, B., "The process of industrial development and alternative development strategies," *Essays in International Finance*, 141, 1980.

Balassa, B., "Adjustment to external shocks in developing countries," in B. Csikós-Nagy, D. Hague, and G. Hall, eds, *The Economics of Relative Prices*, London, Macmillan, 1984a.

Balassa, B., "Adjustment policies and development strategies in Sub-Saharan Africa," in M. Syrquin, L. Taylor, and L.E. Westphal, eds, *Economic Structure and Performance. Essays in Honor of Hollis B. Chenery*, Orlando, Academic Press, 1984b.

Balassa, B., "The terms of trade controversy and the evolution of soft financing: Early years in the UN – Comment," in G.M. Meier and D. Seers, eds, *Pioneers in Development*, Oxford, Oxford University Press, 1984c.

Balassa, B., "Exports, policy choices and economic growth in developing countries after the 1973 oil shock," *Journal of Development Economics*, 18, 1985a, pp. 23–36.

Balassa, B., "The Cambridge group and the developing countries," *The World Economy*, 8, 1985b, pp. 201–18.

Balassa, B., "Policy responses to exogenous shocks in developing countries," *American Economic Review*, Papers and Proceedings, 76, 1986a, pp. 75–8.

Balassa, B., "Dependency and trade orientation," *The World Economy*, 9, 1986b, pp. 259–73.

Balassa, B., "Economic incentives and agricultural performance," paper presented at the Eighth Congress of the International Economic Association held in December 1986, in New Delhi, India, mimeo, 1986c.

Balassa, B. and Associates, *The Structure of Protection in Developing Countries*, Baltimore, Md, Johns Hopkins University Press, 1971.

Balassa, B., E. Voloudakis, P. Fylaktos and S.T. Suh, "Export incentives and export expansion in developing countries: An econometric investigation," World Bank Development Research Department, Discussion Paper no. 159, 1986.

Banerji, R. and J. Riedel, "Industrial employment expansion under alternative trade strategies: Case of India and Taiwan: 1950–1970," *Journal of Development Economics*, 7, 1980, pp. 567–77.

Behrman, J.B., "Country and sectoral variations in manufacturing elasticities of substitution between capital and labor," in A.O. Krueger, ed., *Trade and Employment in Developing Countries 2. Factor Supply and Substitution*, Chicago, Ill., Chicago University Press, 1982.

Bergsten, C.F., "The new era in world commodity markets," *Challenge*, 17, 1974, pp. 34–42.

Berlinski, J. and D.M. Schydlowsky, "Argentina," in B. Balassa and Associates, *Development Strategies in Semi-Industrial Economies*, Baltimore, Md, Johns Hopkins University Press, 1982.

Bhagwati, J.N., *Foreign Trade Regimes and Economic Development: Anatomy and Consequences of Exchange Control Regimes*, Cambridge, Mass., Ballinger, 1978.

Bhagwati, J.N. and T.N. Srinivasan, *Foreign Trade Regimes and Economic Development: India*. New York, Columbia University Press, 1975.

Bruton, H.J., "Productivity growth in Latin America," *American Economic Review*, 57, 1967, pp. 1099–1107.

Bruton, H.J., "The import substitution strategy of economic development: A survey," *Pakistan Development Review*, 10, 1970, pp. 124–46.

Bruton, H.J., "Industrialization policy and income distribution," Research Memorandum 69, mimeo. Williams College, 1974.

Carvalho, J.L. and C.L.S. Haddad, "Foreign trade strategies and employment in Brazil," in A.O. Krueger, M.B. Lary, T. Monson, and N. Akrasanee, eds, *Trade and Employment in Developing Countries 1. Individual Studies*. Chicago, Ill., Chicago University Press, 1981.

Caves, R.E., "Export-led growth and the new economic history," in J.N. Bhagwati *et al.*, eds, *Trade, Balance and Payments, and Growth*, Amsterdam: North-Holland, 1965.

Chenery, H.B., "Patterns of industrial growth," *American Economic Review*, 50, 1960, pp. 624–54.

Chenery, H.B., "Growth and transformation," in H.B. Chenery, S. Robinson, and M. Syrquin, eds, *Industrialization and Growth: A Comparative Study*, Oxford, Oxford University Press, 1986, ch. 2.

Chenery, H.B. and Syrquin, M., *Patterns of Development 1950–1970*. Oxford, Oxford University Press, 1975.

Chichilnisky, G., "Terms of trade and domestic distribution: Export-led growth with abundant labor," *Journal of Development Economics*, 8, 1981, pp. 163–92.

Cline, W.R., "Can the East Asian experience be generalized?," *World Development*, 10, 1982, pp. 81–90.

Cohen, B.I., "The stagnation of Indian exports," *Quarterly Journal of Economics*, 78, 1964, pp. 604–20.

Cohen, B.I. and D.G. Sisler, "Exports of developing countries in the 1960s," *Review of Economics and Statistics*, 53, 1971, pp. 354–61.

Cooper, R.N., "Currency devaluation in developing countries," *Essays in International Finance*, 86, 1971.

Crafts, N.F.R., "Trade as a handmaiden of growth: an alternative view," *Economic Journal*, 83, 1973, pp. 875–84.

De Vries, B.A., "The export experience of developing countries," World Bank Staff Occasional Papers no. 3, Johns Hopkins University Press, 1967.

Diaz-Alejandro, C.F., "Delinking North and South: Unshackled or unhinged," in A. Fishlow, C.F. Diaz-Alejandro, R.R. Fagen, and R.D. Hansen, eds, *Rich and Poor Nations in the World Economy*, New York, McGraw Hill, 1978.

Donges, J.B. and J. Riedel, "The expansion of manufactured exports in developing countries: An empirical assessment of supply and demand issues," *Weltwirtschaftliches Archiv*, 113, 1977, pp. 58–87.

Donovan, D.J., "Real responses associated with exchange rate action in selected upper credit tranche stabilization programs," *International Monetary Fund Staff Papers*, 28, 1981, pp. 698–727.

Elias, V.J., "Sources of economic growth in Latin American countries," *Review of Economics and Statistics*, 60, 1978, pp. 362–70.

Ellsworth, P.T., "The terms of trade between primary producing and industrial countries," *Inter-American Economic Affairs*, 10, 1956, pp. 47–65.

Faluvégi, L., "Gazdasági hatékonyság – gazdaságirányítás", (Economic efficiency – economic management), *Közgazdasági Szemle*, 31, 1984, pp. 1025–43.

Feder, G., "On exports and economic growth," *Journal of Development Economics*, 12, 1983, pp. 59–73.

Fields, G.S., "Employment, income distribution and economic growth in seven small open economies," *Economic Journal*, 94, 1984, pp. 74–83.

Findlay, R., "The terms of trade and equilibrium growth in the world economy," *American Economic Review*, 70, 1980, pp. 291–9.

Findlay, R., "Growth and development in trade models," in W. Jones and B. Kenen, eds, *Handbook of international economics*, Vol. I. Amsterdam, North-Holland, 1984.

Flanders, M.J. "Prebisch on protectionism: An evaluation," *Economic Journal*, 74, 1964, pp. 305–26.

Grinols, E. and J.N. Bhagwati, "Foreign capital, savings and dependence," *Review of Economics and Statistics*, 58, 1976, pp. 416–24.

Haberler, G., "Terms of trade and economic development," in H. Ellis, ed., *Economic Development of Latin America*, New York, St Martin's Press, 1961.

Haq, M.U., *The Poverty Curtain: Choices for the Third World*, New York, Columbia University Press, 1976.

Heller, P.S. and R.C. Porter, "Exports and growth: An empirical re-investigation," *Journal of Development Economics*, 5, 1978, pp. 191–3.

Hicks, J.P., "An inaugural lecture," *Oxford Economic Papers*, 1953.

Hirschman, A.O., *The Strategy of Economic Development*, New Haven, Conn., Yale University Press, 1958.

Innis, H., *Essays in Canadian Economic History*. Toronto, University of Toronto Press, 1957.

Isserlis, L., "Tramp shipping cargoes and freights," *Journal of the Royal Statistical Society*, 101, 1938, pp. 53–164.

Johnson, H.G., "Increasing productivity, income-price trends and the trade balance," *Economic Journal*, 64, 1954, pp. 462–85.

Johnson, H.G., "The possibility of income losses from increased efficiency factor accumulation in the presence of tariffs," *Economic Journal*, 17, 1967, pp. 151–4.

Johnson, H.G., "Alternative maximization policies for developing country exporters of primary products," *Journal of Political Economy*, 78, 1968, pp. 489–93.

Kindleberger, C.P., *International Economics*, Homewood, Ill., R.D. Irwin, 1953.

Kindleberger, C.P., *Terms of Trade, a European Case Study*, London, Chapman Hill, 1956.

Kravis, I.B., "Trade as a handmaiden of growth: Similarities between the nineteenth and the twentieth centuries," *Economic Journal*, 80, 1970, pp. 850–72.

Kravis, I.B., "A reply to Mr Adams," *Economic Journal*, 83, 1973a, pp. 212–17.

Kravis, I.B., "A reply to Mr Crafts' note," *Economic Journal*, 83, 1973b, pp. 885–9.

Kravis, I.B. and R.E. Lipsey, *Price Competitiveness in World Trade*, New York, National Bureau of Economic Research, 1971.

Kravis, I.B. and R.E. Lipsey, "Prices and terms of trade for developed country exports of manufactured goods," in B. Csikós-Nagy, D. Hague, and G. Hall, eds, *The Economics of Relative Prices*, London, Macmillan, 1984.

Krueger, A.O., *Trade and Employment in Developing Countries 3. Synthesis and Conclusions*, Chicago, Ill., University of Chicago Press, 1983.

Krueger, A.O., "Trade policies in developing countries," in R.W. Jones and P.B. Kenen, eds, *Handbook of International Economics*, Vol. I, Amsterdam, North-Holland, 1984.

Leff, N.H., "Export stagnation and autarkic development in Brazil, 1947–1962," *Quarterly Journal of Economics*, 81, 1967, pp. 286–301.

Leff, N.H., "The 'exportable surplus' approach to foreign trade in underdeveloped countries," *Economic Development and Cultural Change*, 17, 1969, pp. 346–55.

Leff, N.H., "Tropical trade and development in the nineteenth century: The Brazilian experience," *Journal of Political Economy*, 81, 1973, pp. 678–96.

Lewis, W.A., "World production, prices and trade, 1870–1960," *Manchester School of Economic and Social Studies*, 21, 1952, pp. 139–91.

Lewis, W.A., *Aspects of Tropical Trade, 1883–1967*. Uppsala, Wiksell, 1969.

Lewis, W.A., "The slowing down of the engine of growth," *American Economic Review*, 70, 1980, pp. 555–64.

Lipsey, R.E., *Price and Quantity Trends in the Foreign Trade of the United States*. Princeton, NJ, Princeton University Press, 1963.

Love, J., "External market conditions, competitiveness, diversification, and LDC exports," *Journal of Development Economics*, 16, 1984, pp. 279–91.

Martin, R., "Immiserizing growth for a tariff-distorted, small economy Further analysis," *Journal of International Economics*, 7, 1977, pp. 223–8.

Maizels, A., *Industrial Growth and World Trade*, Cambridge, Mass., Cambridge University Press, 1963.

Maizels, A., *Exports and Economic Growth in Developing Countries*, Cambridge, Mass., Cambridge University Press, 1968.

McKinnon, R.I., *Money and Capital in Economic Development*, Washington, DC, The Brookings Institution, 1973.

Michaely, M., "Exports and growth: An empirical investigation," *Journal of Development Economics*, 4, 1977, pp. 49–54.

Michaely, M., *Trade, Income Levels, and Dependence*, Amsterdam, North Holland, 1985.

Michalopoulos, C. and K. Jay, "Growth of exports and income in the developing world: A neoclassical view," US Agency for International Development, Discussion Paper, no. 28, mimeo, 1973.

Mikesell, R.F., "More Third World cartels ahead?" *Challenge*, 17, 1974, pp. 24–31.

Morrisson, C., "Domestic income distribution and the structure of foreign trade," OECD Development Centre, mimeo, 1985.

Myint, H., "The gains from trade and the backward countries," *Review of Economic Studies*, 22, 1955, pp. 129–42.

Myint, H., "Growth policies and income distribution," World Bank Development Policy Issues Series, Discussion Paper no. VPERS1, mimeo, 1985.

Myrdal, G., *Economic Theory and Underdeveloped Regions*, London, Duckworth, 1957.

North, D.C., *The Economic Growth of the United States, 1790–1860*. Englewood Cliffs, NJ, Prentice-Hall, 1961.

Nurkse, R., *Equilibrium and Growth in the World Economy*, Cambridge, Mass., Harvard University Press, 1961.

Nurkse, R., "International trade policy and development policy," in H.S. Ellis and H.C. Wallich, eds, *Economic Development for Latin America*, London, Macmillan, 1966.

Papanek, G., "Aid, foreign private investment, savings, and growth in less developed countries," *Journal of Political Economy*, 81, 1973, pp. 120–30.

Pindyck, R.S., "Gains to producers from the cartellization of exhaustible resources," *Review of Economics and Statistics*, 60, 1978, pp. 238–51.

Porter, R.C., "Some implications of postwar primary-product trends," *Journal of Political Economy*, 78, 1970, pp. 586–97.

Prebisch, R., *The Economic Development of Latin America*, Lake Success, United Nations, 1950.

Prebisch, R., "Commercial policy in underdeveloped countries," *American Economic Review*, Papers and Proceedings, 44, 1959, pp. 251–73.

Radetzki, M., "The potential for monopolistic commodity pricing by developing countries," in G.K. Helleiner, ed., *A World Divided: The Less Developed Countries in the International Economy*, Cambridge, Mass., Cambridge University Press, 1975.

Radetzki, M., "Long-term copper production options of the developing countries," *Natural Resource Forum*, 1, 1977, pp. 145–55.

Radetzki, M., "Strategic metal markets. Prospects for producer cartels," *Resource Policy*, 10, 1984, pp. 227–40.

Riedel, J., "Trade as the engine of growth in developing countries, revisited," *Economic Journal*, 94, 1984, pp. 56–73.

Schumpeter, J.A., *History of Economic Analysis*. New York, Oxford University Press, 1954.

Senghaas, D., "The case for autarchy," *Development*, 2, 1980, pp. 17–22.

Singer, H., "The distribution of gains between investing and borrowing countries," *American Economic Review*, Papers and Proceedings, 1950.

Singer, H., "The terms of trade: Controversy and the evolution of soft financing: Early years in the UN," in G.M. Meier and D. Seers, eds, *Pioneers in Development*, Oxford, Oxford University Press, 1984.

Spraos, J., "The statistical debate on the net barter terms of trade between primary commodities and manufactures," *Economic Journal*, 90, 1980, pp. 107–28.

Spraos, J., *Inequalizing Trade?* Oxford, Clarendon Press, 1983.

Stern, E. and W. Tims, "The relative bargaining strengths of the developing countries," *American Journal of Agricultural Economics*, 57, 1975, pp. 225–36.

Taylor, L., "South–South trade and southern growth: Bleak prospects from the structuralist point of view," *Journal of International Economics*, 11, 1981, pp. 589–602.

Vines, D., "A North–South growth model along Kaldorian lines," Centre for Economic Policy Research, Discussion Paper Series no. 26, mimeo, 1984.

Watkins, M.H., "A staple theory of economic growth," *Canadian Journal of Economics and Political Science*, 29, 1963, pp. 141–58.

Weisskopf, T.E., "The impact of foreign capital inflow on domestic savings in underdeveloped countries," *Journal of International Economics*, 2, 1972, pp. 25–38.

World Bank, *World Development Report 1981*, World Bank, 1981.

Yates, P.L., *Forty Years of Foreign Trade*, London, Allen & Unwin, 1959.

2 Policy Choices in the Newly-Industrializing Countries*

INTRODUCTION

This chapter will compare the policies and economic performance of newly-industrializing countries (NICs) in the Far East and Latin America in the 1963–88 period. The two groups of countries include Hong Kong, Korea, Singapore, and Taiwan and Argentina, Brazil, Chile, and Mexico.

Information will be provided on indicators of economic growth as well as on domestic savings ratios, the efficiency of investment, and export performance. Next, the results will be explained in terms of the policies applied.

GROWTH PERFORMANCE

The Far Eastern newly-industrializing countries had relatively low income levels in 1963. Even Hong Kong and Singapore were behind Argentina, Chile, and Mexico in terms of income per head (Table 2.1).

The situation changed dramatically in the following two-and-a-half decades. By 1988, all four of the Far Eastern NICs surpassed the per capita incomes of every Latin American newly-industrializing country. These changes occurred as the per capita income of the four Far Eastern NICs increased four-and-a-half to six times during the 1963–87 period. Among Latin American NICs per capita incomes increased two-and-a-half times in Brazil, one-and-a-half times in

---

* Originally published in P. Marer and A. Koves, editors, *Foreign Economic Liberalization: Transformations in Socialist and Market Economies*, Westview Press, Boulder, Colorado, 1991.

The author is indebted to Sinod Thomas for helpful comments and to Shigeru Akiyama for research assistance.

Table 2.1   Gross domestic product per capita (US dollars)

| | At purchasing power parities in 1980 prices | | | | | At exchange rates |
	1963	1973	1981	1988	1988/1963	1988
Hong Kong	2247	4552	7751	11952	5.32	9600
Korea	747	1553	2457	4094	5.48	4082
Singapore	1777	3838	6308	11693	6.58	9009
Taiwan	980	1976	3029	4607	4.70	5862
Argentina	2949	4157	3935	3474	1.18	2806
Brazil	1400	2338	3252	3424	2.45	2454
Chile	3231	3502	4443	3933	1.22	1732
Mexico	2312	3403	4576	3649	1.58	2114

Source: 1963–81 figures from Summers, R. and A. Heston, "A New Set of International Comparisons of Real Product and Price Levels Estimates for 130 Countries," *Review of Income and Wealth*, March 1988.
1988 estimates updated from 1985 figures by utilizing national data on economic growth rates.

Mexico and by less than one-quarter in Argentina and Chile.

Further interest attaches to intercountry differences in increases in per capita incomes over time. Table 2.1 provides data for the bench-mark years of the 1963–73 period of world economic boom, the 1973–81 period of two oil shocks, and the 1981–7 period of the debt crisis.

It appears that the Far Eastern NICs started gaining on the Latin American NICs already in the 1963–73 period; per capita incomes doubled in the Far Eastern NICs, much surpassing the performance of any of the Latin American countries. The Far Eastern NICs increased their lead during the period of the oil crises, notwithstanding their reliance on imported petroleum, while Argentina suffered declines in per capita incomes.

Differences in economic performance increased further in the period of the debt crisis. The Far Eastern NICs experienced increases in per capita incomes by one-half to four-fifths. In turn, apart from small gains in Brazil, incomes per head fell in the Latin American NICs. In this connection, reference may be made to differences in the foreign debt situation. There is a contrast between the high degree of foreign indebtedness of Latin American countries and the low external debt of the Far Eastern NICs (see further below).

Table 2.2 GDP growth rates, domestic savings ratios, and incremental capital–output ratios

Country	1963–73			1973–81			1981–8		
	GDP growth rate	Domestic saving ratio	ICOR	GDP growth rate	Domestic saving ratio	ICOR	GDP growth rate	Domestic saving ratio	ICOR
Hong Kong	8.9	24.3	3.6	9.1	29.0	3.4	7.3	29.3	3.9
Korea	9.3	13.0	2.0	7.7	23.7	4.0	10.1	31.0	2.8
Singapore	10.3	16.5	3.1	7.8	32.8	5.0	6.1	41.8	7.0
Taiwan	11.1	24.4	1.9	8.0	32.8	3.7	7.9	33.8	2.8
Argentina	5.0	20.5	4.2	1.1	24.2	20.2	–0.0	16.3	–925.9
Brazil	8.2	26.3	2.2	5.3	21.2	4.9	3.0	21.8	5.9
Chile	2.8	14.3	7.5	3.7	14.2	4.5	1.6	15.9	9.2
Mexico	7.4	19.2	2.7	6.7	22.1	3.4	–0.0	26.2	–905.6

Source: World Bank data base.

Note: ICOR = Incremental capital–output ratio.

DOMESTIC SAVINGS AND THE EFFICIENCY OF INVESTMENT

Various factors may be introduced to explain differences in growth performance between the Far Eastern and the Latin American newly-industrializing countries. They include differences in domestic savings ratios and investment efficiency, as well as the changing relative importance of exports. Increases in domestic savings ratios and in investment efficiency add to GDP directly while exports have indirect effects.

A comparison of the Far Eastern and Latin American NICs does not show overall differences in domestic savings ratios in the 1963–73 period while there were considerable differences within each group. The superior growth performance of the Far Eastern NICs during this period is thus explained by their higher investment efficiency which is measured, however imperfectly, by incremental capital–output ratios (ICOR).[1] Among Latin American NICs, Brazil and Mexico had low incremental capital–output ratios (Table 2.2).

The situation changed in the 1973–81 period. All Far Eastern NICs increased their domestic savings ratios to a substantial extent while the increases were smaller, or domestic savings ratios declined, in the Latin American NICs. At the same time, the Far Eastern NICs maintained higher levels of investment efficiency than their Latin

Table 2.3   Export and import shares (per cent)

	Export/GDP ratio				Import/GDP ratio			
	1963	1973	1981	1988	1963	1973	1981	1988
Hong Kong	39.0	49.8	48.5	51.1	75.4	74.1	83.6	117.2
Korea	2.3	23.7	30.4	35.4	14.6	31.3	37.3	30.2
Singapore	124.5	86.5	151.0	164.2	153.4	121.5	198.5	183.3
Taiwan	15.3	41.2	47.7	51.8	16.7	35.7	44.7	38.2
Argentina	10.0	4.6	7.4	10.2	7.2	3.1	7.6	5.9
Brazil	6.0	7.8	8.8	9.5	6.3	8.8	9.1	4.5
Chile	11.6	12.1	11.5	31.9	13.6	10.7	19.2	21.9
Mexico	5.1	4.4	8.0	11.9	7.4	6.9	9.9	11.2

Sources: United Nations and World Bank. Data relate to merchandise trade.

American counterparts. An apparent exception is Mexico where newly-found oil raised GDP growth rates, thereby reducing incremental capital–output ratios.

In the 1981–7 period, negative GDP growth rates in Argentina and Mexico do not permit deriving meaningful estimates of incremental capital–output ratios. Growth rates in Brazil and Chile continued to fall behind those of the Far Eastern NICs.

THE ROLE OF EXPORTS

The Far Eastern NICs attained high rates of economic growth in an open economy as shown by their high export–GDP ratios (Table 2.3). Nor can these differences be explained by disparities in country size. Thus, while Brazil and Mexico have large economies, Korea's population and GDP are greater than Argentina's, and Taiwan's population and GDP are greater than Chile's.

In Korea and Taiwan, the export–GDP ratio increased greatly between 1963 and 1988, indicating the leading role of exports in the growth process. This was the case, to a lesser extent, in Hong Kong and Singapore that already had high export–GDP ratios at the beginning of the period. At any rate, the figures for these countries are much affected by entrepôt trade. The results are further affected by the importation of inputs for processing to export that raised the ratio for Singapore above 100 percent.[2]

Export–GDP ratios increased much less in the Latin American

NICs than in Korea and Taiwan. In Mexico's case, the oil finds raised the export–GDP ratio; in Chile, an even larger increase occurred as economic policy shifted in an outward-oriented direction after 1973.

Export expansion in the Far Eastern NICs involved an increasing shift towards manufactured goods. In Korea, the share of manufactured goods in total exports rose from 45 percent in 1963 to 93 percent in 1988; in Taiwan, the corresponding figures were 38 and 92 percent (Table 2.4). Smaller changes occurred in Hong Kong that already had a 92 percent manufactured export share in 1963 and in Singapore where entrepôt trade in primary products is of importance.

The share of manufactured exports increased also in the Latin American NICs, but it remained lower than in the Far Eastern NICs. The relevant shares for 1963 and 1988 are: Argentina, 6 and 32 percent; Brazil, 3 and 48 percent; Chile, 4 and 15 percent; and Mexico, 17 and 56 percent.

Data on manufactured export share are affected by the availability of natural resources, in particular copper in Chile. At the same time, interest attaches to per capita manufactured exports that provide an indication of a country's success in these export products.

Table 2.5 shows the rapid expansion of manufactured exports in the Far Eastern NICs. These exports were negligible in Korea and Taiwan in 1963 but reached $1349 per head in the first case and $2786 per head in the second in 1988. The rate of expansion was slower in Hong Kong and Singapore that started with a higher base (nearly $180 per head in both cases in 1963). But the absolute figures are much higher ($4683 in Hong Kong and $10 398 in Singapore in 1988), although a portion of the total represents re-exports.

The per capita manufactured exports of the Latin American NICs are dwarfed by those of the East Asian NICs. In 1988, these exports were only $140 per head in Mexico, $112 per head in Brazil, $90 per head in Argentina, and $83 per head in Chile.

THE POLICIES APPLIED

The data show that, for the 1963–88 period as a whole, superior growth performance in the Far Eastern newly-industrializing countries was associated with high domestic savings ratios and high levels of investment efficiency. At the same time, exports played an important role in the growth process, contributing to the efficient use of investment funds.

Table 2.4   Commodity composition of exports (per cent)

1963	Fuels	Nonfuel primary goods	Manufactured goods	Other	Total
Hong Kong	0.0	7.8	91.7	0.5	100.0
Korea	3.0	51.8	45.1	0.2	100.0
Singapore	16.7	52.3	27.8	3.3	100.0
Taiwan	0.9	61.0	38.0	0.0	100.0
Argentina	0.8	93.4	5.7	0.0	100.0
Brazil	0.7	96.1	3.0	0.2	100.0
Chile	0.0	96.0	3.9	0.2	100.0
Mexico	4.5	78.4	17.0	0.1	100.0

1973	Fuels	Nonfuel primary goods	Manufactured goods	Other	Total
Hong Kong	.	3.3	96.5	0.2	100.0
Korea	1.1	14.7	84.0	0.2	100.0
Singapore	19.8	33.8	44.3	2.1	100.0
Taiwan	0.3	16.0	83.6	0.1	100.0
Argentina	0.2	77.4	22.4	0.1	100.0
Brazil	1.3	77.1	19.6	1.9	100.0
Chile	0.2	96.1	3.7	0.0	100.0
Mexico	0.9	57.1	41.9	0.0	100.0

1981	Fuels	Nonfuel primary goods	Manufactured goods	Other	Total
Hong Kong	0.1	3.0	96.5	0.4	100.0
Korea	0.7	8.7	90.0	0.5	100.0
Singapore	27.3	16.8	48.2	7.7	100.0
Taiwan	1.9	9.2	88.7	0.1	100.0
Argentina	6.8	73.6	19.6	0.0	100.0
Brazil	5.1	54.3	39.1	1.5	100.0
Chile	1.8	90.2	7.7	0.3	100.0
Mexico	72.1	17.8	10.1	0.0	100.0

1988	Fuels	Nonfuel primary goods	Manufactured goods	Other	Total
Hong Kong	0.2	3.2	95.4	1.2	100.0
Korea	1.0	5.7	93.3	.	100.0
Singapore	12.5	13.2	70.3	4.0	100.0
Taiwan	0.6	7.4	91.8	0.2	100.0
Argentina	1.5	66.8	31.6	0.0	100.0
Brazil	4.1	48.1	47.8	.	100.0
Chile	0.9	84.1	15.0	.	100.0
Mexico	30.7	13.6	55.8	.	100.0

Sources: United Nations and World Bank.

Table 2.5   Per capita exports of manufactured goods (US dollars)

	1963	1973	1981	1988
Hong Kong	179.7	866.9	2,664.7	4,682.5
Korea	1.5	79.2	492.8	1,349.3
Singapore	175.0	730.0	4,139.0	10,398.0
Taiwan	10.8	237.7	1,110.8	2,785.8
Argentina	3.7	29.4	62.6	90.4
Brazil	0.5	12.2	73.4	111.8
Chile	2.6	4.7	25.5	83.0
Mexico	3.7	19.6	28.5	139.9

Sources: United Nations and World Bank.

Apart from Hong Kong, all developing countries passed through the first stage of import substitution, involving the replacement by domestic production of the imports of nondurable consumer goods and their inputs. The manufacture of these products, including clothing and textiles, shoes and leather, and furniture and wood, conform to the production possibilities of the developing countries. They utilize in large part unskilled labor, involve the use of simple production processes, are not subject to important scale economies, and do not require the existence of a sophisticated industrial structure.

Once the first stage of import substitution has been completed, however, the rate of growth of industrial production cannot continue to exceed that of consumption. Now, countries face two choices: embarking on the exportation of nondurable consumer goods and their inputs or moving to the second stage of import substitution through the replacement by domestic production of the imports of producer and consumer durables and intermediate products.

Among present-day newly-industrializing countries, the choice was made for the first alternative in Korea, Singapore, and Taiwan in the early 1960s. These countries also carried out financial reforms that permitted raising domestic savings ratios.

Negative real interest rates (nominal interest rates exceeded by the rate of inflation) led to financial repression in the Latin American NICs that was not conducive to increasing domestic saving and to the efficient allocation of the amount saved. And, these countries shifted to the second stage of import substitution that proved costly as the commodities in question did not conform to the production possibilities of the countries concerned.

Thus, the manufacture of producer and consumer durables requires the existence of a sophisticated industrial structure to provide parts, components, and accessories made to precision. Also, such vertical specialization, as well as a horizontal or product specialization, needs a large domestic market for manufactured goods.

Large domestic markets are also necessary for the production of intermediate goods, where traditional economies of scale obtain. Furthermore, the manufacture of producer and consumer durables relies to a considerable extent on skilled and technical labor while intermediate products are highly capital-intensive. At the same time, the margin of transformation for intermediate products is often small and can be squandered through the poor organization of production.

The resulting high domestic costs reduced the efficiency of investment in countries pursuing a strategy of continued import substitution. In order to compensate for the higher costs, these countries also increased import protection, thereby discriminating against exports.

As the costs of continued import substitution became apparent, leading to declines in export expansion and economic growth, the three large Latin American NICs undertook reforms aimed to provide improved incentives to exports in the mid-1960s. The most far-reaching reforms were carried out in Brazil while its favorable balance-of-payments position, due to workers' remittances, tourism, and border industries, hampered the reform effort in Mexico and the opposition of urban interests obstructed the course of economic reforms in Argentina.

The reforms undertaken in the mid-1960s permitted reducing the bias of the incentive system against exports in Brazil, to a lesser extent in Mexico, and even less in Argentina. But, not even Brazil provided equal incentives to exports and import substitution as was the case in the Far Eastern NICs. Finally, after initial efforts, reforms were jettisoned by the Allende Government in Chile in the early 1970s.

Policies changed again following the oil crisis of 1973–4. The quadrupling of oil prices, together with the ensuing world recession, imposed a considerable cost on the economies of the newly-industrializing countries. This cost, shown in Table 2.6, was the largest in the East Asian NICs that were most exposed to foreign trade.[3]

Table 2.6 further shows the balance-of-payments effects of the policies applied in response to external shocks, including additional net external financing, export promotion, import substitution, and deflationary policies. Additional net external financing has been

Table 2.6   External shocks and policy responses to external shocks

		External shocks (% of GDP)	Additional net external financing	Export promotion (% of external shocks)	Import substitution	Deflationary policies
1974–8	Hong Kong	n.a.	n.a.	n.a.	n.a.	n.a.
	Korea	10.5	−88	90	128	−30
	Singapore	20.9	42	11	−24	70
	Taiwan	7.2	−92	14	96	82
	Argentina	0.5	−168	−13	146	136
	Brazil	3.3	30	15	66	−11
	Chile	6.0	−48	71	18	60
	Mexico	1.2	123	−70	33	14
1979–81	Hong Kong	n.a.	n.a.	n.a.	n.a.	n.a.
	Korea	9.4	−18	−7	8	116
	Singapore	30.4	39	89	−59	31
	Taiwan	13.1	−40	27	91	22
	Argentina	1.2	423	−109	−281	67
	Brazil	2.5	−33	38	49	47
	Chile	3.9	257	50	−133	−74
	Mexico	−0.5	309	412	−756	−64

Source: World Bank

For explanation, see text.

derived as the difference between actual financing and that estimated on the assumption that past trends in exports and imports continued. The effects of export promotion have been calculated in terms of changes in export market shares. Import substitution has been defined as savings in imports associated with a decrease in the income elasticity of import demand compared with the preceding period. Finally, the effects on imports of changes in GNP growth rates in response to the macroeconomic policies followed have been estimated on the assumption of unchanged income elasticities of import demand.

The Far Eastern newly-industrializing countries accepted an initial decline in the growth rate of GNP in order to limit reliance on external financing. Economic growth accelerated subsequently, however, as the countries in question maintained their outward-oriented policies. At the same time, adopting realistic exchange rates helped not only exports but also import substitution.

Among the Latin American newly-industrializing countries, Chile

Table 2.7 External debt ratios (per cent)

	External debt/exports				Debt service/exports			
	1973	1978	1981	1988	1973	1978	1981	1988
Hong Kong	.	.	.	.	.	.	.	.
Korea	95.2	100.8	121.0	52.4	16.8	12.8	21.7	13.5
Singapore	12.5	10.0	7.7	10.1	1.8	4.1	1.4	1.9
Taiwan	.	.	.	.	.	.	.	.
Argentina	171.6	169.4	302.0	512.0	36.7	42.3	45.7	43.6
Brazil	183.9	371.0	299.5	314.3	27.0	57.5	66.0	50.2
Chile	223.1	247.1	279.0	232.5	16.1	53.6	64.8	25.3
Mexico	185.9	313.2	283.0	319.1	38.6	65.1	51.9	48.9

Source: World Bank data base.

Note: Exports of non-factor and factor services are included in the figures.

shifted to outward-oriented policies in response to the external shocks it suffered. These policies led to considerable gains in export market shares while reliance on external financing was reduced. In turn, Brazil and Mexico relied to a considerable extent on external borrowing in order to finance the adverse balance-of-payments effects of external shocks while, self-sufficient in petroleum, Argentina experienced practically no external shocks.

The three large Latin American NICs also increased the extent of inward orientation of their incentive system, thereby promoting the replacement of imports by domestic production. Only Brazil, which continued with the export subsidies introduced in the preceding period, made some modest gains in exports; Argentina and Mexico lost export market shares.

The effects of the policies followed in regard to foreign borrowing are apparent in Table 2.7 that shows considerable increases in the external indebtedness of Brazil and Mexico between 1973 and 1978. By contrast, Korea and Singapore experienced a decline and Taiwan's external debt remained very small.

Having found oil that led to rapid export expansion, the ratio of external debt to exports declined in Mexico after 1978. Also, Brazil reduced reliance on external borrowing and adopted a mixture of policies aimed at increasing exports, import substitution, and slowing the economy. In turn, Argentina and Chile experienced a considerable capital inflow as a result of the overvaluation of the exchange rate aimed to reduce inflation.

The Far Eastern NICs again accepted a slowdown in economic growth after 1978 in order to limit reliance on foreign borrowing while maintaining their outward-oriented policies that led to the subsequent acceleration of economic growth. Only Korea engaged in foreign borrowing but its debt–export ratio hardly changed.

The results of alternative policies are apparent in the debt situation of the NICs on the eve of the debt crisis. While in Korea the debt–export ratio was 1.1 in 1981, this ratio reached 3.3 in Chile, 2.8 in Brazil, 2.7 in Mexico, and 2.5 in Argentina. Also, debt-service ratios ranged between 90 percent (Chile) and 56 percent (Mexico) in the Latin American NICs, compared with 24 percent in Korea. These high ratios necessitated corrective action on the part of the Latin American NICs, leading to a decline in their per capita incomes after 1981. By contrast, growth continued in the Far Eastern NICs, where Singapore and Taiwan accumulated a net asset position abroad.

CONCLUSION

This chapter has reviewed economic developments in the Far Eastern and Latin American newly-industrializing countries. The results show that the Far Eastern NICs attained much larger increases in per capita incomes than their Latin American counterparts in the 1963–88 period.

Differences in economic growth rates find their origin in differences in savings ratios and investment efficiency. While savings ratios differed little between the two groups of countries between 1963 and 1973, these ratios increased substantially in the Far Eastern NICs in subsequent years as they employed measures encouraging savings.

Investment efficiency was higher in the Far Eastern NICs than in the Latin American NICs throughout the period. The Far Eastern NICs achieved high levels of investment efficiency in the framework of an open economy, with high and rising ratios of exports to the gross domestic product. Export expansion involved an increasing shift towards manufactured goods.

Exports in the Far Eastern newly-industrializing countries were promoted by the system of incentives that entailed no discrimination, or limited discrimination, against exports. These countries also relied to a considerable extent on export promotion in response to external shocks and did not engage in excessive foreign borrowing.

The favorable external debt situation of the Far Eastern NICs also augurs well for their future economic growth. Korea's external debt ratio declined to 0.5 in 1988 as it had a large trade surplus in 1988 when Taiwan and Singapore also increased their surpluses. In turn, the external debt ratio reached 5.1 in Argentina, 3.2 in Mexico, 3.1 in Brazil, and 2.3 in Chile in 1988.

The experience of the Far Eastern and Latin American newly-industrializing countries provides important lessons to other developing countries. It indicates the superiority of outward-oriented policies that provide similar incentives to exports and import substitution. It also shows that the continuation of outward-oriented policies permits overcoming the effects of external shocks while reliance on external borrowing reinforces the adverse effects of these shocks.

Countries that have accumulated external debt, then, should adopt outward-oriented policies that provide impetus to economic growth through increased exports while improving the balance of payments. Such policies involve the simultaneous promotion of exports and liberalization of imports.

Notes

1. ICORs fail to allow for the effects of factors other than capital on economic growth and are subject to considerable measurement error. They are derived from national accounts statistics.
2. In any case, export values and value added (GDP) are not strictly comparable.
3. The cost of external shocks is measured as the balance-of-payments effects of the deterioration of the terms of trade and of the export shortfall, resulting from the slowdown of the world economy.

Part II

Adjustment Policies

3 A Conceptual Framework for Adjustment Policies*

STABILIZATION POLICIES VS ADJUSTMENT POLICIES

One may base the distinction between stabilization policies and adjustment policies on the policy measures applied or, alternatively, on the policy objectives pursued. While classification by policy measures would seem attractive, it encounters practical difficulties. Thus, the exchange rate is an important instrument for stabilization policies as well as for adjustment policies. Also, monetary and fiscal policies, which are central to stabilization, assume importance for adjustment as well.

The principal objective of stabilization policies under the auspices of the International Monetary Fund is taken to be improving the balance of payments; the IMF generally adds lowering inflation rates as another objective. In turn, increasing the rate of growth of output can be considered the principal objective of adjustment policies under World Bank auspices.

The chapter will begin by examining the existing conceptual framework for stabilization policies and inquire into the question of an appropriate framework for adjustment policies. Next, the instruments of adjustment policies will be briefly reviewed, followed by a discussion of the principal types of policies, including policies aimed at improving the use of existing resources, increasing savings and investment, and ensuring an efficient choice of investments. Furthermore, brief consideration will be given to the coordination of stabilization and adjustment policies and to adjustment with equity.

* Originally prepared as a background paper for *Adjustment Lending: An Evaluation of Ten Years of Experience*, Policy and Research Report no. 1, Country Economics Department, World Bank, Washington, DC, 1988.

THE CONCEPTUAL FRAMEWORK FOR STABILIZATION PROGRAMS

The conceptual framework for stabilization programs has been described in a recent paper by the IMF Research Department.[1] It is stated there that remedying balance-of-payments deficits is the principal objective of these programs. It is added that, since "it is generally easier to reduce absorption than to increase production . . ., policies affecting absorption are often first put in place when a rapid decline in a current account deficit is mandatory" (p. 6). Such expenditure-reducing policies are considered in the model described in the paper.

The paper notes that "at the core of every Fund-related program is a basic financial programming framework" (p. 13), reflecting the monetary approach to the balance of payments. In this framework, "the change in net foreign assets will be positive (the balance of payments will be in surplus) to the extent that the change in the money stock exceeds the change in domestic credit" (ibid.). For a given money stock, then, domestic credit restraint will bring about an improvement in the balance of payments.

Domestic credit restraint may involve the private and the public sector. Now, "a ceiling on the expansion of domestic credit to the public sector [is] derived in conjunction with the overall expansion of credit consistent with a balance of payments target and the targeted flow of credit to the private sector. Coupled with a limitation on external borrowing to the public sector, this [yields] an effective limit on the size of the fiscal deficit" (pp. 24–5).

Thus, the financial programming framework starts out with a balance-of-payments target and proceeds to consider, first, monetary and, subsequently, fiscal variables as policy instruments in the pursuit of this target. Monetary and fiscal policies, then, represent the principal instruments used in stabilization programs.

In another paper, written for the World Bank by economists who were previously, and are now again, employees of the IMF, the financial programming framework is extended to include also reducing domestic inflation as a target.[2] This involves adding the exchange rate as a policy instrument. In turn, real output, exports, capital flows, and the international price of imports are exogenous variables (the first three exogenous variables are introduced in the previous model as well).

Both variants of the financial programming framework are limited to issues of stabilization. In the paper cited earlier, it is claimed however that "the promotion of sustained growth has always been a major concern of the Fund" (p. 27) and that growth aspects have received increased attention in recent years. It is added that "there is therefore increasing relevance to extending the basic financial programming model to incorporate the economic variables and relationships that are crucial for meeting growth objectives. To do so, however, is a formidable task, and studies aimed at doing so have only begun to suggest ways in which the financial programming framework can be extended" (ibid.).

Such an attempt has been made in the Khan–Montiel–Haque paper cited above in attempting to combine the Fund and the Bank approaches. The paper has a fatal defect, however, of identifying the Bank approach with a two-gap model, in which exports are exogenous and the incremental capital–output ratio, the import propensity, and the savings rate are given *ex ante* (Section IV). While this greatly eases the task of combining the two models, it takes relationships as given that are to change under adjustment programs.

Thus, adjustment programs generally aim at increasing exports. They also aim at raising efficiency levels, involving reductions in the incremental capital–output ratio, include measures affecting imports, and aim at increasing savings rates. The proposed model, however, fails to consider the effects of adjustment policies on these variables.

Could one, then, model adjustment policies? Simple models could be derived without much difficulty, taking economic growth as the ultimate target, introducing exports, imports, savings, and investment as intermediate targets, and utilizing a number of policy instruments, such as the exchange rate, the interest rate, export incentives, import protection, and pricing policies. To make the model realistic, however, would require making it very complicated. At the same time, our knowledge of the factors affecting the efficiency of resource use is woefully inadequate, although this plays an important role in adjustment programs. Also, we know little of factors affecting savings and investment.

This being the case, a more "literary" approach is suggested. This would involve adopting an overall framework for adjustment policies. Such a framework would include the policies that can be used to pursue the stated objective.

OBJECTIVES AND INSTRUMENTS OF ADJUSTMENT POLICIES[3]

As noted above, the primary objective of adjustment policies is increasing the rate of economic growth. This objective may be pursued by improving the efficiency of using existing resources, adding to available resources, and ensuring the efficient use of these additions to resources. In the first case, production incentives need to be reformed; in the second, incentives need to be provided to savings and investment; in the third, the choice of alternative investments is the relevant consideration.

One may, then, classify policy instruments for adjustment into three groups, according to whether they affect resource allocation, savings and investment, and the choice of investments. At the same time, it should be recognized that these instruments are interdependent and will generally interact in the pursuit of particular goals.

For example, the choice of the exchange rate will affect not only the allocation of existing resources but also the availability of additional resources through its impact on capital flight. Furthermore, while interest rate policy may aim at increasing savings, high (low) interest rates will disfavor (favor) capital-intensive activities. Finally, sectoral policies, which aim at promoting investment in particular activities, have a bearing on the allocation of existing resources as well.

While recognizing these interactions, the following discussion of the three groups of policy instruments will give emphasis to their primary effects. Following a brief statement on these policy instruments, they will be considered individually.

Policy measures that can be employed to improve the use of existing resources will be considered in two parts: exchange rate and trade policy and government regulations and state enterprises. Under the first heading, a review of the exchange rate–import protection–export subsidy nexus will be followed by a discussion of the need to grant export subsidies, reduce and equalize import protection, and maintain realistic exchange rates. Under the second heading, the need to decontrol prices and eliminate subsidies will be considered, with further attention given to the desirability of deregulation and privatization.

A variety of measures may be taken to increase savings and investment in developing countries. The discussion will focus on reforming tax regulations, establishing realistic interest rates, increasing public savings, developing financial intermediation, and providing investment incentives.

There are further measures that affect the allocation of investment among alternative uses. They may pertain to private investment, public investment, or to particular sectors.

EXCHANGE RATE AND TRADE POLICY

The *exchange rate–import protection–export subsidy* nexus is of primary importance as far as production incentives are concerned. These measures are interdependent in their effects on productive activities, and they can be used in alternative ways to influence the allocation of economic resources. For example, imposing import tariffs of 20 percent and granting a 20 percent export subsidy across the board would have the same impact on productive activities as a 20 percent devaluation.

Conceptually, then, a devaluation is equivalent to a combination of import tariffs and export subsidies. There are differences, however, in the international acceptability of these measures. Also, countries may have taken a commitment to forego the use of a particular measure.

A country may generally vary its exchange rate at will. Also, developing countries can vary their measures of protection unless binding them under GATT rules. In turn, foreign nations may apply retaliatory measures in response to export subsidies that are deemed to injure their domestic industries.

But, countries may forego variations in exchange rates by *de jure* and *de facto* joining a currency area. The example *par excellence* is participation in the franc area that involves maintaining the exchange rate fixed *vis-à-vis* the French franc. And, there are several countries in Central America and elsewhere, which have in practice tied their exchange rates to the US dollar.

Apart from the case when the exchange rate is fixed, a devaluation (or, alternatively, its equivalent, an import tariff–export subsidy scheme) may be utilized to remedy a balance-of-payments deficit in a developing country where optimal policies have been applied. But, in developing countries in general, there is excessive import protection of manufacturing activities, with a consequent bias against manufactured and primary exports and against primary activities in general. It would be desirable, then, to reduce this bias so as to improve the efficiency of resource allocation.

Using tariff reductions for this purpose would, however, bring a further deterioration in the balance of payments, unless accompanied by a devaluation of the exchange rate. If an across-the-board tariff reduction is accompanied by a devaluation of a commensurate magnitude, import prices would remain unchanged while export prices would rise at the same rate as the devaluation, thereby reducing the bias against exports.

The described procedure is equivalent to providing an implicit export subsidy. The same result may be achieved by granting an explicit export subsidy at identical rates. The conceptual equivalence of a partially compensated devaluation and an across-the-board export subsidy may be illustrated by an example.

Assume that initially the exchange rate is 100 pesos to the dollar, all imports are subject to a tariff of 50 percent, and export subsidies are not provided. Under the first alternative, reducing tariffs by one-half, accompanied by a 20 percent devaluation, would leave the domestic prices of imports unchanged while raising export prices by 20 percent. Under the second alternative, the 20 percent increase in the prices of exports would be attained by granting a 20 percent export subsidy across the board.

In affecting the prices of imports and exports in the same way, the described alternatives would have identical effects on the balance of payments, domestic inflation, and the government budget. The balance of payments would improve as exports rise in response to increased incentives. Also, the inflationary effects of the devaluation on imports would be offset by commensurate reductions in tariffs, so that these effects would be limited to increases in export prices, just as in the case of (explicit) export subsidies. And, under both alternatives, there would be a cost to the government budget: the loss of tariff proceeds in the first case and the budgetary cost of export subsidies in the second. However, this budgetary cost would be recouped in part through tax receipts on higher incomes and consumption following the expansion of exports.

Complications are introduced if exports use imported inputs. In the case when imported inputs utilized directly and indirectly in export production enter duty-free, a devaluation will raise export prices as well as the prices of imported inputs. To obtain equivalent results, export subsidies would need to be set on value added in exports – the difference between the fob export value and the cif value of imported inputs used directly and indirectly in export production – rather than on export value.

Deducting the cif value of direct and indirect imported inputs from export value may involve administrative problems. The same comment applies to granting export subsidies to a large number of peasant proprietors. Extending export subsidies to earnings from service items, among which tourism is of considerable importance for many developing countries, may also encounter administrative difficulties.

These considerations, then, favor a devaluation cum tariff reduction over an export subsidy. A further advantage of the former alternative is that it would reduce discrimination against products that are subject to duties at rates lower than the devaluation or enter duty-free. This is because such products will enjoy the partial or the full benefit of a devaluation through increases in their domestic prices.

In developing countries, agricultural products, some intermediate goods, energy products, and capital goods are often subject to low or nil duties, thereby suffering discrimination *vis-à-vis* products with higher tariffs. A devaluation, partially compensated by tariff reductions, then, would encourage efficient import substitution in these products.

The preceding considerations point to the advantages of a partially compensated devaluation over an export subsidy. These conclusions are further strengthened if account is taken of the danger of retaliation by importing countries against an export subsidy.

Export subsidies would have to be utilized, however, if fixed exchange rates are maintained as in the franc area. Also, in the presence of continued import protection, export subsidies would improve the efficiency of resource allocation by reducing the bias of the system of incentives against exports.

In the event that export subsidies are to be employed, developing countries will wish to minimize the chances of retaliation on the part of developed countries. This objective may be served by applying measures that are accepted or countenanced by GATT.

Exempting exports and their direct and indirect inputs from indirect taxes and rebating duties on imported inputs are accepted by GATT. In fact, exemptions from indirect taxes do not represent an export subsidy; rather, they are necessary to ensure tax neutrality on domestic and foreign sales, thereby avoiding taxing exports. At the same time, shifting from income taxes to indirect taxes can be used to increase incentives to exports.

Note further that rebating duties on imported inputs used in export production will reduce but not eliminate the bias against exports. Thus, a 20 percent tariff on the product and its imported inputs will still provide a 20 percent protection on value added in import substitution as against zero protection on value added in exports that obtain their imported inputs duty-free.

There are some further measures benefiting exports, which are not usually met with retaliation. They include preferential export credits that reduce the disadvantages of developing-country exporters, which are due to the undeveloped state of credit facilities and the riskiness of entering export markets. Also, the government may share the cost of entering new markets through tax concessions on marketing expenditures as well as through the collection of information, market research, and trade fairs organized or partly financed by quasi-governmental bodies. Finally, the government may finance improvements in infrastructure that benefit export activities.

Going beyond these measures and granting explicit subsidies to exports will invoke retaliation if they cause injury to the domestic industries of foreign countries. However, small developing-country exporters have little to fear from retaliation because they are not likely to cause injury abroad. Thus, the application of export subsidies by the franc area countries, which cannot devalue their currencies, is unlikely to trigger countervailing measures.

In view of the limitations imposed on export subsidies by developing countries in general, there is need to reduce and to rationalize *import protection*. In order to minimize dislocation, the reform of the system of protection should be carried out over a period of, say, four to five years. At the same time, the measures to be applied should be made public in advance so as to prepare firms for the necessary adjustment.

In reforming the system of protection, priority should be given to eliminating quantitative import restrictions that have a variety of disadvantages compared to tariffs. While the extent of tariff protection can be easily ascertained, gauging the protective effect of quantitative import restrictions, and their cost to the national economy, would necessitate comparisons of domestic and foreign prices. Price comparisons, however, encounter practical difficulties on all but standardized products, because of differences in quality, specifications, and other product characteristics. Decision-making in the granting of import licenses thus involves considerable arbitrariness and increases uncertainty to the users of imported inputs.

Also, tariffs add to government revenue while the difference between the domestic and the import price accrues to the importer under licensing. Such quota profits, reflecting the scarcity of imports, may lead to overcrowding in individual industries through the establishment of firms for the purpose of sharing these profits and provide inducement for bribery.

It has been suggested that tariffs be raised in order to offset the loss of protection to domestic producers, owing to the elimination of quantitative import restrictions. But, unless provisions are made for the elimination of additional tariff protection over time, there is the danger that the higher tariffs will become imbedded in the system of import protection. Furthermore, producers will clamor for tariffs in excess of the extent of protection provided by the quantitative restrictions, and their claims will be difficult to evaluate, given the uncertainties involved in measuring the tariff equivalent of quantitative import restrictions.

In fact, it would be desirable to undertake tariff reforms parallel with the elimination of quantitative import restrictions. This would permit the application of a coordinated approach and allow for adjustment in protected industries. An appropriate procedure is to make changes in steps within an announced timetable as suggested above.

In regard to quantitative import restrictions, one may begin by liberalizing the importation of material inputs and machinery used in export production, with the freeing of such inputs utilized in domestic production undertaken at the second stage. Next, consumer goods for general use may be liberalized, with luxury products left to the last stage.

Reforming tariffs should aim at equalizing effective rates of protection on value added across the board. This can be accomplished by setting equal tariffs at each stage of the production process. Such a goal may be approached through several steps.

First of all, there would be need to set a tariff ceiling and reduce the ceiling over time. This should also involve transforming tariffs on luxury goods into excise taxes that would apply to imported and to domestic products as well.

Also, high tariffs should be reduced more than low tariffs. This squeezing of the tariff structure would have more than proportionate effects on effective rates of protection (the rate of protection on value added in the production process), which magnify differences in (nominal) tariff rates at different stages of fabrication.

A more controversial proposal involves imposing tariffs on duty-free items. This would, on the one hand, reduce discrimination against the products in question and, on the other hand, lower effective protection on the products that use them as inputs. At the same time, these tariffs should not be higher than the long-term tariff target, say 10–12 percent, lest temporary incentives are provided to the industries in question while discriminating against exports.

Additional measures may be granted to the benefit of infant industries on a temporary basis and on a degressive scale. But these measures should also promote exports. This may be accomplished by providing investment incentives that will be discussed below.

Reducing import protection over time may necessitate changes in *exchange rates* so as to safeguard the balance of payments. But this is far from certain since export incentives, as well as reductions in the bias against exports associated with import liberalization, would contribute to export expansion.

Assuming that changes in protection do not require changes in exchange rates beyond the initial compensated devaluation, there is need to avoid variations in real exchange rates unless external or internal shocks alter the equilibrium exchange rate. Particular importance attaches to the fact that an appreciation of the exchange rate would discriminate against exports and engender capital flight.

Capital flight, through the underinvoicing of exports and the overinvoicing of imports, is also an important drawback of dual exchange rates. At the same time, dual exchange rates subsidize imports and the sale of foreign financial assets while taxing exports and the purchase of foreign financial assets. The improved allocation of existing resources calls for eliminating such taxes and subsidies by adopting a single exchange rate.

GOVERNMENT REGULATIONS AND PUBLIC ENTERPRISES

Price control is often used in conjunction with import protection, in order to limit profits to producers in monopoly situations or if collusive oligopolists dominate the protected market. Conversely, liberalizing trade will permit eliminating price control.

Price control may also aim at avoiding increases in the prices of particular inputs and of consumer goods. But, as production is discouraged and consumption encouraged as a result, exports will decline or imports rise, leading to the deterioration of the balance of payments and to inefficient resource use.

In the case of inputs, distortions in relative prices further reduce the efficiency of resource allocation. Also, price controls on inputs, such as electricity, fuel oil, and gasoline, encourage their wasteful use. To the extent that these products and services are produced by public enterprises, price control further contributes to the public sector deficit, thereby increasing inflationary pressures.

Price control on consumer goods is often used to avoid increases in the prices of necessities, supposedly to the benefit of the poor. But it may eventually have the opposite effect by limiting supply in discouraging production. Also, price control benefits all users, irrespective of their income position. And, the benefits are mitigated by shortages, necessitating formal or informal rationing, if sufficient supplies are not available at the controlled price. Last but not least, in most developing countries, the poor strata of the population importantly include agricultural producers who are adversely affected by price control.

It has been suggested that income distributional objectives be served by using *consumption subsidies* instead of price control. But, these subsidies have a budgetary cost; they increase demand for the product in question; and, being untargeted, they are an inefficient way of pursuing income distributional objectives. A superior alternative is to use targeted subsidies to benefit the poor.

These considerations indicate the need to eliminate price control and to pursue income distributional objectives through targeted subsidies rather than by subsidizing consumption. It would further be desirable to liberalize *government regulations* that circumscribe the activities of private business in many developing countries. The regulations may have been established by legislation and government decrees, but their implementation generally involves case-by-case decision-making on the part of government administration. In practice, this may lead to endless *trámites* (bureaucratic red tape), to use a Latin American expression, and may engender bribery.

Government regulations may extend to the establishment of the firm as well as to its operations. In so doing, they may compromise the success of trade liberalization that requires freedom in setting up new enterprises and in firm operations in order to respond to the needs of foreign markets.

In view of the cost of complying with extensive regulations, the regulations discriminate against small- and medium-size firms that cannot afford the cost and the time involved. Also, inducement is provided to the informal sector, which avoids the cost of regulations but does not enjoy the protection of the law, so that its further development is thwarted.

Deregulation would improve the use of resources. This would occur by reducing the need for a large government apparatus, lowering the cost of complying with the regulations for the firm, and avoiding discrimination against small- and medium-size firms. At the same time, opportunities would be provided for the integration of the informal sector in the national economy.

Establishing a modern legal framework to safeguard property and contractual rights would further contribute to the better use of existing resources. This objective would also be served by setting up a modern bankruptcy system that facilitates the transfer of assets of loss-making enterprises to more efficient users.

Moreover, labor regulations would need to be modified. In developing countries, labor costs are often raised by high redundancy payments or by outright prohibition of discharging workers. At the same time, these regulations have been shown to have the opposite of the desired effect by discouraging hiring.

High social charges also have adverse effects on employment by increasing the cost of labor. The same conclusion holds for excessively high statutory minimum wages that further create distortions between the formal sector and the informal sector, where such regulations do not apply.

Deregulation would permit firms to better respond to market signals and thus make trade policy reform more effective. *Public enterprises*, however, tend to respond to bureaucratic imperatives rather than to market signals. The improved use of existing resources would then require that public enterprises conform to the rules to which private enterprises are subject.

To accomplish this objective, public enterprises in the competitive sector should be given freedom of decision-making, with profit maximization as the overriding objective. Also, they should be put on the same footing as private enterprises in terms of credits, taxation, and government regulations. Public utilities, too, should be managed on the basis of economic principles.

Most public utilities are natural monopolies, hence there is a rationale for public ownership. Noneconomic considerations also often call for the public ownership of natural resource industries.

But, downstream activities and other industries and services can best be left to private enterprise.

It follows that privatization can lead to improvements in concentrating the government's activities in areas, such as the provision of social services, where it has a comparative advantage. Privatization should be defined as the transfer of control. The sale of minority participation in public enterprises does not qualify as privatization; in fact, it represents the increased use of private funds in the public sector.

At the same time, one would have to create the appropriate conditions for privatization. This would necessitate, first of all, establishing clear and unambiguous procedural rules and applying these rules in practice. The rules should provide for the valuation of the enterprises to be privatized by an independent board, which may use auctioning or other methods appropriate for the conditions of the country concerned. This is to avoid both underpricing and putting an excessively high value on assets of doubtful productivity.

It would also be desirable for the state to undertake the rationalization of the enterprise prior to privatization, so as to eliminate excessive debt and reduce overmanning. In some cases, parts of the enterprise may be rehabilitated while others would have to be closed down. And, there will be public enterprises beyond rescue that will have to be closed down altogether.

INCENTIVES TO SAVINGS AND INVESTMENT

A variety of measures may be used to encourage domestic savings in developing countries. Some of these measures also discourage capital flight, thereby increasing the availability of savings for domestic investment. This result may also be obtained through increased foreign investment.

Improvements in the *tax system* would encourage private savings, discourage capital flight, and encourage foreign direct investment in developing countries. The improvements may extend to corporate and personal income taxes as well as to indirect taxes.

High and progressive corporate income tax rates reduce business savings and discourage foreign direct investment. The situation is aggravated by the lack of inflation accounting in many developing countries that leads to the taxation of "phantom" profits, by failing to provide full adjustment for the depreciation of machinery and equipment.

In many developing countries, the double taxation of dividends reduces the amounts available for private savings. Personal savings are also adversely affected by highly progressive income taxes. Such taxes further discourage foreign direct investment, by necessitating higher pre-tax salaries for leading employees, and encourage emigration.

Personal savings are discouraged and capital flight encouraged by the taxation of nominal interest income, which does not allow for the fact that the principal loses value through inflation. Also, personal savings are discouraged by the taxation of savings under income taxes, which favors present over future consumption that is the result of today's savings.

The availability of savings for domestic investment could be increased by lowering corporate income tax rates, introducing inflation accounting in corporate and personal income taxes, eliminating the double taxation of dividends, and reducing the progressivity of personal income taxes. Ideally, income taxes should be replaced by a tax on consumption, when income distributional objectives can be pursued by taxing luxury consumption and providing exemptions for basic necessities.

There is evidence that savings are discouraged by negative real *interest rates*. For one thing, the holding of financial assets with negative rates of return is discouraged. For another thing, incentives are provided to accumulate consumer durables as an inflation hedge. At the same time, there are inducements for capital flight in search of higher returns abroad.

Negative real interest rates also create an excess demand for funds, thereby leading to credit rationing and inefficient credit allocation. Available credits are often allocated to state enterprises and large firms, thereby limiting the availability of credit to medium-size and small enterprises. Also, import-substitution activities are generally favored, irrespective of whether credit allocation is done by the banks or by governments. Banks favor these activities because they involve lower risks than exports while governments favor them as part of a strategy of import protection.

Negative real interest rates further provide inducement for investment in capital-intensive activities and for the use of capital-intensive production methods. At the same time, firms may borrow at negative real interest rates as an inflation hedge and accumulate inventories rather than undertaking new investments. Also, self-investment at low, and even negative, rates of return is favored over lending at negative real interest rates and, more generally, the development of financial intermediation is discouraged.

These considerations indicate the need for positive real interest rates that equate the demand for, and the supply of, credit. However, excessively high real interest rates have adverse effects of their own, by discouraging investment and leading to the bankruptcy of firms whose continued operation is socially desirable.

Excessively high interest rates can be avoided if the *deficit of the public sector* is reduced. In fact, lowering the deficit creates a "virtuous circle," inasmuch as the resulting decline in interest rates further lowers the deficit by reducing the cost of servicing the domestic debt, generating an additional decline in interest rates and so on.

Thus, reducing public sector deficits is an important part of interest rate policy and, more generally, adjustment policies. One can in this way avoid excessively high interest rates and the crowding-out of private investment that has occurred in recent years in a number of developing countries with high public sector deficits.

Apart from cutting excessive public investment, to be discussed further below, lowering the public sector deficit requires reducing the size of the government apparatus and limiting subsidies. The former can be accomplished in conjunction with deregulation while the latter can be accompanied by targeted measures to help the poor.

It has been suggested that taxes be increased in order to raise public savings. In view of the high taxation of economic activities in most developing countries, however, higher taxes will have adverse effects on work and risk-taking. Rather, the emphasis should be put on generating public savings through reductions in government expenditures that would also increase the availability of financial resources to the private sector.

Public savings could further be increased through privatization, the closing-down of hopelessly inefficient public enterprises, and the rationalization of those remaining. In this way, savings in the public enterprise sector would add to savings in the government budget.

Market-clearing interest rates at realistic levels would contribute to the development of *financial intermediation* by providing inducement for financial savings and furthering their efficient allocation. Pursuing this objective would also necessitate avoiding the use of preferential credit schemes and of directed credit in particular sectors.

At the same time, improvements in the system of financial intermediation are necessary in order to capture the full benefits of interest rate reform. Reforms of the financial system should serve the twin objectives of ensuring that investors face identical credit conditions and that there is competition among banks and other financial intermediaries. Legalizing curb markets, easing the conditions of entry into commercial banking, and encouraging the establishment of other financial intermediaries will promote these objectives.

In a number of developing countries, it would further be necessary to rehabilitate viable banks and other financial institutions that are in difficulties and closing down those that are not viable. This is a particular problem in highly-indebted countries where foreign debts burden the banks or their major borrowers.

At the same time, strict rules would need to be established on banking operations, including the preparation of financial statements, the classification of loans, the establishment of loan reserves, and write-offs for non-performing loans. Financial statements should convey adequate information on the quality of bank assets and should be regularly audited, with rigorous banking supervision under the aegis of the central bank.

Governments should further avoid excessively high reserve requirements and taxes on financial transactions, which create a wedge between interest rates paid by borrowers and received by lenders. This again tends to discourage savings and encourage self-investment to the detriment of investments that are socially desirable.

Finally, financial intermediation in long-term obligations should be developed, both to respond to demand for such obligations on the part of savers and to provide financing for long-term investments. Apart from the transformation of the banking system, possibly involving the extension of the activities of commercial banks to long-term finance and the establishment of investment banks, the development of capital markets would serve these objectives. Countries which possess the necessary degree of financial sophistication are well-advised to create the conditions for the establishment and, if they exist, the further development of stock and bond markets.

While positive real interest rates will increase the amount of savings available for investment and improve the allocation of these savings, *investment incentives* will induce firms to increase the share of retained earnings available for investment. Investment incentives have a role to play as adjustment policies aim at the acceleration of economic growth.

The incentives should be granted in a form that does not create a bias in favor of capital-intensive activities. Accelerated depreciation provisions, low or nil tariffs on imported machinery and equipment, and the imposition of minimum investment requirements as a condition for obtaining investment incentives give rise to such a bias. Tax holidays will be a more appropriate measure as they are neutral in their effects on factor use.

MEASURES AFFECTING INVESTMENT ALLOCATION

Investment incentives should be provided across the board, with higher incentives to export activities that suffer discrimination under import protection. Investment promotion is not warranted, however, in the event of foreign market limitations in the form of export quotas. Examples are coffee exports under the International Coffee Agreement and petroleum exports under OPEC. The exports of textiles and clothing do not come into this category, however, because of the possibilities for product upgrading under the Multi-fiber Arrangement and for sales outside the MFA.

Also, investment incentives are eminently suitable for promoting infant industries as they do not discriminate in favor of import substitution and against export activities. This is the case, in particular, in industries producing durable producer and consumer goods, where economies of scale and cost reductions through specialization in the production of parts, components, and accessories would be foregone and possibilities for subsequent exports reduced, if excessive reliance was based on the protection of infant industries.

These considerations apply to *private enterprises* as well as to firms producing traded goods under competition in the public sector. Other public sector investments pertain to public utilities, social and physical infrastructure, as well as to natural resource industries. Also, in developing countries where the private sector does not have sufficient financing, the government may play a role in promoting large investments in basic industries.

Public investments should be subject to economic project evaluation. This may be done by a separate entity established for this purpose, so as to ensure uniformity in the methods and criteria applied in project evaluation and to provide for a review of proposals prepared under the aegis of governmental agencies that will eventually implement the project. Following a review of possible alternatives, final decision on public investment could then be made by an interministerial committee.

In the case of large projects, it is desirable to make public the results of project evaluation prior to taking decisions and to invite debate on the desirability of the projects in question. Information should also be made available on direct and indirect subsidies, which may be granted to the project in the form of tariff protection, project-specific infrastructure, and the provision of inputs below world market prices.

Project evaluation assumes particular importance by reason of the need to rationalize the public investment program in the framework of structural investment policies. In fact, the adoption of adjustment policies provides an opportunity for a review of public investment extending beyond the evaluation of new investments, so as to consider the possibility of stopping or discontinuing ongoing investments if they do not hold sufficient promise.

The adoption of adjustment policies also provides an opportunity for the formulation of *sectoral policies*. In this connection, distinction may be made between sectors where the state has a major responsibility, such as public utilities and education, and sectors where the government may support the operation of market processes.

In the case of sectors where the government has a major responsibility, there is need to specify medium-term objectives that may be pursued in the framework of a coordinated program. Further importance attaches to fitting individual projects in the program and undertaking the evaluation of these projects as noted above.

Government support of the operation of market processes is called upon to different degrees in sectors producing traded goods under competition. They are related to market failures, where markets cannot ensure the efficient utilization of resources and the long-term development of a particular sector.

A case in point is agriculture, where sectoral policies may involve undertaking government-sponsored research, establishing extension services, providing high-quality seeds, and improving transportation facilities. However, public agencies assuming the tasks traditionally performed by private interests, such as the processing and marketing of agricultural produce and the purchase of inputs for agriculture, has generally involved inefficiencies and high costs.

More generally, sectoral policies should not be used to distort resource allocation through government intervention in market processes. Rather, the objective should be to support the operation of market processes that permit accelerating economic growth.

COORDINATION OF ADJUSTMENT AND STABILIZATION POLICIES

While adjustment policies aim at accelerating economic growth, most developing countries – in particular, highly-indebted countries – also need to reduce their balance-of-payments deficits. In this connection, distinction may be made among countries on the basis of whether they have or do not have IMF programs.

In the case of countries with IMF programs, there is need to ensure that Bank and IMF programs are mutually supportive. This may be accomplished through coordination by the staff of the two institutions.

In countries without an IMF program, the Bank is called upon also to deal with monetary and fiscal policies. At the same time, as a general guideline, the policies applied to improve the balance of payments should aim at doing so by output-increasing rather than expenditure-reducing measures.

The (partially) compensated devaluation, discussed earlier, is a *par excellence* output-increasing policy. This is because it promotes exports and the production of import substitutes that were subject to low or nil protection while keeping the prices of other import substitutes unchanged.

But, expenditure-reducing policies could not be forgone. In the absence of such policies, there is the danger that inflation accelerates. Also, as noted above, reductions in government expenditures permit increasing the availability of funds to the private sector, thus exploiting its growth potential.

ADJUSTING WITH EQUITY

A judicious choice of policies can ensure that improvements in the balance of payments are not made at the expense of economic growth. Nevertheless, the process of adjustment may involve costs to the poor. Such costs may be the result of shifts in resources or the phasing-out of price control and consumer subsidies.

To the extent that adjustment involves unemployment in particular sectors, attention would need to be given to retraining, so as to transform existing skills in a way that they become marketable. Retraining may be complemented by the creation of opportunities for productive employment in areas such as road maintenance and small-scale irrigation.

In replacement of price control and consumer subsidies, well-targeted programs benefiting the poor should be relied upon. Such programs may focus on food distribution, targeting in particular pregnant women and school children in poor areas; on primary health care, emphasizing prevention; and on education, concentrating on primary schooling.

Some of these programs may be financed through the elimination of price control on goods and services produced by public enterprises and the abolition of subsidies. Others may involve the imposition of user charges; e.g. by having the well-to-do finance the education of their children.

CONCLUDING REMARKS

This chapter has defined adjustment policies in terms of the objective of accelerating economic growth. This objective may be pursued by various policies aimed at improving the use of existing resources, adding to these resources, and ensuring the efficient allocation of resource increments.

The described policies range over a wide spectrum, encompassing macro as well as micro policies. There is also a mixture of changes in relative prices and institutional reform. As to the former, reducing the bias of the incentive system against exports would need to be accompanied by changes in factor prices as existing measures tend to burden labor and favor capital in most developing countries. As to the latter, changes in the status and operation of public enterprises and the introduction of economic project evaluation in public investments are of particular importance.

The various elements of adjustment policies need to be coordinated in order to ensure their maximum effectiveness. But, different policies may receive emphasis in different countries and at different times, depending on the existing conditions.

In this connection, a distinction may be made between structural adjustment polices and sectoral policies. Structural adjustment policies concern the entire economy and will cover most, although not necessarily all, of the areas discussed in this chapter. In turn, as the name indicates, sectoral adjustment policies concentrate on a particular sector, with supporting policies in other areas.

In this connection, questions may be raised about the sequencing of structural adjustment and sectoral polices. As a general rule, it is appropriate to start with structural adjustment policies that will provide a framework in which sectoral adjustment polices can operate.

Note should further be taken of the time element involved. There are time lags in the working of adjustment policies, so that the time horizon of adjustment programs should not be too short. Nor should these programs extend over an excessively long period that would increase expectations about policy reversals.

The last point leads to the important issue of ensuring that structural adjustment programs are credible. This means that decisions need to be reached in advance, with a timetable provided for their implementation. At the same time, the measures to be taken should be well publicized, so as to prepare the affected industries for the prospective changes.

In practice, ideal policies cannot be established by one fell swoop. Thus, one needs to envisage a sequence of adjustment programs. At the same time, it is important to understand the overall objectives at the outset, so as not to lose sight of the "big picture" in reforming policies.

The chapter further noted the need for the coordination of adjustment and stabilization policies. Also, consideration needs to be given to the political constraints and to the income distributional effects of the policies applied. The chapter described possible measures that may be taken to ease any adverse consequences the policies applied may have on the poor.

Notes

1. "Theoretical Aspects of the Design of Fund-supported Adjustment Programs," Occasional Paper 55, Washington, DC, International Monetary Fund, 1987, p. 6.
2. Mohsin S. Khan, Peter Montiel, and Nadeem U. Haque, "Adjustment with Growth: Relating the Analytical Approaches of the World Bank and the IMF," Development Policy Issues Series Discussion Papers No. VPERS8, Washington, DC, World Bank, 1986.
3. The following discussion draws on Bela Balassa, "Structural Adjustment Policies in Developing Countries," *World Development*, January 1982, and "Structural Adjustment Policies: Conceptual Issues," October 1987.

4 A Quantitative Appraisal of Adjustment Lending*

INTRODUCTION

Adjustment lending by the World Bank has a history of nearly a decade. The first structural adjustment loans were extended to Bolivia, Kenya, Philippines, Senegal and Turkey in 1980. The first sectoral adjustment loan was granted to Jamaica in 1979, followed by loans to Pakistan and Sudan in 1980.

This chapter aims to provide a quantitative appraisal of adjustment lending, including structural adjustment loans as well as sectoral adjustment loans. This is a difficult task that entails the choice of appropriate benchmarks as well as performance indicators. Both of these choices involve practical problems and the results should be interpreted with caution.

The basic idea is to compare performance indicators for periods before and after adjustment loans. But, countries often had several loans; Turkey even received five structural adjustment loans. In these cases, the date of the first adjustment loan was used as the benchmark. However, in a subsequent part of the chapter, we have employed a weighting procedure, based on the number of adjustment loans a country received.

The next question concerns the choice of the time period before and after the adjustment loan. Calculations were initially made for three-year time spans, both to limit the effects of year-to-year fluctuations and to allow for sufficient time for the effects of the loan to be apparent. Excluding the year of the loan, for an adjustment loan extended in 1984, for example, this involved comparing data for the 1981–3 and 1985–7 periods (for lack of data, countries receiving adjustment loans beyond 1984 could not be considered).

In order to provide information for a longer time span, the statistical tables also show results for the period from the receipt of the

* Originally published in the *Pakistan Development Review*, 28; pp. 73–94, Summer 1989.

first adjustment loan until 1987. In the discussion, particular attention is given to results for this period that also includes the effects of subsequent adjustment loans. And, it is for this period that the weighting procedure referred to above has been applied.

Changes in performance indicators for particular countries between periods before and after adjustment loans were further compared to the changes observed in countries that did not receive such loans. Comparisons were made for countries that belong to the following groups: sub-Saharan Africa (14 recipients and 23 non-recipients of adjustment loans), low-income countries (1 and 7), lower-middle-income countries (8 and 24), and upper-middle-income countries (6 and 21). The latter three groups follow the *World Development Report 1987* classification and were defined to exclude the countries of sub-Saharan Africa.

The next question concerns the choice of the performance indicators. In the present investigation, a large number of indicators were used, grouped under nine headings. They are economic growth (GDP, per capita GDP, industrial production, agricultural production, consumption, per capita consumption, investment, and aggregate expenditure), export performance (export growth), import substitution (import–GDP ratio), savings and investment (domestic savings–GDP, private saving–GDP, public saving–GDP, investment–GDP, and foreign saving–GDP), balance of payments (current account balance–GDP, basic balance–GDP, and overall balance–GDP) external debt (external debt–exports, debt service–exports), inflation (wholesale prices, consumer prices), monetary policy (money supply growth, real discount rate), fiscal policy (government revenue–GDP, government expenditure–GDP, budget surplus–GDP).

PERFORMANCE INDICATORS

GDP growth is a particularly important performance indicator since adjustment policies aim at accelerating economic growth. But the gross domestic product may or may not increase more rapidly than population, hence the importance of per capita GDP as a performance indicator.

Within GDP, traded goods are produced by the industrial and the agricultural sectors. Since reductions in balance-of-payments deficits through output-increasing policies involve increases in production in these sectors, their inclusion among performance indicators is of interest.

Aggregate expenditure will rise less than the gross domestic product if expenditure-reducing policies are applied. Within aggregate expenditure, changes in consumption provide an indication of variations in living standards while changes in investment are a gauge of prospects for future economic growth.

Increases in output in traded goods sectors may involve export expansion, import substitution, or production catering to increases in domestic demand. Export performance is measured by export growth while the import–GDP ratio is used as an indicator of import substitution.

Changes in domestic savings may originate in the private or in the public sector, when public savings are measured in terms of the government budget balance and private savings are defined as the difference between domestic and public savings. Domestic investment may be financed by domestic or by foreign savings.

The group of savings and investment indicators is followed by indicators of the balance of payments. The current account deficit would equal foreign savings, except for unilateral transfers and for differences in national accounts and balance-of-payments statistics. These differences are quite substantial, e.g. in Bolivia.

The basic balance further includes long-term capital movements while the overall balance comprises short-term capital movements as well. The overall balance thus equals changes in foreign reserves.

In the present chapter, debt indicators have been expressed in relation to exports since export receipts are used to service the debt. The statistical tables provide information on the debt–export and debt service–export ratios, the latter inclusive of amortization as well as interest, although rescheduling arrangements involve postponing the payment of amortization.

The wholesale price index and the consumer price index are used as indicators of inflation. In turn, indicators of monetary policy include money supply growth and the real discount rate. With money supply growth defined in nominal terms, it is also an indicator of inflationary pressures emanating from monetary policy.

Among fiscal indicators, the government budget balance is identical to public savings as noted above. Further information is provided on changes in government revenue and government expenditure.

THE STATISTICAL TABLES

The appendix tables provide information on the performance indicators for each of the 29 countries that were recipients of adjustment loans up to 1984. As noted above, the values taken by the performance indicators are shown for the three years preceding and following the first adjustment loan to the country concerned as well as for the period up to 1987 following the receipt of the loan.

For each period, averages of the performance indicators are reported for the particular country under the heading "own average" while the "group average" refers to the average for the countries that are not recipients of adjustment loans and belong to the same category as the country concerned. Such comparator groups include countries of sub-Saharan Africa, low-income countries, lower-middle-income countries, and higher-middle-income countries. The country tables further provide information on the difference between the "own average" and the "group average" in each of the three periods.

Table 4.1 reports overall averages of the data of the country tables. This table, as well as tables reporting averages for the four country groupings (Tables 4.6 to 4.9), has the same structure as the country tables.

Another set of tables (Tables 4.2 to 4.5) shows changes in the performance indicators between periods before and after the first adjustment loan. In the tables, a positive sign indicates an increase in the particular indicator and a negative sign a decrease (there are no instances where no change would have occurred in a particular indicator). Finally, N refers to not available.

It should be emphasized that a positive sign may represent an improvement or a deterioration, depending on the particular indicator. It will show an improvement in the case of the economic growth, export performance, investment and savings (except for foreign savings), balance of payments, government revenue, and budget surplus indicators. In turn, increases in foreign savings, the external debt, debt service, inflation, money supply growth, and government expenditure indicators are interpreted negatively.

The import substitution and real discount rate indicators are ambiguous. Import substitution may be the result of output-increasing policies or of excessive protection. And, increases in the real discount rate represent an improvement in cases when negative real interest rates gave place to positive real interest rates and a deterioration when interest rates rose to excessive levels.

Table 4.1 Performance indicators: overall averages

Indicators	Preceding 3 years			Following 3 years			Years until 1987		
	Own average	Group average	Difference	Own average	Group average	Difference	Own average	Group average	Difference
Population, mil.	24.2	17.2	.	26.8	18.6	.	27.6	19.1	.
Per capita GDP, US$	1107.9	1333.9	.	939.5	1451.1	.	938.5	1448.1	.
Economic growth									
Gross domestic product	2.7	3.7	-1.0	2.2	2.6	-0.4	2.5	2.8	-0.3
Per capita GDP	0.2	1.2	-1.0	-0.2	0.2	-0.4	-0.0	0.4	-0.4
Industrial production	1.8	5.1	-3.3	1.8	2.7	-0.9	1.8	2.8	-0.9
Agricultural production	1.6	2.1	-0.5	2.8	2.5	0.3	3.2	2.8	0.4
Consumption	4.0	4.1	-0.2	1.6	2.5	-0.8	2.0	2.4	-0.4
Per capita consumption	1.5	1.5	-0.1	-0.8	-0.1	-0.8	-0.4	-0.1	-0.3
Investment	-1.5	6.8	-8.3	0.4	3.0	-2.5	2.0	5.0	-3.1
Aggregate expenditure	2.7	4.1	-1.4	1.3	1.3	-0.1	1.8	1.5	0.3
Export performance									
Export growth	7.1	5.7	1.3	5.7	3.1	2.6	5.8	3.5	2.3
Import substitution									
Import/GDP ratio	30.7	46.1	-15.5	29.0	43.7	-14.7	28.7	43.1	-14.5
Investment and savings									
Domestic saving/GDP	16.3	12.3	4.0	15.1	10.7	4.4	15.3	10.8	4.6
Private saving/GDP	24.3	18.4	5.9	23.5	16.4	7.1	23.7	16.4	7.3

Public saving/GDP	-8.0	-5.5	-2.4	-7.8	-6.1	-1.6	-7.9	-5.9	-2.0
Investment/GDP	23.2	25.0	-1.8	19.5	21.4	-1.9	19.0	20.8	-1.8
Foreign saving/GDP	6.9	12.7	-5.8	4.3	10.7	-6.4	3.7	10.0	-6.3
Balance of payments									
Current account/GDP	-7.5	-6.2	-1.3	-2.6	-5.6	3.1	-2.1	-4.9	2.7
Basic balance/GDP	-3.6	-0.2	-3.4	-1.4	-1.3	-0.0	-1.0	-1.1	0.1
Overall balance/GDP	-3.4	-0.2	-3.2	-3.2	-2.0	-1.2	-2.8	-1.8	-1.1
External debt									
External debt/exports	271.7	173.9	97.8	379.1	253.0	126.1	392.2	265.9	126.3
Debt service/exports	21.8	12.4	9.4	25.3	17.7	7.6	25.7	18.7	7.0
Inflation									
Wholesale prices	32.5	18.5	13.9	43.2	25.7	17.5	44.9	25.0	19.9
Consumer prices	24.6	17.0	7.6	33.6	20.4	13.2	102.0	20.6	81.5
Monetary policy									
Money supply growth	24.0	20.3	3.7	43.0	20.9	22.1	88.8	21.9	66.9
Real discount rate	-6.0	-4.3	-1.8	-4.0	-1.1	-2.9	-3.5	-0.8	-2.7
Fiscal policy									
Gov. revenue/GDP	19.0	23.5	-4.5	22.7	25.7	-3.0	22.5	25.9	-3.4
Gov. expenditure/GDP	27.0	29.0	-2.1	30.4	31.8	-1.4	30.5	31.8	-1.4
Budget surplus/GDP	-8.0	-5.5	-2.4	-7.8	-6.1	-1.6	-7.9	-5.9	-2.0

Table 4.2 Performance indicators: three years following loan

	Cote d'Ivoire	Ghana	Guinea-Bissau	Kenya	Malawi	Mauritius	Nigeria	Senegal	Sierra Leone	Sudan	Tanzania	Togo	Uganda	Zimbabwe
Economic growth														
Gross domestic product	−	+	−	−	−	+	−	+	−	+	−	+	−	−
Per capita GDP	−	+	−	−	−	+	−	+	−	+	−	−	−	−
Industrial production	−	+	−	−	−	+	+	+	−	+	−	−	−	−
Agricultural production	−	+	−	+	+	+	−	+	+	+	−	+	−	+
Consumption	−	+	−	−	−	+	−	+	−	−	−	+	N	−
Per capita consumption	−	+	−	−	−	+	−	+	−	−	−	+	N	−
Investment	−	+	+	−	−	+	−	+	+	+	−	+	N	−
Aggregate expenditure	−	+	−	−	−	+	−	+	−	+	−	+	N	−
Export performance														
Export growth	−	+	+	−	−	+	+	+	+	+	−	−	N	+
Import substitution														
Import/GDP ratio	−	+	+	−	−	−	−	+	−	+	−	−	+	−
Investment and savings														
Domestic saving/GDP	−	+	−	−	+	+	−	−	+	−	−	−	+	+
Private saving/GDP	−	−	−	+	+	−	N	+	−	−	−	−	+	+
Public saving/GDP	+	+	−	−	−	+	N	−	+	+	+	−	+	+
Investment/GDP	−	+	+	−	−	−	−	−	−	−	+	−	+	−
Foreign saving/GDP	−	+	+	+	−	−	−	+	−	+	−	−	−	−
Balance of payments														
Current account/GDP	+	−	−	+	+	+	+	−	+	−	N	+	+	+
Basic balance/GDP	+	+	+	−	+	+	+	−	−	−	N	+	+	+
Overall balance/GDP	−	−	+	−	+	+	+	−	−	−	N	−	+	+
External debt														
External debt/exports	+	+	+	+	+	+	+	+	+	+	+	+	N	+
Debt service/exports	+	+	+	+	+	+	+	−	−	+	+	+	N	+
Inflation														
Wholesale prices	N	+	N	N	N	N	N	N	+	N	N	N	N	N
Consumer prices	−	−	N	+	+	−	+	+	+	+	+	−	N	+
Monetary policy														
Money supply growth	+	+	N	−	+	−	−	+	+	−	−	−	+	−
Real discount rate	+	+	N	+	+	+	+	−	−	N	−	+	N	−
Fiscal policy														
Gov. revenue/GDP	+	+	+	+	+	+	N	+	−	−	−	+	+	+
Gov. expenditure/GDP	+	+	+	+	+	−	N	+	−	−	−	+	+	+
Budget surplus/GDP	+	+	−	−	−	+	N	−	+	+	+	−	+	+

Table 4.2   *cont.*

Pakistan	Bolivia	Costa Rica	Guyana	Jamaica	Morocco	Philippines	Thailand	Turkey	Brazil	Korea	Mexico	Panama	Uruguay	Yugoslavia	Increase	Decrease	Not Available
+	−	+	−	+	+	−	−	+	+	+	−	−	+	+	14	15	0
+	−	+	−	+	+	−	−	+	+	+	−	−	+	+	13	16	0
+	−	+	−	+	−	−	−	+	+	+	−	−	+	+	13	16	0
+	−	+	−	−	+	−	+	+	−	+	−	+	+	−	17	12	0
−	−	+	−	+	+	−	−	−	+	−	−	−	+	+	10	18	1
−	−	+	−	+	+	−	+	−	+	−	−	−	+	+	11	17	1
−	−	+	−	+	+	−	+	+	+	+	+	−	+	+	17	11	1
−	−	+	−	+	+	−	+	+	+	+	−	−	+	+	14	14	1
+	−	+	−	+	−	−	−	+	−	+	−	−	+	+	15	13	1
+	−	−	−	+	+	+	−	+	−	+	−	−	−	+	12	17	0
−	−	+	−	−	+	−	−	+	+	+	+	−	+	+	14	15	0
−	+	−	N	+	+	+	−	−	+	+	+	−	−	+	13	14	2
+	−	+	N	−	+	−	−	+	+	−	−	+	+	+	16	11	2
−	−	−	−	+	−	−	−	−	−	−	−	−	−	+	6	23	0
+	−	−	+	+	−	+	−	−	−	−	−	−	−	−	9	20	0
+	+	+	−	−	+	−	+	+	+	+	+	+	+	+	21	7	1
+	−	−	−	−	+	−	−	+	−	+	+	+	−	+	16	12	1
+	−	+	−	+	+	−	+	+	−	−	+	−	+	+	15	13	1
−	+	+	+	+	+	+	+	−	+	+	+	+	+	+	26	2	1
−	+	+	−	−	−	+	+	+	−	+	+	−	+	−	19	9	1
−	N	−	N	N	−	+	−	N	+	−	+	−	+	+	7	6	16
−	+	−	+	−	−	−	−	−	+	−	+	−	+	+	14	13	2
−	+	−	+	−	+	−	−	−	+	+	+	−	+	+	14	14	1
+	−	+	−	+	+	+	+	+	+	+	N	N	N	+	17	6	6
+	−	+	N	+	−	−	+	−	−	+	+	−	−	−	16	11	2
+	+	+	N	+	−	−	+	−	−	+	+	−	−	−	16	11	2
+	−	+	N	−	+	−	−	+	+	−	−	+	+	+	16	11	2

Table 4.3 Performance indicators: years until 1987

	Cote d'Ivoire	Ghana	Guinea-Bissau	Kenya	Malawi	Mauritius	Nigeria	Senegal	Sierra Leone	Sudan	Tanzania	Togo	Uganda	Zimbabwe
Economic growth														
Gross domestic product	−	+	−	−	−	+	−	+	−	−	−	+	−	−
Per capita GDP	−	+	−	−	−	+	−	+	−	−	−	+	−	−
Industrial production	−	+	−	−	−	+	+	−	−	+	−	−	−	−
Agricultural production	−	+	−	−	+	+	−	+	+	+	+	+	−	+
Consumption	−	+	−	−	−	+	−	−	−	−	−	+	N	−
Per capita consumption	−	+	−	−	−	+	−	−	−	−	−	+	N	−
Investment	−	+	+	−	−	+	−	+	+	+	+	+	N	−
Aggregate expenditure	−	+	−	−	−	+	−	+	−	−	−	+	N	−
Export performance														
Export growth	−	+	+	+	−	+	+	−	+	+	−	−	N	+
Import substitution														
Import/GDP ratio	−	+	+	−	−	−	−	+	−	+	−	−	+	−
Investment and savings														
Domestic saving/GDP	−	+	−	−	−	+	−	−	+	−	−	−	+	+
Private saving/GDP	−	−	−	+	−	−	N	−	+	−	−	−	+	+
Public saving/GDP	+	+	−	−	+	+	N	−	+	+	+	−	+	+
Investment/GDP	−	+	+	−	−	−	−	−	−	+	−	−	+	−
Foreign saving/GDP	−	+	+	−	−	−	−	+	−	+	−	−	−	−
Balance of payments														
Current account/GDP	+	−	−	+	+	+	+	−	+	−	N	+	+	+
Basic balance/GDP	+	+	+	−	+	+	+	+	−	−	N	+	+	+
Overall balance/GDP	+	−	+	−	+	+	+	−	−	−	N	−	+	+
External debt														
External debt/exports	+	+	+	+	+	+	+	+	+	+	+	+	N	+
Debt service/exports	+	+	+	+	+	+	+	−	−	−	+	+	N	+
Inflation														
Wholesale prices	N	+	N	N	N	N	N	N	+	N	N	N	N	N
Consumer prices	−	−	N	−	+	−	+	+	+	+	+	−	N	+
Monetary policy														
Money supply growth	+	+	N	−	+	+	−	+	+	−	−	−	+	−
Real discount rate	+	+	N	+	+	+	+	−	−	N	−	+	N	−
Fiscal policy														
Gov. revenue/GDP	+	+	+	+	+	+	N	+	−	−	−	+	+	+
Gov. expenditure/GDP	+	+	+	+	−	−	N	+	−	−	−	+	+	+
Budget surplus/GDP	+	+	−	−	+	+	N	−	+	+	+	−	+	+

Table 4.3   *cont.*

Pakistan	Bolivia	Costa Rica	Guyana	Jamaica	Morocco	Philippines	Thailand	Turkey	Brazil	Korea	Mexico	Panama	Uruguay	Yugoslavia	Increase	Decrease	Not Available
+	−	+	−	+	+	−	−	+	+	+	−	−	+	+	13	16	0
+	−	+	−	+	+	−	−	+	+	+	−	−	+	+	13	16	0
+	−	+	−	+	−	−	−	+	+	+	−	−	+	+	12	17	0
+	−	+	−	−	+	−	−	+	−	+	−	+	+	−	16	13	0
−	−	+	+	+	+	−	−	+	+	−	−	−	+	+	11	17	1
−	−	+	+	+	+	−	−	+	+	−	−	−	+	+	11	17	1
−	+	+	−	+	+	−	+	+	+	+	+	−	+	+	19	9	1
−	−	+	−	+	+	−	−	+	+	+	−	−	+	+	12	16	1
+	−	+	−	+	−	−	−	+	−	+	−	−	+	+	15	13	1
+	−	−	−	+	+	−	−	+	−	+	−	−	−	+	11	18	0
−	−	+	−	+	+	−	−	+	+	+	+	−	+	+	14	15	0
−	+	−	N	+	+	−	−	+	+	+	+	−	−	+	12	15	2
−	−	+	N	−	+	−	−	−	+	−	−	+	+	+	15	12	2
−	−	−	−	+	−	−	−	+	−	−	−	−	−	+	7	22	0
+	−	−	+	+	−	−	−	−	−	−	−	−	−	−	7	22	0
+	+	+	−	−	+	+	+	+	+	+	+	+	+	+	22	6	1
+	−	−	−	−	+	+	+	+	−	+	+	+	−	+	19	9	1
+	−	+	−	+	+	−	+	+	−	−	+	−	+	+	16	12	1
−	+	+	+	+	+	+	+	−	+	+	+	+	+	−	25	3	1
+	+	+	−	−	−	+	+	+	−	+	+	−	+	−	19	9	1
−	N	−	N	N	−	+	−	N	+	−	+	−	+	+	7	6	16
−	+	−	+	−	−	+	−	−	+	−	+	−	+	+	14	13	2
−	+	−	+	−	+	−	−	−	+	−	+	−	+	+	14	14	1
+	−	+	+	+	+	−	+	+	+	+	N	N	N	+	17	6	6
+	−	+	N	+	−	−	+	−	−	+	+	−	−	−	16	11	2
+	+	+	N	+	−	−	+	−	−	+	+	−	−	−	15	12	2
−	−	+	N	−	+	−	−	−	+	−	−	+	+	+	15	12	2

Table 4.4 Performance indicators: relative to comparator groups in three years following loan

	Cote d'Ivoire	Ghana	Guinea-Bissau	Kenya	Malawi	Mauritius	Nigeria	Senegal	Sierra Leone	Sudan	Tanzania	Togo	Uganda	Zimbabwe
Economic Growth														
Gross domestic product	–	+	–	–	+	+	–	+	–	+	–	+	–	–
Per capita GDP	–	+	–	–	+	+	–	+	–	+	–	–	–	–
Industrial production	–	+	–	–	–	+	+	+	+	+	–	–	–	–
Agricultural production	–	+	–	+	+	+	–	+	–	+	+	+	–	+
Consumption	–	+	–	–	–	+	–	+	–	–	–	+	N	–
Per capita consumption	–	+	–	–	–	+	–	+	–	–	–	+	N	–
Investment	–	+	–	–	–	+	–	+	–	+	+	+	N	–
Aggregate expenditure	–	+	–	–	–	+	–	+	–	+	–	+	N	–
Export performance														
Export growth	+	+	+	+	+	+	+	+	+	+	–	–	N	+
Import substitution														
Import/GDP ratio	–	+	+	–	–	–	–	+	–	+	–	–	+	–
Investment and savings														
Domestic saving/GDP	–	+	–	+	+	+	–	–	–	+	+	–	+	+
Private saving/GDP	+	+	–	+	+	+	N	–	–	–	+	+	+	+
Public saving/GDP	+	+	–	–	+	+	N	–	+	+	+	–	+	–
Investment/GDP	–	+	+	–	–	–	–	+	–	+	–	–	+	+
Foreign saving/GDP	–	+	+	–	–	–	+	+	–	+	–	+	–	–
Balance of payments														
Current account/GDP	+	–	–	+	+	+	–	–	+	+	N	+	+	+
Basic balance/GDP	+	–	+	+	+	+	–	+	–	+	N	+	+	+
Overall balance/GDP	+	+	+	–	+	+	+	+	–	+	N	–	+	+
External debt														
External debt/exports	+	+	+	+	–	–	+	–	+	+	+	–	N	–
Debt service/exports	+	+	+	+	–	+	+	–	–	–	–	+	N	+
Inflation														
Wholesale prices	N	+	N	N	N	N	N	N	+	N	N	N	N	N
Consumer prices	–	–	N	+	+	–	+	+	+	+	+	–	N	+
Monetary policy														
Money supply growth	+	+	N	–	+	+	–	+	+	–	–	–	+	–
Real discount rate	+	+	N	+	–	+	–	–	–	N	–	+	N	–
Fiscal policy														
Gov. revenue/GDP	+	+	–	–	–	–	N	–	–	–	–	–	+	–
Gov. expenditure/GDP	–	–	+	–	–	–	N	+	–	–	–	+	+	–
Budget surplus/GDP	+	+	–	–	+	+	N	–	+	+	+	–	+	–

Table 4.4   *cont.*

Pakistan	Bolivia	Costa Rica	Guyana	Jamaica	Morocco	Philippines	Thailand	Turkey	Brazil	Korea	Mexico	Panama	Uruguay	Yugoslavia	Increase	Decrease	Not Available
+	−	+	−	+	+	+	+	+	+	+	−	−	+	+	17	12	0
+	−	+	−	+	+	+	+	+	+	+	−	−	+	+	16	13	0
+	+	+	−	+	−	+	+	+	+	+	−	−	+	+	17	12	0
−	−	+	+	−	+	−	+	+	−	+	−	−	+	−	16	13	0
−	−	+	−	+	+	+	+	+	+	+	−	+	+	+	15	13	1
−	−	+	−	+	+	+	+	+	+	+	−	+	+	+	15	13	1
+	−	+	−	+	+	+	+	+	+	+	+	+	+	+	19	9	1
+	−	+	−	+	+	+	+	+	+	+	+	+	+	+	18	10	1
+	+	−	−	+	−	+	−	+	−	+	−	−	+	+	19	9	1
−	−	−	+	+	+	+	+	+	+	+	+	−	+	+	16	13	0
−	−	+	−	+	+	+	−	+	+	+	+	−	+	+	18	11	0
−	+	+	N	+	+	+	−	−	+	+	+	−	+	+	19	8	2
+	−	−	N	−	+	+	−	+	+	+	+	+	+	+	18	9	2
−	−	+	+	+	+	+	+	+	+	−	+	−	+	+	17	12	0
−	−	+	+	+	+	−	+	−	−	−	−	+	−	+	13	16	0
+	+	+	−	+	+	+	+	+	+	+	+	+	−	+	22	6	1
+	+	−	−	+	+	+	+	+	−	+	+	+	−	+	21	7	1
+	+	+	−	+	+	+	+	+	−	+	+	−	+	+	22	6	1
−	+	−	+	+	+	+	−	−	−	−	+	+	+	−	16	12	1
−	−	+	−	−	−	−	+	+	−	−	+	−	−	−	12	16	1
+	N	−	N	N	−	+	−	N	+	−	+	−	+	+	8	5	16
−	+	−	+	−	−	+	−	−	+	−	+	−	+	+	15	12	2
+	+	−	+	+	−	+	−	+	+	−	+	−	+	+	17	11	1
+	−	+	−	+	−	−	+	+	+	−	N	N	N	+	12	11	6
+	−	+	N	+	−	−	+	−	−	+	−	−	−	−	8	19	2
−	+	+	N	+	−	−	+	−	−	−	−	−	−	−	8	19	2
+	−	−	N	−	+	+	−	+	+	+	+	+	+	+	18	9	2

Table 4.5 Performance indicators: relative to comparator groups in years until 1987

	Cote d'Ivoire	Ghana	Guinea-Bissau	Kenya	Malawi	Mauritius	Nigeria	Senegal	Sierra Leone	Sudan	Tanzania	Togo	Uganda	Zimbabwe
Economic Growth														
Gross domestic product	−	+	−	−	−	+	−	+	−	+	+	+	−	−
Per capita GDP	−	+	−	−	−	+	−	+	−	+	+	+	−	−
Industrial production	−	+	−	−	−	+	+	−	+	+	−	−	−	−
Agricultural production	−	+	−	−	+	+	−	+	−	+	+	+	−	+
Consumption	−	+	−	−	−	+	−	+	−	−	−	+	N	−
Per capita consumption	−	+	−	−	−	+	−	+	−	−	−	+	N	−
Investment	−	+	−	−	−	+	−	+	−	+	+	+	N	−
Aggregate expenditure	−	+	−	−	−	+	−	+	−	−	−	+	N	−
Export performance														
Export growth	+	+	+	+	−	+	+	+	+	+	+	−	N	+
Import substitution														
Import/GDP ratio	−	+	+	−	−	−	−	+	−	+	−	−	+	−
Investment and savings														
Domestic saving/GDP	+	+	−	+	+	+	−	−	−	+	−	−	+	+
Private saving/GDP	+	+	−	+	+	+	N	−	−	−	+	+	+	+
Public saving/GDP	+	+	−	−	+	+	N	−	+	+	+	−	+	−
Investment/GDP	−	+	+	+	−	−	−	+	−	+	−	−	+	+
Foreign saving/GDP	−	+	+	−	−	−	−	+	−	+	−	+	−	−
Balance of payments														
Current account/GDP	+	−	−	+	+	+	−	−	+	−	N	+	+	+
Basic balance/GDP	+	−	+	+	+	+	−	+	−	+	N	+	+	+
Overall balance/GDP	+	+	+	−	+	+	+	+	−	+	N	−	+	+
External debt														
External debt/exports	+	+	+	−	−	−	+	−	+	+	+	−	N	−
Debt service/exports	−	+	+	+	+	+	+	−	−	−	−	+	N	+
Inflation														
Wholesale prices	N	+	N	N	N	N	N	N	+	N	N	N	N	N
Consumer prices	−	−	N	+	+	−	+	+	+	+	+	−	N	+
Monetary policy														
Money supply growth	+	+	N	−	+	+	−	+	+	+	−	−	+	−
Real discount rate	+	+	N	+	−	+	−	−	−	N	−	+	N	−
Fiscal policy														
Gov. revenue/GDP	+	+	−	−	−	−	N	−	−	−	−	−	+	−
Gov. expenditure/GDP	−	−	+	−	−	−	N	+	−	−	−	+	+	−
Budget surplus/GDP	+	+	−	−	+	+	N	−	+	+	+	−	+	−

Table 4.5   *cont.*

Pakistan	Bolivia	Costa Rica	Guyana	Jamaica	Morocco	Philippines	Thailand	Turkey	Brazil	Korea	Mexico	Panama	Uruguay	Yugoslavia	Increase	Decrease	Not Available
+	−	+	−	+	+	−	−	+	+	+	−	−	+	+	15	14	0
+	−	+	+	+	+	−	+	+	+	+	−	−	+	+	17	12	0
+	+	+	+	+	−	−	+	+	+	+	−	−	+	+	16	13	0
+	−	+	+	−	+	−	+	+	−	+	−	−	+	−	16	13	0
−	−	+	+	+	+	−	+	+	+	+	−	+	+	+	15	13	1
−	−	+	+	+	+	+	+	+	+	+	−	+	+	+	16	12	1
+	+	+	+	+	+	−	+	+	+	+	+	+	+	+	20	8	1
+	+	+	+	+	+	−	+	+	+	+	+	+	+	+	18	10	1
+	+	−	+	+	−	+	−	+	−	+	−	−	+	+	20	8	1
−	−	−	+	+	+	−	+	+	+	+	+	−	+	+	15	14	0
−	−	+	−	+	+	−	−	+	+	+	+	−	+	+	17	12	0
−	+	+	N	+	+	−	−	+	+	+	+	−	+	+	19	8	2
+	−	−	N	+	+	+	−	+	+	+	+	+	+	+	19	8	2
−	−	+	+	+	+	−	+	+	+	+	+	−	+	+	18	11	0
−	−	+	+	+	+	−	+	−	−	−	+	+	−	+	13	16	0
+	+	+	−	−	+	+	+	+	+	+	+	+	−	−	+	20	8	1
+	−	−	−	+	+	+	+	+	−	+	+	+	−	−	+	20	8	1
+	+	+	−	+	+	+	+	+	−	+	+	−	−	+	+	22	6	1
−	+	−	+	+	+	+	−	−	−	−	+	+	+	−	15	13	1
−	+	+	−	−	−	−	+	+	−	−	+	−	−	−	13	15	1
+	N	−	N	N	−	+	−	N	+	−	+	−	+	+	8	5	16
−	+	−	−	−	−	−	−	−	+	−	+	−	+	+	13	14	2
−	+	−	+	+	−	+	−	+	+	−	+	−	+	+	17	11	1
+	−	+	−	+	−	−	+	+	+	+	N	N	N	+	13	10	6
+	−	+	N	+	−	−	+	−	−	+	−	−	−	−	8	19	2
−	+	+	N	−	−	−	+	−	−	−	−	−	−	−	7	20	2
+	−	−	N	+	+	+	−	+	+	+	+	+	+	+	19	8	2

In Tables 4.2 to 4.5, changes in indicator values are shown for each country, with the countries being separated into the four groups in the tables. The tables further show the sums of positive and negative signs, as well as of the not available data, for each performance indicator.

Table 4.2 pertains to changes in each country's own performance indicators between the three-year periods preceding and following the first adjustment loan. The corresponding changes in indicator values between the pre-loan period and the period up to 1987 following the loan are shown in Table 4.3.

In turn, Tables 4.4 and 4.5 show changes in performance indicators *vis-à-vis* the comparator groups for the two post-loan periods, respectively. A positive (negative) sign indicates an increase (decrease) in the value of a country's performance indicator relative to that for the comparator group.

In interpreting the average values of the performance indicators, it should be noted that some indicators are not available for all countries or for all years. Correspondingly, there may be discrepancies in the values of linked indicators, e.g. those for domestic savings, private savings, and public savings.

THE OVERALL RESULTS

Countries receiving adjustment loans experienced a decline in the rate of growth of GDP in the three years following the first adjustment loan, with a slight plurality in the negative results being translated into a decline in average growth rates from 2.7 to 2.2 percent. However, there were improvements *vis-à-vis* the comparator groups, with 17 of the 29 countries bettering their relative position and the 0.7 percent average shortfall in the three years preceding the loan declining to 0.4 percent in the three years afterwards.

A smaller decline in GDP growth rates is shown for the recipients of adjustment loans if the post-loan period is extended to 1987. Furthermore, the average improvement *vis-à-vis* the comparator groups is slightly greater than beforehand, although only 15 countries experienced an improvement *vis-à-vis* these groups.

Decreases in the *per capita GDP* of the loan recipient countries approximately matched those for the gross domestic product as population growth rates underwent little change during the period under consideration. At the same time, improvements are observed *vis-à-vis* the comparator groups. While in the three years preceding the first adjustment loan average per capita income growth was 1.0

percentage points lower in the loan recipient countries than in the nonrecipients, this difference declined to 0.4 percentage points in the period after the loan, irrespective of whether one considers the first three years after the first adjustment loan or the period until 1987. At the same time, in the first three years, there were 16 countries and, until 1987, 17 countries experiencing an improvement *vis-à-vis* the comparator groups.

Economic growth following the first adjustment loan was concentrated in industry and in agriculture. The average rate of *industrial growth* remained unchanged following the first adjustment loan, even though a larger number of countries experienced a deceleration than an acceleration. At the same time, there was a substantial improvement *vis-à-vis* the comparator groups, with the average shortfall declining from 3.3 percent in the three years preceding the loan to 0.9 percent in the period until 1987 as 16 countries experienced an improvement in relative terms.

Agricultural growth exhibited a continued acceleration in the loan recipient countries during the period under consideration and the majority of these countries experienced increases over time. The average improvement is particularly noteworthy *vis-à-vis* the comparator groups (from −0.5 percent to 0.4 percent), with 16 countries improving their relative position.

The decline in the average growth of *aggregate expenditure* for the recipients of adjustment loans was considerably greater than that in GDP growth. However, the relative increase *vis-à-vis* the comparator countries was also larger. In fact, in the years until 1987 from the first adjustment loan, the recipients of these loans attained average increases in aggregate expenditures 0.3 percentage points greater than the comparator groups while they had a shortfall of 1.4 percentage points in the three years preceding the loan.

The fall in aggregate expenditure was concentrated in *consumption*. A decline is shown in consumption growth in the loan recipient countries *vis-à-vis* the nonrecipients, with a differential of −0.2 percentage points in the three years preceding the first adjustment loan giving place to a differential of −0.4 percentage points in the years until 1987. At the same time, there was a substantial improvement in the relative position of the loan recipient countries in regard to *investment*.

While the recipients of adjustment loans experienced an average 8.3 percentage points shortfall in investment growth *vis-à-vis* the comparator groups in the three years preceding the first adjustment loan, the shortfall decreased to 3.1 percentage points in the years until 1987 following the loan. This occurred as a 1.5 percent average annual rate of decline in investment gave place to a 2.0 percent rate of increase in the loan recipient countries while the comparator groups exhibited decreases in investment growth rates. There is also a large plurality in the number of loan recipient countries experiencing improvements in investment growth rates *vis-à-vis* the comparator groups.

Average *export growth* rates declined less in countries receiving adjustment loans than elsewhere as a much larger number of loan recipient countries experienced an improvement rather than a deterioration in their relative position. In turn, average import–GDP ratios fell in the same proportion in the loan recipient as in the nonrecipient countries while fewer loan recipient countries showed relative increases than decreases.

Average *domestic savings* ratios decreased slightly in countries receiving adjustment loans, with somewhat larger declines occurring in the comparator countries over the entire period. At the same time, a substantially larger number of loan recipient countries experienced increases than decreases in domestic savings ratios *vis-à-vis* the nonrecipients.

The latter conclusion also applies to *private savings* and *public savings*, taken individually. Furthermore, the loan recipient countries experienced an improvement in their average private and public savings ratios *vis-à-vis* the comparator groups.

In turn, average *investment* ratios decreased in a parallel fashion in the two groups of countries, although a substantial majority of loan recipients improved their relative position *vis-à-vis* the nonrecipients. Finally, the ratio of *foreign savings* to GDP decreased in both cases, but the decline was larger in the loan recipient countries.

A large majority of loan recipients attained an improvement in their *current account balance* during the period under consideration. This result was repeated for the *basic balance* and, to a lesser extent, the *overall balance*. Furthermore, average improvements in these balances were substantially greater in loan recipient countries than in the comparators and there was a very large plurality of loan recipient countries experiencing a relative improvement.

In relative terms, the loan recipient countries also attained improvements in their *external debt indicators vis-à-vis* the nonrecipients, although these indicators increased in absolute terms over time. Thus, between the three years preceding the first adjustment loan and the subsequent period until 1987 average external debt–

export ratios increased from 272 to 392 percent and debt service–export ratios from 22 to 26 percent in the loan recipient countries while average increases were from 174 to 266 percent and from 12 to 19 percent, respectively, in the comparator countries.

Data for *wholesale prices* are available for only a few countries, hence the discussion will concentrate on *consumer prices*. Inflation, as measured by the consumer price index, accelerated in 14 countries receiving adjustment loans and decelerated in 13 countries, with 14 loan recipient countries showing an improvement and 13 countries a deterioration *vis-à-vis* the comparator groups. But average annual inflation rates in the loan recipient countries increased substantially, from 25 percent in the three years preceding the adjustment loan to 102 percent in the post-loan period until 1987, reflecting in large part the 1965 percent annual rate of inflation in the latter period in Bolivia. By comparison, inflation rates increased from 17 to 21 percent in the comparator groups.

The average results for *money supply growth* also largely reflect the Bolivian increase of 1397 percent a year. At the same time, 14 countries showed an increase and 14 a decline in money supply growth rates. Money supply growth rates accelerated however *vis-à-vis* the comparator groups in the large majority of the loan recipient countries.

The *real discount rate* increased in 17 loan recipient countries and declined in six countries between the three-year period preceding the loan and the subsequent period up to 1987. As a result, the average increased from −6.0 percent to −3.5 percent. This compares with an increase from −4.3 percent to −0.8 percent in the comparator groups while a majority of loan recipients experienced increases in the real discount rate *vis-à-vis* these groups.

Changes in the *budget surplus* (public savings) were discussed above. At the same time, loan recipient countries experienced increases in *government expenditure ratios* as well as in *revenue ratios*. In these countries, the average ratio of government expenditures to GDP increased from 27.0 percent to 30.5 percent between the pre-loan and the post-loan (up to 1987) period while the average government revenue ratio rose from 19.0 to 22.5 percent.

At the same time, the loan recipient countries exhibited relative increases in government expenditures and government revenues *vis-à-vis* the comparator countries. However, these results were due to developments in relatively few countries; in particular, 20 countries experienced a decline and seven countries an increase in their expenditure ratio compared with the nonrecipients.

RESULTS FOR PARTICULAR COUNTRY GROUPS

Further interest attaches to the results for particular country groups. As noted earlier, adjustment loans were extended until 1984 to 14 sub-Saharan African countries while 23 countries of the region did not receive such loans. The corresponding figures are 1 and 7 for low-income countries, 8 and 24 for lower-middle-income countries, and 6 and 21 for upper-middle-income countries. The following discussion will make comparisons for the loan recipients and nonrecipients in each of the four country groupings between the three-year period preceding the first adjustment loan and the subsequent period up to 1987. The relevant results are shown in Tables 4.6 to 4.9.

The recipients of adjustment loans in *sub-Saharan Africa* had a slightly lower GDP growth rate than the nonrecipients in the three years preceding the loan; the difference increased in the period up to 1987 following the loan as the recipient countries experienced a greater deceleration of economic growth than the nonrecipients. Similar conclusions apply to per capita income growth.

Loan recipients slightly improved their relative position, however, as far as industrial and agricultural growth are concerned. In turn, they experienced a much larger fall in the growth of aggregate expenditure than the comparator group. The decline was concentrated in consumption where average annual increases fell from 6.3 percent in the three years preceding the loan to 0.9 percent after the loan in the first group as against an average decline from 3.6 to 2.5 percent in the second.

Export growth rates declined proportionately less in the loan recipient countries than in the nonrecipients. At the same time, 11 loan recipient countries accelerated their export growth rate while two experienced a deceleration relative to the nonrecipients. In turn, the import–GDP ratio declined slightly more in the loan recipient countries than in the comparator group.

The domestic savings ratio fell somewhat in sub-Saharan countries receiving adjustment loans while larger decreases are shown for the comparator group, with the fall in private savings dominating the outcome in the latter case. At the same time, investment ratios declined somewhat more in the loan recipient than in the nonrecipient countries of the region. This occurred as foreign savings fell to a greater extent in the first case than in the second.

Loan recipient countries exhibited substantial improvements in their current account balance, with smaller changes shown in the basic balance and the overall balance. Lesser improvements were observed in the current account balance and the basic balance of the comparator group, which also experienced a deterioration in its overall balance. However, loan recipients exhibited much larger increases in their external debt–export and in debt service–export ratios than nonrecipient sub-Saharan African countries.

The rate of inflation declined less in the loan recipient than in the nonrecipient countries as money supply growth accelerated to a greater extent in the first group than in the second. Also, the real discount rate increased to a lesser extent in the loan recipient countries than in the nonrecipients. Finally, both expenditure–GDP and revenue–GDP ratios rose more in the former case than in the latter.

Pakistan is the only *low-income country* outside sub-Saharan Africa that received adjustment loans during the period under consideration. It showed a much superior growth performance than the comparator group, with its GDP growth rate rising from 5.3 to 6.9 percent as against declines elsewhere. Also, the growth of industrial production and agricultural output accelerated in Pakistan while industrial growth rates declined and agricultural growth rates increased less in the comparator group. At the same time, the growth of aggregate expenditure decreased to a lesser extent in Pakistan than elsewhere and the decline was equally shared by consumption and investment.

Pakistan experienced a substantial acceleration of export growth between the pre-loan and the post-loan periods while a slight decrease occurred in the low-income group of nonrecipients of adjustment loans. At the same time, Pakistan exhibited a small increase in its import–GDP ratio that was matched by the comparator group.

Domestic savings ratios declined more in Pakistan than in the comparator group as the fall in private savings was not compensated by improvements in public savings. There was also a decline in the investment ratio, despite a rise in foreign savings. The foreign savings ratio increased to a greater extent in the comparator group, leading to a rise in the investment ratio.

All indicators show an improvement in Pakistan's balance of payments as compared to a deterioration in the nonrecipient group of low-income countries. At the same time, Pakistan attained a decline in its external debt ratio, compared with an increase in the comparator group that also exhibited a larger rise in its debt service ratio than Pakistan.

Pakistan experienced a deceleration of inflation, whether measured by the wholesale or the consumer price index. The two indices, however, point in different directions for the rest of the low-income countries. This occurred as money supply growth decreased in a parallel fashion in the two cases. Finally, the real discount rate increased in Pakistan while declining in the comparator group.

Table 4.6 Performance indicators: group = sub-Saharan Africa

Indicators	Preceding 3 years			Following 3 years			Years until 1987		
	Own average	Group average	Difference	Own average	Group average	Difference	Own average	Group average	Difference
Population, mil.	14.1	6.1	.	16.1	6.8	.	16.6	7.0	.
Per capita GDP, US$	676.0	636.9	.	457.8	639.6	.	459.5	633.5	.
Economic growth									
Gross domestic product	3.0	3.1	-0.1	1.7	2.5	-0.8	1.9	2.8	-0.9
Per capita GDP	0.1	0.2	-0.1	-1.3	-0.4	-0.9	-1.1	-0.1	-1.0
Industrial production	1.8	5.3	-3.4	1.0	3.9	-2.8	0.9	3.7	-2.7
Agricultural production	1.7	1.7	-0.0	3.5	2.4	1.0	3.5	3.1	0.4
Consumption	6.3	3.6	2.7	0.7	2.5	-1.7	0.9	2.5	-1.6
Per capita consumption	3.2	0.6	2.6	-2.2	-0.5	-1.7	-2.1	-0.5	-1.6
Investment	-0.3	5.5	-5.8	0.2	7.8	-7.6	1.2	11.9	-10.7
Aggregate expenditure	4.7	3.1	1.6	0.1	1.6	-1.5	0.6	1.9	-1.3
Export performance									
Export growth	9.9	5.8	4.1	5.0	2.3	2.7	6.4	2.4	4.0
Import substitution									
Import/GDP ratio	31.8	45.7	-13.9	29.5	44.2	-14.7	28.9	44.0	-15.2
Investment and savings									
Domestic saving/GDP	12.3	7.5	4.8	11.2	6.2	5.0	11.5	6.2	5.2
Private saving/GDP	23.2	14.3	8.9	23.4	11.2	12.2	23.2	11.2	12.0

113

Public saving/GDP	-10.8	-5.7	-5.1	-11.6	-6.0	-5.6	-11.4	-5.9	-5.5
Investment/GDP	21.6	22.3	-0.7	17.7	19.0	-1.3	17.2	18.6	-1.4
Foreign saving/GDP	9.2	14.7	-5.5	6.5	12.8	-6.3	5.7	12.4	-6.7
Balance of payments									
Current account/GDP	-9.0	-8.0	-1.0	-0.6	-5.9	5.3	-0.2	-5.2	5.0
Basic balance/GDP	-5.6	-1.5	-4.1	1.6	-1.7	3.3	2.0	-1.4	3.4
Overall balance/GDP	-4.2	-1.3	-2.9	-1.8	-2.6	0.9	-1.5	-2.5	1.0
External debt									
External debt/exports	288.3	196.2	92.1	472.7	306.2	166.5	489.0	320.4	168.7
Debt service/exports	11.5	9.1	2.4	21.1	15.1	6.0	21.3	16.6	4.7
Inflation									
Wholesale prices	35.3	12.4	22.9	58.2	17.1	41.1	58.2	19.1	39.1
Consumer prices	20.9	15.7	5.2	20.5	14.4	6.2	20.2	13.9	6.2
Monetary policy									
Money supply growth	22.3	16.9	5.4	30.6	15.4	15.2	32.1	15.7	16.4
Real discount rate	-8.0	-6.1	-1.8	-4.9	-2.8	-2.2	-4.6	-2.2	-2.4
Fiscal policy									
Gov. revenue/GDP	20.0	22.1	-2.2	28.6	25.6	3.0	28.5	25.7	2.8
Gov. expenditure/GDP	30.8	27.8	2.9	40.1	31.6	8.5	39.9	31.6	8.3
Budget surplus/GDP	-10.8	-5.7	-5.1	-11.6	-6.0	-5.6	-11.4	-5.9	-5.5

Table 4.7 Performance indicators: group = low-income countries

Indicators	Preceding 3 years			Following 3 years			Years until 1987		
	Own average	Group average	Difference	Own average	Group average	Difference	Own average	Group average	Difference
Population, mil.	77.8	251.6	.	87.8	269.5	.	93.4	278.6	.
Per capita GDP, US$	225.2	167.8	.	330.9	224.3	.	331.8	237.6	.
Economic growth									
Gross domestic product	5.3	5.1	0.2	6.8	4.2	2.6	6.9	4.4	2.4
Per capita GDP	2.1	3.0	-0.9	3.6	2.2	1.4	3.7	2.4	1.2
Industrial production	8.1	8.1	-0.1	9.5	3.6	5.9	9.4	5.1	4.3
Agricultural production	2.8	2.8	0.1	3.7	4.2	-0.5	4.0	3.4	0.5
Consumption	6.5	4.2	2.3	5.1	4.5	0.6	5.9	4.4	1.5
Per capita consumption	3.4	2.3	1.1	2.0	2.6	-0.6	2.8	2.5	0.2
Investment	7.0	16.6	-9.6	6.7	3.5	3.2	6.6	3.7	3.0
Aggregate expenditure	6.6	6.3	0.3	5.3	3.9	1.4	6.0	4.3	1.7
Export performance									
Export growth	2.8	7.7	-4.9	12.6	4.6	8.0	11.8	5.2	6.6
Import substitution									
Import/GDP ratio	20.1	17.5	2.6	22.7	20.8	1.9	22.5	19.9	2.6
Investment and savings									
Domestic saving/GDP	8.0	14.8	-6.8	6.2	13.3	-7.1	6.0	13.9	-8.0
Private saving/GDP	11.1	15.8	-4.7	8.8	17.4	-8.6	9.3	20.0	-10.7

Public saving/GDP	-3.1	-3.8	0.7	-2.7	-6.9	4.2	-3.3	-5.7	2.3
Investment/GDP	18.3	19.7	-1.4	17.4	21.8	-4.4	17.1	21.5	-4.4
Foreign saving/GDP	10.4	5.0	5.4	11.3	8.6	2.7	11.2	7.6	3.6
Balance of payments									
Current account/GDP	-4.8	-2.3	-2.5	-2.0	-6.0	3.9	-2.6	-4.7	2.1
Basic balance/GDP	-1.9	0.8	-2.8	-0.2	-1.7	1.5	-0.8	-1.2	0.4
Overall balance/GDP	-1.2	0.7	-1.9	0.1	-0.8	0.9	-0.9	-0.6	-0.3
External debt									
External debt/exports	490.7	223.8	266.9	338.7	258.2	80.5	345.4	275.7	69.7
Debt service/exports	23.9	10.8	13.1	22.3	12.0	10.4	25.5	13.7	11.8
Inflation									
Wholesale prices	8.4	11.6	-3.2	7.5	9.2	-1.7	6.8	7.2	-0.4
Consumer prices	8.2	5.3	2.9	8.0	9.3	-1.3	6.4	8.6	-2.2
Monetary policy									
Money supply growth	18.6	19.5	-0.9	14.8	14.0	0.8	14.7	16.1	-1.4
Real discount rate	1.7	1.9	-0.2	1.9	-0.1	2.0	3.4	1.1	2.3
Fiscal policy									
Gov. revenue/GDP	14.3	13.9	0.4	16.0	12.9	3.0	16.3	14.7	1.6
Gov. expenditure/GDP	17.5	17.7	-0.3	18.6	19.8	-1.2	19.7	20.4	-0.7
Budget surplus/GDP	-3.1	-3.8	0.7	-2.7	-6.9	4.2	-3.3	-5.7	2.3

Table 4.8 Performance indicators: group = lower-middle-income countries

Indicators	Preceding 3 years			Following 3 years			Years until 1987		
	Own average	Group average	Difference	Own average	Group average	Difference	Own average	Group average	Difference
Population, mil.	20.7	12.8	.	22.7	13.8	.	23.5	14.2	.
Per capita GDP, US$	948.1	834.9	.	986.6	1040.0	.	954.4	1049.6	.
Economic growth									
Gross domestic product	1.6	5.2	−3.6	1.3	2.6	−1.3	1.7	2.9	−1.2
Per capita GDP	−0.5	2.7	−3.2	−0.8	0.1	−0.9	−0.4	0.4	−0.8
Industrial production	0.5	7.3	−6.8	−0.1	1.9	−2.0	0.4	2.3	−1.9
Agricultural production	1.6	3.0	−1.4	2.0	2.3	−0.2	3.5	2.3	1.1
Consumption	1.1	5.1	−4.0	1.3	2.8	−1.5	2.2	2.7	−0.4
Per capita consumption	−1.0	2.5	−3.5	−0.8	0.2	−1.0	0.1	0.1	0.0
Investment	−5.0	9.1	−14.1	−2.7	−1.3	−1.3	1.2	−1.3	2.5
Aggregate expenditure	−0.4	5.6	−6.0	0.8	1.5	−0.7	1.7	1.5	0.3
Export performance									
Export growth	2.1	7.6	−5.6	6.3	2.7	3.6	4.2	3.7	0.5
Import substitution									
Import/GDP ratio	34.6	47.4	−12.8	33.6	45.7	−12.1	33.7	44.5	−10.8
Investment and savings									
Domestic saving/GDP	18.3	11.7	6.6	16.0	9.4	6.6	16.1	9.6	6.5
Private saving/GDP	25.7	18.1	7.7	24.1	17.1	7.1	24.8	17.0	7.8

Public saving/GDP	-7.5	-7.0	-0.5	-7.2	-7.2	-0.0	-8.1	-6.8	-1.3
Investment/GDP	24.0	27.4	-3.4	21.1	24.1	-3.0	20.4	22.9	-2.5
Foreign saving/GDP	5.8	15.7	-9.9	5.1	14.7	-9.6	4.3	13.3	-9.0
Balance of payments									
Current account/GDP	-8.1	-5.3	-2.8	-8.5	-7.8	-0.7	-7.9	-6.6	-1.3
Basic balance/GDP	-3.7	0.7	-4.3	-8.2	-2.3	-5.9	-7.5	-2.0	-5.5
Overall balance/GDP	-3.9	1.0	-4.9	-7.8	-2.6	-5.2	-6.9	-2.3	-4.6
External debt									
External debt/exports	257.7	177.6	80.0	315.7	236.3	79.4	336.8	255.2	81.6
Debt service/exports	28.9	17.1	11.8	27.9	20.5	7.4	28.3	20.8	7.5
Inflation									
Wholesale prices	25.5	16.0	9.5	7.1	14.1	-7.0	8.9	15.5	-6.5
Consumer prices	21.8	16.3	5.5	30.6	20.6	10.0	259.3	26.0	233.3
Monetary policy									
Money supply growth	21.4	23.4	-2.0	34.5	18.4	16.0	190.5	21.1	169.3
Real discount rate	-6.5	-3.3	-3.2	-2.4	-0.8	-1.6	-3.8	-0.5	-3.2
Fiscal policy									
Gov. revenue/GDP	20.2	22.1	-1.8	18.5	23.3	-4.8	17.9	23.4	-5.5
Gov. expenditure/GDP	27.7	29.0	-1.4	25.7	30.5	-4.7	26.0	30.2	-4.2
Budget surplus/GDP	-7.5	-7.0	-0.5	-7.2	-7.2	-0.0	-8.1	-6.8	-1.3

Table 4.9 Performance indicators: group = upper-middle-income countries

Indicators	Preceding 3 years			Following 3 years			Years until 1987		
	Own average	Group average	Difference	Own average	Group average	Difference	Own average	Group average	Difference
Population, mil.	43.4	9.7	.	47.1	10.5	.	47.6	10.6	.
Per capita GDP, US$	2403.8	3820.0	.	2022.0	4097.2	.	2056.2	4082.2	.
Economic growth									
Gross domestic product	3.0	3.0	-0.1	4.0	2.5	1.5	4.1	2.5	1.7
Per capita GDP	1.2	1.3	-0.1	2.4	1.1	1.3	2.5	1.0	1.5
Industrial production	2.3	1.2	1.1	4.7	0.9	3.8	4.7	0.9	3.8
Agricultural production	0.9	1.7	-0.8	2.0	2.7	-0.7	2.2	2.5	-0.3
Consumption	2.1	4.1	-2.0	3.5	1.7	1.8	3.6	1.5	2.1
Per capita consumption	0.4	2.4	-2.0	1.8	0.2	1.6	2.0	0.1	1.9
Investment	-1.3	5.2	-6.5	4.0	-2.7	6.7	3.7	-2.4	6.1
Aggregate expenditure	1.4	4.2	-2.8	3.8	0.2	3.6	3.8	0.1	3.7
Export performance									
Export growth	7.7	2.6	5.2	5.4	5.4	-0.1	5.7	5.3	0.4
Import substitution									
Import/GDP ratio	24.5	50.4	-25.9	22.7	43.5	-20.8	22.5	43.1	-20.6
Investment and savings									
Domestic saving/GDP	24.3	24.0	0.3	24.6	22.5	2.0	25.0	22.5	2.5
Private saving/GDP	27.1	28.9	-1.8	25.6	27.4	-1.8	25.9	27.3	-1.4

Public saving/GDP	-2.8	-3.5	0.7	-1.0	-5.0	3.9	-1.0	-4.9	3.9
Investment/GDP	26.7	29.1	-2.4	21.9	23.4	-1.5	21.9	23.1	-1.2
Foreign saving/GDP	2.4	5.1	-2.7	-2.7	0.8	-3.6	-3.0	0.6	-3.6
Balance of payments									
Current account/GDP	-3.8	-3.7	-0.2	1.1	-2.1	3.2	1.4	-2.0	3.3
Basic balance/GDP	0.8	1.4	-0.6	1.1	0.8	0.3	1.2	0.9	0.3
Overall balance/GDP	-1.1	0.7	-1.8	-0.8	0.1	-0.9	-0.8	0.2	-1.0
External debt									
External debt/exports	217.9	108.7	109.2	267.5	150.1	117.4	264.0	151.4	112.6
Debt service/exports	34.3	14.1	20.2	31.4	21.1	10.2	31.8	21.5	10.3
Inflation									
Wholesale prices	40.1	37.3	2.8	68.1	63.8	4.4	70.9	54.5	16.4
Consumer prices	38.4	22.9	15.4	67.9	35.9	32.0	72.1	30.9	41.1
Monetary policy									
Money supply growth	32.1	24.4	7.7	85.9	38.2	47.8	88.5	38.5	49.9
Real discount rate	-1.7	-2.2	0.5	-6.9	2.3	-9.1	-1.3	1.8	-3.1
Fiscal policy									
Gov. revenue/GDP	15.9	30.2	-14.3	15.9	31.3	-15.4	15.9	31.4	-15.5
Gov. expenditure/GDP	18.7	33.7	-15.0	16.9	36.3	-19.3	16.9	36.3	-19.4
Budget surplus/GDP	-2.8	-3.5	0.7	-1.0	-5.0	3.9	-1.0	-4.9	3.9

The approximate maintenance of budget deficits in Pakistan was the result of parallel increases in government revenues and expenditures, expressed as a percentage of GDP. In turn, revenues rose more than expenditures in the rest of the low-income countries, leading to smaller budget deficits.

Loan recipient *lower-middle-income countries* experienced a small increase in their average GDP growth rate between the pre-loan and the post-loan periods while a decline was observed in the nonrecipient countries. This occurred as the former group of countries attained a substantial improvement in its industrial and agricultural growth performance relative to the latter.

In turn, a decline in aggregate expenditure in the pre-loan period gave place to an increase following the adjustment loan in the loan recipient countries whereas a deceleration of expenditure growth was observed in the comparator group. Within aggregate expenditure, increases in loan recipient countries relative to nonrecipients were much greater in regard to investment than consumption.

The group of loan recipients attained a substantial acceleration in export growth while the opposite conclusion applies to the nonrecipient group. At the same time, both country groups experienced import substitution as measured by the import–GDP ratio.

The average domestic savings ratio declined in the group of loan recipients as a fall in the private savings ratio was accompanied by a rise in public dissaving. The domestic savings ratio decreased in a parallel fashion in the rest of the lower-middle-income countries where private as well as public savings also declined.

The average investment ratio fell more than the domestic savings ratio in the group of loan recipients as foreign savings decreased over time. Changes in the same direction but of a larger magnitude occurred in the comparator group.

The current account deficit of loan recipients among lower middle-income countries declined slightly, with increases experienced in the case of nonrecipients. In turn, the basic balance and the overall balance of both groups of countries deteriorated.

Wholesale price data are available for few lower-middle-income countries. At the same time, the average rise of consumer prices accelerated in the loan recipients owing to Bolivia's rapid inflation; most other countries of the group experienced a decline in inflation rates. In turn, inflation rates increased to a substantial extent in the comparator group.

Average money supply growth rates were again dominated by Bolivia; a majority of the other loan-recipients experienced a decline as against an acceleration in the nonrecipient countries. Finally, the average real discount rate increased proportionately less in the former group of countries than in the latter.

The rise in the ratio of the government budget deficit to GDP for loan recipients among lower-middle-income countries was due to decreases in revenues in excess of the decline in expenditures. In turn, revenues increased more than expenditures in the comparator countries.

The average rate of growth of GDP increased in the *upper-middle-income* countries receiving adjustment loans while a decline was observed in the comparator group. The same conclusions apply to per capita income growth.

The average growth of both industrial production and agricultural output accelerated in the loan recipient countries after the first adjustment loan. In turn, a decline occurred in industrial production growth, and a smaller increase was experienced in the growth of agricultural output, in the nonrecipient group.

The rise of aggregate expenditure accelerated in the recipients of adjustment loans. This occurred as a decline in investment gave place to an increase and consumption growth rates rose over time. By contrast, consumption growth rates decreased and investment fell in absolute terms in the nonrecipient countries.

Loan recipients among upper-middle-income countries experienced a deterioration in their export performance as against improvements in the comparator group. In turn, the import–GDP ratio fell in both groups of countries.

The domestic savings ratio increased in the loan recipient countries as the decline in private savings was more than offset by the fall in the government budget deficit. The share of investment in GDP decreased, however, as the inflow of foreign savings was superseded by an outflow. A larger fall in investment shares occurred in the nonrecipient countries, where domestic as well as foreign savings ratios declined.

The loan recipients among upper-middle-income countries experienced a substantial improvement in their current account balance, turning a deficit into a surplus, while less sizeable improvements occurred in the comparator countries that continued to have a deficit. Improvements were smaller in the basic balance and the overall balance of the loan recipients; both of these balances deteriorated in the comparator countries. Finally, loan recipient countries attained a reduction in their average debt service–export ratios while their external debt ratio increased. Both of these ratios increased substantially in the comparator group.

The average rise of wholesale as well as consumer prices accelerated in both the loan recipient and the nonrecipient countries, with larger increases in both indices in the first group. Similar results obtained in regard to money supply growth. Finally, the real discount rate increased less in the case of loan recipients than nonrecipients.

The budget deficit declined in the loan recipient countries as their expenditures fell and revenues remained unchanged as a proportion of GDP. In turn, the budget position of the comparator countries deteriorated as expenditures increased more than revenues.

CONCLUSIONS

This chapter has presented a quantitative analysis of adjustment programs. This was done by charting changes in various performance indicators following the receipt of the first adjustment loan, further contrasting the results with those for the comparator group of countries that did not receive adjustment loans.

Concentrating attention on the period up to 1987, we find that the average decline in the GDP growth rate in the loan recipient countries was less than in the comparator groups. Similar results were obtained in regard to per capita GDP. At the same time, in both cases, a majority of loan recipient countries experienced an improvement in their relative position *vis-à-vis* the nonrecipients.

It is further apparent that the loan recipient countries made an adjustment effort in the period following the first loan. To begin with, economic expansion was concentrated in the traded goods sectors, industry and agriculture, both of which experienced an improvement in the loan recipient countries relative to the comparator groups. Also, the growth of consumption declined substantially in absolute terms as well as relative to the nonrecipient countries. In turn, an acceleration is observed in the growth of investment that holds the promise for future economic growth.

Furthermore, the average export growth rate fell less in the loan recipient countries than in the comparator group and a much larger number of countries experienced an improvement than a deterioration relative to the nonrecipients. At the same time, the loan recipient countries attained a substantial improvement in their current account balance position as their domestic savings ratios declined less than in the comparator groups. Finally, despite increases in absolute terms, the loan recipient countries improved their relative position as far as external debt indicators are concerned.

Inflation, as measured by the consumer price index, decelerated in a majority of countries receiving adjustment loans *vis-à-vis* the comparators, although the average increased substantially due to hyperinflation in Bolivia. In turn, money supply growth rates increased more in the loan recipient countries than in the nonrecipients while real discount rates increased in the majority of the loan recipients. Finally, expenditure–GDP ratios increased less in the loan recipient than in the nonrecipient countries.

Data have also been provided for loan recipients and nonrecipients in sub-Saharan Africa, low-income countries, lower-middle-income countries, and upper-middle-income countries. The following discussion will be limited to changes in per capita incomes in the period until 1987 following the first adjustment loan.

Average per capita incomes decreased more in sub-Saharan loan recipient countries than in the comparator group. However, the relative position of the loan recipients improved *vis-à-vis* the nonrecipients in the other three groups of countries. In fact, per capita incomes rose more in the post-loan period than in the pre-loan period in Pakistan, the only loan recipient among low-income countries. The same result was obtained in the upper-middle-income countries while the lower-income countries experienced a smaller decline after than before the loan.

Thus, the relative position of loan recipients improved in three out of four country groupings in regard to per capita incomes. It is also apparent that, on the whole, loan recipients improved their relative position *vis-à-vis* the comparator groups in industrial production, agricultural output, investment, exports, the balance of payments, external debt indicators, and the government budget. In turn, the results point in different directions, depending on whether average changes or the number of countries experiencing improvements *vis-à-vis* the comparator groups are considered in the case of inflation and the real discount rate and a deterioration is observed in regard to money supply growth.

The quantitative appraisal of adjustment programs thus points to the overall success of these programs, with the qualifications just noted. This conclusion is strengthened if consideration is given to weighted performance indicators, the weights being the number of times a country received an adjustment loan. Thus, weighting improves the relative performance of the loan recipients in regard to practically all economic growth indicators, export growth, domestic savings, external debt indicators, inflation, money supply growth, the real discount rate, and the government budget while little change is shown in regard to the rest of the indicators (Table 4.10).

Table 4.10 Performance indicators

Indicators	Preceding 3 years			Years until 1987 Unweighted			Years until 1987 Weighted		
	Own average	Group average	Difference	Own average	Group average	Difference	Own average	Group average	Difference
Population, mil.	24.2	17.2	.	27.6	19.1	.	29.6	20.8	.
Per capita GDP, US$	1107.9	1333.9	.	938.5	1448.1	.	967.4	1373.6	.
Economic growth									
Gross domestic product	2.7	3.7	-1.0	2.5	2.8	-0.3	2.7	2.8	-0.1
Per capita GDP	0.2	1.2	-1.0	-0.0	0.4	-0.4	0.3	0.4	-0.0
Industrial production	1.8	5.1	-3.3	1.8	2.8	-0.9	2.5	2.8	-0.3
Agricultural production	1.6	2.1	-0.5	3.2	2.8	0.4	2.9	2.6	0.3
Consumption	4.0	4.1	-0.2	2.0	2.4	-0.4	2.3	2.6	-0.3
Per capita consumption	1.5	1.5	-0.1	-0.4	-0.1	-0.3	-0.1	0.0	-0.1
Investment	-1.5	6.8	-8.3	2.0	5.0	-3.1	2.1	3.7	-1.6
Aggregate expenditure	2.7	4.1	-1.4	1.8	1.5	0.3	2.1	1.6	0.5
Export performance									
Export growth	7.1	5.7	1.3	5.8	3.5	2.3	6.6	3.4	3.3
Import substitution									
Import/GDP ratio	30.7	46.1	-15.5	28.7	43.1	-14.5	29.9	43.6	-13.7
Investment and savings									
Domestic saving/GDP	16.3	12.3	4.0	15.3	10.8	4.6	16.2	10.5	5.7
Private saving/GDP	24.3	18.4	5.9	23.7	16.4	7.3	23.5	16.6	7.0

Public saving/GDP	-8.0	-5.5	-2.4	-7.9	-5.9	-2.0	-7.1	-6.3	-0.8
Investment/GDP	23.2	25.0	-1.8	19.0	20.8	-1.8	19.8	21.5	-1.7
Foreign saving/GDP	6.9	12.7	-5.8	3.7	10.0	-6.3	3.6	11.0	-7.4
Balance of payments									
Current account/GDP	-7.5	-6.2	-1.3	-2.1	-4.9	2.7	-3.4	-5.5	2.1
Basic balance/GDP	-3.6	-0.2	-3.4	-1.0	-1.1	0.1	-1.7	-1.3	-0.3
Overall balance/GDP	-3.4	-0.2	-3.2	-2.8	-1.8	-1.1	-2.4	-1.9	-0.5
External debt									
External debt/exports	271.7	173.9	97.8	392.2	265.9	126.3	345.8	257.8	88.0
Debt service/exports	21.8	12.4	9.4	25.7	18.7	7.0	25.4	18.6	6.8
Inflation									
Wholesale prices	32.5	18.5	13.9	44.9	25.0	19.9	46.3	23.0	23.3
Consumer prices	24.6	17.0	7.6	102.0	20.6	81.5	68.2	20.5	47.7
Monetary policy									
Money supply growth	24.0	20.3	3.7	88.8	21.9	66.9	64.4	21.4	42.9
Real discount rate	-6.0	-4.3	-1.8	-3.5	-0.8	-2.7	-1.7	-0.9	-0.8
Fiscal policy									
Gov. revenue/GDP	19.0	23.5	-4.5	22.5	25.9	-3.4	20.8	25.2	-4.5
Gov. expenditure/GDP	27.0	29.0	-2.1	30.5	31.8	-1.4	27.9	31.5	-3.7
Budget surplus/GDP	-8.0	-5.5	-2.4	-7.9	-5.9	-2.0	-7.1	-6.3	-0.8

Appendix Tables

Performance indicators: Côte d'Ivoire

Indicators	Preceding 3 years			Following 3 years			Years until 1987		
	Own average	Group average	Difference	Own average	Group average	Difference	Own average	Group average	Difference
Population, mil.	8.0	6.0	.	9.4	6.7	.	9.9	6.9	.
Per capita GDP, US$	1129.6	615.7	.	750.6	641.8	.	768.0	635.8	.
Economic growth									
Gross domestic product	7.7	3.5	4.3	-3.9	1.7	-5.6	-0.3	2.5	-2.8
Per capita GDP	3.2	0.6	2.6	-7.4	-1.2	-6.2	-3.9	-0.4	-3.5
Industrial production	12.0	5.4	6.6	-3.0	4.0	-7.1	-3.7	3.5	-7.2
Agricultural production	7.6	1.9	5.8	-3.2	0.2	-3.4	2.4	2.1	0.2
Consumption	8.0	3.5	4.5	-0.8	2.1	-2.9	1.2	2.3	-1.1
Per capita consumption	3.5	0.5	3.0	-4.4	0.9	-3.6	-2.4	-0.6	-1.8
Investment	5.2	5.2	0.1	-26.1	-4.7	-21.5	-17.6	5.9	-23.5
Aggregate expenditure	7.2	3.1	4.1	-6.5	0.3	-6.8	-2.6	1.2	-3.8
Export performance									
Export growth	6.7	10.1	-3.4	-0.7	2.1	-2.8	3.6	2.3	1.3
Import substitution									
Import/GDP ratio	38.8	44.8	-6.0	36.5	45.8	-9.3	34.4	45.5	-11.1
Investment and savings									
Domestic saving/GDP	24.7	8.6	16.1	20.8	5.0	15.8	21.8	5.2	16.6
Private saving/GDP	30.0	18.8	11.3	25.8	11.9	13.8	25.8	11.9	13.9

Public saving/GDP	-7.4	-5.1	-2.3	-3.4	-6.8	3.3	-3.4	-6.7	3.3
Investment/GDP	28.1	22.3	5.8	17.6	19.6	-2.0	15.4	19.2	-3.8
Foreign saving/GDP	3.4	13.7	-10.3	-3.2	14.5	-17.7	-6.4	14.0	-20.4
Balance of payments									
Current account/GDP	-14.3	-6.8	-7.5	-9.6	-7.9	-1.7	-7.0	-7.1	0.1
Basic balance/GDP	-4.8	-0.2	-4.5	-3.4	-2.6	-0.8	-1.6	-2.2	0.6
Overall balance/GDP	-2.5	-0.3	-2.2	-3.8	-3.0	-0.7	-2.0	-2.6	0.6
External debt									
External debt/exports	150.7	172.3	-21.6	291.4	286.1	5.2	295.7	307.0	-11.3
Debt service/exports	19.1	7.7	11.4	29.3	13.3	16.0	25.9	15.4	10.5
Inflation									
Wholesale prices	14.8	12.5	·	·	12.9	·	·	17.1	·
Consumer prices	·	16.1	-1.3	5.8	15.1	-9.2	5.2	14.0	-8.8
Monetary policy									
Money supply growth	4.7	17.1	-12.4	7.6	13.6	-6.0	6.7	14.8	-8.1
Real discount rate	-5.1	-6.9	1.7	5.0	-3.7	8.7	5.1	-2.5	7.6
Fiscal policy									
Gov. revenue/GDP	23.6	21.9	1.6	31.9	25.0	6.9	31.9	25.1	6.8
Gov. expenditure/GDP	31.0	27.0	4.0	35.3	31.7	3.6	35.3	31.8	3.5
Budget surplus/GDP	-7.4	-5.1	-2.3	-3.4	-6.8	3.3	-3.4	-6.7	3.3

Performance indicators: Ghana

Indicators	Preceding 3 years			Following 3 years			Years until 1987		
	Own average	Group average	Difference	Own average	Group average	Difference	Own average	Group average	Difference
Population, mil.	11.2	6.3	.	12.7	7.0	.	12.9	7.1	.
Per capita GDP, US$	2174.7	706.4	.	519.6	624.5	.	519.6	625.8	.
Economic growth									
Gross domestic product	-3.3	2.8	-6.1	6.3	2.8	3.5	6.3	2.8	3.5
Per capita GDP	-6.1	-0.1	-6.0	3.0	-0.1	3.0	3.0	-0.1	3.0
Industrial production	-10.9	5.4	-16.3	11.1	4.0	7.0	11.1	4.1	7.0
Agricultural production	-1.9	1.1	-3.1	5.3	3.1	2.2	5.3	3.2	2.1
Consumption	-3.9	3.6	-7.5	6.9	1.9	5.0	6.9	2.1	4.8
Per capita consumption	-6.6	0.6	-7.2	3.5	-1.0	4.6	3.5	-0.9	4.4
Investment	-13.5	7.4	-20.9	19.7	14.2	5.5	19.7	13.8	5.9
Aggregate expenditure	-4.7	3.7	-8.5	7.9	1.6	6.2	7.9	1.7	6.1
Export performance									
Export growth	-2.4	3.5	-5.9	8.0	2.5	5.5	8.0	2.5	5.4
Import substitution									
Import/GDP ratio	5.8	47.6	-41.8	9.6	44.0	-34.4	9.6	44.4	-34.8
Investment and savings									
Domestic saving/GDP	4.2	6.8	-2.6	7.2	5.8	1.3	7.2	5.7	1.5
Private saving/GDP	9.4	12.8	-3.4	9.1	6.1	3.0	9.1	6.1	3.0

Public saving/GDP	-5.2	-6.2	1.0	-1.9	-4.9	3.0	-1.9	-4.9	3.0
Investment/GDP	4.5	22.7	-18.2	8.3	17.9	-9.6	8.3	17.9	-9.7
Foreign saving/GDP	0.3	15.9	-15.6	1.1	12.1	-11.0	1.1	12.3	-11.2
Balance of payments									
Current account/GDP	-0.6	-9.4	8.8	-1.3	-3.3	2.0	-1.3	-3.3	2.0
Basic balance/GDP	-0.2	-2.7	2.5	0.3	-0.4	0.8	0.3	-0.4	0.8
Overall balance/GDP	-0.2	-2.2	1.9	-0.3	-2.5	2.2	-0.3	-2.5	2.2
External debt									
External debt/exports	112.0	209.9	-98.0	330.5	339.7	-9.2	330.5	338.3	-7.7
Debt service/exports	5.7	10.2	-4.5	13.9	17.1	-3.2	13.9	17.9	-3.9
Inflation									
Wholesale prices	42.0	12.5	29.6	67.1	20.8	46.3	67.1	20.5	46.6
Consumer prices	63.0	15.2	47.8	24.8	14.2	10.7	24.8	14.1	10.8
Monetary policy									
Money supply growth	34.6	17.1	17.4	49.1	16.8	32.3	49.1	16.2	32.8
Real discount rate	-26.3	-5.2	-21.0	-3.8	-1.8	-2.0	-3.8	-1.9	-1.9
Fiscal policy									
Gov. revenue/GDP	5.6	22.2	-16.6	9.6	25.9	-16.3	9.6	25.9	-16.3
Gov. expenditure/GDP	10.9	28.4	-17.6	11.6	30.8	-19.2	11.6	30.8	-19.2
Budget surplus/GDP	-5.2	-6.2	1.0	-1.9	-4.9	3.0	-1.9	-4.9	3.0

Performance indicators: Guinea-Bissau

Indicators	Preceding 3 years			Following 3 years			Years until 1987		
	Own average	Group average	Difference	Own average	Group average	Difference	Own average	Group average	Difference
Population, mil.	0.8	6.5	.	0.9	7.2	.	0.9	7.2	.
Per capita GDP, US$	201.5	671.9	.	181.5	624.7	.	181.5	624.7	.
Economic growth									
Gross domestic product	6.3	2.3	4.0	1.6	3.7	-2.0	1.6	3.7	-2.0
Per capita GDP	4.4	-0.6	5.0	-0.3	0.8	-1.1	-0.3	0.8	-1.1
Industrial production	1.1	4.3	-3.2	-6.0	2.5	-8.5	-6.0	2.5	-8.5
Agricultural production	10.7	1.4	9.3	5.5	6.7	-1.3	5.5	6.7	-1.3
Consumption	9.6	3.1	6.5	1.6	3.5	-1.9	1.6	3.5	-1.9
Per capita consumption	7.6	0.2	7.5	-0.4	0.5	-0.9	-0.4	0.5	-0.9
Investment	2.9	2.2	0.6	5.0	25.4	-20.3	5.0	25.4	-20.3
Aggregate expenditure	8.5	1.9	6.6	1.9	3.6	-1.7	1.9	3.6	-1.7
Export performance									
Export growth	-15.4	2.1	-17.5	-8.5	2.7	-11.2	-8.5	2.7	-11.2
Import substitution									
Import/GDP ratio	36.4	46.9	-10.5	52.2	37.5	14.7	52.2	37.5	14.7
Investment and savings									
Domestic saving/GDP	-2.5	5.4	-7.9	-10.7	10.7	-21.4	-10.7	10.7	-21.4
Private saving/GDP	35.1	11.4	23.7	34.8	22.4	12.4	34.8	22.4	12.4

Public saving/GDP	−38.7	−7.0	−31.7	−45.9	−5.6	−40.3	−45.9	−5.6	−40.3
Investment/GDP	25.6	21.3	4.3	31.8	17.3	14.5	31.8	17.3	14.5
Foreign saving/GDP	28.1	15.9	12.2	42.5	6.6	35.9	42.5	6.6	35.9
Balance of payments									
Current account/GDP	−15.3	−9.5	−5.8	−22.0	−2.8	−19.2	−22.0	−2.8	−19.2
Basic balance/GDP	−5.8	−3.3	−2.5	−2.1	−0.5	−1.6	−2.1	−0.5	−1.6
Overall balance/GDP	−8.9	−2.8	−6.1	−2.6	−1.9	−0.8	−2.6	−1.9	−0.8
External debt									
External debt/exports	1279.2	250.6	1028.6	1894.3	345.9	1548.3	1894.3	345.9	1548.3
Debt service/exports	19.2	11.9	7.4	43.7	18.6	25.1	43.7	18.6	25.1
Inflation									
Wholesale prices	.	11.9	.	.	23.9	.	.	23.9	.
Consumer prices	.	14.8	.	.	12.8	.	.	12.8	.
Monetary policy									
Money supply growth	.	15.2	.	.	16.1	.	.	16.1	.
Real discount rate	.	−4.5	.	.	−0.8	.	.	−0.8	.
Fiscal policy									
Gov. revenue/GDP	10.6	23.5	−13.0	11.6	29.1	−17.5	11.6	29.1	−17.5
Gov. expenditure/GDP	49.3	30.6	18.7	57.5	34.7	22.8	57.5	34.7	22.8
Budget surplus/GDP	−38.7	−7.0	−31.7	−45.9	−5.6	−40.3	−45.9	−5.6	−40.3

Performance indicators: Kenya

Indicators	Preceding 3 years			Following 3 years			Years until 1987		
	Own average	Group average	Difference	Own average	Group average	Difference	Own average	Group average	Difference
Population, mil.	15.4	5.8	.	18.1	6.5	.	19.6	6.9	.
Per capita GDP, US$	342.5	526.1	.	345.7	671.9	.	325.0	648.9	.
Economic growth									
Gross domestic product	7.2	3.5	3.7	2.0	2.3	-0.4	3.1	2.5	0.6
Per capita GDP	3.2	0.6	2.5	-2.1	-0.6	-1.5	-1.0	-0.4	-0.7
Industrial production	10.1	5.5	4.7	1.9	4.3	-2.4	3.0	4.0	-1.0
Agricultural production	4.4	2.9	1.5	5.1	1.4	3.6	3.4	1.9	1.4
Consumption	9.4	4.2	5.3	-1.1	3.1	-4.3	1.4	2.7	-1.3
Per capita consumption	5.3	1.2	4.1	-5.0	0.2	-5.2	-2.6	-0.2	-2.4
Investment	11.7	4.9	6.9	-13.9	2.2	-16.1	-2.2	8.0	-10.1
Aggregate expenditure	9.5	2.9	6.6	-4.3	1.9	-6.1	0.4	1.9	-1.5
Export performance									
Export growth	-0.0	6.5	-6.5	-1.0	2.1	-3.1	2.5	2.2	0.3
Import substitution									
Import/GDP ratio	34.2	42.8	-8.6	30.2	46.9	-16.7	29.0	45.8	-16.7
Investment and savings									
Domestic saving/GDP	21.3	8.9	12.4	19.3	5.4	13.9	20.7	5.6	15.1
Private saving/GDP	24.8	12.6	12.1	25.1	11.4	13.6	26.0	11.2	14.8

Public saving/GDP	-3.5	-4.9	1.4	-5.8	-7.0	1.3	-5.3	-6.6	1.3
Investment/GDP	25.4	22.2	3.2	24.0	21.3	2.7	23.4	19.8	3.7
Foreign saving/GDP	4.1	13.4	-9.2	4.7	15.9	-11.2	2.7	14.2	-11.4
Balance of payments									
Current account/GDP	-6.7	-6.4	-0.3	-4.7	-9.5	4.8	-3.2	-7.3	4.1
Basic balance/GDP	-0.5	0.1	-0.6	-2.7	-3.3	0.6	-1.7	-2.3	0.6
Overall balance/GDP	1.4	-0.3	1.6	-2.4	-2.8	0.3	-1.3	-2.5	1.2
External debt									
External debt/exports	141.3	168.9	-27.6	224.3	250.6	-26.3	237.8	291.4	-53.5
Debt service/exports	7.8	7.3	0.5	19.9	11.9	8.1	21.7	14.5	7.2
Inflation									
Wholesale prices	13.3	12.6	-3.4	14.6	11.9	-0.2	10.9	16.1	-3.4
Consumer prices		16.7			14.8			14.3	
Monetary policy									
Money supply growth	22.4	17.4	5.0	10.8	15.2	-4.4	12.7	15.8	-3.1
Real discount rate	-5.3	-7.8	2.5	-0.3	-4.5	4.2	1.5	-3.1	4.6
Fiscal policy									
Gov. revenue/GDP	20.3	21.2	-0.9	21.9	23.5	-1.6	21.3	24.1	-2.8
Gov. expenditure/GDP	23.8	26.1	-2.3	27.7	30.6	-2.9	26.6	30.7	-4.1
Budget surplus/GDP	-3.5	-4.9	1.4	-5.8	-7.0	1.3	-5.3	-6.6	1.3

Performance indicators: Malawi

Indicators	Preceding 3 years			Following 3 years			Years until 1987		
	Own average	Group average	Difference	Own average	Group average	Difference	Own average	Group average	Difference
Population, mil.	5.9	6.0	.	6.6	6.7	.	7.0	6.9	.
Per capita GDP, US$	182.5	615.7	.	180.8	641.8	.	175.3	635.8	.
Economic growth									
Gross domestic product	5.1	3.5	1.6	3.6	1.7	1.9	3.1	2.5	0.6
Per capita GDP	1.9	0.6	1.3	0.5	-1.2	1.6	-0.2	-0.4	0.3
Industrial production	4.3	5.4	-1.1	1.2	4.0	-2.8	1.6	3.5	-1.8
Agricultural production	-0.2	1.9	-2.1	5.5	0.2	5.3	3.4	2.1	1.3
Consumption	4.3	3.5	0.8	1.2	2.1	-0.9	1.8	2.3	-0.5
Per capita consumption	1.1	0.5	0.6	-1.9	-0.9	-1.0	-1.4	-0.6	-0.8
Investment	10.0	5.2	4.8	-0.6	-4.7	4.1	-2.9	5.9	-8.8
Aggregate expenditure	4.4	3.1	1.3	0.4	0.3	0.2	0.6	1.2	-0.6
Export performance									
Export growth	12.8	10.1	2.7	8.3	2.1	6.2	2.7	2.3	0.5
Import substitution									
Import/GDP ratio	42.4	44.8	-2.3	27.7	45.8	-18.2	27.1	45.5	-18.4
Investment and savings									
Domestic saving/GDP	14.0	8.6	5.5	15.6	5.0	10.6	13.5	5.2	8.3
Private saving/GDP	23.0	18.8	4.3	24.8	11.9	12.9	21.7	11.9	9.8

Public saving/GDP	-9.0	-5.1	-3.9	-9.2	-6.8	-2.4	-8.2	-6.7	-1.5
Investment/GDP	31.5	22.3	9.2	19.4	19.6	-0.2	17.2	19.2	-1.9
Foreign saving/GDP	17.4	13.7	3.7	3.8	14.5	-10.8	3.7	14.0	-10.3
Balance of payments									
Current account/GDP	-20.7	-6.8	-13.9	-7.5	-7.9	0.4	-7.0	-7.1	0.1
Basic balance/GDP	-9.2	-0.2	-8.9	-5.4	-2.6	-2.8	-3.8	-2.2	-1.6
Overall balance/GDP	-2.6	-0.3	-2.3	-2.4	-3.0	0.7	-2.5	-2.6	0.2
External debt									
External debt/exports	257.8	172.3	85.4	313.9	286.1	27.8	346.4	307.0	39.4
Debt service/exports	18.0	7.7	10.3	22.9	13.3	9.6	27.9	15.4	12.5
Inflation									
Wholesale prices	.	12.5	.	.	12.9	.	.	17.1	.
Consumer prices	12.9	16.1	-3.2	14.4	15.1	-0.6	13.6	14.0	-0.4
Monetary policy									
Money supply growth	-0.8	17.1	-17.9	10.8	13.6	-2.8	16.5	14.8	1.7
Real discount rate	-3.9	-6.9	2.9	-3.8	-3.7	-0.1	-2.7	-2.5	-0.2
Fiscal policy									
Gov. revenue/GDP	18.3	21.9	-3.7	18.6	25.0	-6.4	19.0	25.1	-6.1
Gov. expenditure/GDP	27.3	27.0	0.2	27.8	31.7	-4.0	27.2	31.8	-4.6
Budget surplus/GDP	-9.0	-5.1	-3.9	-9.2	-6.8	-2.4	-8.2	-6.7	-1.5

Performance indicators: Mauritius

Indicators	Preceding 3 years			Following 3 years			Years until 1987		
	Own average	Group average	Difference	Own average	Group average	Difference	Own average	Group average	Difference
Population, mil.	0.9	6.0	.	1.0	6.7	.	1.0	6.9	.
Per capita GDP, US$	1186.3	615.7	.	1074.7	641.8	.	1125.9	635.8	.
Economic growth									
Gross domestic product	0.4	3.5	-3.0	3.6	1.7	1.9	5.3	2.5	2.9
Per capita GDP	-1.0	0.6	-1.5	2.2	-1.2	3.4	4.0	-0.4	4.4
Industrial production	-0.4	5.4	-5.8	3.1	4.0	-1.0	7.5	3.5	4.0
Agricultural production	-10.0	1.9	-11.9	2.3	0.2	2.1	5.3	2.1	3.1
Consumption	1.5	3.5	-2.0	1.6	2.1	-0.4	3.1	2.3	0.7
Per capita consumption	0.1	0.5	-0.4	0.3	-0.9	1.2	1.8	-0.6	2.4
Investment	-9.5	5.2	-14.7	0.6	-4.7	5.3	12.7	5.9	6.8
Aggregate expenditure	-1.7	3.1	-4.8	1.3	0.3	1.0	5.2	1.2	4.0
Export performance									
Export growth	1.5	10.1	-8.5	5.5	2.1	3.4	12.0	2.3	9.7
Import substitution									
Import/GDP ratio	57.1	44.8	12.4	49.7	45.8	3.8	52.1	45.5	6.6
Investment and savings									
Domestic saving/GDP	16.1	8.6	7.5	17.0	5.0	12.0	19.4	5.2	14.3
Private saving/GDP	24.7	18.8	5.9	23.4	11.9	11.5	24.0	11.9	12.2

Public saving/GDP	-8.5	-5.1	-3.5	-6.4	-6.8	0.4	-5.9	-6.7	0.8
Investment/GDP	27.6	22.3	5.3	19.2	19.6	-0.3	19.7	19.2	0.5
Foreign saving/GDP	11.4	13.7	-2.2	2.2	14.5	-12.4	0.2	14.0	-13.8
Balance of payments									
Current account/GDP	-11.9	-6.8	-5.0	-3.9	-7.9	4.0	-3.6	-7.1	3.5
Basic balance/GDP	-9.1	-0.2	-8.9	-4.6	-2.6	-2.0	-4.1	-2.2	-1.8
Overall balance/GDP	-6.0	-0.3	-5.7	-3.7	-3.0	-0.7	-3.2	-2.6	-0.6
External debt									
External debt/exports	68.8	172.3	-103.6	111.7	286.1	-174.4	102.9	307.0	-204.1
Debt service/exports	5.2	7.7	-2.5	15.4	13.3	2.1	13.3	15.4	-2.1
Inflation									
Wholesale prices	.	12.5	.	.	12.9	.	.	17.1	.
Consumer prices	21.7	16.1	5.6	8.1	15.1	-6.9	6.6	14.0	-7.4
Monetary policy									
Money supply growth	12.6	17.1	-4.5	10.3	13.6	-3.3	13.4	14.8	-1.4
Real discount rate	-8.4	-6.9	-1.5	3.0	-3.7	6.7	4.4	-2.5	6.9
Fiscal policy									
Gov. revenue/GDP	20.5	21.9	-1.4	21.1	25.0	-3.8	21.3	25.1	-3.8
Gov. expenditure/GDP	29.0	27.0	2.0	27.5	31.7	4.2	27.2	31.8	-4.7
Budget surplus/GDP	-8.5	-5.1	-3.5	-6.4	-6.8	0.4	-5.9	-6.7	0.8

138

Performance indicators: Nigeria

Indicators	Preceding 3 years			Following 3 years			Years until 1987		
	Own average	Group average	Difference	Own average	Group average	Difference	Own average	Group average	Difference
Population, mil.	87.6	6.3	.	99.8	7.0	.	101.5	7.1	.
Per capita GDP, US$	941.4	706.4	.	695.9	624.5	.	695.9	625.8	.
Economic growth									
Gross domestic product	−1.7	2.8	−4.5	−2.3	2.8	−5.1	−2.3	2.8	−5.1
Per capita GDP	−4.6	−0.1	−4.5	−5.5	−0.1	−5.4	−5.5	−0.1	−5.4
Industrial production	−6.3	5.4	−11.7	−3.5	4.0	−7.5	−3.5	4.1	−7.6
Agricultural production	3.2	1.1	2.1	1.7	3.1	−1.4	1.7	3.2	−1.5
Consumption	9.7	3.6	6.1	−5.5	1.9	−7.4	−5.5	2.1	−7.6
Per capita consumption	6.5	0.6	5.9	−8.6	−1.0	−7.6	−8.6	−0.9	−7.7
Investment	1.7	7.4	−5.7	−5.3	14.2	−19.5	−5.3	13.8	−19.1
Aggregate expenditure	8.0	3.7	4.3	−6.3	1.6	−8.0	−6.3	1.7	−8.1
Export performance									
Export growth	−29.5	3.5	−33.0	11.1	2.5	8.7	11.1	2.5	8.6
Import substitution									
Import/GDP ratio	25.9	47.6	−21.8	13.8	44.0	−30.2	13.8	44.4	−30.6
Investment and savings									
Domestic saving/GDP	22.1	6.8	15.4	12.6	5.8	6.8	12.6	5.7	7.0
Private saving/GDP	14.0	12.8	1.2	.	6.1	.	.	6.1	.

Public saving/GDP	12.1	-6.2	18.3	11.3	-4.9	-6.6	11.3	-4.9	-6.6
Investment/GDP	24.6	22.7	1.9	.	17.9	.	.	17.9	.
Foreign saving/GDP	2.4	15.9	-13.5	-1.3	12.1	-13.4	-1.3	12.3	-13.6
Balance of payments									
Current account/GDP	-3.5	-9.4	5.9	0.9	-3.3	4.2	0.9	-3.3	4.2
Basic balance/GDP	-2.4	-2.7	0.3	-0.5	-0.4	-0.0	-0.5	-0.4	-0.0
Overall balance/GDP	-3.1	-2.2	-1.0	-2.1	-2.5	0.4	-2.1	-2.5	0.4
External debt									
External debt/exports	66.2	209.9	-143.7	207.9	339.7	-131.8	207.9	338.3	-130.3
Debt service/exports	7.7	10.2	-2.5	28.3	17.1	11.2	28.3	17.9	10.4
Inflation									
Wholesale prices	.	12.5	.	.	20.8	.	.	20.5	.
Consumer prices	12.8	15.2	-2.3	16.8	14.2	2.6	16.8	14.1	2.8
Monetary policy									
Money supply growth	19.6	17.1	2.5	4.1	16.8	-12.7	4.1	16.2	-12.1
Real discount rate	-5.2	-5.2	0.0	-4.2	-1.8	-2.4	-4.2	-1.9	-2.3
Fiscal policy									
Gov. revenue/GDP	18.4	22.2	-3.8	.	25.9	.	.	25.9	.
Gov. expenditure/GDP	6.3	28.4	-22.1	.	30.8	.	.	30.8	.
Budget surplus/GDP	12.1	-6.2	18.3	.	-4.9	.	.	-4.9	.

Performance indicators: Senegal

Indicators	Preceding 3 years			Following 3 years			Years until 1987		
	Own average	Group average	Difference	Own average	Group average	Difference	Own average	Group average	Difference
Population, mil.	5.4	5.8	.	6.0	6.5	.	6.4	6.9	.
Per capita GDP, US$	425.0	526.1	.	414.3	671.9	.	424.9	648.9	.
Economic growth									
Gross domestic product	0.2	3.5	−3.3	5.7	2.3	3.4	3.5	2.5	1.0
Per capita GDP	−2.5	0.6	−3.2	2.8	−0.6	3.4	0.6	−0.4	1.0
Industrial production	7.0	5.5	1.5	7.6	4.3	3.4	4.5	4.0	0.5
Agricultural production	−1.1	2.9	−4.0	8.0	1.4	6.6	3.8	1.9	1.9
Consumption	4.0	4.2	−0.2	4.5	3.1	1.4	2.8	2.7	0.1
Per capita consumption	1.1	1.2	−0.0	1.6	0.2	1.5	−0.1	−0.2	0.2
Investment	−7.4	4.9	−12.2	4.7	2.2	2.5	0.9	8.0	−7.1
Aggregate expenditure	2.1	2.9	−0.8	4.5	1.9	2.7	2.5	1.9	0.7
Export performance									
Export growth	6.3	6.5	−0.2	7.9	2.1	5.7	3.0	2.2	0.8
Import substitution									
Import/GDP ratio	45.4	42.8	2.6	54.2	46.9	7.3	48.8	45.8	3.0
Investment and savings									
Domestic saving/GDP	6.7	8.9	−2.1	−0.7	5.4	−6.1	1.6	5.6	−4.0
Private saving/GDP	7.6	12.6	−5.0	5.1	11.4	−6.3	5.1	11.2	−6.0

Public saving/GDP	-0.9	-4.9	4.0	-5.9	-7.0	1.2	-5.9	-6.6	0.8
Investment/GDP	16.4	22.2	-5.8	16.0	21.3	-5.2	15.2	19.8	-4.5
Foreign saving/GDP	9.7	13.4	-3.7	16.8	15.9	0.9	13.6	14.2	-0.5
Balance of payments									
Current account/GDP	-8.0	-6.4	-1.6	-13.7	-9.5	-4.2	-13.2	-7.3	-5.9
Basic balance/GDP	-3.8	0.1	-4.0	-4.5	-3.3	-1.2	-3.7	-2.3	-1.4
Overall balance/GDP	-1.1	-0.3	-0.9	-2.6	-2.8	0.1	-2.1	-2.5	0.4
External debt									
External debt/exports	106.3	168.9	-62.6	176.7	250.6	-73.9	224.1	291.4	-67.3
Debt service/exports	12.0	7.3	4.7	7.0	11.9	-4.9	10.5	14.5	-4.1
Inflation									
Wholesale prices		12.6			11.9			16.1	
Consumer prices	8.1	16.7	-8.6	11.6	14.8	-3.2	8.8	14.3	-5.5
Monetary policy									
Money supply growth	8.9	17.4	-8.4	11.4	15.2	-3.8	9.0	15.8	-6.8
Real discount rate	-0.0	-7.8	7.8	-0.3	-4.5	4.2	-0.4	-3.1	2.8
Fiscal policy									
Gov. revenue/GDP	18.7	21.2	-2.5	20.8	23.5	-2.7	20.8	24.1	-3.2
Gov. expenditure/GDP	19.6	26.1	-6.5	26.7	30.6	-3.9	26.7	30.7	-4.0
Budget surplus/GDP	-0.9	-4.9	4.0	-5.9	-7.0	1.2	-5.9	-6.6	0.8

Performance indicators: Sierra Leone

Indicators	Preceding 3 years			Following 3 years			Years until 1987		
	Own average	Group average	Difference	Own average	Group average	Difference	Own average	Group average	Difference
Population, mil.	3.4	6.5	.	3.8	7.2	.	3.8	7.2	.
Per capita GDP, US$	330.9	671.9	.	219.8	624.7	.	219.8	624.7	.
Economic growth									
Gross domestic product	3.1	2.3	0.7	0.0	3.7	-3.7	0.0	3.7	-3.7
Per capita GDP	0.8	-0.6	1.4	-2.3	0.8	-3.1	-2.3	0.8	-3.1
Industrial production	-2.3	4.3	-6.5	-3.4	2.5	-5.9	-3.4	2.5	-5.9
Agricultural production	0.6	1.4	-0.8	0.7	6.7	-6.0	0.7	6.7	-6.0
Consumption	0.7	3.1	-2.5	-7.1	3.5	-10.6	-7.1	3.5	-10.6
Per capita consumption	-1.5	0.2	-1.7	-9.3	0.5	-9.8	-9.3	0.5	-9.8
Investment	-12.5	2.2	-14.7	-10.9	25.4	-36.2	-10.9	25.4	-36.2
Aggregate expenditure	-1.1	1.9	-2.9	-7.5	3.6	-11.1	-7.5	3.6	-11.1
Export performance									
Export growth	2.3	2.1	0.2	42.9	2.7	40.2	42.9	2.7	40.2
Import substitution									
Import/GDP ratio	23.1	46.9	-23.8	11.0	37.5	-26.5	11.0	37.5	-26.5
Investment and savings									
Domestic saving/GDP	3.5	5.4	-1.9	7.7	10.7	-3.0	7.7	10.7	-3.0
Private saving/GDP	15.3	11.4	3.8	15.7	22.4	-6.8	15.7	22.4	-6.8

Public saving/GDP	-11.7	-7.0	-4.7	-7.7	-5.6	-2.1	-7.7	-5.6	-2.1
Investment/GDP	14.7	21.3	-6.6	8.1	17.3	-9.2	8.1	17.3	-9.2
Foreign saving/GDP	11.1	15.9	-4.7	0.4	6.6	-6.2	0.4	6.6	-6.2
Balance of payments									
Current account/GDP	-8.6	-9.5	0.9	-0.5	-2.8	2.3	-0.5	-2.8	2.3
Basic balance/GDP	-8.0	-3.3	-4.8	-47.8	-0.5	-47.2	-47.8	-0.5	-47.2
Overall balance/GDP	-8.1	-2.8	-5.3	-44.1	-1.9	-42.2	-44.1	-1.9	-42.2
External debt									
External debt/exports	396.8	250.6	146.1	580.4	345.9	234.5	580.4	345.9	234.5
Debt service/exports	14.6	11.9	2.7	11.0	18.6	-7.6	11.0	18.6	-7.6
Inflation									
Wholesale prices	28.6	11.9	16.7	49.2	23.9	25.3	49.2	23.9	25.3
Consumer prices	39.6	14.8	24.8	78.7	12.8	65.9	78.7	12.8	65.9
Monetary policy									
Money supply growth	36.1	15.2	20.9	95.4	16.1	79.3	95.4	16.1	79.3
Real discount rate	-17.8	-4.5	-13.3	-35.7	-0.8	-34.9	-35.7	-0.8	-34.9
Fiscal policy									
Gov. revenue/GDP	12.3	23.5	-11.3	7.5	29.1	-21.6	7.5	29.1	-21.6
Gov. expenditure/GDP	24.0	30.6	-6.6	15.2	34.7	-19.5	15.2	34.7	-19.5
Budget surplus/GDP	-11.7	-7.0	-4.7	-7.7	-5.6	-2.1	-7.7	-5.6	-2.1

Performance indicators: Sudan

Indicators	Preceding 3 years			Following 3 years			Years until 1987		
	Own average	Group average	Difference	Own average	Group average	Difference	Own average	Group average	Difference
Population, mil.	18.1	5.8	.	20.2	6.5	.	21.4	6.9	.
Per capita GDP, US$	406.5	526.1	.	390.3	671.9	.	376.9	648.9	.
Economic growth									
Gross domestic product	1.1	3.5	-2.4	4.1	2.3	1.8	0.7	2.5	-1.8
Per capita GDP	-1.8	0.6	-2.5	1.3	-0.6	1.9	-2.0	-0.4	-1.6
Industrial production	-1.8	5.5	-7.3	8.1	4.3	3.8	2.7	4.0	-1.3
Agricultural production	1.4	2.9	-1.4	6.7	1.4	5.3	3.0	1.9	1.1
Consumption	6.6	4.2	2.4	4.4	3.1	1.2	1.1	2.7	-1.6
Per capita consumption	3.5	1.2	2.4	1.6	0.2	1.4	-1.6	-0.2	-1.4
Investment	-16.5	4.9	-21.4	18.9	2.2	16.7	0.6	8.0	-7.4
Aggregate expenditure	2.0	2.9	-0.9	5.8	1.9	3.9	0.7	1.9	-1.2
Export performance									
Export growth	-15.0	6.5	-21.5	-5.2	2.1	-7.4	-1.9	2.2	-4.1
Import substitution									
Import/GDP ratio	15.8	42.8	-27.0	24.5	46.9	-22.4	22.0	45.8	-23.8
Investment and savings									
Domestic saving/GDP	7.9	8.9	-1.0	5.0	5.4	-0.4	5.1	5.6	-0.5
Private saving/GDP	12.7	12.6	0.1	10.8	11.4	-0.7	10.8	11.2	-0.4

Public saving/GDP	-4.8	-4.9	0.1	-4.1	-7.0	3.0	-4.1	-6.6	2.5
Investment/GDP	14.9	22.2	-7.3	19.7	21.3	-1.6	16.7	19.8	-3.0
Foreign saving/GDP	7.0	13.4	-6.4	14.7	15.9	-1.1	11.7	14.2	-2.5
Balance of payments									
Current account/GDP	-1.6	-6.4	4.7	-3.6	-9.5	5.8	-3.6	-7.3	3.7
Basic balance/GDP	-1.3	0.1	-1.5	-3.2	-3.3	0.1	-3.2	-2.3	-0.9
Overall balance/GDP	-1.6	-0.3	-1.3	-3.4	-2.8	-0.7	-3.4	-2.5	-0.9
External debt									
External debt/exports	467.0	168.9	298.1	838.1	250.6	587.4	891.2	291.4	599.8
Debt service/exports	13.2	7.3	5.9	15.2	11.9	3.3	11.7	14.5	-2.8
Inflation									
Wholesale prices	22.5	12.6	.	.	11.9	.	.	16.1	.
Consumer prices	.	16.7	5.8	27.0	14.8	12.2	31.1	14.3	16.8
Monetary policy									
Money supply growth	33.8	17.4	16.5	29.3	15.2	14.1	32.9	15.8	17.1
Real discount rate	.	-7.8	.	.	-4.5	.	.	-3.1	.
Fiscal policy									
Gov. revenue/GDP	12.3	21.2	-8.9	9.5	23.5	-14.0	9.5	24.1	-14.5
Gov. expenditure/GDP	17.2	26.1	-9.0	13.6	30.6	-17.0	13.6	30.7	-17.1
Budget surplus/GDP	-4.8	-4.9	0.1	-4.1	-7.0	3.0	-4.1	-6.6	2.5

Performance indicators: Tanzania

Indicators	Preceding 3 years			Following 3 years			Years until 1987		
	Own average	Group average	Difference	Own average	Group average	Difference	Own average	Group average	Difference
Population, mil.	18.2	6.0	.	20.8	6.7	.	21.9	6.9	.
Per capita GDP, US$	251.3	615.7	.	289.8	641.8	.	273.5	635.8	.
Economic growth									
Gross domestic product	3.1	3.5	-0.4	0.6	1.7	-1.1	2.4	2.5	-0.0
Per capita GDP	-0.2	0.6	-0.8	-2.8	-1.2	-1.6	-1.0	-0.4	-0.6
Industrial production	1.5	5.4	-3.9	-3.9	4.0	-7.9	-2.3	3.5	-5.8
Agricultural production	1.0	1.9	-0.9	-0.2	0.2	-0.4	2.2	2.1	0.0
Consumption	12.0	3.5	8.5	1.6	2.1	-0.4	2.9	2.3	0.5
Per capita consumption	8.5	0.5	8.0	-1.8	-0.9	-0.9	-0.6	-0.6	-0.0
Investment	-1.5	5.2	-6.7	-5.1	-4.7	-0.4	6.3	5.9	0.4
Aggregate expenditure	8.6	3.1	5.5	0.3	0.3	0.0	3.5	1.2	2.3
Export performance									
Export growth	-0.6	10.1	-10.7	-16.7	2.1	-18.8	-5.4	2.3	-7.6
Import substitution									
Import/GDP ratio	27.7	44.8	-7.1	14.6	45.8	-31.2	16.6	45.5	-28.9
Investment and savings									
Domestic saving/GDP	11.0	8.6	2.5	9.6	5.0	4.6	7.4	5.2	2.2
Private saving/GDP	22.1	18.8	3.4	18.4	11.9	6.4	17.3	11.9	5.4

Public saving/GDP	-11.1	-5.1	-6.0	-8.8	-6.8	-2.0	-8.5	-6.7	-1.8
Investment/GDP	24.7	22.3	2.5	16.3	19.6	-3.2	16.3	19.2	-2.9
Foreign saving/GDP	13.7	13.7	0.0	6.7	14.5	-7.8	8.9	14.0	-5.1
Balance of payments									
Current account/GDP	-9.7	-6.8	-2.9	.	-7.9	.	.	-7.1	.
Basic balance/GDP	-6.1	-0.2	-5.8	.	-2.6	.	.	-2.2	.
Overall balance/GDP	-4.7	-0.3	-4.4	.	-3.0	.	.	-2.6	.
External debt									
External debt/exports	349.5	172.3	177.2	701.4	286.1	415.3	771.9	307.0	464.9
Debt service/exports	9.3	7.7	1.6	13.5	13.3	0.2	14.0	15.4	-1.4
Inflation									
Wholesale prices	.	12.5	.	.	12.9	.	.	17.1	.
Consumer prices	18.5	16.1	2.4	30.4	15.1	15.4	31.3	14.0	17.3
Monetary policy									
Money supply growth	29.2	17.1	12.1	10.5	13.6	-3.1	19.1	14.8	4.3
Real discount rate	-11.1	-6.9	-4.2	-20.2	-3.7	-16.5	-20.5	-2.5	-18.0
Fiscal policy									
Gov. revenue/GDP	20.4	21.9	-1.5	19.4	25.0	-5.6	19.2	25.1	-5.9
Gov. expenditure/GDP	31.5	27.0	4.5	28.2	31.7	-3.6	27.7	31.8	-4.1
Budget surplus/GDP	-11.1	-5.1	-6.0	-8.8	-6.8	-2.0	-8.5	-6.7	-1.8

Performance indicators: Togo

Indicators	Preceding 3 years			Following 3 years			Years until 1987		
	Own average	Group average	Difference	Own average	Group average	Difference	Own average	Group average	Difference
Population, mil.	2.7	6.3	.	3.0	7.0	.	3.1	7.1	.
Per capita GDP, US$	366.8	706.4	.	257.3	624.5	.	257.3	625.8	.
Economic growth									
Gross domestic product	2.6	2.8	-0.2	2.8	2.8	-0.1	3.0	2.8	0.2
Per capita GDP	-0.4	-0.1	-0.3	-0.6	-0.1	-0.5	-0.3	-0.1	-0.2
Industrial production	3.8	5.4	-1.6	1.5	4.0	-2.6	1.7	4.1	-2.4
Agricultural production	2.1	1.1	1.0	6.2	3.1	3.1	7.0	3.2	3.8
Consumption	-0.8	3.6	-4.4	2.3	1.9	0.4	1.1	2.1	-1.0
Per capita consumption	-3.8	0.6	-4.3	-1.0	-1.0	0.0	-2.1	-0.9	-1.3
Investment	-18.1	7.4	-25.5	18.7	14.2	4.5	12.4	13.8	-1.4
Aggregate expenditure	-6.5	3.7	-10.2	5.7	1.6	4.1	3.4	1.7	1.7
Export performance									
Export growth	23.9	3.5	20.4	2.5	2.5	0.0	2.1	2.5	-0.4
Import substitution									
Import/GDP ratio	52.2	47.6	4.6	48.2	44.0	4.2	46.1	44.4	1.7
Investment and savings									
Domestic saving/GDP	17.5	6.8	10.7	12.2	5.8	6.4	12.6	5.7	7.0
Private saving/GDP	21.2	12.8	8.4	19.1	6.1	13.0	19.1	6.1	13.0

Public saving/GDP	-3.7	-6.2	2.5	-6.4	-4.9	-1.4	-6.4	-4.9	-1.4
Investment/GDP	28.8	22.7	6.1	22.0	17.9	4.1	22.7	17.9	4.8
Foreign saving/GDP	11.3	15.9	-4.6	9.8	12.1	-2.2	10.1	12.3	-2.2
Balance of payments									
Current account/GDP	-7.9	-9.4	1.5	2.4	-3.3	5.7	2.4	-3.3	5.7
Basic balance/GDP	-0.7	-2.7	2.0	4.9	-0.4	5.3	4.9	-0.4	5.3
Overall balance/GDP	2.6	-2.2	4.7	1.5	-2.5	4.0	1.5	-2.5	4.0
External debt									
External debt/exports	269.4	209.9	59.5	312.0	339.7	-27.7	312.0	338.3	-26.3
Debt service/exports	12.5	10.2	2.3	32.6	17.1	15.4	32.6	17.9	14.7
Inflation									
Wholesale prices	·	12.5	·	·	20.8		·	20.5	
Consumer prices	14.4	15.2	-0.8	-0.4	14.2	-14.6	-0.4	14.1	-14.5
Monetary policy									
Money supply growth	20.7	17.1	3.6	2.9	16.8	-13.9	2.9	16.2	-13.3
Real discount rate	-2.7	-5.2	2.5	10.4	-1.8	12.2	10.4	-1.9	12.3
Fiscal policy									
Gov. revenue/GDP	28.3	22.2	6.1	31.5	25.9	5.6	31.5	25.9	5.6
Gov. expenditure/GDP	32.0	28.4	3.6	37.9	30.8	7.0	37.9	30.8	7.0
Budget surplus/GDP	-3.7	-6.2	2.5	-6.4	-4.9	-1.4	-6.4	-4.9	-1.4

Performance indicators: Uganda

Indicators	Preceding 3 years			Following 3 years			Years until 1987		
	Own average	Group average	Difference	Own average	Group average	Difference	Own average	Group average	Difference
Population, mil.	13.0	6.3	.	14.7	7.0	.	14.9	7.1	.
Per capita GDP, US$	.	706.4	.	.	624.5	.	.	625.8	.
Economic growth									
Gross domestic product	3.3	2.8	0.5	-2.1	2.8	-4.9	-2.1	2.8	-4.9
Per capita GDP	0.4	-0.1	0.5	-5.0	-0.1	-4.9	-5.0	-0.1	-5.0
Industrial production	2.7	5.4	-2.7	-2.2	4.0	-6.2	-2.2	4.1	-6.3
Agricultural production	3.5	1.1	2.4	-6.4	3.1	-9.5	-6.4	3.2	-9.6
Consumption	20.3	3.6	16.7	.	1.9	.	.	2.1	.
Per capita consumption	16.9	0.6	16.3	.	-1.0	.	.	-0.9	.
Investment	10.9	7.4	3.5	.	14.2	.	.	13.8	.
Aggregate expenditure	19.8	3.7	16.1	.	1.6	.	.	1.7	.
Export performance									
Export growth	137.7	3.5	134.2	.	2.5	.	.	2.5	.
Import substitution									
Import/GDP ratio	9.1	47.6	-38.5	16.0	44.0	-28.1	16.0	44.4	-28.5
Investment and savings									
Domestic saving/GDP	10.2	6.8	3.5	21.9	5.8	16.1	21.9	5.7	16.3
Private saving/GDP	62.0	12.8	49.2	65.6	6.1	59.5	65.6	6.1	59.5

Public saving/GDP	-51.7	-6.2	-45.5	-38.4	-4.9	-33.4	-38.4	-4.9	-33.4
Investment/GDP	14.0	22.7	-8.6	14.9	17.9	-2.9	14.9	17.9	-3.0
Foreign saving/GDP	3.8	15.9	-12.1	-7.0	12.1	-19.1	-7.0	12.3	-19.3
Balance of payments									
Current account/GDP	-8.7	-9.4	0.7	57.4	-3.3	60.7	57.4	-3.3	60.7
Basic balance/GDP	-19.9	-2.7	-17.2	88.6	-0.4	89.0	88.6	-0.4	89.0
Overall balance/GDP	-23.4	-2.2	-21.3	43.1	-2.5	45.6	43.1	-2.5	45.6
External debt									
External debt/exports	.	209.9	.	.	339.7	.	.	338.3	.
Debt service/exports	.	10.2	.	.	17.1	.	.	17.9	.
Inflation									
Wholesale prices	.	12.5	.	.	20.8	.	.	20.5	.
Consumer prices	.	15.2	.	.	14.2	.	.	14.1	.
Monetary policy									
Money supply growth	46.5	17.1	29.3	141.3	16.8	124.5	141.3	16.2	125.1
Real discount rate	.	-5.2	.	.	-1.8	.	.	-1.9	.
Fiscal policy									
Gov. revenue/GDP	43.8	22.2	21.6	139.2	25.9	113.4	139.2	25.9	113.4
Gov. expenditure/GDP	95.5	28.4	67.1	177.6	30.8	146.8	177.6	30.8	146.8
Budget surplus/GDP	-51.7	-6.2	-45.5	-38.4	-4.9	-33.4	-38.4	-4.9	-33.4

Performance indicators: Zimbabwe

Indicators	Preceding 3 years			Following 3 years			Years until 1987		
	Own average	Group average	Difference	Own average	Group average	Difference	Own average	Group average	Difference
Population, mil.	7.3	6.3	.	8.4	7.0	.	8.6	7.1	.
Per capita GDP, US$	849.7	706.4	.	630.5	624.5	.	630.5	625.8	.
Economic growth									
Gross domestic product	7.2	2.8	4.4	1.8	2.8	-1.0	1.8	2.8	-1.0
Per capita GDP	3.6	-0.1	3.7	-1.8	-0.1	-1.7	-1.8	-0.1	-1.7
Industrial production	5.2	5.4	-0.3	2.0	4.0	-2.1	2.0	4.1	-2.1
Agricultural production	2.9	1.1	1.7	11.6	3.1	8.5	11.6	3.2	8.4
Consumption	6.9	3.6	3.3	-0.2	1.9	-2.1	-0.2	2.1	-2.3
Per capita consumption	3.3	0.6	2.7	-3.7	-1.0	-2.7	-3.7	-0.9	-2.8
Investment	32.7	7.4	25.3	-2.7	14.2	-16.8	-2.7	13.8	-16.5
Aggregate expenditure	10.1	3.7	6.4	-2.2	1.6	-3.9	-2.2	1.7	-4.0
Export performance									
Export growth	10.7	3.5	7.2	11.0	2.5	8.5	11.0	2.5	8.5
Import substitution									
Import/GDP ratio	31.3	47.6	-16.3	25.4	44.0	-18.7	25.4	44.4	-19.1
Investment and savings									
Domestic saving/GDP	15.7	6.8	8.9	19.7	5.8	13.8	19.7	5.7	14.0
Private saving/GDP	22.9	12.8	10.1	26.6	6.1	20.5	26.6	6.1	20.5

Public saving/GDP	-7.2	-6.2	-1.0	-6.8	-4.9	-1.9	-6.8	-4.9	-1.9
Investment/GDP	21.1	22.7	-1.6	19.0	17.9	1.1	19.0	17.9	1.1
Foreign saving/GDP	5.4	15.9	-10.5	-0.7	12.1	-12.7	-0.7	12.3	-12.9
Balance of payments									
Current account/GDP	-8.3	-9.4	1.1	-1.7	-3.3	1.6	-1.7	-3.3	1.6
Basic balance/GDP	-6.4	-2.7	-3.6	1.0	-0.4	1.4	1.0	-0.4	1.4
Overall balance/GDP	-0.6	-2.2	1.5	-0.1	-2.5	2.5	-0.1	-2.5	2.5
External debt									
External debt/exports	82.8	209.9	-127.2	162.5	339.7	-177.2	162.5	338.3	-175.8
Debt service/exports	5.4	10.2	-4.8	22.1	17.1	5.0	22.1	17.9	4.2
Inflation									
Wholesale prices		12.5			20.8			20.5	
Consumer prices	9.7	15.2	-5.5	14.3	14.2	0.1	14.3	14.1	0.3
Monetary policy									
Money supply growth	21.9	17.1	4.8	14.4	16.8	-2.4	14.4	16.2	-1.8
Real discount rate	-2.0	-5.2	3.2	-4.5	-1.8	-2.7	-4.5	-1.9	-2.6
Fiscal policy									
Gov. revenue/GDP	26.3	22.2	4.1	28.3	25.9	2.5	28.3	25.9	2.5
Gov. expenditure/GDP	33.5	28.4	5.1	35.2	30.8	4.4	35.2	30.8	4.4
Budget surplus/GDP	-7.2	-6.2	-1.0	-6.8	-4.9	-1.9	-6.8	-4.9	-1.9

Performance indicators: Pakistan

Indicators	Preceding 3 years			Following 3 years			Years until 1987		
	Own average	Group average	Difference	Own average	Group average	Difference	Own average	Group average	Difference
Population, mil.	77.8	251.6	.	87.8	269.5	.	93.4	278.6	.
Per capita GDP, US$	225.2	167.8	.	330.9	224.3	.	331.8	327.6	.
Economic growth									
Gross domestic product	5.3	5.1	0.2	6.8	4.2	2.6	6.9	4.4	2.4
Per capita GDP	2.1	3.0	-0.9	3.6	2.2	1.4	3.7	2.4	1.2
Industrial production	8.1	8.1	-0.1	9.5	3.6	5.9	9.4	5.1	4.3
Agricultural production	2.8	2.8	0.1	3.7	4.2	-0.5	4.0	3.4	0.5
Consumption	6.5	4.2	2.3	5.1	4.5	0.6	5.9	4.4	1.5
Per capita consumption	3.4	2.3	1.1	2.0	2.6	-0.6	2.8	2.5	0.2
Investment	7.0	16.6	-9.6	6.7	3.5	3.2	6.6	3.7	3.0
Aggregate expenditure	6.6	6.3	0.3	5.3	3.9	1.4	6.0	4.3	1.7
Export performance									
Export growth	2.8	7.7	-4.9	12.6	4.6	8.0	11.8	5.2	6.6
Import substitution									
Import/GDP ratio	20.1	17.5	2.6	22.7	20.8	1.9	22.5	19.9	2.6
Investment and savings									
Domestic saving/GDP	8.0	14.8	-6.8	6.2	13.3	-7.1	6.0	13.9	-8.0
Private saving/GDP	11.1	15.8	-4.7	8.8	17.4	-8.6	9.3	20.0	-10.7

Public saving/GDP	-3.1	-3.8	0.7	-2.7	-6.9	4.2	-3.3	-5.7	2.3
Investment/GDP	18.3	19.7	-1.4	17.4	21.8	-4.4	17.1	21.5	-4.4
Foreign saving/GDP	10.4	5.0	5.4	11.3	8.6	2.7	11.2	7.6	3.6
Balance of payments									
Current account/GDP	-4.8	-2.3	-2.5	-2.0	-6.0	3.9	-2.6	-4.7	2.1
Basic balance/GDP	-1.9	0.8	-2.8	-0.2	-1.7	1.5	-0.8	-1.2	0.4
Overall balance/GDP	-1.2	0.7	-1.9	0.1	-0.8	0.9	-0.9	-0.6	-0.3
External debt									
External debt/exports	490.7	223.8	266.9	338.7	258.2	80.5	345.4	275.7	69.7
Debt service/exports	23.9	10.8	13.1	22.3	12.0	10.4	25.5	13.7	11.8
Inflation									
Wholesale prices	8.4	11.6	-3.2	7.5	9.2	-1.7	6.8	7.2	-0.4
Consumer prices	8.2	5.3	2.9	8.0	9.3	-1.3	6.4	8.6	-2.2
Monetary policy									
Money supply growth	18.6	19.5	-0.9	14.8	14.0	0.8	14.7	16.1	-1.4
Real discount rate	1.7	1.9	-0.2	1.9	-0.1	2.0	3.4	1.1	2.3
Fiscal policy									
Gov. revenue/GDP	14.3	13.9	0.4	16.0	12.9	3.0	16.3	14.7	1.6
Gov. expenditure/GDP	17.5	17.7	-0.3	18.6	19.8	-1.2	19.7	20.4	-0.7
Budget surplus/GDP	-3.1	-3.8	0.7	-2.7	-6.9	4.2	-3.3	-5.7	2.3

Performance indicators: Bolivia

Indicators	Preceding 3 years			Following 3 years			Years until 1987		
	Own average	Group average	Difference	Own average	Group average	Difference	Own average	Group average	Difference
Population, mil.	5.3	12.8	.	5.9	13.4	.	6.2	14.1	.
Per capita GDP, US$	713.2	739.8	.	1076.1	1038.1	.	1082.6	1047.4	.
Economic growth									
Gross domestic product	2.5	6.2	-3.6	-3.7	2.3	-6.1	-2.2	2.8	-5.0
Per capita GDP	-0.1	3.6	-3.7	-6.3	-0.2	-6.1	-4.8	0.3	-5.1
Industrial production	-2.1	9.4	-11.5	-5.4	1.1	-6.5	-6.0	2.1	-8.1
Agricultural production	1.6	2.1	-0.5	-7.2	1.5	-8.7	-0.7	2.0	-2.7
Consumption	4.5	5.5	-1.0	1.0	3.1	-2.1	-0.2	2.9	-3.1
Per capita consumption	1.9	2.9	-1.0	-1.7	0.5	-2.2	-2.8	0.3	-3.1
Investment	-3.2	12.8	-16.1	-34.6	-1.6	-32.9	2.4	-0.8	3.2
Aggregate expenditure	2.8	7.1	-4.3	-3.1	1.6	-4.7	-1.5	1.7	-3.2
Export performance									
Export growth	-1.2	11.1	-12.3	-4.7	1.6	-6.3	-4.1	3.1	-7.2
Import substitution									
Import/GDP ratio	29.3	46.0	-16.7	12.8	47.1	-34.3	13.7	45.3	-31.6
Investment and savings									
Domestic saving/GDP	18.2	13.0	5.2	10.6	9.0	1.6	7.3	9.5	-2.2
Private saving/GDP	23.5	18.2	5.2	27.2	17.3	9.9	30.5	17.2	13.3

Public saving/GDP	−5.3	−6.4	1.1	−16.5	−8.1	−8.4	−22.2	−7.5	−14.7
Investment/GDP	23.8	27.5	−3.7	8.4	25.7	−17.3	7.3	23.9	−16.6
Foreign saving/GDP	5.6	14.4	−8.8	−2.2	16.7	−18.9	−0.0	14.4	−14.4
Balance of payments									
Current account/GDP	−6.9	−2.9	−4.0	−4.1	−9.5	5.4	−4.4	−7.4	3.0
Basic balance/GDP	0.4	2.8	−2.3	−4.9	−2.7	−2.2	−6.2	−2.1	−4.1
Overall balance/GDP	−1.5	3.0	−4.5	−6.4	−3.0	−3.4	−5.2	−2.5	−2.8
External debt									
External debt/exports	229.6	175.0	54.7	358.3	210.5	147.8	447.9	238.9	209.0
Debt service/exports	29.7	16.1	13.7	33.0	20.4	12.6	34.6	20.7	13.9
Inflation									
Wholesale prices	12.7	16.8	.	.	11.9	.	.	14.1	.
Consumer prices	.	16.1	−3.3	143.7	14.7	128.9	1964.7	22.2	1942.5
Monetary policy									
Money supply growth	16.7	27.0	−10.3	151.8	14.2	137.6	1396.8	19.2	1377.6
Real discount rate	1.8	−3.7	5.6	−33.2	−1.6	−31.6	−45.4	−1.2	−44.2
Fiscal policy									
Gov. revenue/GDP	10.3	21.3	−10.9	5.7	22.8	−17.1	5.4	23.0	−17.6
Gov. expenditure/GDP	15.6	27.7	−12.1	22.2	30.9	−8.7	27.5	30.5	−3.0
Budget surplus/GDP	−5.3	−6.4	1.1	−16.5	−8.1	−8.4	−22.2	−7.5	−14.7

Performance indicators: Costa Rica

Indicators	Preceding 3 years			Following 3 years			Years until 1987		
	Own average	Group average	Difference	Own average	Group average	Difference	Own average	Group average	Difference
Population, mil.	2.3	13.1	.	2.6	14.4	.	2.6	14.5	.
Per capita GDP, US$	1441.1	1016.0	.	1503.6	1057.9	.	1503.6	1059.0	.
Economic growth									
Gross domestic product	-2.9	3.2	-6.2	4.4	3.2	1.2	4.4	3.2	1.2
Per capita GDP	-5.6	0.8	-6.4	1.8	0.7	1.1	1.8	0.7	1.1
Industrial production	-5.5	3.3	-8.8	6.4	3.0	3.4	6.4	3.0	3.4
Agricultural production	-0.0	4.0	-4.1	2.7	3.2	-0.5	2.7	3.2	-0.5
Consumption	-5.9	4.7	-10.6	5.2	2.2	3.1	5.2	2.2	3.0
Per capita consumption	-8.5	2.0	-10.5	2.6	-0.4	3.0	2.6	-0.4	3.0
Investment	-18.7	3.5	-22.2	11.0	0.4	10.6	11.0	0.7	10.4
Aggregate expenditure	-9.0	3.6	-12.6	6.5	1.6	4.9	6.5	1.6	4.8
Export performance									
Export growth	0.4	-0.1	0.5	2.6	5.7	-3.1	2.6	5.8	-3.1
Import substitution									
Import/GDP ratio	42.4	49.8	-7.4	32.8	43.1	-10.2	32.8	43.1	-10.3
Investment and savings									
Domestic saving/GDP	22.7	9.6	13.0	24.0	9.9	14.1	24.0	9.9	14.1
Private saving/GDP	26.4	18.0	8.4	26.0	16.9	9.2	26.0	16.9	9.2

Public saving/GDP	−3.8	−7.9	4.1	−2.0	−5.6	3.6	−2.0	−5.6	3.6
Investment/GDP	26.8	27.7	−1.0	23.5	21.4	2.1	23.5	21.4	2.1
Foreign saving/GDP	4.1	18.1	−14.0	−0.5	11.5	−12.0	−0.5	11.5	−12.0
Balance of payments									
Current account/GDP	−13.3	−9.6	−3.6	−6.3	−5.3	−1.0	−6.3	−5.3	−1.0
Basic balance/GDP	−9.1	−2.7	−6.5	−10.9	−1.8	−9.0	−10.9	−1.8	−9.0
Overall balance/GDP	−12.5	−2.1	−10.4	−10.1	−1.9	−8.2	−10.1	−1.9	−8.2
External debt									
External debt/exports	263.7	185.0	78.7	340.4	276.2	64.2	340.4	275.6	64.8
Debt service/exports	24.4	19.3	5.1	33.8	21.0	12.9	33.8	21.1	12.7
Inflation									
Wholesale prices	65.7	13.0	52.7	9.0	17.9	−8.8	9.4	17.6	−8.2
Consumer prices	48.4	16.0	32.5	12.9	31.1	−18.1	13.9	30.7	−16.7
Monetary policy									
Money supply growth	45.4	15.8	29.6	18.7	23.6	−4.8	14.1	23.3	−9.1
Real discount rate	−12.3	−2.7	−9.7	13.2	−0.9	14.1	13.0	−0.8	13.8
Fiscal policy									
Gov. revenue/GDP	17.7	23.7	−6.0	22.1	24.0	−2.0	22.1	24.0	−2.0
Gov. expenditure/GDP	21.5	31.5	−10.1	24.0	29.6	−5.6	24.0	29.6	−5.6
Budget surplus/GDP	−3.8	−7.9	4.1	−2.0	−5.6	3.6	−2.0	−5.6	3.6

160

Performance indicators: Guyana

Indicators	Preceding 3 years			Following 3 years			Years until 1987		
	Own average	Group average	Difference	Own average	Group average	Difference	Own average	Group average	Difference
Population, mil.	0.8	12.5	.	0.8	13.7	.	0.8	14.2	.
Per capita GDP, US$	711.1	817.8	.	605.9	1036.4	.	610.5	1046.4	.
Economic growth									
Gross domestic product	-0.6	5.2	-5.9	-6.5	1.9	-8.4	-3.5	2.4	-5.9
Per capita GDP	-1.4	2.8	-4.2	-7.3	-0.6	-6.7	-4.3	-0.1	-4.2
Industrial production	-2.0	8.3	-10.2	-12.6	1.5	-14.1	-7.3	1.7	-9.0
Agricultural production	0.7	3.5	-2.7	-0.6	1.0	-1.6	0.4	1.4	-1.0
Consumption	-3.9	5.4	-9.3	-11.8	1.9	-13.7	-3.6	2.3	-5.9
Per capita consumption	-4.7	2.7	-7.4	-12.5	-0.6	-11.9	-4.5	-0.3	-4.1
Investment	1.7	7.2	-5.5	-10.9	-3.5	-7.4	-6.0	-3.6	-2.4
Aggregate expenditure	-3.2	5.5	-8.6	-12.0	0.2	-12.2	-4.4	0.6	-5.0
Export performance									
Export growth	0.5	9.0	-8.5	-6.0	3.0	-9.1	-4.6	3.4	-8.0
Import substitution									
Import/GDP ratio	70.6	50.1	20.5	66.2	44.7	21.5	64.7	44.1	20.7
Investment and savings									
Domestic saving/GDP	20.4	12.3	8.2	9.6	9.5	0.1	11.7	9.5	2.2
Private saving/GDP	37.9	18.3	19.5	.	17.4	.	.	17.2	.

Public saving/GDP	-17.4	-6.9	-10.5		-7.8			-7.3	.
Investment/GDP	27.1	28.5	-1.4	23.7	23.6	0.0	24.8	22.8	2.0
Foreign saving/GDP	6.6	16.3	-9.6	14.1	14.1	-0.0	13.1	13.2	-0.2
Balance of payments									
Current account/GDP	-14.5	-5.2	-9.3	-27.8	-7.7	-20.1	-26.1	-6.7	-19.4
Basic balance/GDP	-8.6	0.7	-9.3	-36.5	-2.4	-34.2	-34.6	-1.9	-32.7
Overall balance/GDP	-7.8	1.5	-9.3	-36.9	-2.7	-34.2	-35.7	-2.3	-33.3
External debt									
External debt/exports	188.4	167.2	21.1	386.7	234.6	152.1	407.5	253.4	154.0
Debt service/exports	20.7	15.7	5.0	19.0	20.3	-1.4	15.5	20.9	-5.4
Inflation									
Wholesale prices	15.7	15.6			12.3			14.4	.
Consumer prices		17.1	-1.4	19.6	14.8	4.8	16.8	23.5	-6.8
Monetary policy									
Money supply growth	5.1	25.9	-20.8	20.9	18.5	2.4	20.2	21.1	-0.9
Real discount rate	-4.5	-3.8	-0.7	-4.5	-0.9	-3.6	-1.7	-1.0	-0.7
Fiscal policy									
Gov. revenue/GDP	34.0	22.3	11.7	.	22.9	.	.	23.1	.
Gov. expenditure/GDP	51.4	29.2	22.2	.	30.7	.	.	30.4	.
Budget surplus/GDP	-17.4	-6.9	-10.5	.	-7.8	.	.	-7.3	.

Performance indicators: Jamaica

Indicators	Preceding 3 years			Following 3 years			Years until 1987		
	Own average	Group average	Difference	Own average	Group average	Difference	Own average	Group average	Difference
Population, mil.	2.0	12.4	.	2.1	13.1	.	2.2	13.9	.
Per capita GDP, US$	1456.7	651.9	.	1415.7	1016.0	.	1282.7	1034.5	.
Economic growth									
Gross domestic product	-2.8	7.8	-10.5	-0.7	3.2	-3.9	-0.4	3.0	-3.5
Per capita GDP	-3.6	5.1	-8.7	-2.0	0.8	-2.8	-1.8	0.6	-2.4
Industrial production	-6.2	12.1	-18.3	-3.5	3.3	-6.9	-2.0	2.9	-4.9
Agricultural production	4.4	5.5	-1.1	-3.3	4.0	-7.3	0.2	2.9	-2.7
Consumption	-2.5	5.3	-7.7	-1.0	4.7	-5.7	-0.2	3.5	-3.7
Per capita consumption	-3.3	2.6	-5.9	-2.3	2.0	-4.3	-1.6	0.9	-2.6
Investment	-17.7	15.5	-33.2	7.3	3.5	3.8	1.2	0.5	0.7
Aggregate expenditure	-6.0	7.3	-13.3	0.0	3.6	-3.5	-0.1	2.3	-2.5
Export performance									
Export growth	-2.2	10.9	-13.2	0.1	-0.1	0.2	-1.9	2.8	-4.6
Import substitution									
Import/GDP ratio	37.2	42.7	-5.5	53.7	49.8	3.9	56.0	46.4	9.6
Investment and savings									
Domestic saving/GDP	12.2	13.2	-1.1	11.0	9.6	1.4	13.4	9.7	3.8
Private saving/GDP	26.4	18.9	7.5	27.7	18.0	9.7	28.4	17.4	10.9

Public saving/GDP	-14.2	-6.1	-8.1	-16.6	-7.9	-8.8	-14.9	-7.6	-7.4
Investment/GDP	15.2	26.4	-11.3	19.0	27.7	-8.7	21.1	24.7	-3.6
Foreign saving/GDP	3.0	13.2	-10.2	8.0	18.1	-10.1	7.6	15.0	-7.4
Balance of payments									
Current account/GDP	-4.5	-2.7	-1.8	-10.0	-9.6	-0.4	-11.5	-7.5	-4.1
Basic balance/GDP	-4.7	2.3	-7.1	-5.5	-2.7	-2.9	-5.3	-2.1	-3.2
Overall balance/GDP	-5.4	2.6	-8.0	-4.9	-2.1	-2.8	-3.4	-2.3	-1.1
External debt									
External debt/exports	154.6	171.4	-16.9	176.5	185.0	-8.5	241.0	227.1	13.9
Debt service/exports	55.4	16.1	39.2	23.9	19.3	4.6	26.5	19.9	6.6
Inflation									
Wholesale prices	.	20.9	.	.	13.0	.	.	14.6	.
Consumer prices	18.6	16.3	2.3	15.5	16.0	-0.5	16.7	21.9	-5.2
Monetary policy									
Money supply growth	21.8	29.0	-7.3	11.7	15.8	-4.1	17.7	20.0	-2.3
Real discount rate	-7.3	-3.7	-3.6	-3.4	-2.7	-0.7	-0.6	-1.5	0.9
Fiscal policy									
Gov. revenue/GDP	23.5	20.8	2.7	28.1	23.7	4.4	26.8	23.8	3.1
Gov. expenditure/GDP	37.7	26.8	10.9	44.7	31.5	13.2	41.7	31.3	10.4
Budget surplus/GDP	-14.2	-6.1	-8.1	-16.6	-7.9	-8.8	-14.9	-7.6	-7.4

Performance indicators: Morocco

Indicators	Preceding 3 years			Following 3 years			Years until 1987		
	Own average	Group average	Difference	Own average	Group average	Difference	Own average	Group average	Difference
Population, mil.	20.4	13.4	.	22.5	14.7	.	22.5	14.7	.
Per capita GDP, US$	706.4	1038.1	.	598.5	1064.6	.	598.5	1064.6	.
Economic growth									
Gross domestic product	2.6	2.3	0.3	5.1	3.2	2.0	5.1	3.2	2.0
Per capita GDP	0.1	-0.2	0.3	2.5	0.7	1.9	2.5	0.7	1.9
Industrial production	1.7	1.1	0.6	0.9	1.9	-1.0	0.9	1.9	-1.0
Agricultural production	-2.2	1.5	-3.8	17.5	3.0	14.5	17.5	3.0	14.5
Consumption	2.8	3.1	-0.3	6.2	2.8	3.4	6.2	2.8	3.4
Per capita consumption	0.3	0.5	-0.2	3.6	0.2	3.4	3.6	0.2	3.4
Investment	-5.9	-1.6	-4.3	0.3	-3.9	4.3	0.3	-3.9	4.3
Aggregate expenditure	1.4	1.6	-0.1	5.4	1.4	4.0	5.4	1.4	4.0
Export performance									
Export growth	4.4	1.6	2.8	3.1	2.4	0.8	3.1	2.4	0.8
Import substitution									
Import/GDP ratio	34.1	47.1	-13.0	34.2	43.3	-9.1	34.2	43.3	-9.1
Investment and savings									
Domestic saving/GDP	9.1	9.0	0.1	13.1	9.4	3.7	13.1	9.4	3.7
Private saving/GDP	20.2	17.3	2.9	20.8	16.0	4.8	20.8	16.0	4.8

Public saving/GDP	-11.1	-8.1	-2.9	-7.6	-5.8	-1.9	-7.6	-5.8	-1.9
Investment/GDP	22.2	25.7	-3.6	21.6	21.0	0.7	21.6	21.0	0.7
Foreign saving/GDP	13.1	16.7	-3.7	8.5	11.6	-3.0	8.5	11.6	-3.0
Balance of payments									
Current account/GDP	-10.6	-9.5	-1.0	-4.5	-5.1	0.6	-4.5	-5.1	0.6
Basic balance/GDP	-2.8	-2.7	-0.2	-0.4	-2.0	1.6	-0.4	-2.0	1.6
Overall balance/GDP	-2.5	-3.0	0.5	0.3	-2.2	2.5	0.3	-2.2	2.5
External debt									
External debt/exports	369.1	210.5	158.6	492.8	305.4	187.4	492.8	305.4	187.4
Debt service/exports	42.2	20.4	21.7	35.1	22.5	12.7	35.1	22.5	12.7
Inflation									
Wholesale prices	12.3	11.9	0.4	6.1	19.4	-13.2	6.1	19.4	-13.2
Consumer prices	9.7	14.7	-5.0	6.4	38.9	-32.5	6.4	38.9	-32.5
Monetary policy									
Money supply growth	10.7	14.2	-3.5	14.1	23.1	-9.0	14.1	23.1	-9.0
Real discount rate	-2.7	-1.6	-1.1	0.3	4.1	-3.8	0.3	4.1	-3.8
Fiscal policy									
Gov. revenue/GDP	26.5	22.8	3.8	25.3	24.5	0.8	25.3	24.5	0.8
Gov. expenditure/GDP	37.6	30.9	6.7	33.0	30.3	2.7	33.0	30.3	2.7
Budget surplus/GDP	-11.1	-8.1	-2.9	-7.6	-5.8	-1.9	-7.6	-5.8	-1.9

Performance indicators: Philippines

Indicators	Preceding 3 years			Following 3 years			Years until 1987		
	Own average	Group average	Difference	Own average	Group average	Difference	Own average	Group average	Difference
Population, mil.	45.7	12.8	.	50.8	13.4	.	53.4	14.1	.
Per capita GDP, US$	541.6	739.8	.	743.3	1038.1	.	653.3	1047.4	.
Economic growth									
Gross domestic product	6.0	6.2	-0.2	2.6	2.3	0.3	0.4	2.8	-2.4
Per capita GDP	3.1	3.6	-0.6	0.1	-0.2	0.2	-2.0	0.3	-2.3
Industrial production	7.3	9.4	-2.1	2.5	1.1	1.5	-1.1	2.1	-3.2
Agricultural production	4.5	2.1	2.5	1.7	1.5	0.2	2.1	2.0	0.1
Consumption	4.8	5.5	-0.7	3.1	3.1	0.0	2.1	2.9	-0.8
Per capita consumption	1.9	2.9	-1.0	0.6	0.5	0.1	-0.4	0.3	-0.7
Investment	6.6	12.8	-6.2	-2.0	-1.6	-0.4	-8.5	-0.8	-7.7
Aggregate expenditure	5.3	7.1	-1.8	1.7	1.6	0.2	-0.5	1.7	-2.2
Export performance									
Export growth	9.2	11.1	-1.9	3.0	1.6	1.5	4.0	3.1	0.9
Import substitution									
Import/GDP ratio	23.5	46.0	-22.5	24.7	47.1	-22.4	22.1	45.3	-23.2
Investment and savings									
Domestic saving/GDP	24.1	13.0	11.2	23.1	9.0	14.0	19.8	9.5	10.3
Private saving/GDP	23.7	18.2	5.4	23.7	17.3	6.4	20.1	17.2	2.9

Public saving/GDP	0.5	−6.4	6.9	−0.6	−8.1	7.5	−0.3	−7.5	7.2
Investment/GDP	29.6	27.5	2.1	28.5	25.7	2.8	20.7	23.9	−3.1
Foreign saving/GDP	5.5	14.4	−8.9	5.5	16.7	−11.2	0.9	14.4	−13.5
Balance of payments									
Current account/GDP	−4.4	−2.9	−1.5	−7.1	−9.5	2.4	−3.7	−7.4	3.7
Basic balance/GDP	−0.5	2.8	−3.2	−3.6	−2.7	−0.9	0.5	−2.1	2.6
Overall balance/GDP	1.4	3.0	−1.7	−3.8	−3.0	−0.8	−0.7	−2.5	1.7
External debt									
External debt/exports	231.0	175.0	56.0	336.1	210.5	125.6	339.6	238.9	100.7
Debt service/exports	23.2	16.1	7.1	25.7	20.4	5.3	26.9	20.7	6.2
Inflation									
Wholesale prices	10.4	16.8	−6.4	13.7	11.9	1.9	19.3	14.1	5.2
Consumer prices	11.6	16.1	−4.5	11.1	14.7	−3.6	15.9	22.2	−6.3
Monetary policy									
Money supply growth	16.1	27.0	−10.9	14.2	14.2	−0.0	13.6	19.2	−5.6
Real discount rate	−4.1	−3.7	−0.3	−3.7	−1.6	−2.1	−6.2	−1.2	−5.0
Fiscal policy									
Gov. revenue/GDP	13.2	21.3	−8.0	11.5	22.8	−11.3	11.9	23.0	−11.1
Gov. expenditure/GDP	12.7	27.7	−14.9	12.1	30.9	−18.7	12.2	30.5	−18.3
Budget surplus/GDP	0.5	−6.4	6.9	−0.6	−8.1	7.5	−0.3	−7.5	7.2

Performance indicators: Thailand

Indicators	Preceding 3 years			Following 3 years			Years until 1987		
	Own average	Group average	Difference	Own average	Group average	Difference	Own average	Group average	Difference
Population, mil.	46.6	12.8	.	50.7	14.1	.	51.6	14.4	.
Per capita GDP, US$	690.3	935.9	.	792.5	1030.9	.	792.7	1049.8	.
Economic growth									
Gross domestic product	6.0	4.3	1.7	4.9	2.5	2.4	4.5	2.9	1.7
Per capita GDP	3.6	2.1	1.6	2.8	-0.0	2.8	2.5	0.4	2.1
Industrial production	6.8	5.3	1.5	5.6	2.4	3.2	5.6	2.5	3.0
Agricultural production	2.4	3.0	-0.6	3.4	2.4	1.0	2.4	2.1	0.2
Consumption	5.3	5.8	-0.5	5.1	1.5	3.6	4.4	2.0	2.5
Per capita consumption	3.0	3.1	-0.2	3.0	-1.0	4.1	2.4	-0.6	3.0
Investment	2.2	10.0	-7.8	6.7	-2.3	9.0	3.2	-1.8	5.1
Aggregate expenditure	4.5	5.9	-1.4	5.4	0.3	5.1	4.2	0.9	3.3
Export performance									
Export growth	9.8	6.4	3.4	5.6	5.7	-0.1	6.1	5.7	0.4
Import substitution									
Import/GDP ratio	29.8	51.2	-21.4	26.9	43.6	-16.7	26.1	43.4	-17.3
Investment and savings									
Domestic saving/GDP	23.8	10.6	13.1	20.5	9.8	10.7	21.7	9.7	12.0
Private saving/GDP	27.8	17.4	10.4	24.9	16.4	8.5	24.9	16.5	8.4

Public saving/GDP	-4.0	3.6	-4.4	-6.0	1.6	-4.4	-6.0	1.6
Investment/GDP	26.9	1.7	23.5	22.0	1.4	23.0	21.9	1.1
Foreign saving/GDP	3.2	-15.0	2.9	12.2	-9.3	1.3	12.2	-10.9
Balance of payments								
Current account/GDP	-7.0	0.0	-5.4	-6.2	0.8	-3.9	-5.8	1.9
Basic balance/GDP	-1.3	-0.7	-1.5	-1.9	0.4	-0.9	-1.7	0.8
Overall balance/GDP	-0.3	-0.1	0.3	-2.6	2.8	0.7	-2.3	3.1
External debt								
External debt/exports	108.0	-54.1	159.3	257.6	-98.3	158.9	263.5	-104.7
Debt service/exports	15.0	-2.0	22.5	19.7	2.8	23.6	20.3	3.3
Inflation								
Wholesale prices	13.6	-2.6	-0.4	14.9	-15.2	0.9	15.4	-14.5
Consumer prices	14.1	-4.0	2.3	19.9	-17.6	2.3	26.3	-24.0
Monetary policy								
Money supply growth	10.5	-10.6	5.0	23.8	-18.8	8.1	23.9	-15.7
Real discount rate	-0.4	3.1	9.4	-1.2	10.6	8.0	-1.4	9.4
Fiscal policy								
Gov. revenue/GDP	13.9	-9.2	15.5	22.9	-7.3	15.5	22.9	-7.4
Gov. expenditure/GDP	17.9	-12.8	19.9	28.9	-9.0	19.9	28.9	-9.0
Budget surplus/GDP	-4.0	3.6	-4.4	-6.0	1.6	-4.4	-6.0	1.6

Performance indicators: Turkey

Indicators	Preceding 3 years			Following 3 years			Years until 1987		
	Own average	Group average	Difference	Own average	Group average	Difference	Own average	Group average	Difference
Population, mil.	42.6	12.8	.	46.7	13.4	.	49.0	14.1	.
Per capita GDP, US$	1324.2	739.8	.	1157.1	1038.1	.	1111.0	1047.4	.
Economic growth									
Gross domestic product	2.1	6.2	-4.1	4.3	2.3	2.0	5.4	2.8	2.6
Per capita GDP	0.0	3.6	-3.6	1.8	-0.2	2.0	2.8	0.3	2.6
Industrial production	3.9	9.4	-5.5	5.2	1.1	4.2	6.5	2.1	4.4
Agricultural production	1.4	2.1	-0.7	2.1	1.5	0.5	3.3	2.0	1.3
Consumption	3.3	5.5	-2.3	2.6	3.1	-0.5	4.1	2.9	1.3
Per capita consumption	1.2	2.9	-1.7	0.1	0.5	-0.4	1.7	0.3	1.4
Investment	-4.5	12.8	-17.3	0.8	-1.6	2.4	5.7	-0.8	6.5
Aggregate expenditure	1.2	7.1	-5.9	2.2	1.6	0.6	4.4	1.7	2.8
Export performance									
Export growth	-4.4	11.1	-15.5	46.3	1.6	44.8	28.3	3.1	25.1
Import substitution									
Import/GDP ratio	9.8	46.0	-36.2	17.8	47.1	-29.3	20.2	45.3	-25.1
Investment and savings									
Domestic saving/GDP	15.9	13.0	2.9	16.4	9.0	7.4	17.4	9.5	8.0
Private saving/GDP	20.2	18.2	1.9	18.7	17.3	1.4	22.7	17.2	5.4

Public saving/GDP	-4.3	-6.4	2.1	-2.7	-8.1	5.4	-5.2	-7.5	2.3
Investment/GDP	20.9	27.5	-6.6	20.7	25.7	-5.0	21.3	23.9	-2.5
Foreign saving/GDP	5.0	14.4	-9.3	4.3	16.7	-12.4	3.9	14.4	-10.5
Balance of payments									
Current account/GDP	-3.7	-2.9	-0.8	-2.9	-9.5	6.6	-2.7	-7.4	4.7
Basic balance/GDP	-2.7	2.8	-5.4	-2.6	-2.7	0.1	-2.5	-2.1	-0.3
Overall balance/GDP	-2.9	3.0	-5.9	-1.0	-3.0	2.1	-1.1	-2.5	1.4
External debt									
External debt/exports	517.1	175.0	342.1	275.4	210.5	64.9	266.8	238.9	27.9
Debt service/exports	20.5	16.1	4.4	30.0	20.4	9.6	30.6	20.7	9.9
Inflation									
Wholesale prices	.	16.8	.	.	11.9	.	.	14.1	.
Consumer prices	43.7	16.1	27.6	33.4	14.7	18.7	38.0	22.2	15.8
Monetary policy									
Money supply growth	44.7	27.0	17.6	39.3	14.2	25.0	39.0	19.2	19.8
Real discount rate	-22.9	-3.7	-19.2	2.8	-1.6	4.4	2.7	-1.2	3.9
Fiscal policy									
Gov. revenue/GDP	22.5	21.3	1.2	21.3	22.8	-1.4	18.6	23.0	-4.3
Gov. expenditure/GDP	26.8	27.7	-0.9	24.1	30.9	-6.8	23.9	30.5	-6.7
Budget surplus/GDP	-4.3	-6.4	2.1	-2.7	-8.1	5.4	-5.2	-7.5	2.3

Performance indicators: Brazil

Indicators	Preceding 3 years			Following 3 years			Years until 1987		
	Own average	Group average	Difference	Own average	Group average	Difference	Own average	Group average	Difference
Population, mil.	124.0	9.8	.	135.5	10.5	.	136.9	10.6	.
Per capita GDP, US$	2078.1	3923.1	.	1736.1	4111.8	.	1736.1	4085.6	.
Economic growth									
Gross domestic product	2.2	2.8	−0.6	7.4	2.6	4.8	7.4	2.6	4.8
Per capita GDP	−0.0	1.1	−1.2	5.1	1.2	3.9	5.1	1.2	3.9
Industrial production	−0.1	0.7	−0.8	9.1	0.9	8.2	9.1	0.9	8.2
Agricultural production	4.6	1.6	3.0	1.5	3.1	−1.5	1.5	2.7	−1.1
Consumption	1.7	4.0	−2.3	6.5	1.5	5.0	6.5	1.4	5.1
Per capita consumption	−0.5	2.3	−2.8	4.3	0.0	4.2	4.3	−0.0	4.3
Investment	−3.4	5.8	−9.1	12.6	−2.7	15.4	12.6	−2.2	14.9
Aggregate expenditure	0.7	4.3	−3.6	7.5	0.1	7.4	7.5	0.1	7.4
Export performance									
Export growth	11.6	1.9	9.7	2.5	5.5	−3.0	2.5	5.6	−3.1
Import substitution									
Import/GDP ratio	9.8	50.9	−41.1	7.4	43.0	−35.6	7.4	42.8	−35.3
Investment and savings									
Domestic saving/GDP	20.6	24.0	−3.4	22.9	22.9	0.0	22.9	22.9	0.0
Private saving/GDP	20.5	29.1	−8.5	22.1	27.8	−5.6	22.1	27.8	−5.6

Public saving/GDP	0.0	-3.6	3.6	0.5	-5.0	5.5	0.5	-5.0	5.5
Investment/GDP	21.7	29.3	-7.7	18.4	23.0	-4.6	18.4	22.9	-4.5
Foreign saving/GDP	1.1	5.4	-4.3	-4.6	0.0	-4.6	-4.6	-0.0	-4.6
Balance of payments									
Current account/GDP	-5.3	-3.9	-1.4	-0.6	-1.7	1.2	-0.6	-1.7	1.2
Basic balance/GDP	-1.8	1.4	-3.2	-3.2	0.9	-4.1	-3.2	0.9	-4.1
Overall balance/GDP	-1.5	0.5	-2.0	-4.0	0.2	-4.1	-4.0	0.2	-4.1
External debt									
External debt/exports	360.1	108.5	251.7	381.4	147.8	233.6	381.4	147.8	233.5
Debt service/exports	67.4	14.3	53.2	35.4	21.2	14.4	35.4	21.1	14.3
Inflation									
Wholesale prices	102.6	37.2	65.4	201.9	68.5	133.4	203.2	57.3	145.9
Consumer prices	95.4	22.8	72.6	189.7	38.6	151.1	199.7	32.3	167.4
Monetary policy									
Money supply growth	73.6	23.9	49.7	269.2	39.1	230.1	269.2	39.9	229.4
Real discount rate	-25.6	-2.9	-22.7	-11.6	2.3	-13.9	3.6	2.1	1.5
Fiscal policy									
Gov. revenue/GDP	9.3	30.2	-20.9	9.1	31.4	-22.3	9.1	31.4	-22.3
Gov. expenditure/GDP	9.3	33.8	-24.5	8.7	36.4	-27.8	8.7	36.4	-27.8
Budget surplus/GDP	0.0	-3.6	3.6	0.5	-5.0	5.5	0.5	-5.0	5.5

Performance indicators: Korea

Indicators	Preceding 3 years			Following 3 years			Years until 1987		
	Own average	Group average	Difference	Own average	Group average	Difference	Own average	Group average	Difference
Population, mil.	37.5	9.4	.	39.9	10.1	.	40.7	10.4	.
Per capita GDP, US$	1570.3	3237.7	.	1976.2	4036.3	.	2080.6	4050.5	.
Economic growth									
Gross domestic product	5.1	4.8	0.3	8.4	2.5	5.9	8.5	2.4	6.2
Per capita GDP	3.5	2.8	0.7	6.8	1.0	5.8	7.0	0.8	6.1
Industrial production	9.8	3.4	6.4	11.5	1.6	9.8	10.9	1.5	9.4
Agricultural production	-7.5	3.4	-10.9	3.3	1.7	1.6	3.8	2.0	1.8
Consumption	6.0	5.3	0.7	5.5	2.7	2.8	5.7	2.2	3.5
Per capita consumption	4.4	3.3	1.1	4.0	1.1	2.8	4.2	0.7	3.5
Investment	8.3	8.7	-0.4	12.1	-2.3	14.4	9.7	-2.5	12.2
Aggregate expenditure	6.4	6.0	0.4	7.5	1.2	6.3	6.9	0.6	6.3
Export performance									
Export growth	7.2	4.6	2.6	10.6	6.6	4.0	12.1	5.7	6.5
Import substitution									
Import/GDP ratio	36.5	49.4	-12.9	37.9	47.7	-9.8	36.9	46.4	-9.5
Investment and savings									
Domestic saving/GDP	26.4	25.4	1.1	27.5	22.5	5.0	29.7	22.3	7.4
Private saving/GDP	25.5	29.1	-3.7	26.8	28.5	-1.7	28.9	28.0	0.9

Public saving/GDP	5.8	-5.0	0.8	5.9	-5.2	0.7	3.6	-2.7	0.9
Investment/GDP	4.3	25.0	29.3	2.6	26.5	29.0	3.6	29.1	32.7
Foreign saving/GDP	-3.2	2.7	-0.4	-2.4	4.0	1.5	2.6	3.7	6.3
Balance of payments									
Current account/GDP	2.5	-3.2	-0.7	1.5	-3.9	-2.4	-4.0	-1.7	-5.7
Basic balance/GDP	0.6	0.3	0.9	0.4	-0.1	0.3	-4.1	2.4	-1.7
Overall balance/GDP	0.6	-0.4	0.2	1.4	-1.2	0.2	-1.9	3.0	1.1
External debt									
External debt/exports	-5.5	143.2	137.6	5.9	135.5	141.4	36.2	93.1	129.3
Debt service/exports	0.5	19.5	20.0	-0.0	17.3	17.3	3.6	11.4	15.0
Inflation									
Wholesale prices	-53.8	54.6	0.8	-63.2	65.1	1.9	-8.2	31.3	23.1
Consumer prices	26.9	30.4	3.5	-30.7	35.0	4.3	-1.0	21.5	20.5
Monetary policy									
Money supply growth	-18.3	35.8	17.5	-15.7	36.8	21.0	-3.1	23.7	20.6
Real discount rate	-0.4	2.5	2.1	-3.9	4.5	0.7	-0.6	-3.4	-4.1
Fiscal policy									
Gov. revenue/GDP	-11.8	30.4	18.6	-11.4	30.1	18.7	-12.2	29.7	17.5
Gov. expenditure/GDP	-17.6	35.4	17.8	-17.3	35.2	18.0	-15.8	32.3	16.5
Budget surplus/GDP	5.8	-5.0	0.8	5.9	-5.2	0.7	3.6	-2.7	0.9

Performance indicators: Mexico

Indicators	Preceding 3 years			Following 3 years			Years until 1987		
	Own average	Group average	Difference	Own average	Group average	Difference	Own average	Group average	Difference
Population, mil.	71.2	9.8	.	78.8	10.5	.	79.8	10.6	.
Per capita GDP, US$	2779.3	3923.1	.	2017.6	4111.8	.	1927.9	4085.6	.
Economic growth									
Gross domestic product	5.2	2.8	2.4	0.9	2.6	-1.8	1.4	2.6	-1.2
Per capita GDP	2.5	1.1	1.3	-1.7	1.2	-2.8	-1.1	1.2	-2.3
Industrial production	5.4	0.7	4.7	1.6	0.9	0.7	2.0	0.9	1.1
Agricultural production	4.2	1.6	2.6	0.9	3.1	-2.2	1.2	2.7	-1.5
Consumption	5.6	4.0	1.5	0.2	1.5	-1.3	0.6	1.4	-0.8
Per capita consumption	2.8	2.3	0.5	-2.3	0.0	-2.4	-1.8	-0.0	-1.8
Investment	3.0	5.8	-2.8	3.5	-2.7	6.2	4.1	-2.2	6.4
Aggregate expenditure	4.6	4.3	0.4	0.8	0.1	0.7	1.3	0.1	1.1
Export performance									
Export growth	8.6	1.9	6.7	4.7	5.5	-0.8	5.5	5.6	-0.0
Import substitution									
Import/GDP ratio	12.8	50.9	-38.1	11.3	43.0	-31.8	11.8	42.8	-31.0
Investment and savings									
Domestic saving/GDP	27.3	24.0	3.3	28.1	22.9	5.1	28.1	22.9	5.2
Private saving/GDP	34.2	29.1	5.1	35.8	27.8	8.1	35.8	27.8	8.1

Public saving/GDP	-6.9	-3.6	-3.3	-7.8	-5.0	-2.8	-7.8	-5.0	-2.8
Investment/GDP	26.1	29.3	-3.2	21.5	23.0	-1.4	21.5	22.9	-1.4
Foreign saving/GDP	-1.2	5.4	-6.6	-6.5	0.0	-6.6	-6.5	-0.0	-6.5
Balance of payments									
Current account/GDP	-4.6	-3.9	-0.8	1.6	-1.7	3.3	1.6	-1.7	3.3
Basic balance/GDP	0.2	1.4	-1.2	1.1	0.9	0.2	1.1	0.9	0.2
Overall balance/GDP	-2.0	0.5	-2.5	-1.2	0.2	-1.4	-1.2	0.2	-1.4
External debt									
External debt/exports	271.9	108.5	163.4	377.1	147.8	229.3	371.2	147.8	223.3
Debt service/exports	39.9	14.3	25.6	53.8	21.1	32.8	54.4	21.1	33.3
Inflation									
Wholesale prices	35.0	37.2	-2.2	70.8	68.5	2.3	87.0	57.3	29.7
Consumer prices	37.7	22.8	14.9	69.8	38.6	31.3	85.3	32.3	53.1
Monetary policy									
Money supply growth	42.6	23.9	18.7	58.9	39.1	19.8	77.6	39.9	37.7
Real discount rate	.	-2.9	.	.	2.3	.	.	2.1	.
Fiscal policy									
Gov. revenue/GDP	15.7	30.2	-14.5	16.9	31.4	-14.5	16.9	31.4	-14.5
Gov. expenditure/GDP	22.6	33.8	-11.2	24.7	36.4	-11.8	24.7	36.4	-11.8
Budget surplus/GDP	-6.9	-3.6	-3.3	-7.8	-5.0	-2.8	-7.8	-5.0	-2.8

Performance indicators: Panama

Indicators	Preceding 3 years			Following 3 years			Years until 1987		
	Own average	Group average	Difference	Own average	Group average	Difference	Own average	Group average	Difference
Population, mil.	2.0	9.8	.	2.2	10.5	.	2.2	10.6	.
Per capita GDP, US$	1950.6	3923.1	.	2230.1	4111.8	.	2230.1	4085.6	.
Economic growth									
Gross domestic product	8.3	2.8	5.5	2.4	2.6	-0.2	2.4	2.6	-0.2
Per capita GDP	5.9	1.1	4.8	0.3	1.2	-0.9	0.3	1.2	-0.9
Industrial production	6.6	0.7	5.9	0.4	0.9	-0.5	0.4	0.9	-0.5
Agricultural production	0.9	1.6	-0.7	1.5	3.1	-1.6	1.5	2.7	-1.2
Consumption	4.3	4.0	0.3	3.1	1.5	1.6	3.1	1.4	1.7
Per capita consumption	2.1	2.3	-0.2	1.0	0.0	0.9	1.0	-0.0	1.0
Investment	7.5	5.8	1.7	2.8	-2.7	5.5	2.8	-2.2	5.0
Aggregate expenditure	4.9	4.3	0.7	2.9	0.1	2.8	2.9	0.1	2.7
Export performance									
Export growth	16.2	1.9	14.3	0.9	5.5	-4.6	0.9	5.6	-4.6
Import substitution									
Import/GDP ratio	46.2	50.9	-4.7	34.2	43.0	-8.8	34.2	42.8	-8.5
Investment and savings									
Domestic saving/GDP	24.2	24.0	0.2	17.2	22.9	-5.7	17.2	22.9	-5.7
Private saving/GDP	30.6	29.1	1.6	15.8	27.8	-11.9	15.8	27.8	-11.9

Public saving/GDP	-6.4	-3.6	-2.9	1.4	-5.0	6.4	1.4	-5.0	6.4
Investment/GDP	28.5	29.3	-0.8	16.5	23.0	-6.5	16.5	22.9	-6.4
Foreign saving/GDP	4.3	5.4	-1.1	-0.7	0.0	-0.8	-0.7	-0.0	-0.7
Balance of payments									
Current account/GDP	-2.8	-3.9	1.0	6.6	-1.7	8.3	6.6	-1.7	8.3
Basic balance/GDP	4.7	1.4	3.3	6.0	0.9	5.1	6.0	0.9	5.1
Overall balance/GDP	-0.5	0.5	-1.0	-2.1	0.2	-2.3	-2.1	0.2	-2.3
External debt									
External debt/exports	209.4	108.5	100.9	273.9	147.8	126.2	273.9	147.8	126.1
Debt service/exports	32.2	14.3	18.0	27.9	21.1	6.8	27.9	21.1	6.8
Inflation									
Wholesale prices	11.2	37.2	-26.0	-5.1	68.5	-73.6	-5.1	57.3	-62.4
Consumer prices	8.5	22.8	-14.4	0.8	38.6	-37.7	0.8	32.3	-31.4
Monetary policy									
Money supply growth	8.0	23.9	-15.9	4.9	39.1	-34.2	4.9	39.9	-35.0
Real discount rate	.	-2.9	.	.	2.3	.	.	2.1	.
Fiscal policy									
Gov. revenue/GDP	21.8	30.2	-8.3	21.7	31.4	-9.8	21.7	31.4	-9.8
Gov. expenditure/GDP	28.3	33.8	-5.5	20.3	36.4	-16.2	20.3	36.4	-16.2
Budget surplus/GDP	-6.4	-3.6	-2.9	1.4	-5.0	6.4	1.4	-5.0	6.4

Performance indicators: Uruguay

Indicators	Preceding 3 years			Following 3 years			Years until 1987		
	Own average	Group average	Difference	Own average	Group average	Difference	Own average	Group average	Difference
Population, mil.	2.9	10.0	.	3.0	10.7	.	3.0	10.7	.
Per capita GDP, US$	2937.0	3989.9	.	1875.9	4100.0	.	1875.9	4100.0	.
Economic growth									
Gross domestic product	−4.4	2.1	−6.6	3.1	2.0	1.1	3.1	2.0	1.1
Per capita GDP	−5.1	0.5	−5.6	2.4	0.6	1.7	2.4	0.6	1.7
Industrial production	−9.4	0.6	−10.0	2.7	0.2	2.5	2.7	0.2	2.5
Agricultural production	0.1	0.5	−0.4	3.9	2.1	1.7	3.9	2.1	1.7
Consumption	−4.7	3.4	−8.1	4.2	1.2	2.9	4.2	1.2	2.9
Per capita consumption	−5.3	1.8	−7.1	3.4	−0.2	3.6	3.4	−0.2	3.6
Investment	−21.2	−0.7	−20.5	−8.4	−2.7	−5.7	−8.4	−2.7	−5.7
Aggregate expenditure	−7.2	2.2	−9.4	2.8	−0.3	3.1	2.8	−0.3	3.1
Export performance									
Export growth	3.7	3.0	0.7	10.3	4.0	6.4	10.3	4.0	6.4
Import substitution									
Import/GDP ratio	19.4	49.5	−30.0	19.2	41.2	−22.0	19.2	41.2	−22.0
Investment and savings									
Domestic saving/GDP	11.4	22.6	−11.2	12.2	21.0	−8.8	12.2	21.0	−8.8
Private saving/GDP	15.7	28.2	−12.5	13.2	24.6	−11.4	13.2	24.6	−11.4

Public saving/GDP	-4.3	-4.1	-0.1	-1.0	-4.4	3.4	-1.0	-4.4	3.4
Investment/GDP	13.2	28.1	-14.9	7.6	21.9	-14.2	7.6	21.9	-14.2
Foreign saving/GDP	1.8	5.5	-3.7	-4.5	0.9	-5.5	-4.5	0.9	-5.5
Balance of payments									
Current account/GDP	-2.6	-4.9	2.3	-0.3	-1.7	1.4	-0.3	-1.7	1.4
Basic balance/GDP	4.3	0.4	3.9	1.4	1.1	0.2	1.4	1.1	0.2
Overall balance/GDP	-2.4	-0.8	-1.7	2.4	1.3	1.1	2.4	1.3	1.1
External debt									
External debt/exports	196.3	125.1	71.2	288.6	173.8	114.8	288.6	173.8	114.8
Debt service/exports	26.0	16.0	10.0	31.9	25.3	6.7	31.9	25.3	6.7
Inflation									
Wholesale prices	36.6	43.6	-7.0	69.0	43.5	25.5	69.0	43.5	25.5
Consumer prices	34.1	24.8	9.3	70.7	26.2	44.6	70.7	26.2	44.6
Monetary policy									
Money supply growth	18.9	27.1	-8.3	95.3	35.9	59.3	95.3	35.9	59.3
Real discount rate	41.8	1.9	39.8	.	-0.2	.	.	-0.2	.
Fiscal policy									
Gov. revenue/GDP	22.3	30.8	-8.5	22.2	32.4	-10.2	22.2	32.4	-10.2
Gov. expenditure/GDP	26.5	34.9	-8.4	23.2	36.8	-13.6	23.2	36.8	-13.6
Budget surplus/GDP	-4.3	-4.1	-0.1	-1.0	-4.4	3.4	-1.0	-4.4	3.4

Performance indicators: Yugoslavia

Indicators	Preceding 3 years			Following 3 years			Years until 1987		
	Own average	Group average	Difference	Own average	Group average	Difference	Own average	Group average	Difference
Population, mil.	22.5	9.8	.	23.1	10.5	.	23.2	10.6	.
Per capita GDP, US$	3107.8	3923.1	.	2296.2	4111.8	.	2486.7	4085.6	.
Economic growth									
Gross domestic product	1.4	2.8	-1.4	2.0	2.6	-0.6	2.0	2.6	-0.6
Per capita GDP	0.7	1.1	-0.5	1.3	1.2	0.1	1.3	1.2	0.2
Industrial production	1.2	0.7	0.5	3.1	0.9	2.3	2.9	0.9	2.0
Agricultural production	3.4	1.6	1.8	0.8	3.1	-2.2	1.1	2.7	-1.6
Consumption	-0.3	4.0	-4.3	1.2	1.5	-0.3	1.5	1.4	0.0
Per capita consumption	-1.0	2.3	-3.3	0.6	0.0	0.5	0.8	-0.0	0.9
Investment	-2.0	5.8	-7.8	1.5	-2.7	4.2	1.7	-2.2	3.9
Aggregate expenditure	-0.9	4.3	-5.1	1.3	0.1	1.3	1.5	0.1	1.4
Export performance									
Export growth	-1.1	1.9	-3.0	3.1	5.5	-2.4	2.7	5.6	-2.9
Import substitution									
Import/GDP ratio	22.4	50.9	-28.5	26.4	43.0	-16.7	25.4	42.8	-17.3
Investment and savings									
Domestic saving/GDP	35.9	24.0	11.9	39.6	22.9	16.6	39.6	22.9	16.7
Private saving/GDP	36.3	29.1	7.2	39.6	27.8	11.8	39.6	27.8	11.8

Public saving/GDP	-0.4	-3.6	3.1	0.0	-5.0	5.0	0.0	-5.0	5.0
Investment/GDP	38.1	29.3	8.8	38.1	23.0	15.2	38.3	22.9	15.4
Foreign saving/GDP	2.3	5.4	-3.1	-1.4	0.0	-1.5	-1.4	-0.0	-1.3
Balance of payments									
Current account/GDP	-2.0	-3.9	1.9	1.5	-1.7	3.3	1.5	-1.7	3.3
Basic balance/GDP	-0.7	1.4	-2.1	0.7	0.9	-0.2	0.7	0.9	-0.2
Overall balance/GDP	-1.1	0.5	-1.6	0.3	0.2	0.1	0.3	0.2	0.1
External debt									
External debt/exports	140.5	108.5	32.0	142.7	147.8	-5.1	131.1	147.8	-16.7
Debt service/exports	25.0	14.3	10.7	21.8	21.1	0.7	21.1	21.1	-0.0
Inflation									
Wholesale prices	32.3	37.2	-4.9	70.5	68.5	2.0	70.5	57.3	13.3
Consumer prices	34.1	22.8	11.3	72.2	38.6	33.7	72.2	32.3	40.0
Monetary policy									
Money supply growth	28.7	23.9	4.9	66.3	39.1	27.2	66.3	39.9	26.5
Real discount rate	-18.8	-2.9	-15.9	-9.8	2.3	-12.1	-9.8	2.1	-11.9
Fiscal policy									
Gov. revenue/GDP	8.6	30.2	-21.5	7.0	31.4	-24.4	7.0	31.4	-24.4
Gov. expenditure/GDP	9.1	33.8	-24.7	7.0	36.4	-29.5	7.0	36.4	-29.5
Budget surplus/GDP	-0.4	-3.6	3.1	0.0	-5.0	5.0	0.0	-5.0	5.0

Part III

The Public Sector in Developing Countries

5 Public Enterprises in Developing Countries: Issues of Privatization*

INTRODUCTION

There has been a sea change in attitudes towards public enterprises around the world in recent years. In Western Europe, the United Kingdom and, since April 1986, France have set out to privatize public enterprises on a large scale. In the case of France, this represents not only a reversal of the nationalizations undertaken by the previous socialist government in 1981, but companies nationalized in 1945 are also being privatized.

At the same time, there is little indication that the Labour party in Britain or the Socialist party in France would undo the denationalizations that are being carried out, if they were returned to power. Furthermore, in European countries with socialist-oriented governments, such as Austria, Finland, and Spain, several public enterprises are being privatized or their privatization is envisaged.

Attitudes have been changing in the developing countries as well. While many of these countries, whether their government professed itself to be socialist or not, had considered public enterprise as the mainstay of economic development, there has been an increasing disillusionment with public enterprises in recent years and proposals have been made for privatization in various areas.

This chapter will attempt to provide an explanation for the change in attitudes towards public enterprises in the developing countries, draw the lessons of developing-country experience with public enterprises and with privatization, and indicate possible future changes. The discussion will be limited to manufacturing industries, excluding natural resource products which are often considered the preserve of the state; public utilities which as natural monopolies are owned or

---

* Originally published in *Public Finance and Performance of Enterprises*, edited by Manfred Neumann and Karl W. Roskamp, Detroit, Wayne University Press, 1989, pp. 417–33.

regulated by the state throughout the world; and services on which there are limited data.

The first section of the chapter will provide information on the relative importance of public enterprises in the manufacturing sector of the developing countries. The second section will consider possible reasons for the trend towards privatization, with the third section concentrating on efficiency differences between public and private enterprises. In turn, the fourth section will review the record of the developing countries with privatization and the final section will examine prospects for the future.

PUBLIC ENTERPRISES IN THE MANUFACTURING SECTOR OF THE DEVELOPING COUNTRIES

Table 5.1 contains data on the relative shares of public enterprises in the manufacturing sector of the developing countries.[1] Apart from Ghana, where only gross output figures are available, the production data refer to value added and are, on the whole, internationally comparable.[2] However, for a number of countries, there are investment but not production data. Investment data generally overstate the share of public enterprises, which tend to be in capital-intensive industries. Thus, in 1982, public enterprises accounted for 42 percent of the gross domestic product and for 66 percent of gross fixed investment in eight developing countries, on the average (Ayub and Hegstad, 1986, p. 77).[3]

In the 1970s, the share of public enterprises in the manufacturing sector of the industrial countries was the highest in Austria (23 percent), followed by Italy (19 percent), Portugal (12 percent), and France (11 percent). The French ratio reached 33 percent following the nationalizations of 1981, but it has been declining since as a result of denationalizations undertaken by the new government. At the other end of the spectrum, the ratio was practically nil in Belgium, 1 percent in Greece, 4 percent in Australia, and 5 percent in the United Kingdom in the late 1970s.[4]

Among developing countries, the share of public enterprises in the manufacturing sector exceeds 90 percent in Iraq and Syria; it was above this level in Egypt in the mid-1970s but declined to 80 percent by 1979. The share of public enterprises in the manufacturing sector is in the 50–60 percent range in Ethiopia and Burma.

All these countries, together with Tanzania, where the share of

Table 5.1   Relative shares of public enterprises in the
manufacturing sector

		Year	Relative share (percent)
Industrial countries			
Australia	GDP	1978–9	4.0
Austria	GDP	1970–5	23.0*
Belgium	GDI	1978–9	0.4
France	GDI	1971	11.4*
Greece	GDP	1979	1.3
Ireland	GDI	1974–7	9.4
Italy	GDI	1978	18.6*
Portugal	GDP	1976	12.0
United Kingdom	GDI	1978–81	5.3
Sub-Saharan Africa			
Ethiopia	GDP	1979–80	60.9
Ghana	GDP	1970	32.9
Ivory Coast	GDP	1979	25.2*
Kenya	GDP	1970–3	13.1
Senegal	GDP	1974	19.0
Sierra Leone	GDP	1979	14.2
Tanzania	GDP	1974–7	37.9
North Africa and Middle East			
Egypt	GDI	1979	80.4*
Iraq	GDI	1975	96.7
Morocco	GDI	1974–6	26.2
Syria	GDI	1975	95.9
Tunisia	GDP	1982	31.4
Turkey	GDP	1979	30.1
Yemen Arab Rep.	GDI	1975–6	59.5
Asia			
Bangladesh	GDP	1981–2	46.1
Burma	GDP	1980	56.2
India	GDP	1978	15.7
Korea	GDP	1974–7	14.9
Nepal	GDP	1974–5	4.4
Pakistan	GDP	1974–5	7.8
Singapore	GDP	1972	14.2
Sri Lanka	GDP	1974	33.2
Taiwan	GDP	1985	12.0
Thailand	GDP	1970–3	5.2
Latin America			
Bolivia	GDP	1973–5	5.9
Venezuela	GDP	1985	16.2

* including mining.

Sources: Short (1984) and World Bank data files.

public enterprises rose from 15 percent in 1966–8 to 38 percent in 1974–7, profess themselves to be socialist. In turn, the share of public enterprises in the manufacturing sector is 33 percent in Ghana, 31 percent in Tunisia, and 30 percent in Turkey, which are considered mixed economies.

While India has also been influenced by socialist ideas, the share of public enterprises in its manufacturing sector (16 percent) is not much higher than in Korea (15 percent) and in Taiwan (12 percent). But, the direction of change has been different, with the share of public enterprises rising from 13 percent in 1970–3 to 16 percent in 1978 in India and declining from 56 percent in 1952 to 12 percent in 1985 in Taiwan.[5]

The share of public enterprises in the manufacturing sector does not reach 10 percent in Nepal, Sri Lanka, and Thailand. It was below this level also in Pakistan in the mid-1970s, when a number of textile mills were nationalized under Bhutto's socialist-leaning government, some of which have since been reprivatized. In turn, the 46 percent share of public enterprises in the manufacturing sector of Bangladesh has been substantially reduced as a result of the denationalizations undertaken since that time.

In socialist developing countries, the tendency has been for public enterprises to dominate the manufacturing sector. In other developing countries, tobacco and, often, sugar, alcoholic beverages, and cement are in public ownership. Such is frequently the case also for petroleum refining, pharmaceuticals, fertilizer, and iron and steel, in countries where these industries exist. Furthermore, there are government printing presses in many developing countries and in a number of cases the public sector includes textile factories.

The existing situation reflects past decisions that have responded to a variety of considerations. In some industries, such as tobacco, sugar, and alcoholic beverages, public enterprises have been used to indirectly tax consumption. Industries such as steel are often in the public sector because they are considered to be of strategic importance for economic development. There are again others, such as petroleum refining, fertilizer, and cement, where high-capital requirements have led to the establishment of public enterprises. Elsewhere, the creation of public enterprises has been rationalized by reference to the alleged lack of private entrepreneurs. Finally, for social reasons, developing-country governments have taken over private firms in difficulties in a variety of industries.

REASONS FOR PRIVATIZATION

Various reasons have been put forward to explain changes in attitudes towards privatization in recent years. It has been suggested that ideology, and changes thereof, has played an important role, in particular in France and the United Kingdom. Also, budgetary considerations have often been cited as reasons for privatization. Finally, it has been noted that private enterprises tend to be more efficient than their public counterparts.

While the relevance of ideology cannot be denied in the case of France and the United Kingdom, objective factors have importantly entered decision-making in these cases.[6] Furthermore, as noted in the introduction, there is little expectation that renationalization would be undertaken in the two countries in the event of a change in government and, in Western Europe, privatization is carried out by socialist-oriented governments as well. In developing countries also, privatization by and large cuts across the political spectrum, including for example Egypt and Tanzania, although it is not envisaged at this time in some Middle Eastern and African socialist countries.

As to budgetary considerations, in the 1974–7 period, for which data are available, public enterprises in developing countries had an overall deficit averaging 5.4 percent of their gross domestic product.[7] This result reflects the fact that the small current account surpluses of these enterprises, averaging 0.6 percent of GDP before depreciation and government transfers, financed only a fraction of their investments that accounted for the deficit on the capital account of public enterprises equal to 6.0 percent of the developing countries' GDP, on the average. In fact, the current account surplus of public enterprises in the developing countries did not even cover depreciation, averaging 1.1 percent of their GDP.

Yet, the data overstate the current account surplus of the public enterprises as they do not allow for the credit preferences many of them receive. Also, the data include mineral-rich countries, such as Chile, Gambia, Guyana, Venezuela, and Zambia, where public enterprise revenues comprise substantial royalties from the sale of petroleum, copper, bauxite, and other minerals.

Budgetary subsidies and borrowing from the government financed, on the average, slightly over one-half of the overall deficit of public enterprises in the developing countries in the 1974–7 period, when these enterprises accounted for three-fourths of the public sector deficit. The rest of the financing was provided in more or less equal proportions by foreign and domestic borrowing, the latter from banks and in capital markets.

Foreign borrowing assumed particular importance after 1973, contributing substantially to the rising external indebtedness of the developing countries. Thus, in the three largest Latin American countries, Argentina, Brazil, and Mexico, public enterprises hold over one-half of the country's external debt (Balassa *et al.*, 1986, Table 4.4). It has also been reported that public enterprises contracted one-third of developing country borrowing on capital markets in 1976–8 (World Bank, 1980).

Furthermore, public enterprises account for a large proportion of domestic bank credit. It has been noted that, for countries for which data are available, the average share of public enterprise credit in total domestic credit rose by 20 percentage points between the early 1970s and the end of the 1970s to a level of almost 30 percent (Short, 1984, p. 176).

Public enterprises in developing countries, then, simultaneously increased their foreign and domestic borrowing during the 1970s. These results reflect the rising financial requirements of these enterprises, associated with their growing deficits (Short, 1984; Balassa, *et al.*, 1986, ch. 4). With the drying up of foreign loans following the debt crisis of 1982, these deficits have come to be financed increasingly from domestic sources, thereby raising the spectre of "crowding out" for the private sector.

Budgetary and, more generally, financial considerations have thus contributed to the change in attitudes towards public enterprises in the developing countries. But, privatization will not reduce the financial burden that public enterprises represent, unless their performance can be improved. In fact, there are cases, such as Tunisia, where private firms are not willing to take over public enterprises unless the government undertakes their rationalization beforehand.

THE RELATIVE EFFICIENCY OF PUBLIC AND PRIVATE ENTERPRISES

Budgetary and financial issues, then, lead to the question of the relative efficiency of public and private enterprises. Efficiency comparisons should ideally be made in cases where public and private enterprises carry out the same economic activity. There are few such comparisons for the industrial countries, and they generally relate to public utilities and service industries.

A recent study, which has taken particular care in selecting among empirical investigations those which compare identical activities and use appropriate indicators of efficiency, has found 17 cases where private enterprises were more efficient than public enterprises, six where the opposite was the case, and five where no difference could be discerned (Yarrow, 1986).[8] The 28 cases investigated included only one manufacturing industry, steel, where the private sector has been shown to be more efficient than the public sector.

The virtual lack of efficiency comparisons for manufacturing industries in the industrial countries is indicative of the fact that in these countries public and private enterprise can be found side by side mostly in public utilities and service industries. In developing countries, comparisons in the service sector have been made for 33 development finance companies (DFC). The study concludes that "the private DFCs are markedly more vigorous and efficient than state-owned institutions in mobilizing domestic resources" (Gordon, 1983, p. 38) and generally have a much higher level of profitability (ibid., p. 32). At the same time, for selected developing countries, information is available on manufacturing enterprises in the public sector.

In the case of Brazil, it has been reported that the rate of return on equity in public enterprises was one-half that in private enterprises in 1974 and in 1978. Also, in Israel, before-tax profits averaged 1.6 percent on sales in public enterprises, compared with 11.6 percent in private enterprises, in 1976–8 (Ayub and Hegstad, 1986, p. 15). Finally, in India, public enterprises in the manufacturing sector earned a rate of return of just over 2 percent, while private firms earned a rate of return of over 9 percent, in 1976 (Choksi, 1979, pp. 23–4).

Yet, the profit figures overstate the efficiency of public enterprises that pay very low, and even nil, interest on public loans in the three countries. Also, no adjustment has been made for differences between market and shadow prices. Such adjustments have been made in the case of public enterprises in 26 Egyptian manufacturing industries, for which financial and economic rates of return have been calculated for fiscal year 1980/1. The results show considerable differences between the two sets of calculations, reflecting the importance of price distortions in Egypt. They also indicate that, on balance, differences between market and shadow prices have raised financial over economic rates of return in Egyptian public enterprises. Thus, while only one-half of public industries had a financial rate of return of less than 10 percent, one-half of them had a negative rate of economic return (Shirley, 1983, p. 33). Although comparisons with private firms are not available, this result puts the Egyptian public enterprises in the manufacturing sector in an unfavorable light.

Comparisons of various performance indicators for public and private firms have been made for Turkey. The results show that, in 1979, labor productivity was 30 percent higher in private than in public enterprises, even though the latter had a capital–labor ratio 50 percent higher (Shirley, 1983, p. 16). Another study showed that, in 1976, public enterprises utilized 1 percent more labor and 44 percent more capital per unit of output than private enterprises in the Turkish manufacturing sector (Krueger and Tuncer, 1980, p. 43).

These results are confirmed by estimates of economic rates of return for 123 Turkish manufacturing firms in 1981. In manufacturing, taken as a whole, the economic rate of return averaged -0.7 percent in public enterprises and 6.2 percent in private enterprises. Only in two sectors (iron and steel products and electrical machinery) out of 14 was the economic rate of return higher in the public than in the private sector; rates of return were equal for textiles.

At the same time, public enterprises were favored by the system of incentives applied. Thus, the effective rate of subsidy, indicating the combined effects of import protection, tax, and credit performances, averaged 31 percent in the public sector and 49 percent in the private sector. The incentive measures applied, then, benefited the largely inefficient public enterprises at the expense of private enterprises (Yagci, 1984, pp. 86 and 97).

Firm-by-firm comparisons of efficiency levels for Brazil, India, Indonesia, and Tanzania also show the superiority of private over public enterprises. In the case of the Brazilian plastics and steel industries, the level of technical efficiency was shown to be lower in public than in private firms (Tyler, 1979). In India, it was found that productivity in the fertilizer industry was lower in the public than in the private sector, and the differences were explained only in part by higher input costs due to the government imposing the use of high-cost domestically-produced feedstock on public enterprises and by outdated technology stemming from the lack of renewal of old equipment (Gupta, 1982).

In the Indonesian manufacturing sector, production costs in public

enterprises were shown to be generally higher than in private enterprises (Funkhouser and MacAvoy, 1979). In particular, "by almost
any indicator, the economic performance of the state mills has been
inferior to that of private mills" in weaving (Hill, 1982, p. 1015).
Finally, a study of more than 300 firms in ten Tanzanian industries
has found that 23 out of 32 public enterprises used both more capital
and more labor than privately-owned firms in the same industry
(Perkins, 1983).

A variety of factors account for the apparent poor performance of
public enterprises in the manufacturing sector of the developing
countries, some of which have been referred to already in regard to
particular cases. A comparative study lists "(i) inadequate planning
and poor feasibility studies resulting in ill-conceived investments; (ii)
lack of skilled managers and administrators; (iii) centralized decision
making; (iv) state intervention in the day-to-day operation of the
firm; (v) unclear multiple objectives; and (vi) political patronage"
(Choksi, 1979, p. iv). One may add overmanning, the payment of
excessively high wages and/or social benefits, slowness in decision-
making, and the lack of the threat of bankruptcy. All these factors
are related to two basic conditions: the absence of clear-cut objectives for managers and state intervention in firm decision-making.

Profits are never the sole, and are often a subsidiary, objective of
public enterprises in the developing countries. This means that there is
little incentive to reduce costs and to improve technology. The situation
is aggravated by the lack of the threat of bankruptcy, which provides the
ultimate penalty for poor performance in private enterprise.

Public enterprises are also called upon to serve social goals, such as
the regionalization of industry and increased employment, or political objectives, such as favoring the members of a particular race and
party and augmenting military power. At the same time, the relative
importance of economic, social, and political objectives is far from
being unambiguous and it may show changes even in the lifetime of
the same administration and, in particular, following changes in
government.

The overmanning often observed in the public enterprises of developing countries may also be the result of demands by the supervising authorities to hire – or not to fire – labor. The lack of managerial
independence further leads to slowness in decision-making and to
conflicts in sequential decisions. Finally, the dependence of managers
on the government in power will induce them to pursue short-term
objectives at the expense of long-term targets.

THE STATUS OF PRIVATIZATION IN DEVELOPING COUNTRIES

It may be suggested, then, that the observed shortcomings of public enterprises, resulting in their relatively low efficiency, have importantly motivated the movement towards privatization. But why the sudden change in attitudes? Has information not been available for a sufficiently long period on the performance of public enterprises?[9]

It may be claimed that evidence on the relative inefficiency of public enterprises has accumulated over time, increasing its weight and hence its effect on decision-makers. Also, the increasing losses of public economic enterprises, which occurred parallel to the growing budgetary stringency associated with the debt crisis, have made governments recognize the cost of public enterprises to the budget and to the national economy. But, the principal reason may lie in changes in development strategies.

Privatization should be seen as part and parcel of the shift in development strategies initiated in a number of countries, involving greater outward orientation. This shift, necessitating improvements in efficiency, has led to proposals for privatization as private enterprise is considered to be better able to respond to the stick and carrot of competition, which is seen as a condition of improved efficiency.

This is the case, in particular, in regard to foreign markets where private enterprises are well-placed to take the risks and reap the rewards of success in exporting. In fact, it has been shown that, in the 1970–81 period, export growth was negatively correlated with the share of public enterprises in the gross domestic product (GDP) and in gross domestic investment (GDI) of developing countries. The regression coefficient, estimated in a cross-section investigation of 21 countries in the first case and 38 countries in the second, is statistically significant at the 2 percent and the 1 percent level, respectively (Nunnenkamp, 1986, p. 190).

In the same study, a negative correlation has been obtained between the share of public enterprise in GDP and in GDI, on the one hand, and the growth of GDP and that of GDI, on the other, although the results are not significant statistically. Statistically significant results have been obtained, however, in a multiple regression analysis of 73 developing countries, which included the GDP growth rate as dependent variable and per capita incomes, population, the domestic savings ratio, foreign aid, and the index of state intervention as explanatory variables.

The index of state intervention has been defined as a combination of the extent of state regulations in industry and the extent of nationalization. The regression coefficient of this variable has been consistently negative and highly significant, under the various specifications used in the study, for both the 1960–70 and the 1970–80 periods (Singh, 1985, p. 223).

One explanation for the observed negative relationship between state intervention and economic growth is the higher efficiency of private as against public investment. In fact, a study of 27 developing countries has shown the existence of a positive correlation between the share of private investment in the total and the rate of growth of GDP in the 1971–9 period (Blejer and Khan, 1984, p. 27).

The next question concerns the privatization programs of developing countries and the extent to which these plans have been implemented. Table 5.2 provides information on planned sales to private interests and on sales actually accomplished, as well as on closings and liquidations and on leases and management contracts with private interests. The table excludes the sale of 133 enterprises in Chile during the 1970s, representing more than one-fourth of the net worth of the 250 largest Chilean private firms (Shirley, 1983, pp. 57–8); the privatization of jute and textile mills, representing some 40 percent of capacity and about 1000 smaller businesses in 1982 in Bangladesh; and the reprivatization of some 2000 rice, flour, and cotton mills in Pakistan following the nationalizations of the 1970s (Young, 1986, pp. 25–7).

The table shows that limited progress has been made so far in implementing privatization programs in the developing countries. The opposition of vested interests, the poor financial situation of the enterprises to be privatized, the political obstacles to their rationalization and the limited availability of private capital, have all contributed to the delays that have been encountered.

In fact, a considerable number of actions have involved the closing-down of inefficient public enterprises rather than their sale and, more often than not, the sales have entailed reprivatization rather than the divestiture of firms that were originally established as public enterprises. Finally, as shown in Table 5.2, there have been relatively few instances of leasing or management contracts.

Table 5.2   Trade-weighted averages of standard deviations of exchange
rates in bilateral relationships, 1970–86

| | Nominal exchange rates | | Real exchange rates | |
	Actual rate	Trade-weighted rate	Actual rate	Trade-weighted rate
Benin	5.535	5.579	n.a.	n.a.
Burkina Faso	2.996	3.850	8.75	8.26
Cameroon	3.524	3.900	4.75	5.06
Central African Republic	3.046	3.926	4.22	3.85
Congo	4.198	4.822	6.07	5.81
Côte d'Ivoire	4.583	5.008	7.38	6.86
Gabon	6.145	8.642	8.39	7.97
Mali	2.005	2.730	n.a.	n.a.
Niger	3.917	6.091	8.41	8.16
Senegal	3.219	4.378	7.50	6.81
Chad	3.728	4.437	n.a.	n.a.
Togo	4.644	4.774	7.14	7.04
Egypt	23.661	6.650	24.88	7.12
El Salvador	28.699	7.705	8.01	7.19
Ethiopia	8.623	7.187	10.11	9.87
Guatemala	7.423	8.709	7.54	8.06
Haiti	3.720	4.967	6.76	6.56
Honduras	4.948	6.246	5.19	5.37
Iraq	12.367	9.871	n.a.	n.a.
Liberia	8.613	6.078	7.63	6.75
Nicaragua	55.249	8.426	n.a.	n.a.
Oman	11.674	6.528	n.a.	n.a.
Panama	6.100	7.610	5.88	6.98
Paraguay	18.743	22.487	15.96	22.25
Peru	53.016	9.922	14.41	19.36
Syria	10.906	6.829	n.a.	n.a.
Trinidad and Tobago	13.106	3.706	7.27	5.68
Venezuela	15.606	5.411	13.66	4.85
Vietnam	349.725	6.172	n.a.	n.a.
Yemen, Arab Republic	11.291	6.182	n.a.	n.a.
Yemen, P.D.	7.734	6.324	n.a.	n.a.

Source: World Bank data base.

PROSPECTS FOR THE FUTURE

Just as in recent years, the closing-down option will have to be
invoked in the future in cases where the conditions of a public
enterprise are beyond repair. At the same time, the political obstacles to closing down large firms may be surmounted through their

division into smaller units, some of which will be viable and others not. As to privatization, it should be emphasized that selling some of the shares of a public enterprise while retaining control in the public sector, as in the case of Petrobas in Brazil, does not constitute privatization. Rather, such sales reduce the availability of finance for the private sector, thereby contributing to "crowding out."

Privatization should be defined as involving the transfer of control. It may not mean selling all shares to private interests, in particular in countries where the availability of domestic capital is limited. It has been reported, for example, that in Zambia 50:50 joint ventures are invariably managed by the private partner (Berg and Shirley, 1986, p. 1).

At the same time, one would have to create the appropriate conditions for privatization. This would necessitate, first of all, establishing clear and unambiguous procedural rules and applying these rules in practice. The rules should provide for the valuation of the enterprises to be privatized by an independent body, which may use auctioning or other methods appropriate for the conditions of the country concerned. This will prevent both underpricing (as happened in Chile after 1974) and putting an unreasonable value on assets of questionable productivity (there may be need, in fact, to set a notional price as it was done in one case in Canada).

It may also be desirable for the state to undertake the rationalization of the enterprise prior to privatization, so as to eliminate its excessive debt and to reduce overmanning. It may not be expected that firms whose debt exceeds the value of assets would be taken over by private interests. Reductions in the labor force should also be effected before privatization, unless agreement is reached with the labor unions on a timetable for subsequent reductions in manning levels.

Domestic financial limitations may hinder privatization in developing countries, in particular in low-income countries. At the same time, combining privatization with democratization may bear fruit, e.g. in selling state-owned farms to peasants and selling public trading companies engaged in the marketing of agricultural produce and inputs to producers – just as council houses have been sold to their occupants in Britain. These cases have been noted in regard to sub-Saharan Africa, where possibilities exist also in privatizing local industry and fishing[10] notwithstanding the stringency of domestic financial limitations.

Furthermore, the example of France indicates that privatization may be used to revitalize the stock market.[11] It is also the intention of

Pakistani policy-makers to use privatization as a means to strengthen the stock market. And, the sale of bonds secured by revenues from the sale of the Bosphorus Bridge and the Keban Dam are said to have contributed to the revitalization of the bond market in Turkey.

In indebted countries, debt–equity conversions offer potentialities for privatization, involving the country's own nationals who have funds abroad as well as foreigners. More generally, the domestic financing of privatization may be complemented by foreign financing. Apart from well-established cases of national interest, there is no reason to discriminate against foreign capital in the process of privatization.

Consideration may nevertheless be given to leasing or management contracts as alternatives to privatization, with the contracts awarded through auctions, an option that has long been proposed (Demsetz, 1968). It has been used more recently in socialist countries, in particular Hungary, where ideological considerations limit the sale of public assets.

At the same time, for privatization to succeed, certain policy conditions should be met. In particular, there is need for policy reform in developing countries where the system of incentives is biased against exports and in favor of import substitution. While reform efforts have contributed to the process of privatization in these countries, the success of privatization is conditioned on the full implementation of these reforms.

There is further need to strengthen and, where it is lacking, to establish competition in order to derive the benefits of privatization. Without competition, profit maximization by the newly-established private firms may not serve the national interest.[12] In fact, it has been shown that the superiority of private enterprises over public enterprises is the most evident in competitive industries (Yarrow, 1986).

For similar reasons, in the absence of privatization, establishing competitive conditions for public enterprises would lead to improvements in efficiency. Such a direction is being taken by the Hungarian policy-makers. But this can be successfully done only if the management of public enterprises is made independent of the government and it is given appropriate incentives to maximize profits.

The independence of managers can be ensured if they are made responsible to a board of directors, in which the government representatives are in a minority. At the same time, linking the remuneration of management to the firm's profits and establishing the possibility of bankruptcy would provide the carrot and the stick of competition, provided that provisions are simultaneously made for free entry and/or the breaking up of large firms and for import liberalization. Also, the existing privileges of public enterprises in matters of credit and taxation should be eliminated, putting them on an equal footing with private firms.

The question remains, however, if one can establish truly competitive conditions for public enterprises while maintaining public ownership. This question has been much debated in Hungary and while there are some examples of highly efficient public enterprises in developing countries, e.g. in Brazil, a knowledgeable observer of the African scene has expressed skepticism as to the prospects for industrial development via public enterprise.[13]

CONCLUSIONS

This chapter has noted the significant role public enterprises play in the manufacturing sector of the developing countries. These enterprises have often been considered the mainstay of economic development and have assumed particular importance in industries that are seen as being of strategic importance for industrialization as well as in highly capital-intensive industries.

Over time, public enterprises have come to constitute an increasing financial burden for the developing countries, however. Also, with the drying up of foreign loans, their deficits have been increasingly financed from domestic sources, thereby raising the spectre of "crowding out" the private sector.

The poor financial performance of public enterprises to a large extent reflects their relative inefficiency *vis-à-vis* private enterprises, which is documented by the experience of a number of developing countries. Privatization, then, may be regarded as a response to perceived differences in efficiency between private and public enterprises. And, while it is given urgency by the difficult financial situation of public enterprises, it is part and parcel of the shift in development strategies initiated in a number of developing countries, involving greater outward orientation, which requires improved efficiency.

At the same time, for privatization to be successful, it is necessary to establish the conditions of competition. One would further need to overcome the obstacles to privatization in the form of the opposition of vested interests, the poor financial situation of the enterprises to be privatized, the political obstacles to rationalization, and the limitations of domestic private capital.

It has been suggested that, in the absence of privatization, consideration be given to leasing or management contracts, to closing down firms where the conditions are without repair, and to improving the operation of public enterprises. Effecting such improvements, in turn, would require complete independence and improved incentives for managers while exposing them to domestic and foreign competition. The question remains, however, if this can be accomplished while maintaining public ownership.

Notes

1. For purposes of comparison, the table also includes data for the industrial countries, whenever available.
2. In several cases, mining is included with manufacturing. But, in the countries in question mining is generally of little importance and hence it can be disregarded in the discussion.
3. The data include mining and manufacturing.
4. This explains that, apart from British Telecom, the British denationalizations have related largely to public utilities and transportation.
5. During the period under consideration, no change occurred in Korea.
6. In the case of France, expectations for increased efficiency and reduced bureaucratic interference have been given as reasons for privatization (see Balassa, 1987).
7. Unless otherwise noted, the data derive from Short, 1984, Tables 5 to 8. While the country coverage of the tables varies somewhat, the data are by and large comparable.
8. Within the last group there was one case where public enterprise may be slightly favored.
9. In this connection, reference may be made to a statement by Adam Smith in *The Wealth of Nations*, according to which "In every great monarchy in Europe the sale of the crown lands would produce a very large sum of money, which, if applied to the payment of the public debts, would deliver from mortgage a much greater revenue than any which those lands have ever afforded to the crown. . . . When the crown lands had become private property, they would, in the course of a few years, become well improved and well cultivated" (cited in Yarrow, 1986, p. 324).
10. It has been reported that, after collectively purchased motor boats had been sold to fishermen, the share of boats in operating condition rose from 15 percent to 85 percent, with corresponding increases in output (Berg, 1986, p. 18).
11. The success of the present French government to do so has disproved the

contention of the supporters of the socialist government that the French stock market would not be able to absorb the shares offered in the course of privatizing large enterprises (Balassa, 1987).

12. As suggested in the case of the United Kingdom (Kay and Thompson, 1986, p. 25), efficiency may conceivably deteriorate rather than improve as a result.

13. "To an African Government contemplating the creation of a substantial public sector as a means of promoting industrialization the advice of this writer would have to be: don't do it; there are better ways of stimulating industrial growth. A large industrial public sector will contribute little to dynamic industrial growth, will tend to become a drain on the public finances, will require a net inflow of resources to cover its capital requirements and will discourage the growth of private industry" (Killick, 1983, p. 87).

References

Ayub, Mahmood Ali and Sven Olef Hegstad, "Public Industrial Enterprises. Determinants of Performance," Industry and Finance Series Volume 17, Washington, DC, World Bank, July 1986.

Balassa, Bela "French Economic Policy Since March 1986," *The Tocqueville Review*, 1987 and, in French translation, *Commentaire*, Eté, 1987.

Balassa, Bela, Gerardo M. Bueno, Pedro-Pablo Kuczynski, and Mario Henrique Simonsen, *Toward Renewed Economic Growth in Latin America*, Washington, DC, Institute for International Economics, 1986.

Berg, Elliot, "Private Sector Potential in Africa," *Journal of Economic Growth*, Third Quarter 1986, pp. 17–23.

Berg, Elliot and Mary M. Shirley, "Divestiture in Developing Countries" Washington, DC, 1986 (unpublished manuscript).

Blejer, Mario I. and Mohsin S. Khan, "Private Investment in Developing Countries," *Finance and Development*, June 1984, pp. 26–9.

Choksi, Armeane M., "State Intervention in the Industrialization of Developing Countries. Selected Issues," World Bank Staff Working Paper No. 341, Washington, DC, July 1979.

Demsetz, Harold, "Why Regulate Utilities?" *Journal of Law and Economics*, April 1968, pp. 55–65.

Funkhouser, R. and MacAvoy Paul W., "A Sample of Observations on Comparative Prices in Public and Private Enterprise," *Journal of Public Economics*, 1979, pp. 353–68.

Gordon, David L., "Development Finance Companies, State and Privately Owned," World Bank Staff Working Paper No. 578, Washington, DC, July 1983.

Gupta, M., "Productivity Performance of the Public and the Private Sectors in India: A Case Study of the Fertilizer Industry," *Indian Economic Review*, 1982.

Hemming, Richard and Ali M. Mansoor, "Privatization and Public Enterprises," IMF Working Paper No. WP/87/9. Washington, DC, International Monetary Fund, 25 February 1987 (unpublished manuscript).

Hill, Hal, "State Enterprises in a Competitive Industry: An Indonesian Case Study," *World Development*, November 1982, pp. 1015–23.

Interamerican Development Bank, *External Debt and Economic Development in Latin America: Background and Prospects*, 1984.

Kay, J.A. and D.J. Thompson, "Privatization: A Policy in Search of a Rationale," *Economic Journal*, March 1986, pp. 18–32.

Killick, Tony, "The Role of the Public Sector in the Industrialization of African Developing Countries," *Industry and Development No. 7*, New York, United Nations, 1983, pp. 57–88.

Krueger, Anne O. and Baran Tuncer, "Estimating Total Factor Productivity Growth in a Developing Country," World Bank Staff Working Paper No. 422, Washington, DC, October 1980.

Nunnenkamp, Peter, "State Enterprise in Developing Countries," *Intereconomics*, July–August 1986, pp. 186–97.

Perkins, F.S., "Technology Choice, Industrialization, and Development Experiences in Tanzania," *Journal of Developing Studies*, January 1983, pp. 213–47.

Shirley, Mary M., "Managing State-Owned Enterprises," World Bank Staff Working Paper No. 577, Washington, DC, July 1983.

Short, R.P., "The Role of Public Enterprise: An International Statistical Comparison," in Robert H. Floyd, Clive S. Gray, and R.P. Short, eds, *Public Enterprise in Mixed Economies*, Washington, DC, International Monetary Fund, 1984, pp. 110–196.

Singh, Ram D., "State Intervention, Foreign Economic Aid, Savings and Growth in LDCs: Some Recent Evidence," *Kyklos*, 1985(2), pp. 216–32.

Tyler, William G., "Technical Efficiency in Production in a Developing Country: An Empirical Examination of the Brazilian Plastics and Steel Industries," *Oxford Economic Papers*, November 1979, pp. 477–85.

World Bank, *Borrowing in International Capital Markets*, Washington, DC, January 1980.

Yagci, Fahrettin, "Protection and Incentives in Turkish Manufacturing. An Evaluation of Policies and their Impact in 1981," World Bank Staff Working Paper No. 660, Washington, DC, July 1984.

Yarrow, George, "Privatization in Theory and Practice," *Economic Policy*, April 1986, pp. 323–70.

Young, Peter, "Privatization in LDCs: A Solution that Works," *Journal of Economic Growth*, Third Quarter 1986, pp. 24–30.

6 Public Finance and Economic Development*

INTRODUCTION

This chapter will analyze the interrelationships of public finance and economic development. The following aspects of public finance will be considered: the budget deficit (or surplus), the size of the public sector, and public investment. Apart from the financing of the budget deficit, the chapter will examine its possible effects on various economic variables. The relationship between the size of the government budget and economic growth will also be analyzed. Finally, the impact of public investment on private investment, total investment, and economic growth will be investigated.

A budget deficit may be financed through external borrowing, money creation, or internal borrowing; in the latter two cases, there is a corresponding savings surplus in the private sector. According to the Cambridge School, private savings equal private investment *ex ante* as well as *ex post*, so that a budget deficit will generate a trade deficit of equal magnitude, necessitating external borrowing to finance it. This proposition may be transformed into testable hypotheses. One may test for the existence of a positive relationship between the budget deficit and the trade deficit. Furthermore, if the propositions of the Cambridge School hold, one would expect a negative correlation to obtain between the cumulated budget deficit and changes in the foreign debt over time, with allowance made for official and private transfers that do not increase a country's indebtedness.

Alternatively, the budget deficit may be financed through the issue of money. In this event, there will be a positive correlation between the budget deficit and the growth of the (narrowly-defined) money supply. As money creation leads to inflation, it can further be hypothesized that budget deficits will contribute to increases in prices.

---

* Originally published as World Bank Policy, Planning, and Research Working Paper No. 31, August 1988.

The inflationary financing of a budget deficit will absorb private savings. This will also be the case if the budget deficit is financed through domestic borrowing. In either eventuality, the availability of funds for private investment will be reduced and it can be expected that the budget deficit will unfavorably affect private investment. It may further be hypothesized that declines in private investment will have an adverse influence on the rate of economic growth, giving rise to a negative relationship between budget deficits and economic growth.

Thus far, we have been concerned with the economic effects of a budget deficit. Further questions concern the economic implications of the size of the government budget. According to traditional Keynesian textbooks, in the short run there is a balanced budget multiplier: increased government expenditures, financed by taxation, add to national income by their full amount. More recently, it has been shown that the balanced budget multiplier is negative in developed countries as higher taxation reduces profits that, in turn, leads to lower investment. Another channel is the incentive effects of taxation, with higher taxes discouraging work and risk-taking. One may, then, test the hypothesis that the size of the government budget is negatively correlated with economic growth.

Finally, the relationship between public and private investment may be analyzed. This raises questions of complementarity and competition between the two types of investment as well as their relative efficiency. In the first case, the hypothesis is tested if public and private investment are positively or negatively correlated. In the second case, one tests the hypothesis put forward in the development literature that a higher share of public investment is associated with lower investment efficiency. The two hypotheses may also be combined in correlating the relative share of public investment and the rate economic growth.

Apart from reporting on available empirical results, the stated hypotheses will be tested in a cross-section framework for the 1973–84 period. In the regression equations, we will experiment with the introduction of per capita income to test if the relationship is affected by the level of economic development. The sample used in the first section of the chapter includes 21 developed and 94 developing countries, except that a more limited sample has been used in regressions that require data on official and private transfers. Furthermore, in the next two sections, the number of countries covered has been limited by the availability of data on the relevant variables.

Table 6.1   The relationship between the budget deficit and the trade deficit (t-values in parentheses)

	Constant	*Budget deficit*	R^2
(1) Developed countries	1.37 (1.91)Δ	0.44 (3.19)**	0.349
(2) Developing countries	−5.53 (1.97)Δ	0.75 (2.54)*	0.066
(3) All countries	−4.13 (2.44)*	0.73 (2.77)**	0.063

Note: ** 1 percent, * 5 percent, and Δ 10 percent level of significance.

Source: World Bank economic and social data base.

THE FINANCING AND THE ECONOMIC EFFECTS OF BUDGET DEFICITS

As noted in the introduction, a budget deficit may be financed through external borrowing, money creation, and internal borrowing. For lack of data on internal borrowing, only the first two hypotheses could be tested for the entire sample of countries.

The Cambridge School hypothesis on a one-to-one correspondence between the budget deficit and the trade deficit does not receive confirmation from the empirical results. Thus, all the regression coefficients in the estimates linking the trade deficit to the budget deficit are significantly different from (less than) one.

Nevertheless, the results reported in Table 6.1 show that the budget deficit and the trade deficit are positively correlated. This is the case for the developed countries, for the developing countries, and for the two together. The regression coefficients are statistically significant (different from zero) at the 1 percent level in the total and the developed-country regressions and at the 5 percent level in the developing-country regression.

In the case of the developed countries, a dollar increase (decrease) in the budget deficit appears to lead to a 44 cent increase (decrease) in the trade deficit. The apparent effect is larger, 75 cents, for developing countries; it is 73 cents for developed and developing countries, taken together.

The explanatory power of the developing-country and total regressions is, however, very low, with R^2's of 0.07 and 0.06, respectively; it is higher for the developed-country regression (0.35). It would appear that data for the developing countries include a lot of statistical noise. Also, funds for the external financing of the budget deficit may be readily available in some countries but not in others, thereby affecting the results obtained.

In the case of a more limited number of developing countries, for which the relevant data are available, the effects of government budget deficits on changes in the external debt have been investigated over time in the 1973–8 and 1978–82 periods.[1] This has been done under two alternatives: including official and private transfers (for short, transfers) with the change in the external debt as the dependent variable or introducing transfers as an explanatory variable in the regression equation. In the first case, it is hypothesized that government budget deficits are financed through foreign borrowing and transfers; in the second case, it is hypothesized that transfers influence the extent to which the financing of government budget deficits entails foreign borrowing.

Equation (1) of Table 6.2 shows that the sum of the change in the external debt and cumulative transfers is highly correlated with the sum of government budget deficits in both the 1973–8 and the 1978–82 periods. The explanatory power of the regression equation rises – in particular in the second period – if per capita GNP is added as an explanatory variable. As shown in equation (2), this variable has a positive sign, indicating that the possibilities of financing budget deficits by foreign borrowing increase at higher levels of development.[2]

In equation (3), the change in the external debt was regressed on the sum of government budget deficits, the sum of transfers, and per capita GNP. The level of statistical significance of the regression coefficients is relatively high and they have the expected sign, with the negative coefficient for transfers indicating that, for a given budget deficit, higher transfers give rise to less borrowing (significance levels are lower, however, in the second period).

In turn, the effects of the budget deficit on the money supply, inflation, and economic growth could not be ascertained by the econometric investigation of developed and developing countries. However, statistically significant estimates have been obtained as regards the negative effect of the budget deficit on private investment, expressed as a ratio of GDP, in the case of developing countries for which such data are available. The estimates, made for the 24

Table 6.2   Government budget deficits and the external debt
(t-values in parenthesis)

Dependent variables	Independent variables			
Change in the external debt plus sum of transfers (percent of GNP)	Sum of government budget deficits (percent of GNP)	Sum of official and private transfers (percent of GNP)	Per capita GNP initial year ($ million, logs)	R^2
(1a) 1973–8	1.082 (7.953)**			0.657
(1b) 1978–82	0.719 (6.740)**			0.594
(2a) 1973–8	0.899 (4.565)**		1.328 (1.277)	0.664
(2b) 1978–82	0.421 (2.952)**		2.120 (2.830)**	0.669
Change in the external debt (percent of GNP)				
(3a) 1973–8	0.433 (3.688)**	–0.208 (2.352)*	0.864 (1.545)	0.536
(3b) 1978–82	0.205 (2.026)*	–0.228 (1.838)Δ	1.442 (2.823)**	0.506

Note: The change in the external debt refers to the difference between terminal and initial year values; per capita GNP pertains to the initial year of the period; government budget deficits and transfers are cumulated values for each period.
** 1 percent, * 5 percent, and Δ 10 percent level of significance.

Sources: External Debt: Organization for Economic Cooperation and Development, *External Debt of Developing Countries*, various issues. Government Budget Deficit, Official and Private Transfers, Gross National Product, and Population: World Bank economic and social data base.

developing-country sample used in the third section, show the regression coefficient of the budget deficit variable to be statistically significant at the 5 percent level.

All in all, available evidence points to the external financing of a substantial part of the budget deficit. And while its monetary financing could not be ascertained from the data, there is evidence that the budget deficit adversely affects private investment. But, the effects of the budget deficit on the money supply, inflation, and economic growth could not be ascertained from the data.

THE GOVERNMENT BUDGET AND ECONOMIC GROWTH

Knoester (1983) examined the consequences of the postwar expansion of the public sector, financed by direct taxes and social security taxes, in Germany, the Netherlands, the United Kingdom, and the United States by the use of macroeconomic models. He found that in all four countries rates of economic growth declined owing to the shifting forward of these taxes, which reduced profits and ultimately investment.

These results are supported by Eltis (1979) who attributed the "destabilization" of Britain between 1964 and 1973 to the rapid expansion of public spending, accompanied by rapid increases in wages to compensate for higher taxes that financed the rise of public spending.[3] Finally, one may cite the results for Japan, derived by Ihori in a model of utility maximization, according to which "the level of government spending was regarded as too little in the 1960s, but is regarded as too much in recent years for the Japanese economy" (1987, p. 95). Yet, Japan has the lowest share of government spending in GDP among the developed countries.

While his time series investigation led to inconclusive results, in a cross-section investigation of the developed countries in the 1965–77 period, Peterson (1981) also established that tax rates (average as well as marginal) and economic growth rates are negatively correlated. The relationship apparently finds its origin in the high negative correlation between direct tax rates and economic growth rates, while there is a positive correlation (albeit not statistically significant) between indirect taxes and growth rates. The author purports to explain these results with reference to the greater "visibility" of direct taxes as well as by the fact that indirect taxes do not bear on savings.

Marsden (1983) utilized data for seven developed and 13 developing countries for the 1970–9 period. He found a strong negative correlation between the tax–GDP ratio and the GDP growth rate for the entire group of countries as well as for two subgroups of equal size, classified by per capita incomes. The extent of the correlation is reduced if the growth rates of gross domestic investment and the labor force are added as explanatory variables. However, these variables themselves are negatively correlated with the tax–GDP ratio.

Marsden's extended specification was applied by Ram (1986) to all developed and developing countries for which data are available, as well as to developing countries, but he used data on government consumption rather than taxes, the investment–GDP ratio rather than its growth rate, and the rate of population growth rather than the growth of the labor force. The results show the ratio of government consumption to GDP (the government consumption ratio) to be negatively correlated with GDP growth in the 1970–80 period at the 5 percent significance level while a negative sign was obtained but the results were not statistically significant for the 1960–70 period. At the same time, Ram did not follow Marsden in testing for the correlation between government consumption and gross domestic investment.[4]

Ram suggests, however, that an appropriate test would involve using the growth rate of government consumption or that of the government consumption ratio instead of the ratio itself in the estimating equation. In both cases, the estimated coefficients were positive and statistically significant, leading Ram to conclude that "the overall impact of government size on growth is positive in almost all cases" (1986, p. 191).

Ram's conclusion cannot be accepted because of his neglect of the intercorrelation between the growth of output and that of government consumption. In the application of Wagner's law, the result can be reinterpreted as indicating that the growth of output leads to higher levels of government consumption.[5] Thus, Ram's preferred result appears to show a demand relationship while using the government consumption ratio will indicate a supply relationship. It is the latter, however, that is relevant for the problem at hand.

Landau (1983) correlated the share of government consumption in GDP with the rate of economic growth, including per capita GDP, investment, education, and dummy variables for the Mediterranean Climate Zone and for the Tropical Rain Forest Climate Zones as additional variables. For longer and shorter periods, with population weighted or unweighted, the results show a negative correlation between government consumption shares and GDP growth rates for a group of developed and developing countries. The statistical results are slightly weaker if only developing countries are considered; within this group, they are stronger for middle-income countries while the hypothesis is not confirmed by low-income countries.

Landau also used the government consumption share as an explanatory variable in examining the sources of differences in GDP growth rates among developing countries. This variable has been employed by itself, in conjunction with per capita GDP, as well as in conjunction with the population growth rate (representing the growth of the labor force) and the share of investment in GDP in a production function-type relationship.

The results for 90 developing countries show a negative relationship between the government consumption share and the rate of economic growth in all the regressions, statistically significant at the 1 percent level. Adding per capita GNP or the growth of population and the share of investment does not affect the regression coefficient of the government consumption share variable. At the same time, while the per capita GNP variable is not significant statistically, the coefficients of the population growth and investment share variables are positive and statistically significant at the 5 percent and 1 percent levels, respectively, and their introduction increases the explanatory power of the regression equation to a considerable extent.

The government consumption share variable is also shown to be negatively related to economic growth in the regional subsamples, including Africa, Asia, and Latin America. At the same time, the significance level of this variable varies between 1 and 10 percent. For more detailed results, the reader is referred to Table 6.3.

PUBLIC VS PRIVATE INVESTMENT

We have considered above the relationship between the budget deficit, on the one hand, and private investment and economic growth, on the other, as well as that between the size of the government budget and economic growth. In recent years, attention has further been given to the relationship between public and private investment; in particular, the question has been raised if the two are complementary or competing. In the former case, public investment engenders more private investment; in the latter, there is financial (in terms of the availability of financial resources) or real (in terms of the availability of real resources) crowding out.

These questions have been examined in the framework of a model estimated for 24 developing countries, with pooled annual data for the 1971–9 period, by Blejer and Khan (1984a). The authors have separately considered the effects of variations in the amount of credit and in the volume of public investment on investment by the private sector.

The financing of the public sector will impinge on private investment by encroaching on the availability of credit. Blejer and Khan find that "if the overall quantity of financial resources is given, then any

Table 6.3 Factors affecting intercountry differences in GDP growth rates, 1973–80 (t-values in parenthesis)

	Constant	Government consumption share	Per capita GNP	Population growth rate	Investment share	R^2
Africa						
(1)	8.17 (2.85)**	−0.23 (1.74)Δ				0.08
(2)	9.49 (2.75)**	−0.26 (1.86)Δ	0.76 (−0.70)			0.09
(3)	2.21 (0.59)	−0.31 (2.50)*		1.74 (1.56)	0.18 (2.86)**	0.27
Asia						
(1)	10.91 (5.23)**	−0.27 (2.43)*				0.28
(2)	8.88 (3.41)**	−0.21 (1.80)Δ	0.94 (1.26)			0.36
(3)	4.50 (1.10)	−0.20 (1.92)Δ		0.81 (0.73)	0.17 (2.53)*	0.52
Latin America						
(1)	9.13 (4.43)**	−0.29 (2.44)*				0.21
(2)	12.06 (5.00)**	−0.33 (2.97)**	−1.21 (−2.03)Δ			0.34
(3)	6.84 (2.00)Δ	−0.26 (2.08)Δ		0.62 (1.13)	0.02 (0.19)	0.26
LDC						
(1)	8.16 (5.74)**	−0.19 (2.68)**				0.07
(2)	8.87 (5.11)**	−0.20 (2.76)**	−0.30 (−0.72)			0.08
(3)	2.89 (1.58)	−0.20 (3.03)**		0.96 (2.08)*	0.16 (4.01)**	0.24

Note: ** 1 percent, * 5 percent, and Δ 10 percent level of significance.

Source: World Bank economic and social data base.

attempt by the government to increase its share in either domestic or foreign financing at the expense of the private sector would lead to crowding out and to a decline in the level of private investment" (1984a, p. 395). In reference to the positive relationship between the relative share of private investment and the size of total investment (1984b, p. 27), they add that "a decline [in private investment] would most likely result in a fall in total investment as well" (1984a, p. 395).

Turning to real variables, the authors have disaggregated public investment into its trend or expected component and variation around these values.[6] They conclude that "the level of public sector investment has a positive effect on private investment, whereas the change in government investment has a negative effect" (1984a, p. 396). Thus, so they claim, "it is not the level of public investment that crowds out the private sector . . .; rather, it is the change in public investment that appears to have a strong crowding-out effect" (1984a, p. 396).

The authors interpret the trend or expected component of public investment to represent infrastructural investment and variations around these values to represent noninfrastructural investment. This interpretation may be questioned, however, since infrastructural investment is often undertaken in spurts, in which case it will importantly affect variations in public investment around its trend or expected values.[7]

Alternatively, it may be suggested that the trend or expected component of public investment represents a response to economic expansion. In the process of expansion, we do not find evidence of crowding out because economic growth permits parallel increases of public and private investment.

The introduction of such a "growth effect," then, sidesteps the question of crowding out. This may be re-introduced in terms of the relative magnitudes of private and public investment. Thus, one may inquire if a higher ratio of public investment to the gross domestic product is accompanied by a higher or lower ratio of private investment to GDP.

Utilizing the Blejer–Khan data sample, we find that public and private investment are negatively correlated, with a 1 percent increase in public investment being associated with a 0.55 percent decline in private investment in a cross-section relationship. The regression coefficient is statistically significant at the 1 percent level.

The result may understate, however, the existence of crowding out because unfavorable (favorable) economic conditions lead to low (high) public as well as private investment. This possible bias can be avoided by examining the relationship between the relative share of public investment and the ratio of total investment to GDP. According to the regression results, a 1 percent increase in the relative share of public investment is associated with a 0.28 percent decline in the ratio of total investment to the gross domestic product.

Table 6.4 Regression analysis of public investment shares
(double-log regressions; t-values in parenthesis)

Dependent variable	Explanatory variables		
	Constant	Public investment share	Per capita income
(1) Total investment ratio	1.74	−0.28	0.16
	(5.59)**	(3.06)**	(3.34)**
(2) ICOR	−0.44	0.27	0.34
	(0.83)	(1.77) Δ	(4.17)**
(3) GDP growth rate	2.18	−0.55	−0.18
	(3.49)**	(3.02)**	(1.84) Δ

Note: The public investment share refers to the share of public investment in total investment; the investment ratio refers to the ratio of total investment to GDP; the incremental capital–output ratio (ICOR) refers to the ratio of investment to the increment of GDP.

** 1 percent, * 5 percent, and Δ 10 percent level of significance.

Source: See text.

The regression coefficient is statistically significant at the 1 percent level (Table 6.4).

But how can an increase in public investment induce a decline in total investment? This result cannot be explained by crowding out, whether financial or real. It may be rationalized if high public investment is considered an indication of an unfavorable climate for private investors. This may be an objective fact or may be perceived as such by the private sector.

Thus far, we have considered the possible effects of the volume of public investment on the volume of private and of total investment. A further question relates to the relative efficiency of public and private investment. Notwithstanding its well-known shortcomings, lacking a better measure, the incremental capital–output ratio will be used as a proxy for the efficiency of capital.

The estimates provide some evidence of the lower efficiency of public as against private investment. Thus, a 1 percent increase in the relative share of public investment is associated with a 0.27 percent increase in the incremental capital–output ratio in a cross-section relationship. The regression coefficient is statistically significant at the 10 percent level.

This result conforms to ideas expressed by Vito Tanzi who noted that public investment in developing countries may be unproductive (1976, pp. 911, 915). It may be explained by the fact that while private investors aim at maximizing profits, public investment responds to the preference function of government officials that may reflect economic as well as political considerations.

The negative correlation of the relative share of public investment with the volume of total investment and with its efficiency is reinforced if public investment's share is correlated with the rate of economic growth. According to the estimates, a 1 percent increase in the relative share of public investment is associated with a 0.55 percent decline in the rate of growth of GDP. The regression coefficient is statistically significant at the 1 percent level.

The results are consistent inasmuch as the 0.55 percent decline in the rate of growth of GDP, associated with a 1 percent rise in the relative share of public investment, is also obtained by combining the 0.28 percent decrease in the ratio of total investment to GDP and the 0.27 percent rise in the incremental capital–output ratio. It appears, then, that the unfavorable effects of public investment on the volume of investment are matched by its adverse impact on investment efficiency.

The relative share of public investment varies to a considerable extent from country to country, ranging from 15 to 67 percent during the 1971–9 period. According to the estimates, an increase of this share by one-half would be associated with a 14 percent decline in the ratio of total investment to GDP, a 14 percent increase in an incremental capital–output ratio, and a 28 percent decrease in the rate of economic growth.

The results indicate that high levels of public investment have a negative effect on private investment, leading to lower total investment, as well as on the efficiency of investment. Beyond crowding out, the former result may be taken to provide an indication of the unfavorable investment climate associated with large public investment while the latter may be interpreted to reflect the neglect of economic considerations in public investment decisions.

CONCLUSIONS

This chapter has reported on tests of alternative hypotheses as to the effects of a budget deficit, examined the influence of the size of the government on economic growth, and investigated the impact of public investment on private investment, total investment, and economic growth.

The econometric results support the hypotheses put forward in the chapter to varying degrees. While the one-to-one correspondence between the budget balance and the trade balance, postulated by the Cambridge School, is not borne out by the results, there is evidence that a substantial part of the budget deficit is externally financed. In turn, a correlation between the budget deficit and the money supply, inflation rates, or economic growth has not been observed. However, the budget deficit appears to adversely affect private investment.

There is a negative correlation between the ratio of government consumption to GDP and economic growth. This relationship applies to all developing countries as well as to the regional subsamples of countries in Africa, Asia, and Latin America. It is invariant to the introduction of per capita incomes and of the rate of population growth and the ratio of investment to GDP as additional explanatory variables.

Finally, there is a negative correlation between public investment, on the one hand, and private investment, total investment, and economic growth, on the other. It further appears that the negative effects of public investment on economic growth can be decomposed in two parts: its adverse impact on total investment and its unfavorable influence on the efficiency of investment.

This chapter has investigated the effects of the public sector on various economic variables, in particular economic growth. Further research in this area would be desirable, both to provide an explanation for the observed relationships and to extend them in a time series framework. Also, the reverse effects of economic growth on the public sector would need to be examined.

Notes

1. This analysis was first reported in Balassa, 1986.
2. The per capita income variable has not given significant results, however, for the first period. This was also the case in the equations of Table 6.1, where these results are not reported.
3. The paper by Eltis follows the book by Bacon and Eltis (1976), a critique of which by Hadjimatheou and Skouras (1979) has been effectively answered by the authors (1979).
4. It would have made little economic sense to correlate government consumption and population growth rates.
5. The same problem arises in Rubinson's (1977) estimate, which regresses

GDP on the ratio of government revenue to GDP without recognizing that the former affects the latter.

6. Trend and expected values are alternatives in the model but the two exhibit considerable resemblancy and also give similar results. They will not be considered separately in the following.

7. It may be added that, according to Sundararajan and Thakur, public infrastructure investment is a substitute for private investment. These authors, incidentally, have found crowding out in the case of India while public investment appears to have positively affected private investment in Korea (Sundararajan and Thakur, 1980).

References

Bacon, Robert and Walter Eltis, *Britain's Economic Problem: Too Few Producers*, London, Macmillan, 1976 (first edition), 1978 (second edition).

Bacon, Robert and Walter Eltis, "The Measurement of the Growth of the Non-Market Sector and Its Influence: A Reply to Hadjimatheou and Skouras," *Economic Journal*, 89, June 1979, pp. 402–15.

Balassa, Bela, "The Problem of the Debt in Developing Countries," in Bernard P. Herbert, ed., *Proceedings of the 40th Congress of the Institute of Public Finance*, held in Innsbruck in August 1984, Detroit, Wayne University Press, 1986, pp. 153–66.

Blejer, Mario I. and Mohsin S. Khan, "Government Policy and Private Investment in Developing Countries," *IMF Staff Papers*, 31, June 1984, pp. 379–403.

Blejer, Mario I. and Mohsin S. Khan, "Private Investment in Developing Countries," *Finance and Development*, June 1984, pp. 26–9.

Eltis, Walter, "How Rapid Public Sector Growth Can Undermine the Growth of the National Product," in Wilfred Beckerman, ed., *Slow Growth in Britain. Causes and Consequences*, Oxford, Clarendon Press, 1979, pp. 118–39.

Hadjimatheou, G. and A. Skouras, "Britain's Economic Problem: The Growth of the Non-Market Sector?" *Economic Journal*, 89, June 1979, pp. 392–401.

Ihori, Toshihiro, "The Size of Government Spending and the Private Sector's Evaluation," *Journal of the Japanese and International Economies*, 1, March 1987, pp. 82–96.

Knoester, Anthonie, "Stagnation and the Inverted Haavelono Effect: Some International Evidence," *De Economist*, 1983(4), pp. 548–84.

Landau, David, "Government Expenditure and Economic Growth: A Cross-Section Study," *Southern Economic Journal*, 49, January 1983, pp. 783–92.

Marsden, Keith, "Links between Taxes and Economic Growth. Some Empirical Evidence," World Bank Staff Working Paper No. 605, Washington, DC, World Bank, August 1983.

Peterson, Hans-Georg, "Taxes, Tax Systems and Economic Growth," in Herbert Giersch, ed., *Towards an Explanation of Economic Growth*,

Symposium 1980, Institut für Welwirtschaft an der Universität Kiel, Tübingen, J.C.B. Mohr (Paul Siebeck), 1981.

Ram, Rati, "Government Size and Economic Growth: A New Framework and Some Evidence from Cross-Section and Time-Series Data," *American Economic Review*, 76, March 1986, pp. 191–203.

Rubinson, Richard, "Dependence, Government Revenue, and Economic Growth, 1955–1970," *Studies in Comparative International Development*, 12, Summer 1977, pp. 3–28.

Sundararajan, V. and Subhash Thakur, "Public Investment, Crowding Out, and Growth: A Dynamic Model Applied to India and Korea," *IMF Staff Papers*, 27, December 1980, pp. 814–58.

Tanzi, Vito, "Fiscal Policy, Keynesian Economics and the Mobilization of Savings in Developing Countries," *World Development*, 4, October–November 1976, pp. 907–17.

Symposium and Seminar (To Wegnai, hbok an der. I Muench): Karl Duncker, 1. Carl. Mohr (Paul Siebeck), 1991.

Rana, R.Ad. "Investment Inc. and Economic Growth: A New Framework and some Evidence from Asian Section and Time-Series Data," *Asian Economic Review*, 76, March 1986, pp. 191–20.

Robinson, Richard, "Expansions, Contractions, Reversion, and Economic Growth: IMF, 1971. Saudi for Comparative International Development," E. Romue, 19, 7, pp. 3–23.

Sundararajan, V. and Subhash Thakur, "Public Investment, Crowding Out, and Growth: A Dynamic Model Applied to India and Korea," *IMF Staff Papers*, 77, December, 1980, pp. 814–58.

Weil, Vito, "Fiscal Policy, Revenue Transactions, and the Mobilization of Savings in Developing Countries," *World Development*, 4, October, November 1976, pp. 90–92.

Part IV

Financial Liberalization and Interest Rates

7 Financial Liberalization in Developing Countries*

THE MCKINNON–SHAW ANALYSIS

McKinnon and Shaw consider financial liberalization as a mainstay of economic reforms in developing countries. McKinnon goes as far as to "define 'economic development' as the reduction of the great dispersion in social rates of return to existing and new investments under domestic entrepreneurial control" (1973, p. 9). He adds: "Economic development so defined is necessary and sufficient to generate high rates of saving and investment (accurately reflecting social and private time preference), the adoption of best-practice technologies, and learning-by-doing" (ibid.). Shaw suggests that "the argument for liberalization in finance is that scarcity prices for savings increase rates of saving, improve savings allocation, induce some substitution of labor for capital equipment, and assist in income equalization" (1973, p. 121).

Both McKinnon and Shaw maintain that financial liberalization, involving the establishment of higher interest rates that equate the demand for and the supply of savings, will lead to *increased savings*. McKinnon suggests that savings will increase, reflecting social and private time preference (1973, p. 9). While recognizing that the income and substitution effects of increases in interest rates on savings are conflicting, Shaw expresses the view that "savers may ignore a possibly transitory increase from, say, 4 to 6 percent in rates of return, but they are less likely to maintain consumption-saving patterns when rates of return change, in a context of economic reform, from negative levels to positive 10 or 15 percent and more. Given the relative scarcity of wealth in the lagging economies, the income effect of higher rates of return should not be expected to overwhelm the effects of substitution of more wealth for less consumption now" (1973, p. 73).

* Originally published as World Bank Report *Studies in Comparative International Development*, Winter 1990/91 vol. 25, no. 4; pp. 56–70.

The author is indebted to Yoon Je Cho, Maxwell Fry, Alan Gelb, and Jacques Polak for helpful comments.

Shaw further suggests that "real growth in financial institutions provides more investors with access to borrowing and gives them incentive to save and to accumulate the equity that makes borrowing cheaper" (1973, p. 9). In turn, according to McKinnon's complementarity hypothesis, "the increased desirability of holding cash balances reduces the opportunity cost of saving internally for the eventual purchase of capital goods from outside the firm–household" (1973, p. 60).

Both Shaw and McKinnon note that below equilibrium interest rates lead to capital flight, thereby reducing the availability of savings for domestic investment. According to Shaw, "because savings are mobile, evasion of interest rate ceilings is routine in lagging economies [resulting in] capital flight away from domestic asset markets" (1973, p. 94). McKinnon also notes that "financial reform ends the chronic dissipation of . . . savings in low-return foreign investments" (1973, p. 162).

McKinnon adds that "the release of resources from inferior uses in the underdeveloped environment is as important as new net saving *per se*" (1973, p. 15). In fact, both McKinnon and Shaw give emphasis to increases in the efficiency of investment that result from financial liberalization. They consider a variety of avenues through which *efficiency improvements* can take place.

The two authors suggest that, in the absence of financial liberalization, self-investment will occur in the place of providing savings to more efficient uses through the financial system, owing to below-equilibrium – often negative – real interest rates. According to Shaw, "in a repressed economy savings flow mainly to the saver's own investments: self-finance prevails" (1973, p. 10); according to McKinnon, "the bias toward self-finance is one common thread" (1973, p. 30). Savings may go into inventories (Shaw, 1973, pp. 71–2) or create excess capacity in plant and equipment (McKinnon, 1973, pp. 31–2). In this connection, McKinnon's statement deserves full quotation.

If the real rate of return on holding money is low or negative, a significant proportion of the physical capital of the economy will be embodied in inventories of finished and semifinished goods that are not used directly for production or consumption. A small farmer may keep unduly large rice inventories as the embodiment of his savings – a portion of which the rats eat every year. Alternatively, a wealthy member of some urban enclave may build an unusually elaborate house, which he hopes will also maintain its value under inflation. A businessman might deliberately "overinvest" in plant capacity or in certain stocks of raw material, relative to his current operating needs. (1973, p. 63)

Now, "if inflation drives real rates of return in all financial assets to negative values, it is not difficult to imagine that some internal investments within 'surplus' industrial enterprises also would generate negative rates of return" (1973, p. 32). The "surplus" refers here to a surplus of savings and the argument is applied to agriculture as well. At the same time, in the case of inventory accumulation, the rate of return will always be negative, because of the cost involved in storage and – for agricultural products – loss in storage, unless the real price of the commodity in question increases over time.

Financial liberalization, then, brings forth a shift of savings from lower-productivity self-investment to higher-productivity investment intermediated by the financial sector. The same result obtains as credit rationing gives place to allocation by interest rates following financial liberalization.

As there is excess demand for funds at less-than-equilibrium interest rates, there is "credit rationing among borrowers, sometimes according to the dictates of monetary or other authority, sometimes according to the preferences of the [financial] intermediaries" (Shaw, 1973, p. 84). Lending by government authorities, or influenced by them, responds to governmental preferences while financial intermediaries focus on reducing risk. Thus, "effective low ceilings in real loan rates intensify risk aversion and liquidity preference on the part of intermediaries. Banks and others keep a privileged place in their portfolios for established borrowers, especially trading firms with a long record of stability. They have little incentive to explore new and less certain lending opportunities" (p. 86). Also, "rationing is expensive to administer. It is vulnerable to corruption and conspiracy in dividing between borrowers and officers of the intermediary the monopoly rent that arises from the difference between low, regulated loan rate and the market-clearing rate" (ibid.).

Below-equilibrium interest rates also affect the capital-intensity of the investments actually undertaken (McKinnon, 1973, p. 9). This will occur both because capital-intensive projects are profitable and because the substitution of capital for labor is encouraged. "Investment flows to capital-intensive production even though capital is scarce and labor plentiful" (Shaw, 1973, p. 11). And, in the case of North and

Northwest India, "loans on cheap terms have encouraged capital-intensive techniques by large enterprises" (p. 124).

Interest rate controls further encourage overbuilding by banks as a form of competition. Thus, Shaw speaks of lavish financial buildings and numerous branches of financial institutions (p. 85) and suggests that "some of the expensive layering of financial institutions in lagging economies is the direct consequence of controls on loan and deposit rates" (p. 86). In turn, McKinnon refers to the opening of excessive numbers of bank branches in Brazil (1973, p. 84).

Shaw also speaks of the lengthening of maturities and diversification of the menu of financial assets in the event of financial liberalization (1973, p. 7). Thus, "monetary and other financial reform can be expected to extend capital-market horizons and divert savings into contracts at longer term" (p. 127). Also, "in the liberalized economy savers are offered a wide menu of portfolio choices" (p. 10).

Finally, McKinnon and Shaw consider the fact that increased financial intermediation represents, in part, a substitute for the curb market. Thus, Shaw notes that "the curb should have to face competition from deepening in the organized sector" (1973, p. 137). The importance of curb markets would decline following financial liberalization according to McKinnon (1973, p. 60).

At the same time, both authors consider the shift from curb markets to organized finance to be beneficial because of the greater efficiency associated with the latter. According to Shaw, the street markets are only imperfect substitutes for indirect financial assets (1973, p. 85). Furthermore, "financial growth permits unification of the capital market. It reduces interregional and interindustry differences in investment yields and increases mean yields" (p. 74).

In turn, McKinnon notes that "there appears to be no economical substitute for expanding the role of organized finance in small-scale lending to indigenous entrepreneurs in either rural or urban areas" (1973, p. 77). Also, he approvingly notes the conclusions of a study of Chilean curb markets, according to which "money lenders operate on a small scale and do not compete with each other [as they] do not have detailed knowledge of a broad market" (p. 78). McKinnon further adds: "the main burden of ensuring that there is uniformity in borrowing rates and that competition is broadly based rests with direct bank lending" (ibid.).

All in all, there are various ways in which financial liberalization brings improvements in investment efficiency according to McKinnon and Shaw. They include decreases in self-investment at low and even negative real rates of return, rationing of loans by interest rates rather than by public authorities and banks, a shift away from excessively capital-intensive investments and techniques, the avoidance of overbuilding by banks, the lengthening of financial maturities, and the decreased importance of fragmented curb markets.

EXTENSIONS AND CRITICISMS OF THE MCKINNON–SHAW APPROACH

Extensions of the McKinnon–Shaw approach by Kapur (1976), Galbis (1977), Mathieson (1980), and Fry (1988) add little to the underlying ideas but rather formalize the McKinnon–Shaw models. Kapur and Mathieson limit the analysis by assuming the constancy of investment efficiency following financial liberalization while Galbis and Fry consider the case when efficiency increases.

In Kapur's model, increases in the deposit rate of interest raise real money demand and hence the real supply of bank credit, resulting in an acceleration of economic growth. Similar conclusions are reached in Mathieson's model, which differs from Kapur's largely by assuming that fixed capital is fully utilized while it was assumed to be under-utilized by Kapur.

Galbis constructs a two-sector model to analyze the effects of financial repression on the average efficiency of investment. In this model, financial liberalization will lead to higher efficiency by shifting savings from self-investment to uses with higher rates of return. Fry also puts emphasis on increases in investment efficiency following financial liberalization.

The principal critics of the McKinnon–Shaw approach are van Wijnbergen (1983) and Taylor (1983). They use Tobin's portfolio framework for household sector asset allocation. Households have three categories of assets: gold or currency, time deposits, and curb market loans. In response to increases in interest rates on time deposits, households will substitute these for gold or cash and curb market assets.

Van Wijnbergen contrasts his model to those of McKinnon and Kapur. He expresses the view that "the results obtained by McKinnon/Kapur depend crucially on one hidden assumption on asset market structure, an assumption that is never stated explicitly: all these authors assume that the portfolio shift into TD's [time deposits] is coming out of an 'unproductive' asset like gold, cash, commodity stocks etc." (1983, p. 434). He adds that "it is not at all obvious that TD's are closer substitutes to cash, gold etc. rather than to loans extended on the curb markets" (ibid.).

In fact, Taylor expects that the latter outcome will obtain (1983, p. 100). Also, in a study of Korea, van Wijnbergen concluded that "substitution between the curb market and time deposits is of more importance than substitution between currency and time deposits" (van Wijnbergen, 1982, p. 156). Now, "in this case the total supply of funds to the business sector will decline as funds are shifted from the curb market which provides one for one intermediation (no reserve requirements) into the banking system which provides only partial intermediation: partial because a fraction is syphoned off into required and free reserves rather than passed on to firms" (van Wijnbergen, 1983, p. 439).

Expressed differently, van Wijnbergen and Taylor introduce a distortion into their model in the form of reserve requirements in the banking sector. However, they do not consider the effects of interest rate distortions on investment efficiency. Thus, they assume investment efficiency to be the same, irrespective of whether loans are financed by the banking sector or the curb market. As noted above, this was not the view of McKinnon and Shaw who did not neglect the curb market but considered this to lead to lower investment efficiency.

INTEREST RATES AND FINANCIAL INTERMEDIATION

Having reviewed the McKinnon–Shaw analysis, its extensions, and critics, the next question concerns the empirical evidence on the economic effects of interest rates and financial intermediation. Available evidence will be presented on the relationship between interest rates and financial intermediation, between financial inter-mediation and economic growth, and between interest rates and economic growth.

Lanyi and Saracoglu (1983) provide evidence on the relationship between interest rates and the growth of the broad money supply (M2), measured as the real value of the sum of monetary and quasi-monetary deposits with the banking sector, in a cross-section relationship of 21 countries for the 1971–80 period. Classifying countries according to whether they had positive real interest rates, moderately negative real interest rates, or severely negative real interest rates, the authors regress the rate of growth of the broad money supply on interest rates. The results show a high correlation between the two variables, with the regression coefficient of the interest rate variable being statistically significant at the 1 percent level (1983, p. 29).

The statistical relationship between interest rates and financial intermediation was also examined by Fry (1988). In a pooled time series and cross-section estimate for 10 Asian developing countries for the 1962–72 period, Fry regressed the real stock of broad money on the national saving rate, per capita real expected income, the lagged value of broad money, and the 12-month time deposit rate of interest less the expected rate of inflation, when expected values were represented by polynomial distributed lags on current and past values. Fry found the coefficient of the real interest rate variable to be positive and statistically significant at the 1 percent level (1988, p. 146).

The relationship between interest rates and the broadly defined money supply was investigated for Thailand, Indonesia, and the Philippines by Chamley and Hussain (1988). The estimates for Thailand relate to the 1974–86 period, those for Indonesia to the 1972–85 period, and those for the Philippines to the 1972–87 period.[1] The dependent variable in the regression analysis is the rate of change of the ratio of the broad money supply to GDP; the explanatory variables are the ratio of the money supply to GDP in the preceding period, the interest rate (in its various forms), and the rate of inflation. In the following, the best equation is reported in each case.

The results for Thailand show that the rate of change of the broad money supply is positively correlated with the time deposit rate and negatively correlated with the money market rate, both of which are statistically significant at the 1 percent level. The results indicate that the extent of financial intermediation will rise if the time deposit rate increases relative to the money market rate (Chamley and Hussain, 1988, p. 16).

The results for Indonesia show that the rate of change of the broad money supply is positively correlated with the real time deposit rate. The regression coefficient of the interest rate variable is statistically significant at the 1 percent level (p. 29).

The results for the Philippines also show that the rate of change of the broad money supply is positively correlated with the real time deposit rate. The regression coefficient of the interest rate variable is statistically significant at the 1 percent level (p. 41).

Finally, Gelb (1989) examined the effects of interest rates on the ratio of the broad money supply to gross domestic savings by combining time series data for the 1965–73 and 1974–85 periods for 34 developing countries. In the estimating equation, the real deposit rate was statistically significant at the 1 percent level while the other variables (the ratio of savings to GDP, the rate of inflation, the level of GDP per head, and a shift variable for the post-1973 years) were not significant statistically (p. 29).

While the econometric results indicate the effects of interest rates on the extent of financial intermediation, the question remains where the increased financial intermediation originates. In the case of Korea, van Wijnbergen found that substitution between the curb market and time deposits is of greater importance than substitution between currency and time deposits (1982, p. 156). But, this neglects substitution between physical assets and time deposits as well as increases in time deposits due to higher savings in response to the rise of interest rates.

As to the former, van Wijnbergen admits that there is substitution against "unproductive" assets, such as gold and commodity stocks, to which unproductive self-investments should be added. At the same time, he suggests that it is not at all obvious that time deposits are closer substitutes for these assets than for loans on the curb market (1983, p. 434). One should not count, however, the substitution of time deposits for curb market loans but only the incremental reserves against time deposits as a loss.

Assume, for example, that time deposits increase by 400 pesos, with 100 pesos coming from unproductive assets and 300 pesos from the curb market, while there are reserve requirements of 20 percent against time deposits and none against curb market liabilities. Now, there will be a net increase in financial intermediation of 20 (400–80–300) pesos, even though the decline in curb market loans was three times that of unproductive assets.

At the same time, it can hardly be assumed that no reserves would be held against curb market liabilities. Rather, due to greater uncertainty, larger reserves may be held against curb market liabilities than against time deposits. The relevant comparison is, then, between reserves held against curb market liabilities and compulsory reserve requirements against time deposits. As long as the former exceeds the latter, substitution of time deposits for curb market loans will not reduce but increase the extent of financial intermediation.

The possible effects of interest rates on savings were reviewed in another paper by the author (Balassa, 1988). It has been shown that there is some evidence on the favorable effects of increases in interest rates on domestic savings. The amount available for domestic investment will increase further as higher interest rates reduce the incentive for capital flight.

FINANCIAL INTERMEDIATION AND ECONOMIC GROWTH

The next question concerns the relationship between the extent of financial intermediation and economic growth. In the study referred to above, Lanyi and Saracoglu found a high degree of correlation between the rate of growth of GDP and the rate of growth of the broad money supply, with the latter variable being statistically significant at the 1 percent level (1983, p. 29).

Earlier, Jao examined the relationship between the rate of growth of per capita GDP, on the one hand, and the rate of growth of per capita real balances and the ratio of the broad money supply to GDP, on the other (1976).[2] He found that the two variables, representing the extent of financial intermediation, were highly significant statistically in a cross-section regression for 67 developed and developing countries in the 1967–72 period (1976, p. 52). The level of significance was 1 percent for the former variable and 5 percent for the latter. However, in regression analysis limited to the developing countries alone only the former variable was statistically significant (at the 1 percent level).

In turn, Tun Wai (1980) found a positive relationship between real GDP and the real supply of domestic credit in a study of 13 developing countries. In a time series investigation, the credit variable was statistically significant at the 1 percent level in the case of each of the countries (1980, p. 426).

Finally, in the study referred to above, Gelb regressed the rate of growth of GDP on the ratio of the real increase in broad money to gross domestic savings, the ratio of savings to GDP, and a shift variable for the years after 1973. The financial intermediation variable had a positive and significant coefficient at the 1 percent level while the other variables were not significant statistically (Gelb, 1988, p. 23).

Following McKinnon (1973) and Shaw (1973), the above authors made estimates on the assumption that the causation goes from financial intermediation to economic growth or a "supply-leading" relationship. But, the causation may also run from economic growth to financial intermediation as growth creates demand for financial services. Such a "demand-following" relationship was postulated by Goldsmith (1969).

In turn, Patrick (1966) suggested that the direction of causality changes in the course of economic development. In his view, financial development is necessary for sustained economic growth to take place but "as the process of real growth occurs, the supply-leading impetus gradually becomes less important, and the demand-following financial response becomes dominant" (1966, p. 174).

Fritz (1984) employed a Granger test to examine the direction of causality between financial intermediation and economic development. He used factor analysis to define both financial intermediation and economic development as composite sets of variables. The results, obtained for the Philippines, support Patrick's hypothesis that financial intermediation "causes" economic growth at an early stage of development and the causation is reversed at a later stage (1984, p. 109).

The Granger technique was used more recently by Jung (1986) to test the causation between financial intermediation and economic growth. Jung used the ratio of M1 to GNP, denoted the currency ratio, and the ratio of M2 to GNP, denoted the monetization variable, to represent the extent of financial intermediation while economic growth was measured by the growth of per capita GNP. The investigation covered 19 developed and 37 developing countries; 15 annual observations were used for each.

The results, obtained by combining time series and cross-section data, "indicate a moderate support for the supply-leading phenomenon in LDCs. The causal direction, both unidirectional and simple, running from financial development to economic growth is more frequently observed than the reverse" (1986, p. 341).

Jung also examined the Patrick hypothesis as between developing and developed countries. He found that "when the currency ratio is used as a measure of financial development, a supply-leading and then demand-following causality pattern is moderately supported by the data. Thus, LDCs are characterized by the causal direction running from financial to economic development, and DCs by the reverse causal direction, regardless of which causality concept is employed. On the other hand, the monetization variable does not appear to distinguish DCs from LDCs in terms of causality directions" (p. 344); causation runs from financial intermediation to economic growth for both developing and developed countries.

INTEREST RATES AND ECONOMIC GROWTH

The next question concerns the relationship between interest rates and economic growth. Such a relationship may obtain as increases in interest rates are associated with higher domestic investment and with higher efficiency of investment. At the same time, the problem of causation, discussed in the previous section of the chapter, does not arise in this case.

We have referred above to the results obtained in regard to the effects of higher interest rates on domestic savings and investment. In turn, the effects of interest rates on investment efficiency were investigated in an Asian Development Bank study of nine Asian countries (1985), in a study of Turkey by Fry (1988), and in the Gelb study referred to above.

The study of the Asian Development Bank combined time series observations for India, Korea, Malaysia, Nepal, Pakistan, Singapore, Taiwan, and Thailand. It found that the incremental output–capital ratio was positively associated with the real deposit rate, with the latter variable being statistically significant at the 5 percent level (1985, p. 48). The same result was obtained for Turkey by Fry, with the real deposit rate variable being statistically significant at the 1 percent level (1988, p. 148).

In turn, Gelb regressed the incremental output–capital ratio on the real time deposit rate and a shift variable for the post-1973 period. The former variable had a positive, the latter a negative sign; both were statistically significant at the 1 percent level (1989, p. 24).

As to the relationship between interest rates and economic growth, Khatkhate did not observe a difference in average growth rates between countries having below-average and above-average real interest rates in a sample of 64 developing countries (1988, p. 584). This is not an appropriate test, however, since differences within the two groups of countries are disregarded.

In turn, Gupta obtained conflicting results in a cross-section study (1984) and in a study of India and Korea (1986). In both instances, dynamic multiplier analysis was used to examine the long-term effects of changes in nominal interest rates and inflation rates on economic growth.

The first estimate pertains to 25 Asian and Latin American countries and involved combining time series statistics for periods of different length, depending on data availability. It shows an unfavorable effect of higher interest rates on economic growth (1984, p. 41).

However, the long-term multiplier shows the beneficial effect of raising interest rates on economic growth in Korea and India. In the case of India, the best results are obtained if the nominal rate of interest rises and the expected rate of inflation remains the same. In the case of Korea, a decline in the expected rate of inflation, with the nominal interest rate remaining constant, gives the best results (1986, p. 60).

One can only speculate about the reasons for the differences in the results of the two studies. A possible explanation is the distortions introduced by combining countries with different structures. In fact, in another paper Gupta criticized Giovannini for combining data for several regions in investigating the effects of the real interest rates of savings (1987, pp. 307–8).

The positive results obtained by Gupta for India and Korea are confirmed by the cross-section study of Lanyi and Saracoglu (1983), two cross-section studies by Fry (1988), and a cross-section study by Gelb (1989). The Lanyi–Saracoglu and Gelb studies were referred to earlier; the Fry study pertains to seven and 14 Asian developing countries, respectively.

The Lanyi–Saracoglu study shows a positive correlation between the rate of growth of GDP and the interest rate variable as defined above. The latter variable is statistically significant at the 1 percent level (1983, p. 29). The two studies by Fry pooled time series data for the countries concerned. They indicate that the rate of growth of GDP is positively correlated with the real time deposit rate, with the latter being statistically significant at the 1 percent level in the first study and at the 5 percent level in the second. The results suggest that a 1 percent increase in the real time deposit rate towards its competitive free-market equilibrium level is associated with a rise in the rate of economic growth by about one-half of one percentage point (1988, pp. 151–2). These results have been confirmed by Arrieta (1988).

Furthermore, Polak (1989, pp. 66–9) regressed the rate of economic growth on the median rate of interest in a 40-country sample covering the period 1965–85. He obtained a strong correlation, and the statistical significance of the results is not affected if the investment share and the export growth rate are introduced as additional variables. At the same time, the introduction of the export growth rate increases the explanatory power of the regression equation to a considerable extent.

Finally, Gelb regressed the rate of growth of GDP on the real deposit rate and on a shift variable for the post-1973 years. The former variable had a positive, the latter a negative coefficient; both were statistically significant at the 1 percent level (1989, p. 24).

The cited studies relate interest rates directly to economic growth. A positive relationship between the two variables is also shown if we combine the results obtained for the relationship between interest rates and financial intermediation and that between financial intermediation and economic growth or combine the relationship between interest rates and domestic investment and that between interest rates and the efficiency of investment (Fry, 1988, p. 151, and Gelb, 1989, p. 25).

DOMESTIC AND EXTERNAL FINANCIAL LIBERALIZATION

We have seen that raising real interest rates can have favorable effects on financial intermediation and on economic growth. However, excessively high real interest rates have adverse economic effects. They will not permit the financing of various investment projects that otherwise have a good economic rationale and will favor projects that have a high risk. The latter problem has become known as that of "adverse risk selection" on the assumption that the risk tends to rise with the rate of return (Stiglitz and Weiss, 1981).

Excessively high real interest rates were observed in the countries of the Southern Cone of Latin America (Corbo *et al.*, 1985, Table 1). On a quarterly basis, *ex post* real interest rates reached 53.3 percent in Argentina (1979–4th), 54.6 percent in Chile (1982–1st), and 44.0 percent in Uruguay (1982–4th).

Excessively high real interest rates in the countries of the Southern Cone have been attributed to the breakdown of proper financial supervision. As McKinnon noted, "neither officials in the commercial banks themselves, nor government regulatory authorities, adequately monitored the creditworthiness of a broad spectrum of industrial and agricultural borrowers" (McKinnon, 1988, pp. 399–400). The result was the proliferation of bad loans that were rolled over, creating what Harberger calls a "false" demand for credit (Harberger, 1985, p. 237).

A contributing factor was the problem of moral hazard as banks expected to be bailed out by government. They apparently made highly risky investments on the presumption that in the event of losses these would be covered by governments while gains would accrue to the banks themselves.

The problems encountered in the Southern Cone of Latin America indicate that certain conditions need to be fulfilled before the operation of the banking system can be liberalized. First of all, inflation has to be brought under control since high and variable interest rates make borrowers as well as the banks highly vulnerable. Also, government supervision is needed to ensure that banks do not undertake unduly risky investments. In particular, there is need to set appropriate capital and reserve requirements, to limit the proportion of the banks' portfolio that can be lent to any one borrower, and to make detailed inspection of the quality of the banks' portfolio.

The discussion so far has dealt with domestic financial liberalization without any consideration given to external liberalization (the liberalization of the capital account). This represents an appropriate sequence since domestic financial liberalization should be accomplished before external liberalization is undertaken. This is both to generate expertise and to establish domestic banks that can withstand the rigors of international competition.

We have here the traditional infant industry argument that has been applied to financial liberalization in a number of developing economies, including Korea and Taiwan. It has also been applied in European countries, such as France and Italy.

A further question is the order of liberalization as far as the trade account and the capital account are concerned. If the adjustment is equally rapid in the two markets, trade and capital accounts should be liberalized simultaneously. This is not the case, however, as shifts in the capital account occur more rapidly than in the trade account. Correspondingly, resource shifts would occur in response to capital account liberalization that will be undone once the trade account adjusts (Edwards, 1986, pp. 207–8).

It may be assumed that, prior to the opening of the capital account, the domestic rate of interest exceeds the international rate of interest. In this eventuality domestic agents will borrow abroad once the capital account is opened. This will then lead to an appreciation of the exchange rate, with adverse effects on the tradeables sector. In turn, a depreciation will occur in response to the freeing of the trade account.

Thus, resources will flow first to the nontradeable sector and, subsequently, to the tradeable sector. Such switches of reserves are undesirable because of the adjustment costs they entail. Correspondingly, it will be appropriate to liberalize the trade account first and the capital account afterwards, with a view to ensure the simultaneity of adjustment in the two.

The countries of the Southern Cone of Latin American provide cases where the liberalization of the capital account led to large inflows of capital, resulting in a substantial appreciation of the exchange rate. In Argentina and Uruguay, the capital account was liberalized without appreciable changes in the trade account; in Chile, capital account liberalization occurred while the domestic financial system was in disarray.

In turn, there have been successful cases of capital account liberalization. There is full freedom of capital movements in Hong Kong and Singapore and virtual freedom in Malaysia and Thailand. Also, a study of the relationship between domestic and US interest rates has shown that there is *de facto* considerable opening of the capital markets in Colombia (Edwards and Khan, 1985).

CONCLUSIONS

McKinnon and Shaw define financial liberalization to mean the establishment of higher interest rates that equate the demand for, and the supply of, savings. The two authors express the view that higher interest rates will lead to increased savings and financial intermediation as well as to improvements in the efficiency of using savings.

In turn, van Wijnbergen and Taylor claim that higher interest rates on time deposits do not necessarily lead to increased financial intermediation because of shifts from curb markets, which are not subject to the reserve requirements that apply to time deposits. This means that the authors contrast distortions due to reserve requirements with distortions due to interest rate limitations on time deposits.

Abolishing excessive reserve requirements would eliminate distortions while prudential considerations point to the conclusion that reserves should be held against time deposits and against curb market liabilities as well. At the same time, substituting time deposits for unproductive assets, such as gold, cash, and commodity stocks, will increase the extent of financial intermediation. Increases in savings will have the same effect while increased efficiency in the use of savings will add to economic growth.

The chapter summarizes available empirical evidence, indicating that higher real interest rates increase the extent of financial intermediation while increased financial intermediation raises the rate of economic growth in developing countries. Reference is also made to empirical evidence on the effects of interest rates on savings cited in the author's "The Effects of Interest Rates on Savings in Developing Countries." Furthermore, evidence is provided on the effects of interest rates on investment efficiency and on economic growth.

The chapter notes, however, that excessively high interest rates will have unfavorable economic 'effects. Such a situation can be avoided if the liberalization of the banking system takes place under appropriate conditions, including monetary stability and the government supervision of the banks. This would further the goal of establishing equilibrium interest rates.

Domestic financial liberalization may eventually be followed by the liberalization of the capital account. But, this would have to be preceded by trade liberalization in order to avoid unnecessary resource shifts.

Domestic financial liberalization has been traditionally discussed in terms of interest rate levels whereas the liberalization of the capital account would lead to the equalization of domestic and foreign real interest rates, with allowance made for exchange rate changes. However, there are also other important issues relating to interest rates. These include flexibility over time, the avoidance of interest subsidies, an appropriate structure of rates according to maturity, and interest rate differentials reflecting risk.

More generally, in most developing countries there is need for improvements in the functioning of the financial sector. As noted in the World Bank's "Review of Financial Sector Work," such improvements should encompass "the provision of a means of payment, the mobilization and allocation of capital, and the transformation and distribution of risk" (Long, 1985, p. 6). These issues, however, fall outside the scope of this chapter.

Notes

1. For two of the countries, Thailand and Indonesia, estimates have been made also for M1, the narrowly-defined money supply. These estimates are not reported because M2 rather than M1 represents the extent of financial intermediation.
2. Estimates were also made for the narrowly-defined money supply; for reasons noted earlier, these are not reported in the following.

References

Arrieta, Gerardo M. Gonzales, "Interest Rates, Savings, and Growth in LDCs: An Assessment of Recent Empirical Research," *World Development*, May 1988, pp. 589–605.

Asian Development Bank, *Improving Domestic Resource Mobilization through Financial Development*, Manila, Asian Development Bank Economic Office, September 1985.

Balassa, Bela, "The Effects of Interest Rates on Savings in Developing Countries," Washington, DC, World Bank, August 1988, mimeo.

Chamley, Cristophe and Quaizar Hussain, "The Removal of Taxes on Financial Assets in Thailand, Indonesia, and the Philippines: A Quantitative Evaluation," Washington, DC, World Bank, June 1988 (mimeo).

Cho, Yoon Je, "The Effect of Financial Liberalization on the Efficiency of Credit Allocation: Some Evidence from Korea," *Journal of Development Economics*, July 1988, pp. 101–10.

Corbo, Vittorio, Jaime de Melo, and James Tybout, "What Went Wrong with the Recent Reforms in the Southern Cone," Development Research Department Discussion Paper No. 128, Washington DC, World Bank, July 1985.

Edwards, Sebastian, "The Order of Liberalization of the Current and Capital Accounts of the Balance of Payments," in Armeane M. Choksi and Demetrios Papageorgiou, eds, *Economic Liberalization in Developing Countries*, New York, Basil Blackwell, 1986, pp. 185–216.

Edwards, Sebastian and Mohsin S. Khan, "Interest Rate Determination in Developing Countries: A Conceptual Framework," *International Monetary Fund Staff Papers*, September 1985, pp. 377–403.

Fritz, Richard G., "Time Series Evidence of the Causal Relationship between Financial Deepening and Economic Development," *Journal of Economic Development*, July 1984, pp. 91–112.

Fry, Maxwell J., *Money, Interest, and Banking in Economic Development*, Baltimore, Md, Johns Hopkins University Press, 1988.

Galbis, Vicente, "Financial Intermediation and Economic Growth in Less-Developed Countries: A Theoretical Approach," *Journal of Development Studies*, January 1977, pp. 58–72.

Gelb, Alan, "A Cross Section Analysis of Financial Policies, Efficiency, and Growth," PPR Working Paper No. 202, Washington, DC, World Bank, 1989.

Goldsmith, Raymond W., *Financial Structure and Development*, New Haven, Conn., Yale University Press, 1969.

Gupta, Kanhaya L., "Financial Liberalization and Economic Growth: Some Simulation Results," *Journal of Economic Development*, December 1984, pp. 25–44.

Gupta, Kanhaya L., "Financial Development and Economic Growth in India and South Korea," *Journal of Economic Development*, December 1986, pp. 41–62.

Gupta, Kanhaya L., "Aggregate Savings, Financial Intermediation, and Interest Rates," *Review of Economics and Statistics*, May 1987, pp. 303–19.

Harberger, Arnold C., "Lessons for Debtor Country Managers and Policy Makers," in G.W. Smith and John Cuddington, eds, *International Debt and the Developing Countries*, Washington, DC, World Bank, 1985.

Jao, Y.C., "Financial Deepening and Economic Growth: A Cross-Section Analysis," *Malayan Economic Review*, April 1976, pp. 47–58.

Jung, Woo S., "Financial Development and Economic Growth: International Evidence," *Economic Development and Cultural Change*, January 1986, pp. 333–46.

Kapur, Basant K., "Alternative Stabilization Policies for Less-Developed Economies," *Journal of Political Economy*, August 1976, pp. 777–95.

Khatkhate, Deena R., "Assessing the Impact of Interest Rates in Less Developed Countries," *World Development*, May 1988, pp. 577–88.

Lanyi, Anthony and Rüsdü Saracoglu, "Interest Rate Policies in Developing Countries," Occasional Paper 22, Washington, DC, International Monetary Fund, October 1983.

Long, Millard, "Review of Financial Sector Work," Washington, DC, World Bank, 1985.

McKinnon, Ronald I., *Money and Capital in Economic Development*, Washington, DC, The Brookings Institution, 1973.

McKinnon, Ronald I., "Financial Liberalization in Retrospect: Interest Rate Policies in LDCs," in Gustav Ranis and T. Paul Schultz, eds, *The State of Development Economics: Progress and Perspectives*, Oxford, Basil Blackwell, 1988, pp. 386, 410.

Mathieson, Ronald J., "Financial Reform and Stabilization Policy in a Developing Economy," *Journal of Development Economics*, September 1980, pp. 359–95.

Patrick, Hugh T., "Financial Development and Economic Growth in Underdeveloped Countries," *Economic Development and Cultural Change*, January 1966, pp. 174–89.

Polak, Jacques J., *Financial Policies and Development*, Paris, Development Centre of the Organization for Economic Co-operation and Development, 1989.

Shaw, Edward S., *Financial Deepening in Economic Development*, New York, Oxford University Press, 1973.

Stiglitz, Joseph and Andrew Weiss, "Credit Rationing in Markets with Imperfect Information," *American Economic Review*, June 1981, pp. 393–410.

Taylor, Lance, *Structuralist Macroeconomics: Applicable Models for the Third World*, New York, Basic Books, 1983.

Tun Wai, U., *Economic Essays on Developing Countries*, Rockville, Md, Sijthoff & Noordhoff, 1980.

van Wijnbergen, Sweder, "Stagflationary Effects of Monetary Stabilization Policies: A Quantitative Analysis of South Korea," *Journal of Development Economics*, April 1982, pp. 133–70.

van Wijnbergen, Sweder, "Interest Rate Management in LDCs," *Journal of Monetary Economics*, 1983, pp. 433–52.

8 The Effects of Interest Rates on Savings in Developing Countries*

This chapter reviews available evidence on the effects of interest rates on savings. While it focuses on developing countries, the chapter also reports on recent work on the interest elasticity of savings in the United States that has relevance for the interpretation of the developing-country results.

THE INTEREST ELASTICITY OF SAVINGS IN THE UNITED STATES

A review of estimates of the interest elasticity of savings for the United States concluded "that the bulk of the empirical evidence accumulated since 1967 supports the view that consumption and interest rates are inversely related" (Gylfason, 1981, pp. 235–6). The author added that "the results reported in this paper . . . confirm this view" (p. 235).

Among the reported estimates, from the methodological point of view particular interest attaches to those of Boskin (1978), who utilized after-tax real interest rates in a structural estimation of the US aggregate consumption function by the use of instrumental variables. Boskin obtained an interest elasticity of savings of 0.4, statistically significant at the 1 percent level.

Gylfason (1981) estimated the interest elasticity of savings to be 0.3. The estimation was done by the use of quarterly time series from the data bank of the Federal Reserve Board–MIT–University of Pennsylvania econometric model of the US economy. It involved separately introducing in the estimating equation nominal interest

* Originally published in *Banca Nazionale del Lavaro Quarterly Review*, no. 172; March, 1990, pp. 101–18.

The author is indebted to Warren L. Coats, Maxwell Fry, Alan Gelb, Catherine Mann, Anthony Lanyi, Jaime de Melo, James Tybout, and Alan Walters for helpful comments.

rates and the expected rate of inflation, both of which were statistically significant at the 1 percent level. The estimates are reasonably robust with respect to the choice of the variables.

In turn, Summers derived an aggregate savings function in a continuous time life-cycle framework (1981). Summers' point of departure was the traditional two-period model, in which all income is received in the first period. The individual is assumed to maximize an intertemporal utility function of the form $U(C_1C_2)$, subject to a lifetime budget constraint:

$$C_1 + \frac{C_2}{1 + r} = W_1 \tag{1}$$

where W_1 represents labor income in the first period. In this framework, the interest elasticity of savings depends on the elasticity of substitution between present and future consumption. If this elasticity is greater (less) than one, savings respond positively (negatively) to increases in the interest rate.

Summers suggested that the two-period formulation obscures two important aspects of reality. One is that all savings are eventually dissaved and net positive savings arise only because the young who save are more affluent and more numerous than retired dissavers. The other is that increases in interest rates reduce the present value of lifetime income.

In a multiperiod setting, the endowment W_1 in equation (1) represents the present value of future labor income. When the interest rate rises, this endowment declines as future income is more heavily discounted. As a result of this "human wealth effect," consumption will fall as interest rates rise. Since saving represents a small fraction of income, even a small effect on consumption can translate into a large effect on saving.

For what he considered the "plausible logarithmic utility case," Summers' simulation model showed that the interest elasticity of savings varied between 1.9 and 3.4, depending on the rate of interest. Summers added that "the basic conclusion, a significant long-run interest elasticity of aggregate savings, is quite robust to changes in all of the parameter values . . . Almost any plausible life cycle formulation is likely to imply a high long-run elasticity of savings with respect to the interest rate" (1981, pp. 536–7). In fact, the simulations showed that the human wealth effect far outweighs in importance the elasticity of substitution between present and future consumption.

Under plausible parameter values, the interest elasticity of savings was high even for low values of the substitution elasticity.

Summers further established a relationship between his figures and Boskin's. This was done by assuming that the interest elasticity of wealth is 0.5. Now, as Boskin obtained a "direct" interest elasticity of savings of 0.4 and a savings elasticity of 2.8 with respect to changes in wealth, the "full effect" interest elasticity of savings will be 1.9, which is within the range of Summers' estimates.

Finally, Summers introduced the possibility of bequests. He suggested that the desire to leave bequests was a much more important source of savings than accounted for by the life-cycle hypothesis on the assumption of no bequests. With the human wealth effect increasing in importance in the event of bequests, Summers claimed that his conclusions were strengthened in this case.

Summers' conclusions were criticized by Evans (1983). While in his simulation model Evans obtained interest elasticities of savings approximating those of Summers under the assumption of positive rate of time preference, the elasticity values declined if zero or negative time preference was assumed. However, as Summers (1984) noted, the interest elasticity of savings remained generally above 0.3 even under these assumptions and a negative rate of time preference does not appear realistic.

The interest elasticity of savings declined also if lower rates of return and lower population growth were assumed. But, apart from the case of an unrealistically low (0.2) intertemporal substitution elasticity of consumption, the interest elasticity of savings remained above 0.3 if a positive rate of time preference was assumed.

Evans further claimed that the inclusion of bequests will reduce rather than increase the interest elasticity of savings. Summers objected to this statement, noting that "as long as *any part of the population* is saving for altruistic bequests, the long-run partial equilibrium elasticity of savings with respect to the rate of return will be infinite. Illustrative calculations suggest that it is likely to be very high in the short run as well" (Summers, 1984, pp. 250–1; italics in the original). Summers (1984) also referred to the empirical estimates reported in his NBER Working Paper (1982) and those of Shapiro (1984) and Hansen and Singleton (1983). He wrote:

I find in the more reliable estimates in my working paper values of the intertemporal elasticity of substitution which cluster at the high end of the range Evans and I considered. Similar estimates are found using micro data by Shapiro, and by Hansen–Singleton . . . It is also noteworthy that if proper allowance is made for trend growth in the economy, estimated time preference rates are positive, reinforcing the positive effects of higher rates of return on savings.

Summers (1982) estimated the interest elasticity of savings based on the life-cycle hypothesis from a consumption function incorporating data on the after-tax real rate of interest (R), nonhuman wealth (A), expected income from labor (YL^e), and a risk premium (d). The estimating equation, shown in (2), contains the human wealth effect discussed earlier.

$$C_t = \alpha + [\beta_1 + \beta_2 (R_t)] \left[A_t + \frac{YL^e}{R_t + d} \right] \tag{2}$$

Alternative estimates were made based on the utility function of the representative consumer and linking the wealth–labor income ratio to the after-tax rate of return in reduced form equations. All three methods "suggest a significant response of savings to changes in the rate of return" (Summers, 1982, p. 43).

In turn, in making calculations for the same time period as Boskin had, Friend and Hasbrouck (1983) obtained mixed results. Savings were shown to respond positively to increases in the real interest rate using the Christensen–Jorgensen series employed by Boskin but a negative relationship was shown if an autoregressive procedure was utilized to derive rates of return. The latter conclusion also obtained if quarterly or semi-annual data were used for a later period. However, Friend and Hasbrouck did not allow for the human wealth effect.

Finally, in a time series aggregate consumption function, Blinder and Deaton (1985) found that the elasticity of consumption of nondurable goods and services with respect to the nominal rate of interest was -2.3, which corresponds to a high savings elasticity. However, as the authors note, "the strong elasticity is to the *nominal* interest rate and does not appear if only the *real* rate is allowed in the regression" (1985, p. 489). Also, the elasticity declines to -0.8 if the "surprise" version of the equation favored by the authors, which includes unanticipated income and wealth, is replaced by a "non-surprise" version.

THE INTEREST ELASTICITY OF SAVINGS IN
DEVELOPING COUNTRIES: TIME SERIES ESTIMATES

The effects of interest rates on savings in developing countries were first reviewed by Mikesell and Zinser (1973). At the time, only two published studies on the subject were available; an unpublished study by Brown cited in the paper will be referred to subsequently in its published form. The two studies are by Williamson (1968) and by Gupta (1970).

In five out of six Asian countries, Williamson found the interest elasticity of savings to be negative. However, apart from the case of Japan, the estimates were not significant statistically in the regressions using permanent and transitory disposable income as explanatory variables. In turn, Gupta found the interest elasticity of savings to be positive and statistically significant at the 1 percent level for India, when per capita disposable income was used as the explanatory variable.

Both Williamson and Gupta used the real rate of interest as the explanatory variable in the estimation while the dependent variable was personal savings. In turn, in making estimates for Korea, Brown (1973) employed the real interest rate and, alternatively, the nominal interest rate and the rate of inflation combined as explanatory variables. The dependent variable was the ratio of private saving to private disposable income; other explanatory variables included private disposable income and, in some equations, last period's savings ratio and last period's rate of return to capital.

In the Brown study, the regression coefficients of the real interest rate and the nominal interest rate variables were positive and statistically significant at the 1 percent level in all the regression equations; the coefficient of the rate of inflation variable was negative at the same level of significance. In the equation incorporating last period's savings ratio, the interest elasticity of savings was 0.07 at mean values of the explanatory variables and 0.21 at the peak interest rate reported in 1967. The corresponding elasticities were 0.38 and 0.43 in an equation that includes the nominal interest rate and the rate of inflation, together with last period's rate of return on capital.

The Korean results are of particular interest, given the great variability of interest rates during the period of estimation. Thus, real interest rates ranged from −17.0 percent in 1961 to 19.5 percent in 1967 within the period of estimation of 1957–71.

Brown's results were confirmed by subsequent estimates for Korea by Yusuf and Peters (1984). These authors estimated gross national saving as a function of current GNP, permanent income (defined as a three-year average of GNP), GNP growth, the rate of inflation, the real time deposit rate, and, in some regressions, foreign saving. Estimates were made for the 1965–81 and the 1965–82 periods, experimenting with the introduction of dummy variables for the years 1980–1 and 1980–2, respectively. This was done to exclude years with poor growth performance in Korea.

The results showed the coefficient of the real interest rate variable to be positive and statistically significant at the 1 percent level in all the regressions. It further appears that a 1 percent rise in the interest rate was accompanied by an approximately 1 percent increase in gross national saving; i.e. an interest elasticity of savings of 1. The inclusion of a foreign saving variable and a dummy variable for the years 1980–1 (1980–2) did not affect these results.

The statistical significance and the size of the regression coefficient for the interest rate variable were reduced if gross national saving was replaced by gross domestic saving in the regressions. At the same time, gross national saving is the preferable concept because it measures the country's own efforts, at home or abroad, to mobilize resources for investment.

Savings were shown to positively respond to interest rates in Portugal and Turkey. In both cases, the ratio of national saving to GNP was regressed on the growth rate of GNP, the foreign saving rate, and the real deposit rate of interest (Fry, 1977 and 1979). The coefficient of the real interest rate variable was statistically significant at the 1 percent level in the two instances.

De Melo and Tybout (1986) found that "the real interest rate exhibits a positive, albeit weak, correlation with savings rates" (1986, p. 570) in Uruguay, with t-values of around 1.5. The dependent variable in the regression equation was the ratio of gross domestic saving to GDP; other independent variables were the growth rate of GDP and the ratio of foreign saving to GDP. The calculation pertained to the 1962–83 period.

The coefficient of the real interest rate variable was significant at the 1 percent level if the calculation was limited to the 1962–73 period. But the interest rate variable lost its statistical significance if the exchange rate variable was included in the regressions, in which case foreign saving was excluded from the equation. According to the authors, "one plausible explanation for this interest insensitivity is that movements in *ex post* interest rates during the *tablita* period [the post-1978 period of setting exchange rates in advance with a view of lowering inflation rates] largely reflected movements in the expected rate of devaluation, rather than fluctuations in *ex ante* expected returns" (1986, p. 572).

In a study of 12 Latin American countries, including Argentina, Chile, Colombia, Costa Rica, Guatemala, Haiti, Honduras, Mexico, Panama, Paraguay, Peru, and Uruguay, McDonald (1983) found evidence of a positive relationship between the real interest rate and private savings in most of the countries examined, with the estimated interest elasticities of saving clustering around 0.2.

Gupta (1984) estimated savings functions for 12 Asian countries (Burma, India, Indonesia, Korea, Malaysia, Nepal, Pakistan, Philippines, Singapore, Sri Lanka, Taiwan, and Thailand), separating financial savings and savings in physical assets, the hypothesis being that increases in the interest rate will affect positively the former and negatively the latter. The explanatory variables included permanent income, transitory income, expected inflation, unanticipated inflation, the nominal interest rate, the financial intermediation ratio, and uncertainty with respect to inflation.

Among the ten countries for which the interest rate variable could be defined, its coefficient was positive in nine of the financial savings equations. Of the nine equations, the coefficient of the interest rate variable was statistically significant at the 5 percent level in three cases, and it exceeded its standard error in four cases. In turn, as expected, the coefficient of the interest rate variable was generally negative in the physical savings equations. The coefficient was statistically significant at the 5 percent level in four cases and exceeded its standard error in three cases.

Finally Giovannini (1985) estimated the ratio of consumption in the actual year to that of the preceding year as a function of the real rate of interest for 18 countries, including Argentina, Brazil, Colombia, Jamaica, Mexico, Burma, India, Indonesia, Korea, Malaysia, Philippines, Singapore, Taiwan, Thailand, Greece, Portugal, Turkey, and Kenya, generally from the mid-1960s to the late 1970s. Except for some equations for Brazil, India, and Malaysia, the coefficient of the real interest rate variable was positive in all equations indicating the responsiveness of savings to the real rate of interest. The coefficient was statistically significant at the 1 percent level in three cases, at the 5 percent level in two cases, and exceeded its standard error in three cases. At the same time, one may object to the omission of income variables in the regressions.

THE INTEREST ELASTICITY OF SAVINGS IN DEVELOPING COUNTRIES: CROSS-SECTION AND TIME SERIES ESTIMATES

Errors in observation may reduce to a considerable extent the statistical significance of the regression coefficients in time series estimates. This is particularly the case of developing countries where data on saving are subject to considerable error as discussed further below. Substantial errors are associated also with the data on other economic variables.

Given the error possibilities of the time series data, interest attaches to estimates that combine cross-section and time series observation. At the same time, apart from errors of the data, these estimates have their own limitations because the underlying relationships may differ among countries.

Combined cross-section and time series estimates of the savings function were made for seven Asian developing countries for the 1960s by Fry (1978, 1980) and Fry and Mason (1982). The sample of countries included Burma, India, Korea, Malaysia, Philippines, Singapore, and Taiwan.

Fry (1978, 1980) estimated the effects on the ratio of gross national saving to the gross national product of the following variables: the growth rate of real GNP, per capita income, the real rate of interest, the share of foreign saving in GNP and, in some of the regressions, last period's domestic saving share. The real interest rate was defined, alternatively, by the nominal deposit rate of interest and the nominal government bond yield, adjusted for the expected rate of inflation. Country dummy variables were also included in the regression equation that was estimated by two-stage least squares.

The coefficient of the real interest rate variable had a positive sign and it was statistically significant at the 5 percent level in equations omitting last period's domestic saving ratio. In the equations incorporating this variable, the coefficient was significant at the 5 percent level if the deposit rate of interest and at the 10 percent level if the government bond rate was used in the calculations.

Fry and Mason (1982) replaced the per capita income variable by the population dependency ratio (the population under age 15 divided by the population aged 15 to 64). In the framework of a life-cycle model, the real interest rate variable, defined as the difference between the time deposit rate and the expected rate of inflation, appears multiplied by the GNP growth rate while the dependency ratio appears by itself as well as multiplied by the GNP growth rate.

As in the previous Fry papers, the ratio of national saving to the gross national product was used as the dependent variable. The empirical results showed the coefficient of the real rate of interest variable to be positive and statistically significant at the 1 percent level.

Fry's earlier equation was re-estimated by Giovannini (1983) for the 1970s. With some differences, using domestic rather than national saving and defining the expected rate of inflation by the realized future rate, the estimating equation was identical to that used by Fry. At the same time, the coefficient of the real interest rate variable was not significant statistically in the regression results.

Subsequently, Giovannini (1985) re-estimated Fry's equation for the original period, omitting Korean observations for the years 1967 and 1968. He found that the omission of these two data points eliminate the statistical significance of the real interest rate variable.

In turn, Fry (1987) extended the Fry–Mason equation to a longer period (1961–83), adding seven more Asian developing countries, Bangladesh, Hong Kong, Indonesia, Nepal, Pakistan, Sri Lanka, and Thailand. The coefficient of the real interest rate variable was statistically significant at the 1 percent level in the new regression.

Combining the earlier Fry data for the 1960s and the Giovannini data for the 1970s, and adding more countries, then, gave statistically significant results for the real interest rate variable. Also, excluding the data for Korea increased slightly the value and the statistical significance of the coefficient of this variable in the estimates.

Thus, Fry succeeded in re-establishing the statistical significance of the real interest rate variable for a longer period, including as well as excluding data for Korea. He did not attempt to reproduce, however, Giovannini's cross-section results for 18 countries that did not give statistically significant results for the real interest rate variable. At the same time, Giovannini's methodology was criticized by Gupta: "given our findings that the two groups [Asia and Latin America] should not be pooled, Giovannini's findings may be suspect in view of the fact that his sample is even more heterogeneous than our total sample combining as it does countries from Africa, Asia, Latin America, the Middle East, and Europe" (1987, pp. 307–8).

Gupta considered two groups of countries: Malaysia, Sri Lanka, Singapore, Taiwan, Philippines, India, Thailand, Pakistan, and Korea from Asia and Venezuela, Panama, Honduras, Guatemala, El

Salvador, Paraguay, Mexico, Ecuador, Dominican Republic, Uruguay, Peru, Colombia, and Bolivia from Latin America. He pooled cross-section and time series data for the 1967–76 period.

Gupta regressed gross national saving on permanent income, transitory income, the expected rate of inflation, the unanticipated rate of inflation, the nominal rate of interest, the financial intermediation ratio and the uncertainty with respect to inflation. He added, in some of the regressions, lagged saving and foreign saving as explanatory variables.

While Fry, Fry–Mason, and Giovannini used two-stage least squares, Gupta also made estimates by ordinary least squares as well as by the Fuller–Battese and Parks DV methods. The results showed the coefficient of the interest rate variable to be positive under all four methods of estimation and to be significant statistically at the 1 percent level under the Parks DV method, at the 5 percent level under two-stage least squares, at slightly less than the 10 percent level under ordinary least squares, and below this level under the Fuller–Battese method in the Asian regressions. They were not significant statistically in the Latin American regressions; in the latter case, rapid and variable rates of inflation may have affected the statistical significance of the results.

Leite and Makonnen (1986) used pooled cross-section data consisting of 14 observations for six African countries, Benin, Burkina Faso, Côte d'Ivoire, Niger, Senegal, and Togo, to regress gross private saving on lagged gross private saving, the rate of interest, and the share of exports in gross domestic product. In all equations interest rates were found to be positively related to savings and highly significant. However, the effect is much reduced and not statistically significant if changes is disposable income are introduced in the equation.

Khatkhate (1988) divided developing countries in three groups, depending on whether they had positive real interest rates, moderately negative real interest rates, or strongly negative real interest rates. But only 3.5 percentage points separate the first and the third groups, which is very little considering that real rates averaged for long period between +10 percent and −20 percent. These considerations apply *a fortiori* to the subsequent division of developing countries into two groups, according to whether they had real interest rates above or below the median. Further problems arise about the choice of interest rates that is not indicated in the paper.

Thus, one cannot obtain reliable results in the relationship between real interest rates and saving on the basis of the comparison of group data. To do so, it is necessary to undertake regression analysis for the entire sample as it was done by the authors cited above.

All the described estimates are subject to the deficiency that they fail to account for the limitations of savings by low-income recipients due to liquidity constraints. Liquidity constraints have been introduced in the estimation by Rossi (1988) in terms of the total stock of traded assets. Rossi made estimates by pooling time series and cross-section data for six developing country regions. The regions include sub-Saharan Africa (12 countries), North Africa and the Middle East (five countries), East and South Asia and the Pacific (nine countries), Central America and the Caribbean (eight countries), South America (nine countries), and Southern Europe (six countries). The initial year is 1973 while the terminal year varies between 1979 and 1983, depending on data availability for the individual countries.

In the estimating equation, next period's private consumption is expressed as a function of real disposable income, real government expenditure, the real rate of return, and a borrowing constraint. The rate of return is defined, alternatively, as the time deposit interest rate and the foreign interest rate adjusted for expected changes in the exchange rate. The author's conclusions are stated as follows:

> Contrary to Giovannini's (1985) findings, there is clear-cut evidence of a positive relationship between the rate of growth of per capita consumption and the expected real interest rate. Furthermore, in three regions out of six (Middle East and North Africa, Southern Europe, and Central America) the coefficient of [the real interest variable] also turns out to be positive and significantly different from zero, although this result depends on the definition of the real interest rate . . . It is important to stress that if the sample excluded 1982 and 1983 [the years of the debt crisis] South America would also have a positive [real interest rate] coefficient that was significantly different from zero. (pp. 120–23)

From the estimated equation, Rossi (1988) derives the interest elasticity of consumption, when the negative sign corresponds to a positive saving elasticity. Depending on the specifications employed, the elasticities were: sub-Saharan Africa, −0.06 to −0.25; Middle East and North Africa, −0.24 to −1.25; East and South Asia and the

Pacific, −0.08 to −0.18: Central America and the Caribbean, −0.37; South America, −0.01 to −0.10; and Southern Europe, −0.05 to −0.18.

INTERPRETATION OF THE RESULTS

As noted earlier, in a two-period model the interest elasticity of savings depends on the elasticity of substitution between present and future consumption. This statement may be reformulated in terms of substitution and income effects.

The substitution effect operates because a rise in the interest rate reduces the price of future consumption. Now, unless future consumption is an inferior good, individuals will substitute future consumption for present consumption; i.e. they will save more.

But, there is also an income effect in the sense that higher interest rates raise incomes. This fact will induce individuals to increase their present as well as future consumption; i.e. they will save less. In a particular case, the entire increment in income due to higher interest rates will be consumed today. This will be so if an individual saves a fixed amount, e.g. for retirement. Now, a rise in interest rates will induce the individual to increase present consumption, with no change in future consumption.

The effects of changes in interest rates on savings in a two-period model are thus determined by the relative strengths of substitution and income effects, which are not known *a priori*. This statement, traditionally made in textbooks, needs to be modified by considering that, for borrowers, the income effect goes in the same direction as the substitution effect. Now, if savers and borrowers are private individuals, their income effects will compensate and we are left with the substitution effect.

This symmetry will not obtain if borrowers are businesses. Correspondingly, interest attaches to empirical estimates. These will be summarized below.

A number of empirical studies have been undertaken to estimate the interest elasticity of saving in the United States. The bulk of these studies show the elasticity to be positive. They also show it to be relatively high, 0.3–0.4, even excluding the human wealth effect; i.e. a 1 percent increase in interest rates would raise savings by 0.3–0.4 percent.

The estimates for developing countries tend to be lower, in the range of 0.1 to 0.2. Moreover, a number of estimates are not significant statistically. At the same time, a variety of factors may have reduced the statistical significance of the estimates.

First of all, estimates of saving are subject to considerable error. These estimates are usually obtained as the difference between domestic investment and foreign saving, both of which are observed with error.

In developing countries, fixed investment is customarily estimated from data on the importation and the domestic production of machinery and on materials used in construction, which are subject to error. This is the case even more for inventory accumulation. At the same time, inventories decline as interest rates go up, hence reducing savings at higher interest rates.

Foreign saving is derived as the difference between the exports and the imports of goods and services both of which are subject to considerable error. Also, depending on whether the exchange rate is overvalued or undervalued, we observe underreporting (over-reporting) of exports and overreporting (underreporting) of imports. And, foreign saving is *ipso facto* underestimated (overestimated) if the exchange rate is overvalued (undervalued).

Taking the difference between domestic investment and foreign saving, both estimated with error, will magnify the error of estimate in each. The resulting error in estimating national savings may have contributed to the fluctuations observed over time and reduced the statistical significance of the estimated interest elasticity of savings.

Also, ideally, the estimates should relate to personal savings. While this is the case for developed countries, for most developing countries such estimates are not available, hence the use of national savings data, which also include business saving and government saving that do not respond to interest rates. Correspondingly, the estimated interest elasticity of savings will be reduced and will be subject to error.

There are further errors associated with the measurement of interest rates. While most authors employed time deposit rates, for some countries Giovannini (1985) used commercial paper or Treasury bill rates, which may move independently from time deposit rates. And, time deposit rates are relevant for financial savings but not for nonfinancial savings. Moreover, time deposit rates may not move parallel with rates paid by borrowers whose dissavings reduce the total amount saved. Another source of error is the lack of consideration given to taxes on returns to savings.

A variety of approaches has been tried to estimate the expected rate of inflation. All of these approaches are subject to error as inflation expectations are not directly observed. Correspondingly, the estimation of the expected rate of inflation also tends to reduce the statistical significance of the coefficient of the real interest rate variable.

The same conclusion follows if we consider that the estimated relationships are of a short-term character as the savings and the interest rate observations refer to the same year. For one thing, there are lags in the adjustment process. For another thing, savings may not respond to transitional changes in the interest rates.

We have considered various factors that tend to lower the statistical significance of the estimated interest elasticity of savings. In turn, the size of the elasticity is reduced by reason of the omission of the human wealth variable as discussed in the first section and by the lack of consideration given to the liquidity constraint (except for the Rossi study) as noted in the previous section.

The interest elasticity of savings may also be underestimated by reason of the fact that interest rates are often maintained over long periods under the interest controls observed in many developing countries. This will, then, limit the range of observations, which was not the case, e.g. in Korea, where large changes in interest rates occurred. At the same time, it is for Korea where one observed the highest, and statistically significant, interest elasticity of saving among developing countries. In turn, as suggested by Shaw, small and reversible changes in interest rates may not affect savings.

Savers may ignore a possible transitory increase from, say, 4 to 6 percent in rates of return, but they are less likely to maintain consumption-saving patterns when rates of return change, in the context of economic reform, from negative levels to positive 10 or 15 percent and more. Given the relative scarcity of wealth in the lagging economies, the income effect of higher rates of return should not be expected to overwhelm the effects of substitution of more wealth for less consumption now. (Shaw, 1973, p. 73)

Note finally, that estimates of the interest elasticity of saving have been made in a partial equilibrium framework, including different sets of variables in the estimating equation. At the same time, the equations do not include the prices of alternative assets, such as gold, houses, and consumer durables.

The last point brings one to the choice of assets. There is evidence from several countries, including Portugal and Turkey, that negative real interest rates bring a shift to gold, real estate, and consumer durables, which latter are not included in savings as measured in the national income accounts.

Thus far, the discussion has proceeded in a domestic framework that has been used in all the reported estimates. But savers in developing countries have a choice between domestic and foreign assets. While this choice may be limited by currency restrictions, it exists nevertheless. If capital transactions are prohibited, there are black markets as well as possibilities for the underinvoicing of exports and the overinvoicing of imports.

Studies of capital flight have introduced interest rate variables. While domestic interest rates have not been significant statistically, possibly because of the existence of two-way causation, foreign interest rates have been significant in the equations for Mexico and Venezuela (Cuddington, 1987). Thus, for these countries, capital flight appears to respond to interest rates obtainable abroad.

In conclusion, although a positive coefficient has been obtained in most cases, available estimates are far from unanimous as to whether interest rates significantly affect savings in developing countries. But, errors in estimation tend to lower the statistical significance of the interest elasticity of saving. Also, for various reasons, the size of the estimated coefficient is reduced.

At the same time, there is evidence that negative real interest rates lead to a shift from savings to the purchase of gold, real estate, and consumer durables. Furthermore, higher interest rates abroad contribute to the outflow of savings, thereby reducing the amount available for domestic investment.

References

Arrieta, Gerardo M. Gonzales, "Interest Rates, Savings, and Growth in LDCs: An Assessment of Recent Empirical Research," *World Development*, May 1988, pp. 589–605.
Blinder, Alan S. and Angus Deaton, "The Time Series Consumption Function Revisited," *Brookings Papers on Economic Activity*, 1985(2), pp. 465–511.

Boskin, Michael J., "Taxation, Saving and the Rate of Interest," *Journal of Political Economy*, 86, April 1978, pp. S3–S27.

Brown, Gilbert T., *Korean Pricing Policies and Economic Development in the 1960s*, Baltimore, Md, Johns Hopkins University Press, 1973.

Cuddington, John T. "Macroeconomic Determinants of Capital Flight: An Econometric Investigation" in Donald R. Lessard and John Williamson, eds, *Capital Flight and the Third World Debt*, Washington, DC, Institute for International Economics, 1987, pp. 88–102.

de Melo, Jaime and James Tybout, "The Effects of Financial Liberalization on Savings and Investment in Uruguay," *Economic Development and Cultural Change*, 34, April 1986, pp. 561–88.

Evans, Owen J., "Tax Policy, the Interest Elasticity of Saving, and Capital Accumulation: Numerical Analysis of Theoretical Models," *American Economic Review*, 73, June 1983, pp. 398–410.

Friend, Irwin and Joel Hasbrouck, "Saving and After-Tax Rates of Return," *Review of Economics and Statistics*, 65, November 1983, pp. 537–43.

Fry, Maxwell, "Financial Instruments and Markets," in *Conferencia Internacional sobre Economia Portuguesa*, Lisbon, German Marshall Fund and Fundação Calouste Gulbenkian, 1977, vol. II, pp. 191–208.

Fry, Maxwell J., "Money and Capital or Financial Deepening in Economic Development?," *Journal of Money, Credit and Banking*, 10, November 1978, pp. 474–5.

Fry, Maxwell J., "The Cost of Financial Repression in Turkey," *Savings and Development*, 3, 1979(2), pp. 127–35.

Fry, Maxwell J., "Savings, Investment, Growth and the Cost of Financial Repression," *World Development*, 8, April 1980, pp. 317–28.

Fry, Maxwell J., *Money, Interest, and Banking in Economic Development*, Baltimore, Md, Johns Hopkins University Press, 1987.

Fry, Maxwell J. and Andrew Mason, "The Variable Rate-of-Growth Effect in the Life-Cycle Saving Model: Children, Capital Inflows, Interest and Growth in a New Specification of the Life-Cycle Model Applied to Seven Asian Developing Countries," *Economic Inquiry*, 20, July 1982, pp. 426–42.

Giovannini, Alberto, "The Interest Elasticity of Savings in Developing Countries: The Existing Evidence," *World Development*, 11, July 1983, pp. 601–8.

Giovannini, Alberto, "Saving and the Real Interest Rate in LDCs," *Journal of Development Economics*, 18, August 1985, pp. 197–210.

Gupta, Kanhaya L., "Personal Saving in Developing Nations: Further Evidence," *The Economic Record*, 46, 1970, pp. 243–9.

Gupta, Kanhaya L., "Financial Intermediation, Interest Rate and the Structure of Savings: Evidence from Asia," *Journal of Economic Development*, 9, July 1984, pp. 7–24.

Gupta, Kanhaya L., "Aggregate Savings, Financial Intermediation, and Interest Rate," *Review of Economics and Statistics*, 69, May 1987, pp. 303–11.

Gylfason, Thorvalder, "Interest Rates, Inflation, and the Aggregate Consumption Function," *Review of Economics and Statistics*, 63, May 1981, pp. 233–45.

Hansen, Lars P. and Kenneth Singleton, "Stochastic Consumption, Risk Aversion and the Intertemporal Behavior of Asset Returns," *Journal of Political Economy*, 91, April 1983, pp. 249–65.

Khatkhate, Deena R., "Assessing the Impact of Interest Rates in Less Developed Countries," *World Development*, May 1988, pp. 577–88.

Leite, Sergio P. and Dawit Makonnen, "Saving and Interest Rates in the BCEA Countries: An Empirical Analysis," *Savings and Development*, July–September, 1986, pp. 219–31.

McDonald, Donogh, "The Determinants of Saving Behavior in Latin America," Washington, DC, International Monetary Fund, 1983, mimeo.

Mikesell, Raymond F. and James E. Zinser, "The Nature of the Savings Function in Developing Countries: A Survey of the Theoretical and Empirical Literature," *Journal of Economic Literature*, 11, March 1973, pp. 1–26.

Rossi, Nicola, "Government Spending, the Real Interest Rate, and the Behavior of Liquidity-Constrained Consumers in Developing Countries," *IMF Staff Papers*, 351, March 1988, pp. 104–40.

Shapiro, Matthew, "The Permanent Income Hypothesis and the Real Rate: Some Evidence from Panel Data," *Economics Letters*, 14, 1984(1), pp. 93–100.

Shaw, Edward S., *Financial Deepening in Developing Countries*, New York, Oxford University Press, 1973.

Summers, Lawrence H., "Capital Taxation and Accumulation in a Life Cycle Growth Model," *American Economic Review*, 71, September 1981, pp. 533–44.

Summers, Lawrence, H., "Tax Policy, the Rate of Return, and Savings," Working Paper No. 995, Cambridge, Mass., National Bureau of Economic Research, September 1982.

Summers, Lawrence H., "The After-Tax Rate of Return Affects Private Savings," *American Economic Review*, 74, May 1984, pp. 249–53.

Williamson, Jeffrey G., "Personal Saving in Developing Nations: An Intertemporal Cross-Section Estimate for Asia," *The Economic Record*, 44, 1968, pp. 194–210.

Yusuf, Shahid and R. Kyle Peters, "Savings Behavior and Its Implications for Domestic Resource Mobilization. The Case of the Republic of Korea," World Bank Staff Working Papers No. 628, Washington, DC, World Bank, April 1984.

Part V

Planning and Socialist Reform

9 Indicative Planning in Developing Countries*

INTRODUCTION

Following the example of the Soviet Union, several developing countries prepared multi-annual plans in the early postwar period. These plans were comprehensive and dirigiste. Their failure brought about changes in the planning process towards an approach that has been christened indicative planning.

Under indicative planning, sectoral targets are established but these are not compulsory for the private sector. In a subsequent stage, these targets have also been abandoned and emphasis has been given to prices and markets.

This chapter will deal with indicative planning in developing countries. It will describe the efforts made to undertake indicative planning and evaluate these efforts. It will further consider the more recent orientation towards reliance on incentives and markets. Finally, the role of the public sector will be examined.

AN EVALUATION OF INDICATIVE PLANNING

Indicative planning (for short, planning) involves the establishment of sectoral targets which are not compulsory for the private sector. These targets are imbedded in macroeconomic projections that pertain to a period of several years.

Planning in developing countries goes back to colonial times. In fact, at US insistence, four-year recovery programs were drawn up by the European countries participating in the Marshall Plan, which included their overseas territories. However primitive these plans were, they provided a basis for planning at the time of independence.

* Originally prepared as a paper for the Conference on Indicative Planning, held in Washington, DC, in April 1990.

The author is indebted to participants at the Conference and to Mary Shirley for helpful comments and to Shigeru Akiyama for research assistance.

As Killick notes, "in Africa during the 1960s 'having a plan' became almost a *sine qua non* of political independence. With the active encouragement of the World Bank and other aid agencies, most newly independent states hastened to prepare medium-term development plans, often building upon foundations already laid in the colonial period" (1983, p. 47). He adds that "the general model to which planners aspired was for a 'comprehensive' plan (in the sense of including the private sector and para-statal organizations) that presented a strategy and targets for the development of the economy, typically for a five-year period" (ibid.).

The statement about Africa also applies to Asia where countries prepared development plans upon securing independence. Planning assumed particular importance in India where the Soviet example motivated the earlier plans. Multi-annual plans were also prepared in Sri Lanka, Pakistan and, subsequently, Bangladesh.

Different considerations apply to Latin America, where national independence was attained in the nineteenth century. In the years following the Second World War, the UN Economic Commission for Latin America proposed planning to be undertaken by Latin American countries, expressing the view that "the principal task of government . . . is to give long-run direction to economic development by the means of detailed plans" (Hirschman, 1961, p. 22). However, plans were not prepared until 1961 when the Alliance for Progress program sponsored by the United States came into effect. As Urrutia notes, "in Latin America, development plans were a prerequisite for qualification for loans from the Alliance for Progress programme" (1988, pp. 5–6).

Foreign aid agencies contributed to planning also elsewhere in the developing world. Thus, "the macro-economic plans that calculated foreign-exchange needs and showed that a country could profitably absorb foreign aid were used by aid officers in bilateral and multilateral agencies to justify credits and grants . . . International bureaucracies had trouble convincing donors to lend to countries where such justifications, in the form of plans, did not exist" (p. 6).

This statement applies to the World Bank as well as to the US government. The World Bank's 1949–50 Annual Report stated that member countries "know, too, that if they formulate a well-balanced development program based on the [Bank] Mission's recommendations, the Bank will stand ready to help them carry out the program by financing appropriate projects" (p. 18). Also, it was noted that the United States "in a complete reversal of Point Four philosophy has shifted its support from technical assistance to planning" (Watson and Dirlam, 1965, p. 48).

But, how about the success of the plans? An early appraisal, in the mid-1960s, was made by Albert Waterston, the World Bank's planning expert. Having reviewed the experience of more than 100 countries, Waterston reached the conclusion that "among developing nations with some kind of a market economy and a sizeable private sector, only one or two countries seem to have been consistently successful in carrying out plans" (1966, p. 14).

More recent reviews of planning experiences of developing countries confirm Waterston's conclusion. Thus, two decades later, Killick concluded that "medium-term development planning has in most ldcs almost entirely failed to deliver the advantages expected of it" (1986, p. 103).

Killick also carried out a comprehensive survey of the African experience. In his view, "there is no doubt that the general outcome of the above survey of the available evidence on plan execution has been negative . . . Actual results show wide dispersion about target levels and planners seem impotent to modify more than marginally the impact of market forces" (1983, p. 57).

In Senegal, "scant attention is paid to implementation and the Ministry of Planning has little idea of what is actually happening" (1983, p. 57). In Ghana, "we see an almost total gap between the theoretical advantages of planning and the record of the [seven-year plan, 1963–9]. Far from providing a superior set of signals, it was seriously flawed as a technical document and, in any case, subsequent actions of government bore little relation to it" (Killick, 1978, pp. 144–6). This situation continued in subsequent years and the "five-year plan [published in 1975] had even less impact than the seven-year plan of 1963" (Killick, 1983, p. 56). In Tanzania, a sympathetic observer noted that while the 1964–9 plan soon became un-operational, the 1969–74 plan was "standing up better to the test of time" although it remained weak "on the implementation side" (Waide, 1974, p. 49). The economic catastrophy in Tanzania was yet to come.

A detailed study, *Plan Implementation in Nigeria, 1962–66* by Dean, concluded that the implementation of the plan "was largely unsatisfactory" (1972, p. 241). Apart from the lack of fulfilment of plan targets, "the plan did not play a central role in any other realm of national life. It played a peripheral role in the government's decision-making processes; the satisfactory growth of the economy prior to 1966 was due more to the private sector than to direct action under the plan" (p. 236). This situation continued in the 1970s (Adeniyi, 1980).

Even in Kenya, which has a long tradition in planning, while the pattern of government capital formation was shifted in desired directions, "other policy intentions were only partly fulfilled and some were not acted upon at all. There was, moreover, uncertainty about the extent to which those projects and policies which were executed could correctly be attributed to the plan as such" (Killick, 1983, p. 55).

Another feature of African planning was overoptimism, with realization falling much short of the targets (Killick, 1983, p. 50). This was the case also in India in the periods ranging from dirigiste to indicative planning (Gupta, 1987, Table 1). More importantly, these periods of planning were also periods of poor economic performance. This is indicated by a review of Indian planning in the 1950–75 period.

> Our plans were highly sophisticated and elegantly written. Their details were well articulated. They met consistency and sensitivity tests. But when the results achieved in consequence measure so poorly with those of others [in the developing world], sophistication is indeed in danger of turning into sophistry. (Patel, 1980, p. 5)

The author adds, "our retrogression in the world economy took place precisely during the golden age of its growth in the postwar period . . . We have been left much behind in this race. A close look at the rest of the world economy could give us the impression of our being a decaying rather than a developing country – at least in a relative way of speaking" (ibid.).

In fact, the planning models used in India were formulated for a closed economy, concentrating on import substitution, with emphasis given to heavy industry. It is only with the Sixth Five-Year Plan (1980–5) that exports emerged as an objective and improvements occurred. Nevertheless, exports were treated as exogenous in the models that failed to include the behavioral aspects of the economy (Jain, 1986, p. 54).

Today, there is increasing understanding in India of the need for policy changes that are not accommodated in the planning model. Thus, Gupta concludes his review of Indian planning by noting that "it is claimed by many economists, with few dissenting voices, that freer entry into the world market and the allowal of the natural extinction of less competitive and unproductive units may result in a revamping of India's industrial management, improvement of productive efficiency, and reduction of industrial costs" (1987, p. 96).

Planning was even less successful in Bangladesh (Hasnath, 1987). Also, in Sri Lanka planning under the socialist government coincided with poor economic performance. Performance improved as the newly-elected conservative government "concentrated on the management of the economy and the implementation of policies and incentives which stimulated growth through the market system" (Gunatilleke, 1988, p. 99).

Economic growth rates were higher in Asian countries where no plans were prepared (Hong Kong and Singapore) or plans concentrated on the public sector and on the preparation of macroeconomic projections (Korea, Malaysia, Taiwan, and Thailand). Mexico, which was perhaps the most successful Latin American economy in the 1960s and 1970s, did not prepare plans while in Colombia medium-term planning gave place to short-term policymaking.

In other Latin American countries, planning came into disuse as the period of the Alliance for Progress ended. As noted by Garcia d'Acuna, "the analyses of the Latin American experience leads us to conclude that while there were periods and instances in which planning played a significant role in orienting the development process in Latin America, it definitely did not manage to insert itself in the real process of decision making and of shaping economic policy" (1982, p. 26).

More generally, the 1980s brought a decline in planning in the developing world. As Urrutia noted "only a few UN agencies and academic economists continued to believe that macro-economic planning could be an effective management tool in developing countries. The attention of the planners in fact focused on short-term policy making" (1988, p. 8).

RELYING ON INCENTIVES AND MARKETS

The decline of planning may be explained in different ways. In a narrower sense, this decline may be attributed to the lack of success of planning or, expressed differently, an unfavorable cost-benefit ratio in planning. In a broader sense, the decline in planning reflects the growing understanding of the importance of incentives and markets *vis-à-vis* the observed deficiencies of planning. In this connection, the conclusion of a study of planning in developing countries by a World Bank expert deserves full quotation.

> Experience has revealed the inherent limitations of the techno-cratic blueprint in a rapidly changing environment. Available analytical techniques are just not able to cope with the complexity of economic change to produce plans that are up to date, relevant, and comprehensive. Investment planning based on input–output models has fallen foul of unforeseen changes in technical coefficients and demand patterns. Similarly, manpower forecasting has been highly inaccurate because of the difficulties in specifying particular types of skills and in projecting demand over a long period. These technical weaknesses are unlikely to be cured by any foreseeable improvement in data and analytical techniques. Obsession with efforts to improve comprehensive programming capacity diverts attention and resources from more relevant issues. The alternative of making greater use of markets and prices generates less formidable technocratic problems and allows more efficient adjustment. (Agarwala, 1983, p. 11)

An important aspect of increased reliance on incentives and markets is participation in the international division of labor. With most developing countries having small domestic markets, pro-ductivity can be increased in an open economy. At the same time, there is a conflict between opening the economy and planning. In this regard, conclusions reached by the author nearly a quarter of a century ago remain valid:

> It is suggested here that planning, as understood in a narrower sense, is inward-looking in character: It can best be applied in countries whose economy is more or less closed to foreign influences and it provides an inducement for reducing reliance on international trade. To begin with, the uncertainty of plans and forecasts increases with the degree of openness of the national economy. While information on interindustry relationships can be utilized to derive a feasible pattern of production associated with a growth target in a closed economy, disappointed expectations in regard to exports and unforeseen changes in imports will give rise

to discrepancies between plans and realization if the foreign trade sector is of importance.

Correspondingly, the chances for plan fulfilment can be increased by limiting dependence on international exchange. And since growth in an open economy is "unbalanced" in the sense that the production and consumption of individual commodities, and the output of interrelated sectors, are growing at unequal rates, the desire to lessen the uncertainty introduced by foreign trade will necessarily lead to the advocacy of balanced growth. (Balassa, 1966, p. 385)

At the same time, outward orientation brings important benefits. This may be indicated by the experience of countries following different policies. Among the countries selected for this analysis, Korea, Singapore and Taiwan consistently followed outward-oriented policies; Argentina, Brazil and Mexico embarked on an inward-oriented strategy but subsequently carried out reforms, especially Brazil; and India is the *par excellence* case of inward orientation.

The combined shares of the three Far Eastern countries in the manufactured exports of the developing countries increased from 6 percent in 1963 to 32 percent in 1986. Within this group, Korea showed the largest increase (from 1 to 12 percent), followed by Singapore (from 1 to 6 percent) and by Taiwan (from 4 to 14 percent).

Conversely, India's share in the manufactured exports of the developing countries declined from 20 percent in 1963 to 3 percent in 1986. India was able to increase the volume of its manufactured exports only by 3 percent a year during this period as against an average annual growth rate of 13 percent in all developing countries, taken together.

The combined share of the three large Latin American countries remained unchanged at 8 percent between 1963 and 1986. Argentina and Mexico lost market shares (with a decline from 2 percent to 1 percent in the first case and from 4 percent to 3 percent in the second) while Brazil was a gainer, with an increase from 1 to 4 percent.

While the record of the Far Eastern countries in manufactured export growth is well-appreciated, it is less known that these countries also made substantial gains in exporting nonfuel primary products. Their combined share in the exports of these products by developing countries rose from 2 percent in 1963 to 8 percent in 1986, with the gains being concentrated in Korea and Taiwan. This contrasts with a decline in India's export market share from 4 percent to 3 percent. In the same period, Argentina's market share declined from 7 percent to 5 percent and Mexico's from 4 percent to 3 percent while Brazil's share increased from 7 percent to 10 percent.

It appears, then, that the policies applied affected not only manufactured exports but also the exports of nonfuel primary products. This is hardly surprising, given the discrimination against primary activities, in particular agriculture, associated with inward orientation and the lack of such discrimination under outward-oriented policies.

Taken together, the share of the three Far Eastern countries in the nonfuel exports of the developing countries grew from 9 percent in 1963 to 24 percent in 1986, with Korea showing the largest increase. By contrast, India's market share fell from 6 percent to 3 percent. In Latin America, the combined share of the three countries declined from 16 percent to 11 percent, with the largest decrease shown in Argentina.

Increases in exports contribute to economic growth in a variety of ways. They permit resource allocation according to comparative advantage, allow for the exploitation of economies of scale, ensure fuller use of capacity, and provide incentives for technological change in response to the carrot and the stick of competition, resulting in improvements in the efficiency of investment. Export expansion also tends to lead to higher domestic savings as a greater proportion of incomes are derived from exports, and a higher share of the increments in incomes associated with export growth, is saved.

Incremental capital–output ratios provide a crude indication of the efficiency of investment. In the 1963–86 period, these ratios were the lowest in the Far Eastern countries, averaging 3.3 in Taiwan, 3.6 in Korea, and 4.2 in Singapore. Incremental capital–output ratios in Latin America ranged between 4.4 in Brazil and 9.8 in Argentina; they averaged 5.1 in India.

Savings ratios were by far the lowest in India, 14.8 percent; they averaged 27 percent in the three Far Eastern countries and 23 percent in the three large Latin American countries. Intercountry differences in capital–output ratios and saving ratios, in turn, explain differences in economic growth rates.

In the 1963–86 period, GDP growth rates averaged 9 percent in Korea and Singapore, as well as in Taiwan. They varied between 2 percent in Argentina and 7 percent in Brazil, averaging 6 percent in

Mexico. Finally, average GDP growth rates were 4 percent in India. Differences are even larger in per capita terms, with Singapore leading at 8 percent and Argentina and India at the bottom of the list with 1 percent.

Comparisons of incremental capital–output ratios are predicated on the assumption that labor has no opportunity cost. This will not be the case for skilled and technical labor and, for more of the countries concerned, does not hold for unskilled labor either. Correspondingly interest attaches to comparisons of total factor productivity growth that measures change in the productivity of capital and labor combined.

The advantages of outward orientation are apparent from comparisons of estimates of total factor productivity growth for 20 developing countries covering the postwar period. Thus, Chenery (1986, Table 2.2) reports that total factor productivity increased at annual rates of over 3 percent in outward-oriented countries while increases were 1 percent or less in countries with especially pronounced inward orientation. In particular, India experienced a decline in total factor productivity in the manufacturing sector between 1959–60 and 1979–80 (Ahluwalia, 1985).

Another study has shown that export expansion was positively, and import substitution negatively, correlated with the growth of factor productivity in 13 Korean, Turkish and Yugoslav industries during the period preceding the quadrupling of oil prices in 1973 (Nishimizu and Robinson, 1984, Table 5). The results obtained for Turkey confirm the conclusions reached earlier by Krueger and Tuncer (1982) for this country.

There is further evidence that exports contributed to the growth of total factor productivity. Thus, in a cross-section investigation of 39 countries, intercountry differences in domestic and foreign investment and in the growth of the labor force explained 53 percent of the intercountry variation in GDP growth rates while adding an export variable raised the coefficient of determination to 0.71 (Michalopoulos and Jay, 1973). Applying the same procedure to pooled data of 11 semi-industrial countries for the 1960–6 and 1966–73 periods, Balassa (1978) found that adding an export variable increased the explanatory power of the regression equation from 58 to 77 percent. Subsequently, Feder separated the effects of exports on economic growth into two parts: productivity differences between exports and nonexport activities and externalities generated by exports, and obtained highly significant results for broadly as well as for narrowly defined categories of semi-industrial countries for the 1964–77 period.

The cited estimates refer to the period of rapid growth in the world economy. Further interest attaches to the question as to whether these results hold up in the subsequent period of external shocks, in the form of the quadrupling of oil prices and the world recession. Applying production function estimation to the 1973–8 period, the earlier findings on the importance of exports for economic growth have been reconfirmed (Balassa, 1985).

Data available for 43 developing countries have further permitted analyzing the implications for economic growth of export orientation at the beginning of the period of external shocks and of policy responses to external shocks in the 1973–8 period. The extent of export orientation in the initial year has been defined in terms of deviations of actual from hypothetical per capita exports, the latter having been estimated by reference to per capita incomes, population, and the ratio of mineral exports to GNP. In turn, alternative policy responses have been defined as export promotion, import substitution, and additional net external financing.

The impact of export orientation on economic growth is indicated by the existence of a difference of 1 percentage point in GNP growth rates between developing economies in the upper quartile and the lower quartile of the distribution in terms of their export orientation at the beginning of the period of external shocks. Furthermore, a difference of 1.2 percentage points in GDP growth is obtained in comparing the upper and the lower quartiles of the distribution as regards reliance on export promotion, as against import substitution and additional external financing (Balassa, 1985).

The results are cumulative, indicating that both initial export orientation and reliance on exports in response to external shocks importantly contributed to economic growth in developing countries during the period under consideration. These factors explain a large proportion of intercountry differences in GNP growth rates in the 1973–8 period, with a difference of 3.2 percentage points between the upper quartile and the lower quartile of the distribution in the 43 developing countries.

These results are immune to the criticism according to which the causation between exports and economic growth is not uni-directional. At the same time, recent research has examined the causes of the favorable effects of exports on economic growth. De Melo and Robinson have put emphasis on externalities derived from exports (1990) while Romer has indicated that outward orientation will increase the benefits derived from research and development (1989).

As noted earlier, in the 1980s developing countries gave increasing attention to prices and markets. This is particularly apparent as far as trade policies are concerned. Thus, while the debt crisis led to the imposition of protective measures in several of these countries, these were undone in subsequent years. As a result, in most of the 17 highly-indebted countries, there was less protection – both in terms of tariffs and quantitative import restrictions – in the mid-1980s than before the oil crises (Laird and Nogues, 1988, Table 1).

Trade liberalization was given impetus by World Bank adjustment programs. Among 40 countries that received World Bank trade adjustment loans, policy conditions included establishing realistic exchange rates in 38 cases, improving export policy in 33 cases, and liberalizing imports in 29 cases (Thomas, 1989, Table 1).

The preliminary results show a favorable picture. Trade adjustment loan recipients performed better than nonrecipients in all categories. In particular, they increased exports to a greater extent, and while imports also increased, the adjustment loan recipients improved their resource balance compared with nonrecipients. They also exhibited improved performance in GDP growth, investment ratios, and inflation and reduced their debt–export and debt service–export ratios (1989, Table 4).

CONCLUSIONS

This chapter has provided an evaluation of indicative planning in developing countries. It has further considered recent efforts to increase reliance on prices and markets. Finally, the role of the public sector in developing countries has been examined.

Indicative planning involves the establishment of sectoral targets which are not compulsory for the private sector and are imbedded in macroeconomic projections that pertain to a period of several years. Indicative planning has been widely practiced in developing countries during the postwar period. At the same time, the review presented in this chapter indicates that it has failed to have favorable economic effects.

The 1980s have brought about a decline in indicative planning in the developing world. This decline may be explained by the lack of success of planning and by the growing understanding of the importance of incentives and markets. An important aspect of increased reliance on incentives and markets is participation in the international division of labor that conflicts with planning. At the same time, participation in the international division of labor brings important benefits in increasing total factor productivity, and thereby contributing to economic growth.

Apart from giving preference to incentives and markets over indicative planning, the chapter has indicated the desirability of limiting the size of the government and the advantages of private over public investment. However, infrastructural investment creates opportunities to private investment. At the same time, such investment should be subject to rigorous project evaluation and be undertaken in the framework of multi-annual programs.

References

Adeniyi, Eniola O., "National Development Planning and Plan Administration in Nigeria," *Journal of Administration Overseas*, 19, 3, July 1980.

Agarwala, Ramgopal, "Planning in Developing Countries. Lessons of Experience," World Bank Staff Working Papers No. 576, Washington, DC, December 1983.

Ahluwalia, Isher J., *Industrial Growth in India: stagnation since the mid-sixties*, Delhi, New York; Oxford University Press, 1985.

Balassa, Bela, "Planning in an Open Economy," *Kyklos*, 19, 1966, pp. 383–410.

Balassa, Bela, "Exports and Economic Growth: Further Evidence," *Journal of Development Economics*, 5, June 1978, pp. 181–9.

Balassa, Bela, "Exports, Policy Choices, and Economic Growth in Developing Countries After the 1973 Oil Shock," *Journal of Development Economics*, 18, May–June 1985, pp. 23–35.

Balassa, Bela, "Public Enterprise in Developing Countries: Issues of Privatization," in Manfred Neumann and Karl W. Roskamp, eds, *Public Finance and Performance of Enterprises*, Detroit, Wayne University Press, 1989, pp. 417–33.

Chenery, Hollis B., "Growth and Transformation," in Hollis B. Chenery, Sherman Robinson, and Moshe Syrquin, eds, *Industrialization and Growth*, New York; Oxford University Press, 1986, pp. 13–36.

Dean, Edwin, *Plan Implementation in Nigeria, 1962–66*, Ibadan, Oxford University Press, 1972.

de Melo, Jaime and Sherman Robinson, "Productivity and Externalities: Models of Export-Led Growth," World Bank Policy, Planning, and Research Working Papers No. 387, Washington, DC, March 1990.

Feder, Gershon, "On Exports and Economic Growth," *Journal of Development Economics*, 12, February–April 1983, pp. 89–93.

Funkhouser, R. and Paul W. MacAvoy, "A Sample of Observations on Comparative Prices in Public and Private Enterprise," *Journal of Public Economics*, 11, June 1979, pp. 353–68.

Garcia d'Acuna, Eduardo, "Pasado y futuro de la planificaciòn en América Latina," *Penseamento Iberoamericano*, 5, July–December, 1982, pp. 15–45.

Gunatilleke, Godfrey, "Planning in Uncertainty: The Case of Sri Lanka," in Miguel Urrutia and Setsuko Yukawa, eds, *Development Planning in Mixed Economies*, Tokyo, The United Nations University, 1988, pp. 33–106.

Gupta, M., "Productivity Performance of the Public and the Private Sectors in India: A Case Study of the Fertilizer Industy," *Indian Economic Review*, 17, April–December 1982.

Gupta, S., "Indian Plans: Retrospects and Prospects," *The Indian Economic Journal*, 34, April–June, 1987, pp. 87–111.

Hasnath, Syed Abu, "The Practice and Effect of Development Planning in Bangladesh," *Public Administration and Development*, 7, March 1987, pp. 59–75.

Hirschman, Albert O., *Latin American Issues*, New York, Twentieth Century Fund, 1961.

International Bank for Reconstruction and Development, *Annual Report, 1949–50*, Washington, DC, 1950.

Jain, Anil Kumar, "Strategies and Techniques of India's Five Year Plan," *Economic Bulletin for Asia and the Pacific*, 37, June 1986, pp. 42–54.

Killick, Tony, *Development Economics in Action: A Study of Economic Policies in Ghana*, London, Heinemann Educational Books, 1978.

Killick, Tony, "Development Planning in Africa: Experiences, Weaknesses and Prescriptions," *Development Policy Review*, 1, May 1983, pp. 47–76.

Killick, Tony, "Twenty-Five Years of Development: The Rise and Impending Decline of Market Solutions," *Development Policy Review*, 4, June 1986, pp. 99–116.

Krueger, Anne O. and Baran Tuncer, "Estimating Total Factor Productivity Growth in a Developing Country," World Bank Staff Working Paper No. 422, Washington, DC, October 1980.

Krueger, Anne O. and Baran Tuncer, "An Empirical Test of the Infant Industry Argument," *American Economic Review*, 70, December 1982, pp. 1142–52.

Laird, Sam and Julio Nogues, "Trade Policies and the Debt Crisis," World Bank Policy, Planning, and Research Working Papers No. 98, September 1988.

Michalopoulos, C. and Kenneth Jay, "Growth of Exports and Income in the Developing World: A Neoclassical View," U.S. Agency for International Development, Discussion Paper No. 28, mimeo.

Nishimizu, Mieko and Sherman Robinson, "Trade Policies and Productivity Change in Semi-Industrialized Countries," *Journal of Development Economics*, 16, September–October, 1984, pp. 177–206.

Patel, Surendra J., "Planned Development in India. Review of Major Changes," *Mainstream*, 5, January 1980, pp. 1–10.

Romer, Paul M., "What Determines the Rate of Growth of Technological Change?," World Bank Policy, Planning, and Research Working Papers No. 279, September 1989.

Thomas, Vinod, "Developing Country Experience in Trade Reform," World Bank Policy, Planning, and Research Working Papers No. 295, October 1989.

Urrutia, Miguel, "New Approaches to Development Planning," in Miguel Urrutia and Setsuko Yukawa, eds, *Development Planning in Mixed Economies*, Tokyo, The United Nations University, 1988, pp. 1–15.

Waide, E. Bevan, "Planning and Annual Planning as an Administrative Process," in A.H. Rweyemanu and B.V. Mwansasu, eds, *Planning in Tanzania*, Nairobi, East African Literature Bureau, 1974.

Waterston, Albert, "A Hard Look at Development Planning," *Finance and Development*, 3, June 1966, pp. 85–91.

Watson, Andrew and Joel B. Dirlam, "The Impact of Underdevelopment on Economic Planning," *Quarterly Journal of Economics*, 79, May 1965, pp. 167–94.

10 Reflections on "*Perestroika* and the Foreign Economic Ties of the USSR"*

INTRODUCTION

In his "*Perestroika* and the Foreign Economic Ties of the USSR," prepared for the Conference on "Prospects for and Implications of Greater East–West Cooperation," Dr Vladimir Popov has provided an extremely interesting discussion of the present situation in Soviet foreign trade and outlined a new foreign economic strategy for the Soviet Union. We will briefly summarize his conclusions, with which we are in general agreement. Next, we will examine the preconditions of the proposed changes in terms of domestic economic policy and the measures that may be used to promote exports. Finally, possible implications for Council for Mutual Economic Assistance (CMEA) trade and for trade with capitalist countries and, in particular, the United States will be considered.

Dr Popov notes that the Soviet Union has not exploited its foreign trade potential. He adds that Soviet trade is still being carried out on the basis of "an archaic, outmoded and essentially 'colonial' trade structure" (p. 4), which has largely involved exchanging fuels and raw materials for machinery and industrial consumer goods. In reference to the general upgrading and advance of world trade, he notes that the "Soviet Union has so far remained outside these developing worldwide economic processes" (p. 8). Dr Popov further criticizes the system of import controls, the lack of convertibility of the ruble, and the practice of multiple exchange rates in the Soviet economy.

* Co-authored with M.P. Claudan and originally published in M. Kraus and R.D. Leihanity, editors, *Perestroika and East-West Economic Relations: Prospects for the 1990s*, New York University Press, 1990; pp. 107–121.

The author is indebted to Jean Baneth for helpful comments on an earlier draft. He alone is responsible, however, for the opinions expressed that should not be interpreted to reflect the view of the World Bank.

In connection with *perestroika*, Dr Popov notes that improvements have been made in giving a number of organizations the right to trade directly abroad and providing possibilities for joint ventures. At the same time, he makes proposals for the further development of a new foreign economic strategy in the Soviet Union.

The proposed new foreign economic strategy would include making the ruble convertible while establishing a system of customs duties; easing the conditions of establishing joint ventures and setting up special economic zones; permitting Soviet enterprises to borrow abroad; and making balance-of-payments statistics freely available. The described changes aim to "make the Soviet economy more open, create a modern export potential, give Soviet producers entry onto foreign markets and attract foreign firms to participate in projects carried out in the USSR" (pp. 13–14).

These are worthy objectives and one can on the whole agree with the policies proposed to pursue them. At the same time, consideration needs to be given to domestic policy measures necessary to support the policies introduced in regard to foreign economic relationships. Also, policies to promote exports will have to be spelled out.

Domestic policies will need to change in order to ensure efficiency in foreign trade and to provide exports of high quality in the Soviet Union. For one thing, without domestic reforms increases in trade may give rise to welfare losses because prices do not reflect resource scarcities so that high-cost rather than low-cost commodities may be exported. For another thing, domestic reforms are needed to ensure the upgrading of the Soviet export structure.

PRICE SETTING IN THE CONTEXT OF ECONOMIC REFORMS AND EXPORT EXPANSION

Prices in the Soviet Union do not reflect resource scarcities or conform to consumer demand. The prices paid by consumers are divorced from producer prices, with turnover taxes imposed at variable rates separating the two. Producer prices are based on average costs often of a long-ago period as there is an aversion to raising prices. Average costs are calculated to include wages and capital costs, which tend to understate the cost of capital; they do not compensate for the use of natural resources.

At the same time, there is no linkage between domestic producer prices and world market prices. As Dr Popov notes, this means that every product effectively has its own exchange rate. In fact, for many products there is more than one exchange rate since in CMEA trade products are often sold at different prices in trade with different countries.

But how to establish rational prices? Could one set centrally prices that reflect resource scarcities and conform to consumer demand? Some suggested that this could be accomplished by solving on a giant computer a system of equations that would incorporate producer and consumer relationships.[1]

This is a chimera. The Soviet Union today has a sophisticated economy with tens of thousands of products, when different prices would need to be set for different product varieties and, as far as consumer prices are concerned, for products sold at different distances from the factory. Furthermore, technology is changing so that past data on production coefficients soon become outdated. Consumer tastes also change, giving rise to variations in demand.

And how about adopting world market prices? Such recommendations have been made for small socialist countries, such as Hungary, which can maximize welfare by adopting world market prices domestically. The Soviet Union has a large domestic market and it manufactures products (e.g. Lada automobiles) that are not produced elsewhere. But, standardized commodities (e.g. petroleum) have a single world market price, and it may be assumed that the Soviet Union cannot affect the prices of the products it imports (wheat provides an exception to this conclusion).

World market prices are, then, relevant to the Soviet Union as they indicate opportunities available internationally. The Soviet Union has long been isolated from the international markets, however, and a wholesale changeover to world market prices cannot be effected overnight. While for some commodities world market prices can be adopted at an early date, this is not the case for others. In the following, some suggestions are made as to pricing under present-day conditions.

The domestic prices of raw materials and fuels should be set on the basis of world market prices. In this connection, it may be noted that world market prices were used as a yardstick by Stalin in criticizing "the confusion that still reigns in the sphere of price-fixing policy":

Our business executives and planners submitted a proposal [which] suggested fixing the price of a ton of grain at practically the same level as a ton of cotton and, moreover, the price of a ton of grain was taken equivalent to that of a ton of baked bread. In reply to the remarks of members of the Central Committee [of the Communist Party] that the price of a ton of bread must be higher than that of a ton of grain, because of the additional expense of milling and baking, and that cotton was generally much dearer than grain, as was also borne out by their prices in the world market, the authors of the proposal could find nothing coherent to say.[2]

As noted earlier, raw materials and fuels importantly enter into Soviet exports while other raw materials are imported. Adopting world market prices would permit ensuring specialization according to comparative advantage and economizing with raw materials and fuels.

World market prices should also be used for manufactured exports. This means that producers would receive the prices they obtain abroad times the exchange rate. This would contribute to the expansion of exports that are profitable from the point of view of the national economy and would give incentives to producers to seek better prices abroad. In turn, imports of manufactured goods would be sold at prices obtained by adding a tariff to the cif import price expressed in terms of domestic currency at the exchange rate.

Different considerations apply to manufactured goods produced at home and sold in domestic markets. These products should be sold at prices that equate domestic demand and supply. This would mean linking consumer prices to producer prices and permitting prices to adjust to demand and supply conditions.

Eventually, world market prices would be brought to bear on domestic prices in conjunction with the liberalization of imports. But this will be a long process since, after several decades of strict import limitations, there is a pent-up demand for imports which cannot be satisfied as the Soviet Union does not possess the foreign exchange necessary to pay for these imports.

FOREIGN EXCHANGE NEEDS AND CAPITAL INFLOW

Increases in the value of Soviet exports after 1973 resulted in large part from the rise of petroleum prices that brought the export share of fuels from 16.2 percent in 1960 to 47.3 percent in 1986. With the recent fall in petroleum prices, Soviet foreign exchange earnings derived from fuels have declined. Correspondingly, as Table 1 in

Dr Popov's paper shows, the ratio of foreign trade to national income decreased in both 1986 and 1987, and exports fared more poorly than imports in both years. At the same time, Soviet manufactured goods are not of world quality that would permit replacing the lost fuel exports.

The Central Committee of the Communist Party of the USSR set out as a target for the quality of manufactured goods to reach 90 percent of the world market level by 1990 and 100 percent by 1993 (*Financial Times*, 25 August 1988). These targets appear unrealistic if we consider that, according to sources cited by Dr Popov, on quality grounds 17–18 percent of Soviet manufacturing output is competitive on the world market under optimistic estimates and 7–8 percent under pessimistic estimates (p. 9).

At the same time, the targets point to the need for the increased importation of machinery to improve product quality. This conclusion is strengthened if we consider the need to replace outdated machinery; reportedly, the average age of machinery in the Soviet Union is 20 years, compared with 12 years in the United States and 10 years in West Germany and France (*Financial Times*, 25 August 1988).

In order to increase the importation of machinery under present-day conditions regarding exports, a capital inflow would be needed. As far as foreign borrowing goes, this should take the form of borrowing by the central authorities rather than by individual firms. Otherwise, there is the danger of excessive indebtedness as shown by the example of highly-indebted developing countries.

Joint ventures offer advantages over borrowing, however, for several reasons. First, in the case of joint ventures there are no interest payment obligations and transfers of dividends are made from the firm's profits. Second, joint ventures bring in new technology, thereby improving the technological level and the international competitiveness of Soviet enterprise. Third, joint ventures can export through the marketing channels established by the foreign partner.

In practice, some mixture of foreign borrowing and joint ventures may be envisaged. While the legal and the fiscal treatment of joint ventures may be improved further,[3] and one may also endorse Dr Popov's proposal that the 51 percent domestic ownership limitation be abolished (p. 20), the experience of other countries indicates that the establishment of joint ventures takes time. Nor can it be expected that foreign interests would supply more than a fraction of the requirements of the Soviet Union. Correspondingly, there is need for external borrowing to provide foreign exchange for the increased importation of machinery.

Nevertheless, over time, the bulk of the increment in foreign exchange availabilities would have to come from exports. In this connection, the question arises what are the commodities where the Soviet Union may increase its exports.

THE PREREQUISITES OF EXPORT EXPANSION

We have seen that fuels account for nearly one-half of Soviet exports. Increases cannot be foreseen in regard to fuel exports, in part because of domestic supply limitations and in part because higher Soviet export volume would create problems with OPEC as it would contribute to a further weakening of petroleum prices. Supply limitations are also apparent in regard to the exports of raw materials.

Such being the case, the Soviet Union would have to increase the exportation of manufactured goods. In the short to medium run, the best possibilities appear to lie in increasingly exporting raw materials and fuels in a processed form. In such exportation, the availability of raw materials and fuels gives an advantage to the Soviet Union. At the same time, the technological processes of transforming raw materials and fuels are largely standardized and are either available in the Soviet Union or can be obtained from abroad.

First of all, the Soviet Union could develop the exports of petrochemicals, involving a partial shift from the exportation of petroleum. There are further possibilities for exporting basic chemicals and, eventually, chemical products. Also, nonferrous metals could be exported in a processed form.

The Soviet Union could not, and should not, aim at the exportation of labor-intensive products, such as textiles, clothing, shoes, and various simple manufactures. Textiles and clothing are subject to the Multi-fiber Arrangement and all labor-intensive products can be exported by less-developed countries and China. These countries have considerably lower wages than the Soviet Union.

With the upgrading of industry, there are further possibilities for Soviet exports. These lie in the middle range of manufacturing industries where the level of technological sophistication is moderately high. Examples are automobiles (but this would require considerable improvements in the Lada, which is presently exported in small quantities to the West) and relatively simple machinery and machine tools.

For substantially increasing manufactured exports, however, certain conditions have to be met. This requires, first of all, establishing a realistic exchange rate. The present exchange rate between the ruble and the dollar is an artificial creation that does not correspond to the purchasing power of the two currencies in international markets. Thus, while the official value of the ruble is greater than that of the dollar, the opposite is the case as far as the ruble and the dollar exchange rates of Hungary and Poland are concerned. In fact, one ruble was worth 27 Hungarian forints on 5 June 1987, while the dollar was worth 47.5 forints at the exchange rate of the Hungarian National Bank. This means an implicit exchange rate of 1.76 rubles for the dollar as against the official exchange rate of 1.55 dollars for the ruble.[4]

The exchange rate should be set to make marginal exports profitable. As in the Soviet Union marginal exports are manufactured goods, this can be accomplished by calculating the domestic cost of foreign exchange for manufactured exports and setting the exchange rate on this basis.

Such a method of exchange rate determination was used in Hungary following the 1968 reforms, except that the average domestic cost of foreign exchange rather than its marginal cost was calculated. This procedure did not provide sufficient incentives for exports while necessitating subsidies for exports that produced foreign exchange at a domestic cost higher than the average.

Increasing the domestic price of exports will not suffice, however, under present-day conditions because of pent-up domestic demand for manufactured products. Also, exporting involves considerable uncertainty so that the fulfilment of the production plan may be jeopardized if exports do not work out as expected. Finally, exports have high-quality requirements that involve a considerable extra effort.

At the same time, foreign exchange has a scarcity value that exceeds the exchange rate under conditions of import control. Thus, in order to encourage export expansion, consideration may be given to enlarging the scope of the existing foreign exchange retention scheme for exports. This would involve increasing foreign exchange allotments to exporters and allocating part of the allotment to the producers of inputs for export manufacture.

The latter point is of particular importance, given the difficulties exporters encounter in obtaining inputs for export production in general and inputs of appropriate quality in particular. These difficulties may be obviated if the producers of inputs for export production (indirect exporters) receive a foreign exchange allotment.

One may set the foreign exchange allotment as a percentage of net foreign exchange earnings from exports. This involves deducting from fob export value the cif cost of imported inputs as well as the fob value of materials that would otherwise have been exported. The deduction of exports foregone (e.g. that of fuels used in producing petrochemicals for export) is necessary since otherwise the increment in foreign exchange availabilities due to manufactured exports would be overstated. Subsequently, the foreign exchange allotment can be divided between direct and indirect exporters on the basis of their contribution to net foreign exchange earnings.

Foreign exchange allotments could be used to import machinery as well as intermediate products. One may also envisage an auction market for foreign exchange since some firms may not utilize their entire foreign exchange allotment. This would permit easing the foreign exchange shortage under which Soviet firms operate.

It would further be desirable to increase the number of firms that can directly trade abroad. Dr Popov noted that in 1987 22 ministries and departments, as well as 77 associations, enterprises, and organizations, were given the right to carry out export–import operations directly in foreign markets, accounting for 12 percent of exports (p. 14). This proportion should be increased so as to ensure a direct contact between producers and foreign markets. In the absence of such contacts, it is difficult to ascertain the changing needs of markets abroad.

At the same time, replacing foreign trade enterprises by ministries and ministry departments in carrying out export trade will not suffice. It is the producing enterprises that should have foreign contacts rather than the supervisory organizations. Decentralization in the trade area, in turn, should be part and parcel of decentralization in the overall economic sphere.

DECENTRALIZATION, PROFIT INCENTIVES AND COMPETITION

The decentralization of decision-making is necessary to ensure that supply responds to demand. This is relevant not only at the consumer level but also at different stages of fabrication. Centralized planning cannot ensure the equalization of demand and supply, in part because of the impossibility to collect information on all products at the center and in part because of continuous changes that occur in needs and availabilities.

At the same time, for producers to respond to users' needs, they should aim at maximizing profits that bring the firm's own interests into harmony with the society's interests in efficient resource allocation. Profit maximization involves minimizing costs and catering to demand. Setting production targets from above would interfere with the pursuit of these objectives.

In order to ensure that firms maximize profits, firm managers should be provided appropriate incentives. This involves basing the managers' bonuses on profits rather than on the subjective judgment of supervisory organizations.

For profit maximization to lead to efficient resource allocation, there is further need for competition among producers. Competition can be ensured in the Soviet Union whose large domestic market can support a number of efficient-size producers in most industries. This contrasts with the case of small socialist countries, such as Hungary, where the domestic market can support only one or two efficient-size producers in each industry.

In conclusion, emphasis should be given to the interdependence of rational prices, decentralization, profit maximization, incentives, and competition. For commodities produced domestically, the establishment of rational prices requires equating demand and supply. This, in turn, necessitates the decentralization of decision-making and profit maximization by the firm. At the same time, managers have to be provided with appropriate incentives in order to ensure that firms maximize profits. Furthermore, there is need for competition to guarantee that profit maximization leads to the efficient allocation of resources. Expressed differently, under the conditions indicated, the working of the market system in a socialist economy simultaneously ensures efficient resource allocation and the establishment of rational prices.

The described provisions go beyond the measures included in the document approved by the Supreme Soviet on 30 June 1987. This document, entitled "Basic Provisions for Fundamentally Reorganizing Economic Management," represents a half-way house between central planning and market socialism. While it contains a modicum of decentralization, "the basic provisions stress that the economy will continue to be centrally planned and managed as 'a unified national economy complex' directed toward carrying out the party's economic policies."[5] Also, the possibilities for competition would be limited "by accelerating the ongoing process of amalgamating enterprises into production and science-production associations and creating large new groupings called 'state production associations,' which integrate entities engaged in all phases of the research–production–marketing claim."[6]

An additional consideration is that rational prices of products presuppose that there are also rational prices for the factors of production. This, in turn, requires establishing markets for these factors where prices equate demand and supply. Thus, markets are needed for capital, labor, and natural resources.

Also, for the rational pricing of productive factors, the existing excess demand for these factors will need to be eliminated. Excess demand originates in the desire of the firms to expand that is not checked by financial limitations on the expansion. Utilizing an expression introduced by János Kornai, firms face a "soft" budget constraint in the sense that they can expect their losses to be financed from the government budget.

Hardening the budget constraint means making firms fully responsible for the consequences of their actions. Inappropriate actions may, then, lead to bankruptcy, if losses accumulate as a result. Thus, one needs the carrot as well as the stick of competition, with firms benefiting from making profits and suffering the consequences of losses.

The discussion so far pertained to industry. It has been recognized that agriculture also needs a far-reaching transformation in order to fully utilize its production potential. The recent decision to lease land to individual farmers up to 50 years represents an important move towards introducing greater efficiency in farming (*Washington Post*, 27 August 1988). It would further be necessary to transform the huge cooperatives and state farms into smaller, profit-oriented units.

In this connection, reference may be made to the experience of Hungary where the operation of profit-oriented units in agriculture has led to a considerable expansion of production. But Hungary is also an example of the lack of success of half-way houses in industry where continued state intervention has not permitted the full-fledged development of market socialism, with adverse effects on production and exports.

TRADE RELATIONS WITH OTHER COUNTRIES

The question arises what are the implications of policy changes in the Soviet Union for trade relations with other countries. This question will be considered in the following in regard to the Council for Mutual Economic Assistance (CMEA) and for trade with capitalist countries, among which the United States requires special attention.

Decentralization in the economic system of the Soviet Union also requires decentralizing trade with the CMEA countries. While at the end of 1987 only 500 of nearly 40 000 Soviet firms established direct links with firms in the CMEA countries,[7] trade on the basis of intergovernmental contracts would have to to be increasingly replaced by market relations among firms.

Also, in the manufacturing sector, trade may increasingly take the form of intra-industry specialization. This would ensure the exploitation of large-scale economies associated with longer production runs and the use of specialized machinery as firms narrow their product composition.

There are further possibilities for joint ventures among the CMEA countries. As of November 1987, only four joint ventures were created with firms in CMEA countries and letters of intent were signed for eight others.[8] Yet, there are considerable opportunities for joint ventures among firms that use different technologies.

In the past, trade and joint ventures among the CMEA countries were limited by the lack of a convertible currency. As the surplus in bilateral trade between two CMEA countries could not be used to finance a deficit with a third CMEA country, there was an incentive to retrench rather than to expand exports.

As a first step to remedy this situation, a clearing of bilateral balances in CMEA trade should be established. Next, the resulting multilateral balances should be paid for in convertible currencies. In the final step, the currencies of the CMEA countries should be made convertible.

At the same time, the requirements for convertibility should not be underestimated. In the absence of balanced trade, with allowance made for the inflow of foreign capital, and sufficient foreign exchange reserves, there is the danger that a run is created on the currency, precipitating a substantial decline in its value.

This danger is especially apparent under present conditions in the Soviet Union, where exports do not appreciably respond to changes in the value of the currency. Thus, domestic policy reforms providing for an elastic supply of exports is a precondition for currency convertibility.

Convertible currencies are used to settle balances in trade with the capitalist countries. But Soviet trade with these countries has been limited by the availability of exports that could compete in their markets. Thus, the first priority is to increase the scope of commodities that are competitive in the markets of capitalist countries.

Geographical proximity favors Soviet trade with the European Economic Community. Apart from product availabilities for export, in recent years this trade suffered from the relatively poor economic performance of the Common Market countries. With the completion of the internal market in the EC by 1992, a resurgence of growth is foreseen, however.

Geographical proximity also favors trade between the eastern parts of the Soviet Union and Japan. The question is however if the Soviet Union can compete on the Japanese market in middle-range manufactured products, where not only does Japan have a strong position but there is also competition by the East Asian newly-industrializing countries.

It has been said that the Soviet Union has few possibilities to export to the United States because of distance. This statement applies to fuels and raw materials where the Common Market countries provide nearby markets. But transportation costs have limited importance for manufactured goods as indicated by the success of Japan and the newly-industrializing countries in the US market. Once the Soviet Union establishes a competitive export structure, it should be able to sell in the United States.

As noted earlier, establishing joint ventures would help the export promotion effort. In this connection, US firms may play a particularly important role as they have considerable experience with joint ventures in Western Europe and in developing countries.

At the same time, Soviet exports to the United States are limited by the lack of application of the most favored nation clause. This should change with the greater openness of the Soviet economy and increased emigration, as well as agreements on reducing nuclear and conventional armaments.

CONCLUSIONS

In this chapter, attention has been given to the policy conditions of changes in Soviet foreign trade. The discussion has centered on price reform, foreign exchange needs, and capital inflow, the prerequisites of export expansion, the interdependence of the reform measures, and trade relations with other countries.

It has been suggested that domestic policies need to change in order to ensure efficiency in foreign trade and to provide exports of high quality. The first prerequisite is the establishment of rational prices. This objective may be pursued by adopting world market prices for raw materials and fuels, having the exporters of manufactured goods receive the prices they obtain abroad, setting the domestic prices of imports at world market prices plus a tariff, and establishing market-clearing prices for manufactured products that are produced and sold domestically.

Eventually, world market prices would be brought to bear on domestic prices in conjunction with the liberalization of imports, but this will be a long process since the pent-up demand for imports cannot be satisfied from available foreign exchange. At the same time, given the limitations of raising fuel and raw material exports, it would be necessary to increase the exports of manufactured goods where quality provides a constraint. To upgrade quality, there is need for foreign machinery, the purchase of which would necessitate external borrowing and joint ventures. This would, then, help to expand exports that will have to provide the bulk of the increment in foreign exchange availability over time.

There are possibilities for exporting fuels and raw materials in processed form. The Soviet Union should also have possibilities in middle-range products, such as automobiles and relatively simple machinery and machine tools. It is at a disadvantage, however, in exporting labor-intensive manufactures.

Establishing a realistic exchange rate is a pre-condition for expanding the exports of manufactured goods. It would further be desirable to increase foreign exchange retention quotas and to allot these to direct and indirect exporters alike. Finally, the scope of firms that directly trade abroad would need to be substantially enlarged.

The decentralization of decision-making in foreign trade should be accompanied by decentralization in the domestic economy, to be complemented by the introduction of the profit motive and competition. In fact, rational prices, decentralization, profit maximization, incentives to managers, and competition are interdependent and they will have to be pursued simultaneously for efficient resource allocation. At the same time, improvements would need to be made in the conditions under which agriculture operates.

Decentralization of the economic system also requires decentralizing trade with the CMEA countries. At the same time, the expansion and rationalization of this trade would require the clearing of bilateral balances and the settlement of multilateral balances in convertible currencies, with the currencies of the CMEA countries eventually also becoming convertible.

Geographical proximity favors Soviet trade with the Common Market countries. Nevertheless, once a competitive export structure is established, there will be possibilities for exporting manufactured goods to the US market. In the meantime, joint ventures with American firms hold considerable promise.

Notes

1. See e.g. Oscar Lange, "The Computer and the Market," in Morris Bronstein, ed., *Comparative Economic Systems: Models and Cases*, Homewood, Ill., Richard D. Irwin, 1985, ch. 11.
2. *Economic Problems of Socialism in the USSR*, Moscow, Foreign Languages Publishing House, 1952, pp. 24–5.
3. See A.M. Volkov, "New Trends in World Economic Development and East–West Relations," paper prepared for the Conference on "Prospects for and Implications of Greater East–West Cooperation," held at Middlebury College, Middlebury, Vermont on 19–24 September 1988, p. 6.
4. V. Belov, "Socialist Economic Integration in Its Present Stage," paper prepared for the Conference on "Prospects for and Implications of Greater East–West Cooperation," held at Middlebury College, Middlebury, Vermont on 19–24 September 1988, p. 15.
5. Gertrude E. Schroeder, "Gorbachev's Economic Reforms," in Ronald D. Liebovitz, ed., *Gorbachev's New Thinking*, Cambridge, Mass., Ballinger Publishing Company for the International Institute for Economic Advancement, 1988, p. 56.
6. Ibid., p. 58. For a detailed discussion of the Soviet reforms, see Edward A. Hewett, *Reforming the Soviet Economy*, Washington, DC, The Brookings Institution, 1988.
7. Ivan Ivanov, "Restructuring the Mechanism of Foreign Economic Relations in the USSR," *Soviet Economy*, 3, 1987, p. 207.
8. Ibid., p. 209.

11 *Perestroika* and its Implications for European Socialist Countries*

This chapter provides a critical evaluation of *perestroika* (restructuring) in the Soviet Union and examines its implications for the European socialist countries. *Perestroika* was introduced to reform the Soviet economy after the "period of stagnation" under Brezhnev. It involves combining centralized planning with elements of a market economy.

The first section of the chapter describes the main elements of the Soviet economic reforms. The next two sections analyze the micro and the macro conditions of the success of the reforms. The last section discusses the implications of the reforms for the European socialist countries.

THE MAIN ELEMENTS OF *PERESTROIKA*

The basic document of *perestroika* is the *Osnovnye polozheniia* (Basic Provisions) approved by the Central Committee Plenum of the Communist Party of the Soviet Union in June 1987. This was followed by further documents, of which the Law on the State Enterprise, enacted in July 1987, is the most important.

The Basic Provisions emphasize that the economy will continue to be centrally planned and managed as "a unified economic complex". Its goals and priorities are set by a 15-year plan that serves as a basis for the detailed formulation of the plan for the initial five-year period, with a breakdown by years. The plan is prepared by the State

* Originally presented as a paper at the Hungarian-US Roundtable held in Budapest, Hungary, on 22–5 November 1989.

The author is thankful for helpful comments by the participants of the Roundtable as well as by Alan Gelb and Mary Shirley.

Planning Committee (Gosplan) and divided among the ministries that, in turn, provide indicative planning data for the firms, on the basis of which these work out their own five-year and annual plans.

The ministries have been subordinated to seven superministries. At the same time, sectoral subbranches of the ministries are being replaced by several thousand large associations and enterprises, established by amalgamating existing enterprises. The newly-created large groupings incorporate all phases of the manufacturing process, from research to production to marketing.

While the transfer of the functions of the subbranches of the ministries reduces their operational responsibilities, the ministries continue to have an important role in the planning process. Thus, according to the Basic Provisions, the ministry "is responsible to the nation for satisfying demand for the branch's product, preventing disproportions, ensuring that the product meets world technical and quality standards, and working out and implementing branch scientific and technical programs."

The ministry influences firm behavior by setting

1. "Non-binding control figures" that specify the value of output, total profits, foreign currency receipts, and "major indicators of scientific and technical progress and social development," a list to be fixed by the Council of Ministers.
2. A mandatory bill of state orders for output that includes commissionings of facilities financed by state centralized investment and products essential for fulfilling priority state tasks for "social development, scientific–technical progress, defence, and deliveries of farm products."
3. Limits, which include normatives according to a list approved by the Council of Ministers, regulating such matters as growth of total wages and the allocation of profit among various kinds of taxes and funds. (Schroeder, 1988, pp. 56–7)

Apart from the state orders, firms are to sell their products freely to other firms and to wholesale trade organizations. In turn, aside from basic materials and investment goods that continue to be rationed, they are to buy their materials from other firms and from wholesale trade organizations.

The firm's plan is based on the control figures, mandatory state orders, economic normatives, and contracts with customers and suppliers. The Law on the State Enterprise states that "the enterprise is obligated to strictly observe plan discipline and meet plans and contractual obligations in full." It further states that "fulfilment of orders and contracts serves as the most important criterion for evaluating the activities of the enterprise and providing material rewards for its employees."

The firm is subject to "full economic accountability and self-finance." This means that the firm will not receive subsidies and it will finance all its current and capital expenditures from its sales revenues. Firms that continually make losses are to be liquidated.

The Basic Provisions also modify the process of price formation. For basic products, prices are set centrally on the basis of "socially necessary expenses of production and sale, utility, quality, and effective demand," for a period of five years. They are to cover the costs of the enterprises, including payments for natural resources, labor, and capital. For the remaining products, contract prices are to be determined by the enterprises. But these prices are subject to control and should be set on the same basis as the centrally determined prices.

Producer prices and consumer prices continue to be divorced from each other. Food prices are maintained low by the use of state subsidies which may amount to as much as two-thirds of the producer price. In turn, industrial products are often subject to high taxes.

Under *perestroika*, foreign trade has been decentralized. By 1989, all enterprises producing competitive products can trade directly with foreign firms. However, the prices received and paid by Soviet enterprises are divorced from world market prices by the use of conversion factors that vary among products. Also, exceptions from direct trading by enterprises include petroleum, raw materials, steel products, chemicals, grains, and food products. Also, while exporters are supposed to use part of their foreign exchange earnings to import materials and machinery, in practice imports continue to be subject to controls.

The Basic Provisions and the Law on the State Enterprise do not specifically concern agriculture. Agricultural reform was to be carried out in the framework of two major decrees. The first, adopted in November 1985, established GOSAPROM, a superministry for agriculture that has subsequently been abolished because of the excessive bureaucracy it created. The second decree, adopted in March 1986, permits state and collective farms to sell a larger proportion of their output at market prices and endorses the use of production contracts.

In August 1988, it was stated that individual farmers can lease land up to 50 years from state and collective farms. Furthermore, in August 1989, it was declared that state and collective farms can sell above-plan output for foreign exchange. The law adopted by the Supreme Soviet in November 1986 stated the conditions under which cooperatives can be established. The law provides possibilities for the establishment of cooperatives in a variety of areas but permits state employees to participate in the operation of cooperatives only outside working hours.

THE MICRO-CONDITIONS FOR THE SUCCESS OF *PERESTROIKA*

For *perestroika* to succeed, certain micro-conditions would need to be fulfilled. In this connection, one should emphasize the interdependence of rational prices, decentralization, profit maximization, incentives, and competition. For commodities produced domestically, the establishment of rational prices requires that prices equate demand and supply. This, in turn, necessitates the decentralization of decision-making and profit maximization by the firm. At the same time, managers would have to be provided with appropriate incentives in order to ensure that firms maximize profits. Finally, there is need for competition to guarantee that profit maximization does not lead to the exploitation of monopoly positions and inflation.

The establishment of rational prices

The price reform, originally planned for 1988, has been postponed. The implications of maintaining existing distorted prices have been well-stated by Hewett: "That gives enterprises several years to operate with distorted prices that will arbitrarily give profits to some enterprises and losses to others. That, in turn, gives enterprise directors ample ammunition to argue for exceptions (special subsidies or tax breaks), which could set the tone for the next decade or so" (1988, p. 356).

But the planned price reforms do not provide a solution either. Controlled prices will be set on the basis of average costs, so that they will not equate supply and demand, and they will remain unchanged for five years, thereby imparting rigidity to the pricing system. Nor will contractual prices equate supply and demand since they are also supposed to be set on the basis of production costs.

At the same time, to the extent that enterprises set prices, there appears to be a tendency for price increases. Existing regulations permit raising prices by 15 percent for new or particularly fashionable products. But, "new" products may represent little modification from "old" products.

And, the existing situation of excess demand, together with monopolistic structures to be discussed below, has led to increases in the prices of "old" products as well. This explains the introduction of price controls in 1989 (*Financial Times*, 4 February 1989). Price controls, then, introduce additional rigidities in the price-setting process.

At the same time, as noted above, prices at the consumer level are divorced from prices at the producer level by the use of taxes and subsidies. Yet, the two sets of prices should be linked in order for consumer demand to influence producer decisions. This would necessitate equalizing rates of turnover taxes across the board and eliminating consumer subsidies.

Also, prices on the producer level would have to be determined on the market. This, in turn, requires that the other micro-conditions be fulfilled. These will be discussed in the following.

Decentralization

The reform leaves the central planning apparatus and the ministries in place. In fact, the establishment of the superministries represents centralization rather than decentralization. As Hewett noted, "these supraministerial organs will eventually assume important planning functions for their complexes, as Gosplan takes on the more general role of focusing on the entire economy, which includes coordinating relations among the complexes. Presumably this will involve constructing balances for the key products in the complex, allocating investment, reorganizing the sector, and so on" (1988, p. 338).

At the same time, ministries continue to be judged on the basis of meeting output targets. Thus, at a meeting of the Council of Ministers, held in January 1989, "a string of senior ministers . . . were publicly reprimanded for failing to supply consumer goods up to the state-planned targets' (*Financial Times*, 16 January 1989). With the ministries being held responsible for fulfilling the output plan, it is hardly surprising that they try to hold enterprises to their output plan. Thus, Gregory may not greatly exaggerate in making the following statement:

Ministries are still judged on the basis of aggregated physical outputs in the same detail as before. Unless *perestroika* alters in a fundamental way the manner in which ministries are judged, it is foolish to expect a fundamental change in ministry dealings with the enterprises. The ministry will wish to maintain traditional levers over its enterprises. Ministry officials note that if they are to continue to have compulsory targets, they must continue to assign compulsory targets to their enterprises. (1989, p. 6)

The ministries can influence enterprise actions by making the "non-binding control figures" binding, by relying on state orders, and by setting the normatives for the enterprise. Particular importance attaches to state orders that are based on the plan. In effect, the state guarantees markets and supplies. At the same time, operating outside the state-order network is risky. While buyers are easy to find, it is very difficult to obtain materials for production that is not covered by state orders.

Normatives cover the share of profits going to the state, the ministry, and the enterprise; the size of the wage fund; and charges for working capital, the use of natural resources, etc. As normatives are set separately for each enterprise, the ministries can use them to ensure conforming behavior by the enterprise. They are also subject to bargaining in a situation where distorted prices affect the financial profitability of the enterprise.

In order to avoid these adverse consequences, price determination on the market would have to be accompanied by the abolition of the control figures and the equalization of normatives across enterprises. To the extent that initial conditions differ among firms, this should be taken into account in the valuation of their capital.

Also, state orders should be reduced to a minimum. This, in turn, requires abolishing the responsibility of the ministries for output targets. Output should be determined on the market as firms seek to cater to demand in the pursuit of profits.

Profit maximization

In the Soviet Union, profits were introduced alongside output as firm targets during the Kosygin reforms. Nevertheless, output remained the principal indicator of the firm's success.

Profitability would play an important role under the reform since continuing losses would bring the firm into bankruptcy. However, as noted above, under distorted prices, profitability indicators are also distorted. This, in turn, gives rise to bargaining with the supervising ministries.

At the same time, for the supervising ministries, output remains the main success indicator. This means that the ministries will want to force firms to meet output targets. The firms will be inclined to do so in order to get favorable treatment from the supervising ministry. Such will not be the case if the ministries do not have output targets as suggested above.

Incentives

In the past, managers' bonuses depended on firm-plan fulfillment and on various indicators set by the supervising ministry. This situation hardly changes under the reform, thereby reducing the interest of the managers in maximizing profits. In order to do so, managers should be given a share in profits.

Profit-sharing should not be instituted, however, for the workers since profits are the result of actions taken by managers rather than the workers. At the same time, it would be desirable to generalize the piece-wage system, under which the workers are remunerated for their contribution to the firm's production.

Competition

In the traditional centrally planned system, there is no competition as the transfer of products is regulated by the plan. The introduction of firm-to-firm relations could ideally give rise to competition. This is not the case in the Soviet Union, however.

To begin with, there is no competition from imports. Also, the establishment of a few thousand vertically integrated enterprises gives rise to monopoly positions. At the same time, conditions for entry are controlled by the ministries. And, on the part of the ministries, no encouragement is given to enterprises to produce outside their allotted product composition.

The lack of competition interferes with the efficiency of resource allocation even if all other conditions are fulfilled. Furthermore, inflationary pressures are generated. It has been reported that "a poll conducted in late 1988 among managers of industrial enterprises revealed that 10 percent intend to reduce output by 15–20 percent and raise their prices even more, so that output measured in current prices will increase nevertheless" (Popov, 1989, p. 6).

Nor can one expect competition by the cooperatives. This is because the cooperatives produce services and, to a lesser extent, consumer goods which are not available or are not available in sufficient quantities. At the same time, after their initial successes, the activities of the cooperatives have been circumscribed, price control has been imposed, and taxes on income derived from cooperatives raised.

The strictest rules have been imposed on the flourishing medical cooperatives. A range of medical activities, such as observation and treatment of pregnancy, surgery, the treatment of infectious diseases, and the treatment of drug addiction, has been banned and any other medical aid can be offered only on the basis of a contract with a medical institution. The decree also bans cooperative schools, the production or the hiring of video films, publishing books on science, art, and literature, and the manufacture and sale of religious items. In addition, a whole range of activities, including all other publishing, organizing concerts, artistic events, and other forms of entertainment, and tourism services, will only be allowed if the cooperative has a contract with a state enterprise (*Financial Times*, 6 and 17 January 1989).

Also, price controls have been imposed on the cooperatives. In the event that cheap state supplies are used, cooperatives are not supposed to charge more than state prices. Also, in response to high charges in cooperative restaurants and cafes, local councils will set maximum mark-ups (*Financial Times*, 4 February 1989).

Finally, income tax rates have been raised to a considerable extent from the earlier level of 13 percent. The highest marginal rate has been set at 50 percent. This will apply to a large extent to incomes derived from cooperative activities.

These considerations indicate a lackadaisical attitude on the part of the government *vis-à-vis* the cooperatives. While some economists projected that the cooperatives may eventually provide 10–15 percent of national income, the success of the cooperatives and the high incomes they have obtained have been greeted with dismay. Thus, it is doubtful that the contribution of the cooperatives will increase much further.

Yet, for *perestroika* to be successful, more freedom would need to be given to the cooperatives and their activities be extended to a wide range of manufacturing products. It would further be necessary to reverse the process of industrial concentration and to establish the conditions of genuine competition.

THE MACRO-CONDITIONS FOR THE SUCCESS OF *PERESTROIKA*

For *perestroika* to succeed, certain macro-conditions would also need to be fulfilled. The government should aim at realistic growth rates, establish a balance between investment and consumption, eliminate the overhang in the market for consumer goods and services, and drastically reduce the budget deficit. These conditions will be discussed in the following.

Setting realistic growth rates

Gorbachev's new economic strategy is said to be summed up in the new political concepts of "uskorenie" (acceleration), "perestroika" (restructuring), and "glasnost" (openness). In fact, the twelfth five-year plan for the period 1986–90 aims at a considerable acceleration of economic growth. For the period as a whole, GDP is projected to rise by 22 percent, compared with 16.5 percent in 1981–5. A substantial part of this increase would be accomplished by the rise in efficiency by 15 percent, compared with 7.5 percent in the preceding period (Aganbegyan, 1988, pp. 1, 10).

These projections are not realistic. As we have seen, the economic reform has not progressed far, so that there is no basis for the projected improvement in efficiency. In fact, the dislocations created by the reform efforts and their lack of consistency have led to a slowdown in efficiency improvements. Thus, in the short run, there is a conflict between "uskorenie" and "perestroika."

If improvements in efficiency slow down, increases in output would to a large extent be accomplished through increases in resources. Resource availabilities will, however, increase to a lesser extent than beforehand, because of the deceleration of the growth of the labor supply and the limited availability of natural resources. According to the Five-Year Plan, resources would increase by 7 percent in 1986–90, compared with 9 percent in 1981–5. (ibid.).

This being the case, aiming at high economic growth rates only exacerbates the excess demand prevalent in the Soviet economy.

Excess demand, in turn, creates disproportions among industries, adds to inflationary pressure, and does not permit the market mechanism to operate satisfactorily.

There is need, therefore, to eliminate the excess demand existing in the economy. Apart from reducing the budget deficit and eliminating the overhang in the market for consumer goods, to be discussed below, this will necessitate avoiding excessive plan targets and reforming the credit system.

In recent years, credit provided for enterprises increased much more rapidly than production. According to Aganbegyan, in some years the volume of credit increased by 15–17 percent while output grew by 3–5 percent (1988, p. 138). At the same time, the repayment of credit was not ensured, thereby adding to the liquidity of the enterprises. There is need to develop a new credit policy that avoids creating excess liquidity and provides for the repayment of credit.

Establishing a balance between investment and consumption

Perestroika created considerable expectations for improvements in living standards. This has not occurred. The lines have lengthened before shops that appear to have less merchandise. Rationing has become more widespread, and in August 1989 limitations were imposed on the purchase of a range of consumer goods by non-residents in Moscow.

The statistical results of the first half of 1989 confirm these tendencies. Retail sales of bread, potatoes, vegetables, fish, and sugar declined and no change occurred in the production of meat and butter. Also, the production of many consumer durables, such as cars, motorcycles and sewing machines, fell (*Wall Street Journal*, 30 August 1989).

Part of the problem lies in the relative neglect of consumption in the 1986–90 Five-Year Plan. According to the plan, the capital stock would increase by 30 percent in the 1986–90 period as against a rise of 17 percent in 1981–5 (Aganbegyan, 1988, p. 10). Hewett notes that "available data do not indicate precisely where the sacrifices are to be made, but probable targets are housing, the construction industry, and a broad category of 'other' in which most social infrastructure investment can be found" (1988, p. 317). Thus, the welfare consequences of the large investments extend beyond food.

Much of the new investment would go into machine building. According to Aganbegyan "in the Soviet machine building sector in the 1981–85 period only 9 percent of all equipment was renewed, while in the 1986–90 period 40 percent will be changed. This will mean a rise in the annual rate of planned renewal of the range of machinery produced from 3.1 percent in 1985 to 13 percent in 1990" (1988, p. 14).

The renewal of machinery is in fact an important objective, especially since Soviet machinery is much outdated compared with the West. But it is not sufficient to install modern machinery. In this connection, one may recall the example of Poland that spent large sums on modern machinery in the 1970s without commensurate results.

In the Polish case, the lack of a thoroughgoing economic reform was responsible for the lack of success of the machine-building effort. Similar problems arise in the Soviet Union where an appropriate incentive system is lacking. Without such a system, the efficient utilization of machinery cannot be ensured.

These considerations indicate the desirability of a slowdown in the investment effort; since 1988 some steps have been taken in this direction but one would have much farther to go. This conclusion is strengthened if we consider the need to provide for consumer demand in the age of *glasnost*, when the deficiencies of the supply system are widely publicized. In fact, the dissatisfaction of the population threatens the success of *perestroika*.

The first consideration is to provide sufficient food for the population. There were great expectations about the possibilities opened by the August 1988 decree that permitted the leasing of land to individual farmers up to 50 years. The *Washington Post* cited the Soviet news agency that foresaw "a new wave of the mass transfer of land and other means of production to leaseholders in the autumn and winter period of preparations for the new agricultural season" (27 August 1988).

These expectations have not been realized and there has been little movement to lease land. Various considerations may explain this outcome. To begin with, there has been opposition on the part of *sovhozes*, *kolkhozes*, and the local authorities. Furthermore, agricultural machinery and materials have not been provided and the available machinery does not fit the needs of the smallholders. Last but not least, the experience of the 1930s and more recent reversals in the case of cooperatives have raised questions about the long-term future of this effort.

Yet, the long-term leases deserve the full support of the government since they promise improvements in productivity. Further productivity improvements may be obtained by dividing the *kolkhozes* into smaller units and transforming the *sovhozes* into profit-making enterprises. At the same time, there is need to improve infrastructure, in particular the storing, processing, and transportation of food.

Satisfying the needs of the population would further require increased imports of consumer goods. This issue will be taken up below in connection with the need to eliminate the overhang in the market for consumer goods and services.

Eliminating the overhang in the market for consumer goods and services

Limitations on the availability of goods and services led to the accumulation of financial savings in the Soviet Union. Thus, financial savings as a ratio of retail sales increased from 0.54 in 1978 to 0.81 in 1988 (*PlanEcon Report*, 17 February 1989).

This large amount of accumulated savings represents an overhang in the consumer market that is an inflationary force. In order to establish equilibrium in the market, it would be desirable to eliminate the overhang. Several measures may be taken to pursue this objective.

First of all, it would be desirable to increase the attractiveness of financial savings. This could be accomplished by raising interest rates on savings deposits and issuing bonds at attractive interest rates. Interest rates have remained unchanged at low levels in recent years despite increases in the underlying rate of inflation.

Second, it would be desirable to raise the prices of luxury and semi-luxury goods that are in short supply. The approximately eight-year waiting period for automobiles could be reduced if prices were increased to levels where excess demand declines. Also, the prices of electronic goods could be raised.

Third, reductions in military spending would provide the opportunity to increase the production of automobiles and electronic goods. A shift from the production of military vehicles to that of automobiles could be accomplished relatively easily and military electronic goods could also be transformed into civilian goods.

Fourth, a substantial part of housing construction may be oriented towards the sale of houses and apartments to private individuals. This should involve the payment of advance deposits that may also be used for the sale of automobiles.

Fifth, the population should be provided with increasing options for investment. This would permit channeling some of the financial savings into investment goods..

Sixth, the imports of consumer goods should be stepped up. Imports should concentrate on products that have a high domestic mark-up, such as electronic goods. This may make it possible to obtain 8–10 rubles per dollar.

Increased imports of consumer goods would involve external borrowing. This is made possible by the relatively low foreign indebtedness of the Soviet Union. The *New York Times* reports that at the end of 1988 the Soviet Union had an external debt of $43 billion, against which one should set deposits with Western banks of $28 billion and other foreign assets of $5 billion (31 July 1989). The same issue of the *New York Times* quotes George Clark, the Executive Vice-President of Citybank, according to whom "the Soviet Union could double its foreign debt today without raising any kind of concern." This would, however, necessitate the prompt servicing of the debt, the lack of which can adversely affect borrowing possibilities.

Reducing the budget deficit

For many years, the Soviet Union reported a balanced government budget. With *glasnost*, it has been made public that the Soviet Union has been incurring increasing budget deficits. The reported budget deficit averaged 20 billion rubles in 1980–5, 55 billion rubles in 1986, and 95 billion rubles in 1987 (*The Economist*, 8 October 1988). In August 1989, the Chairman of Gosplan reported that the projected 1989 budget deficit has grown 20 percent in six months to 120 billion rubles or 13.8 percent of the gross domestic product.

The rising budget deficit reflects rapid increases in current and capital expenditures and in subsidies, accompanied by little if any rise in revenues. A large item in current expenditure has been the acceleration of wage increases, rising by 7 percent in 1988, compared with a plan target of 2 percent (*Financial Times*, 23 January 1989) with a further increase of 9 percent in the first quarter of 1989, compared with a plan target of 1 percent for the entire year (*PlanEcon Report*, 28 April 1989). Capital expenditures reflect the expansion of investment under the 1986–90 plan. And, subsidies have risen both to finance the increasing losses of enterprises and to keep down food prices in the face of higher prices paid for agricultural produce.

Finally, there have been unanticipated expenditures in connection with Chernobyl and the Armenian earthquake.

On the revenue side an important negative item has been the reduced revenue from taxes on alcohol, in conjunction with Gorbachev's anti-alcohol campaign. According to *PlanEcon Report*, official sales of alcohol declined by 11.6 percent in 1985, 10.6 percent in 1986, and 0.5 percent in 1987 (17 February 1989). Also, revenues fell as a result of decreases in oil prices and the decline of profit remittances by the enterprises.

A variety of measures may be taken to reduce the budget deficit. These include price increases for luxuries and semi-luxuries, advance deposits on houses, apartments, and automobiles, and the sale of imported consumer goods at high prices, recommended for eliminating the overhang in consumer markets.

Furthermore, current expenditures could be reduced by limiting subsidies to loss-making enterprises, lowering food subsidies, restraining wage increases, reducing the size of the bureaucracy, and cutting military expenditures. In turn, the investment program should be cut by postponing large projects.

A leading candidate for cuts is the large petrochemical complex in Tiumen (western Siberia). The planned investment in petroleum in Tanguin may also be postponed. Other candidates for cuts include investments in the production of fertilizers and in irrigation as well as in the proposed metros in several cities.

The government may also introduce auctions of foreign exchange. Apart from increasing revenues, such auctions would contribute to the better allocation of foreign exchange and represent a first step towards the convertibility of the ruble.

THE IMPLICATIONS OF *PERESTROIKA* FOR THE EUROPEAN SOCIALIST COUNTRIES

The success or failure of *perestroika* will have an influence on economic reforms in the European socialist countries. Success will support the reform efforts of countries, such as Hungary and Poland, that have embarked on economic reforms, and may provide inducements to reforms in countries such as Romania and Bulgaria. In turn, as Rezsö Nyers, the President of the Hungarian Socialist Workers' Party, expressed it, "East European reforms will be influenced by setbacks of Soviet reform. . . . A setback will have a limiting impact.

It will warn everybody to be more cautious" (*New York Times*, 5 January 1988).

If *perestroika* goes ahead, however imperfectly, it will have an influence on Soviet foreign trade. It is planned to increase the share of trade in national income, concentrating on raising manufactured exports while stabilizing the exports of fuels and raw materials (Ivanov, 1988, pp. 147–8).

But the expansion of Soviet trade would occur largely with the convertible currency area. Any increases in fuel and raw material exports will be sold for dollars. At the same time, there will be a tendency to shift purchases of manufactured goods from the CMEA countries to the convertible currency area where higher-quality goods can be obtained. And, much of the expansion of imports will occur in high-technology products that are largely provided by the convertible currency area.

The European socialist countries will also suffer a deterioration of their terms of trade. The Soviet Union will aim to obtain world market prices for its fuels and raw materials and to pay prices for manufactured goods that correspond to their quality.

On the other hand, the European socialist countries will benefit from greater freedom in trade flows. State-to-state contracts will increasingly give place to trade relations among enterprises that will reduce the existing rigidity of trade patterns.

Last but not least, the European socialist countries will have access to the large and growing market of the Soviet Union. But, in order to exploit the possibilities offered by the vast market, the quality of goods needs to be improved and product composition upgraded. This, in turn, requires far-reaching economic reforms in the European socialist countries.

CONCLUSIONS

This chapter has provided a critical evaluation of *perestroika* and noted its implications for the European socialist countries. After describing the main elements of the Soviet economic reforms, the chapter indicated the micro- and macro-conditions for the success of the reforms.

As far as micro-conditions are concerned, emphasis has been given to the interdependence of rational prices, decentralization, profit maximization, incentives, and competition. For commodities that are produced domestically, the establishment of rational prices requires that prices equate demand and supply. This, in turn, necessitates the decentralization of decision-making and profit maximization by the firm. At the same time, managers would have to be provided with appropriate incentives in order to ensure that firms maximize profits. Finally, there is need for competition to guarantee that profit maximization does not lead to the exploitation of monopoly positions and to inflation.

For *perestroika* to succeed, certain macro-conditions would also need to be fulfilled. The government should aim at realistic growth rates, establish a balance between investment and consumption, eliminate the overhang in the market for consumer goods and services, and drastically reduce the budget deficit.

The discussion of the micro- and macro-conditions for the success of *perestroika* indicated that the measures taken have not gone very far and have been characterized by lack of consistency. Much needs to be done, therefore, for *perestroika* to be implemented in practice.

In 1989, some steps were taken towards the fulfilment of the macro-conditions in the framework of a stabilization program (Hewett, 1989) but these do not go very far. In April 1990, new reform measures have been announced to further the establishment of market conditions but their implementation is subject to considerable opposition.

At the same time, the success or failure of *perestroika* will have implications for the success of reforms in the European socialist countries. And, the performance of these economies will be affected by the increased demands for quality by the Soviet Union. But, successful reform efforts on their part will help to meet this demand and to exploit the opportunities offered by the vast Soviet market.

References

Aganbegyan, Abel, *The Economic Challenge of Perestroika*, Bloomington, Indiana University Press, 1988.
Gregory, Paul, "The Soviet Bureaucracy and *Perestroika*," *Comparative Economic Studies*, Spring 1989, pp. 1–13.
Hewett, Ed A., *Reforming the Soviet Economy, Equality versus Efficiency*, Washington, DC, The Brookings Institution, 1988.
Hewett, Ed A., "*Perestroika* and the Congress of People's Deputies," Washington, DC, The Brookings Institution, 1989 (mimeo).
Ivanov, Ivan A., "*Perestroika* and Foreign Economic Relations," in Agan-

begyan, Abel ed., *Perestroika 1989*, New York, Charles Scribner & Sons, 1988, pp. 145–64.

Popov, Vladimir V., *"Perestroika*: An Insider's View," *Trade Monitor*, July 1989, pp. 1–12.

Schroeder, Gertrude E., "Gorbachev's Economic Reforms," in Ronald D. Liebowitz, ed., *Gorbachev's New Thinking*, Cambridge, Mass., Ballinger Publishing Co., 1988, pp. 53–68.

12 Economic Integration in Eastern Europe*

This chapter will analyze the principal features of socialist economic integration in Eastern Europe and examine its future prospects. The first section will consider the activities of the Council for Mutual Economic Assistance (CMEA). The second section will examine the issue of subsidization through trade. The third section will review the future possibilities for the CMEA, and the final section will discuss proposals made for a payments arrangement among CMEA countries.

THE ACTIVITIES OF THE COUNCIL FOR MUTUAL ECONOMIC ASSISTANCE

The Communiqué announcing the establishment of the Council for Mutual Economic Assistance was published on 25 January 1949. The CMEA was created in response to the Marshall Plan for Western Europe. However, while the Marshall Plan provided substantial financial assistance for the Western European countries, CMEA involved no transfer of funds.

The founding members of the CMEA were Bulgaria, Czechoslovakia, Hungary, Poland, Romania, and the Soviet Union. Albania joined soon thereafter and East Germany in September 1950, but Albania subsequently ceased to participate in CMEA activities. Mongolia, Cuba, and Vietnam joined in later years but they will not be considered in the following.

Several meetings of the members of the CMEA took place in 1949 and 1950, but its activity ceased in mid-1950 and did not revive until mid-1954. Instead of economic integration, Stalin favored parallel national development, with the Soviet Union exerting a directing

* Originally published as World Bank Policy, Research and External Affairs Working Paper, No. 636, March 1991.
    The author is indebted to Alan Gelb and Martin Shrenk for helpful comments and to Shigeru Akiyama for research assistance.

influence through the "embassy system" under which major economic decisions by the individual countries required the agreement of the Soviet embassy.

Following Stalin's death, the CMEA called for the coordination of five-year plans and for production specialization. In fact, little transpired in a multilateral context in subsequent years and the developments that occurred took the form of bilateral negotiations.

In 1962, the CMEA countries negotiated *Basic Principles of the International Socialist Division of Labor* as the first major policy statement on regional economic cooperation. However, as Brabant notes, "soon thereafter the document was disowned by several signatories. As a result, the CPEs [centrally planned economies] failed to implement the precepts on regional production specialization in the ISDL [international social division of labor] as laid down in *Basic Principles*" (1989, p. 66).

The failure of implementing *Basic Principles* had to do with the rejection of Khruschev's proposal for a "superplan" on the CMEA level. While newspaper reports concentrated on the role of Romania in opposing joint planning, Hungary and Poland were opposed also. As Kiss noted, "the joint planning concept proved to be unrealistic, not only because it was cumbersome technically and methodologically, but also in terms of economic and, last but not least, political implications" (1975, p. 747).

For one thing, the centrally planned economies "saw, at best, limited salvation coming from transposing the problems of rigid, physical planning to the regional plane" (Brabant, 1989, p. 70). For another thing, they feared increased Soviet domination if a superplan was to be instituted. In this connection, mention may be made of the fact that Khruschev's proposal for a superplan followed the 1956 events in Hungary and Poland.

In the 1960s, trade among the CMEA countries continued to take place in the framework of bilateral negotiations. CMEA's influence was little felt although there were some specialization agreements, in particular in engineering products and chemicals. These agreements called for specialization in different products of a particular industry.

Specialization agreements were given a push by the *Complex Program for the Further Extension and Improvement of Cooperation and the Development of Socialist Economic Integration*, dated 1971. Under this program, 101 multilateral specialization agreements were signed between 1972 and 1977; there were also 620–700 bilateral specialization agreements (Pecsi, 1981, p. 13).

Specialization agreements assumed the greatest importance in engineering; among 120 multilateral agreements in effect in 1980, 87 concerned the engineering industries (Sobell, 1984, p. 237). They extended to ball bearings, electrical equipment, measuring instruments, medical and health care equipment, textile machinery, agricultural machinery, and machinery for construction and construction material. As a result, except for Poland and the Soviet Union, a substantial part of machinery trade occurred in the framework of specialization agreements. For 1985, the relevant percentages were: Bulgaria, 58 percent; Czechoslovakia, 44 percent; East Germany, 54 percent; Hungary, 50 percent; Poland, 21 percent; Romania, 62 percent; and the Soviet Union, 22 percent (Brabant, 1988, p. 306).

Another important area for specialization agreements was the automotive industry. An oft-cited case is Hungary's specialization in buses produced by Ikarus. In turn, Hungary does not produce passenger automobiles that are manufactured in the Soviet Union, Czechoslovakia, East Germany, and Poland. There is also specialization in light, medium, and heavy trucks. At the same time, Western firms play an important role, with Fiats being produced in the Soviet Union and Poland, and Western licenses being used in the production of trucks and buses.

Chemicals provide another area of specialization. There has been some shift of basic chemicals to the Soviet Union where raw materials and energy are available. The other members of the CMEA have concentrated on more developed and fine chemicals, with further specialization among products.

Specialization agreements have permitted the exploitation of economies of scale in the framework of the CMEA. At the same time, in the absence of competition, technological progress has not been ensured. The technological backwardness of industry in the CMEA countries is observed across the board, and it is particularly important in modern branches of industry such as computers and electronics. The situation is aggravated by the dominance of sellers' markets in the CMEA countries, with the buyer accepting low-quality merchandise.

Also, the extent of specialization should not be overstated. Faced with supply difficulties from their partners, CMEA countries aimed at producing a wide range of products. Thus, it has been reported that Czechoslovakia and East Germany manufacture more than 70 percent of the range of machinery produced in the world (Lavigne, 1990b, p. 6).

And, specialization has been largely limited to final products; it has not extended to parts and components. Apart from the reluctance of the CMEA countries to rely on imported parts and components, which may not have corresponded to their specifications and often experienced delays, the pricing issue looms large in the case of these inputs. According to Lavigne, "a non-resolved problem remains; the prices of parts and components. The establishment of world market prices, already difficult in the case of final products, is practically impossible for parts and components, whose characteristics and production conditions are highly variable" (1973, p. 264).

At the same time, the CMEA countries have not exploited their market potential. This was first noted by Pryor who concluded that in the years 1956 and 1962, the volume of trade of the CMEA countries was only 50–60 percent of that of comparable Western European countries, while such differences had not been observed in the interwar period. Pryor's conclusions were reached in the framework of a model incorporating trade, per capita GNP, and population figures (1968, p. 164).

In the period following Pryor's calculations the CMEA countries experienced a slowdown in the growth of their trade and Hewett confirmed Pryor's results in calculations made for 1970. Thus, according to Hewett, "typical eastern trade is, *ceteris paribus*, much lower than typical western trade" (1976, p. 8).

At the same time, a decline occurred in the share of intra-area trade. Thus, the share of intra-CMEA trade in the total fell from 71 percent in 1959 to 63 percent in 1971. This involved mostly a shift to trade with developed market economies whose share in the total increased from 21 percent to 27 percent (Balassa, 1976, p. 23).

The share of intra-CMEA trade declined further after 1971. According to estimates by the United Nations Economic Commission for Europe, in 1989 the share of exports and imports in trade among the CMEA countries in their total exports and imports was: Bulgaria, 83 percent and 73 percent; Czechoslovakia, 54 percent and 55 percent; East Germany, 42 percent and 38 percent; Hungary, 39 percent and 39 percent; Poland, 35 percent and 32 percent; Romania, 38 percent and 53 percent; and the Soviet Union, 46 percent and 50 percent. These estimates are adjusted further downwards if account is taken of the overvaluation of the ruble.

Various factors account for the lack of full utilization of the trade potential of the CMEA countries. To begin with, the centralization of economic decision-making, reflected in the planners' desire to lessen uncertainty associated with foreign trade, as well as the absence of direct trade relations between firms, tends to limit the volume of trade.

Opportunities for trade may also be foregone because of the lack of appropriate price signals. Domestic prices in the CMEA countries do not reflect resource scarcities and are divorced from prices in foreign trade. In turn, foreign trade prices follow world market prices with a lag and often show considerable variations in bilateral relationships (Csaba, 1985, p. 15). Under these circumstances, there is a risk that trade in particular commodities may involve a loss, rather than a gain, for the countries concerned and this risk tends to discourage trade among them.

At the same time, apart from relationships with the Soviet Union, there is an attempt to attain trade balance in individual commodity groups, in particular in "hard goods" and "soft goods" when the former, consisting largely of food, fuels, and raw materials, find ready markets in the developed market economies that is not the case for the latter, consisting mainly of manufactured products.

These developments have reinforced the practice of bilateralism under which countries attempt to avoid having an export surplus that is not settled in convertible currencies. Thus, the transferable ruble is not transferable at all and a surplus earned in trade with one partner cannot be converted into goods from another. Bilateralism, in turn, limits the amount of trade.

Finally, mention may be made of the propositions advanced by Holzman. In his view, the formation of the CMEA led to trade destruction, in part because the CMEA member countries are poorly suited to trade with each other and in part because they greatly increased barriers against nonmember countries (1985).

IS THE SOVIET UNION SUBSIDIZING ITS CMEA PARTNERS THROUGH TRADE?

Traditionally, it was assumed that the Soviet Union exploited the CMEA partner countries by turning the terms of trade in its favor. According to Holzman, "from the formation of CMEA until at least the difficulties in 1956 in Hungary and Poland, the Soviet Union exercised political power to trade with the Eastern European nations at very favorable terms of trade to itself. In fact, the ex-enemy Eastern nations were exploited ruthlessly (and this includes the exploitation via deliveries of reparations)" (1985, p. 417).

While data for the pre-1960 period are not available, Marrese and Vanous turned this thesis on its head by providing evidence that the terms of trade favor the other CMEA countries *vis-à-vis* the Soviet Union. Thus, they concluded that "within the CMEA the Soviet Union has been 'subsidizing' certain East European countries by exporting 'hard goods' (fuels, nonfood raw materials, and to a lesser degree food and raw materials for food) at CMEA's ftp's [foreign trade prices] which are below wmp's [world market prices], in exchange for imports of 'soft goods' (machinery and equipment and industrial consumer goods) at CMEA's ftp's, which are above wmp's; subsidization is especially apparent if account is taken of the relatively low quality of East European manufactures in comparison with their Western counterparts" (1983, p. 9).

As the quotation indicates, gains and losses were calculated by comparing prices used in intra-CMEA trade with world market prices, making further adjustments for the quality of "soft goods." Price differences became especially pronounced after 1973 when world oil prices quadrupled and the CMEA countries adopted a five-year averaging of world market prices in intra-CMEA trade. Thus, in 1970 US dollars, the estimated average annual loss to the Soviet Union in trade with its partner countries was 248 million in 1960–3, 398 million in 1964–8, 869 million in 1969–73, and 2840 million in 1974–8 (Marrese and Vanous, 1983, pp. 43–4).

The Marrese–Vanous estimates were criticized on the grounds that the authors used excessive quality discounts to value Soviet imports and exports of machinery and equipment and Soviet imports of consumer goods; the discounts ranged from 25 percent to 60 percent (Marer, 1984). But these discounts are actually used in selling machinery and equipment as well as consumer goods in Western markets.

Objections may also be raised to Marer's argument, according to which the Soviets could not purchase CMEA-quality machinery in the West at the same discount at which the East Europeans sell in the West. Apart from the fact that CMEA-quality machinery is not available in the West, note that Western exporters offer the Soviet Union a variety of advantages in the form of flexibility, service, and opportunity for product buy-back that are not available on the part of CMEA suppliers.

It has also been suggested that relative scarcities differ between the CMEA and the world market, leading to lower relative prices of primary products in the former case (Brada, 1985, p. 89). However, the world market prices offer the relevant benchmark as they represent opportunities foregone for the CMEA countries.

At the same time, there is a source of subsidization of the Soviet Union by the other CMEA countries that lies outside the Marrese–Vanous framework. This is the provision of capital for joint projects, such as the Odenburg gas pipeline. This subsidization is due to excessively low interest rates of 2 percent, much below Euromarket rates of 9–10 percent that may provide an appropriate benchmark, given the extensive use of convertible currencies in extending credit. In the absence of the necessary data, however, the extent of this subsidization cannot be gauged.

Finally, questions arise about the interpretation of the reasons for which the Soviet Union grants subsidies to its partner countries. According to Marrese and Vanous, the reason lies in these countries providing noneconomic benefits to the Soviet Union in enhancing its security. Thus, "the allegiance of East European countries can serve as a substitute for the use of Soviet labor and capital in providing security services to the Soviet Union. Because the Soviet Union is the dominant power within the CMEA, we contend that it utilizes this trade-off. In other words, the Soviet Union engages in preferential trade with Eastern Europe relative to the rest of the world in order to maintain the allegiance of the East European countries" (1983, p. 10).

Marrese and Vanous further suggest that the ranking of countries by per capita subsidies also provides a ranking by noneconomic benefits the Soviet Union obtains through subsidization. The ranking is East Germany, Czechoslovakia, Bulgaria, Hungary, Poland, and Romania. One may argue, however, that this ranking is simply the result of the composition of trade between the Soviet Union and its partner countries. Thus, East Germany and Czechoslovakia rely largely on Soviet fuels and raw materials in exchange for manufactured goods. In turn, during the period under consideration, Romania purchased practically no Soviet fuel and Poland could limit its reliance on Soviet fuel by reason of its extensive coal deposits.

At the same time, Marrese and Vanous argue that "domestic labor unrest in 1970 and 1976 (as well as the national strikes of 1980–81), the large proportion of the private sector in agriculture, the influence of the Roman Catholic church, the population's deep mistrust of the Soviet Union, and Poland's extensive relations with the West have combined to create an atmosphere of weak political allegiance to the Soviet Union which detracts from Poland's strategic value" (1983,

p. 71). Yet, Poland received large financial assistance from the Soviet Union at the time of its troubles, which much exceeded the subsidy calculated by the authors.

Brada further raises the question as to who provides the noneconomic benefits to the Soviet Union in exchange for subsidization. This will not be the population of the Eastern European countries who object to the loss of sovereignty it entails. In turn, the ruling classes in these countries share the political and strategic interests of the Soviet Union. In fact, as the events of the year 1989 indicated, they were kept in place by Soviet power. Or, as Brada expressed it, "to the eyes of East European leaders, many of the intangible benefits provided to the Soviet Union also yield politico-economic benefits to their own nations and enhance, rather than reduce, the political strength and stability of their own regimes" (1988, p. 645).

It may be added that when the governments of these countries deviated from the path of subservience, as happened in Hungary in 1956 and in Czechoslovakia in 1968, the Soviet Union intervened militarily and changed the governments. One may wonder, therefore, if there was need for subsidization when allegiance could be obtained through military means.

Whatever the reasons for subsidization, the question arises if it has continued beyond the period examined by Marrese and Vanous. This question has been addressed in Soviet Union–Hungary relations by Marrese and Wittenberg (1990). The authors conclude that the Soviet Union continued to provide substantial subsidies to Hungary in 1982, but the extent of subsidization declined to a considerable extent in 1987.

The relevant figures are $4.2–4.4 billion and $250–530 million. The authors further note that the fall in oil prices and in net Soviet exports of oil accounts for four-fifths of the decrease in the value of the subsidies.

The estimate for 1987 may be on the low side. Thus, according to Hungarian estimates it may cost Hungary $1.5–2.0 billion to adopt world market prices in its trade with the Soviet Union from January 1991 onwards (Lavigne, 1990a, p. 13 and *Le Monde*, 12 January 1990).

Brada (1985) and Koves (1983) raised the question if there may be other economic losses that offset the gains to CMEA partner countries obtained from the subsidization of their trade by the Soviet Union. They refer to dynamic losses due to insufficient technological progress, owing to their obligation to supply the Soviet Union with manufactured goods. These dynamic losses, together with the losses related to being forced into the straitjacket of the socialist planned system, will continue for a while whereas the gains from subsidization through trade will disappear in 1991.

THE FUTURE OF THE CMEA

The next question concerns the future of the CMEA. Several possibilities present themselves. They include the maintenance of the present arrangement; marketization within the CMEA; CMEA reform; and the dissolution of the CMEA. These will be considered in turn.

Maintaining the present system of the CMEA does not present a desirable option. With the member countries reforming their economies, basing intra-CMEA trade on quota-type bilateral agreements represents a conflict since market elements would coexist with elements of planning.

This conflict has been apparent already following the 1968 Hungarian reforms. While Hungary eliminated plan indicators, allowing firms to establish market relations, exports to the CMEA countries had to be regulated by government orders. Also, problems have arisen in pricing, with domestic prices differing from the prices used in intra-CMEA trade (Antaloczy, 1989).

These problems would be accentuated with the extension of reforms in Hungary and economic reforms undertaken by other CMEA countries. In particular, the transformation of socialist firms into profit-making units and their eventual privatization is incompatible with the maintenance of the present CMEA arrangements.

Marketization within the CMEA was envisaged at the 44th CMEA Council Session held in Prague on 6 July 1988. In this connection one may quote the statement by George Atanasov, Chairman of the Council of Ministers:

> We believe that the efforts to overhaul the integration mechanism and to construct a qualitatively new model of intra-community cooperation would be centered on the creation of a single market of the CMEA member countries, complete with a free movement of goods, services and other factors of production. The need of such a market stems objectively from the logic of economic reforms in the individual socialist countries, which are centered on the

promotion of commodity–money [market] relations. (cited in Schrenk, 1990, p. 1)

Marketization within the CMEA would establish an EC-type integration. But this presupposes that all CMEA member countries undertake far-reaching economic reforms, involving transformation into market economies. This is not in the cards.

While Poland shocked its economy with its January 1990 reform, despite its earlier reforms Hungary is proceeding at a slower pace and Czechoslovakia envisages a slow transformation of its centrally planned economy. Also, Bulgaria has gone no further than declaring its intention to reform and the situation in Romania remains unsettled.

Finally, the Soviet Union has made little progress in *perestroika* after five years. While in early 1990 indications were that a major reform effort was in the offing, the announcement made in May 1990 concerned only price increases. These increases were subsequently withdrawn and it is questionable how far the reforms under preparation will go.

If neither the maintenance of present arrangements within the CMEA nor its marketization present a desirable or feasible option, the question arises if the CMEA could survive through a reform. This is the alternative envisaged by Lavigne who argues that it fits in with the regionalization proceeding elsewhere in the world. At the same time, Lavigne expressed the view that "the countries of Eastern Europe deceive themselves if they expect eventually to be integrated with Western Europe" (1980a, p. 9).

This statement relegates the Eastern European countries to an economic backwater. Rather than integrating with the Soviet Union, where the prospects for reform are at best murky, the Eastern European countries want to become developed market economies. In so doing, integration into the EC offers an important avenue.

Nor can it be assumed that the EC would reject countries that carry out far-reaching reforms in decentralizing and privatizing their economies. In fact, the EC is prepared to eventually accept European market economies as new members if they agree to adopt its rules and regulations. In this connection, reference may be made to Greece and Portugal that were not more developed economically than the Eastern European countries at the time of their application for membership.

Another argument against the dissolution of the CMEA has been put forward by Schrenk. According to him, "a demise of the CMEA in consequence of a joint decision of *all* its members can be ruled out as implausible" (1990, p. 23), because it would conflict with the geopolitical objective of the Soviet Union. But if all other member countries were to demand the dissolution of the CMEA, could the Soviet Union resist?

Schrenk, however, rules out the exit of individual countries. In his view, "as this would violate the geopolitical objective of the USSR, it would amount to an 'adversary separation,' and is likely to provoke hostile responses from the USSR. Volume and composition of CMEA trade . . . suggest the likely direction of the eminently credible threat of economic retaliation: curtailment of trade with the exiting country to the point of trade embargo" (ibid.).

But one member country, East Germany, is actually exiting from the CMEA without invoking Soviet retaliation. Rather, the Soviets wish to ensure that East Germany will continue to provide the products it had so far supplied to the Soviet Union.

Yet, East Germany is the second largest economy in CMEA and its departure will leave a hiatus in CMEA. Now, if Czechoslovakia, Hungary, and Poland also exited, in practical terms CMEA would cease to exist.

At the same time, the maintenance of preferential ties with their CMEA partners is not compatible with these countries wishing to become developed market economies. In fact, their interest lies in having preferential ties with the EC that combines the majority of European developed countries.

Thus, Czechoslovakia, Hungary, and Poland would favor the demise of CMEA and the establishment of preferential ties with the EC. Initially, this would involve unilateral preferences granted by the EC but full membership could be envisaged in a decade or so.

In awaiting membership in the EC, should the three countries envisage participation in EFTA? This is not recommended since EFTA membership is not a stepping-stone to EC membership. Also, several of the EFTA countries themselves wish to become EC members.

Should, then, Czechoslovakia, Hungary, and Poland envisage establishing a free trade area or a customs union on their own? This may be desirable once these countries have gone far enough in their reform process. Establishing a free trade area or customs union among themselves would in fact help the process of structural transformation in their economies by increasing competition.

The discussion so far has not concerned Bulgaria and Romania.

These countries are at a lower level of development and are far behind in their economic reform. They thus provide little attraction to the EC and cannot aspire to participate in a Hungarian–Czech–Polish free trade area or customs union.

Finally, the Soviet Union is a *sui generis* case. In the foreseeable future, it will be preoccupied with its own economic reforms and with maintaining its political and economic unity. The statement made by the President of the Republic of Russia in June 1990 to drastically reduce contributions to the budget of the Soviet Union and the declarations of several republics as to the supremacy of their laws are indicative of tendencies towards disintegration in the Soviet Union.

But how about the modalities of trade among the former CMEA countries? This presupposes bilateral agreements among the countries in question. Such agreements should call for trade relationship between enterprises instead of between states and the use of current world market prices instead of five-year averages in the conduct of such trade. The introduction of such prices would help the reform process by aligning domestic prices to those obtainable in the world market.

PAYMENTS ARRANGEMENTS AMONG CMEA COUNTRIES

Under present conditions, the CMEA countries carry their accounts on bilateral trade in so-called transferable rubles. As noted above, this is a misnomer, since the rubles cannot be used to purchase goods from third countries. Rather, an export surplus gives rise to a credit that remains frozen.

With the dissolution of the CMEA, trade balances should be paid in convertible currencies. Given the scarcity of convertible currencies in Eastern Europe, proposals have been made for payments arrangements. One such proposal has been put forward by Ethier (1990).

Ethier suggests a monthly clearing of balances among Eastern European countries participating in a payments union, with mutual credit provided up to a certain limit. The clearing would also cover balances with nonparticipating Eastern European countries, assumed to include the Soviet Union.

This proposal draws on the experience of the European Payments Union that also involved a clearing of balances and provided credit up to a predetermined limit. But while in the EPU a third party, the

United States, supplied the credits, the Ethier proposal envisages mutual credits by the participants. This provides no incentive for a creditor country to participate in the payments union since it would use scarce foreign exchange to finance the deficit of the partner countries in their mutual trade.

The conclusion is strengthened if we consider that under the Ethier proposal, credit would also be provided for imbalances in trade with nonparticipating Eastern European countries. Thus, if country A had a deficit and country B a surplus in trade with the Soviet Union, country B would provide a credit.

Apart from the treatment of trade balances with nonparticipating Eastern European countries, the main problem with payments arrangements that involve the granting of mutual credits is that they are based on one segment of the balance of payments rather than on the overall balance. It is for this reason that the idea of a payments union was abandoned by ESCAP. Also, the payments arrangement in the Central American Common Market broke down as Nicaragua ran large deficits in intra-group trade that were financed by Costa Rica and Guatemala, although these countries were in an overall deficit position (Michalopoulos, 1990, p. 10).

A possible argument in favor of a payments union is that it contributes to the expansion of trade. This occurred in the EPU as countries dismantled their quantitative import restrictions. But such restrictions were dismantled *vis-à-vis* nonparticipating countries as well so that trade with these countries expanded also.

The Eastern European countries would also need to liberalize trade across the board. Such trade liberalization however does not require payments arrangements among particular countries that would focus on their mutual trade rather than on their overall trade.

It may be suggested that, in order to avoid the problems resulting from large and persistent debtor and creditor positions and the need to finance intraregional as opposed to global deficits, payments arrangements be established starting out from initial trade positions. But in Eastern Europe, it is precisely the initial trade positions of the countries concerned that need to be changed since the price relations on which they are based are distorted (Michalopoulos, 1990, pp. 11–12).

But how about the outside financing of credits in a payments union of Eastern European countries? Such an alternative has been put forward, entailing the creation of a fund of convertible currencies from which Eastern European countries could borrow to settle trade debts with each other (*New York Times*, 9 May 1990).

Outside aid eases the problem of financing debtor positions within a payments union and removes the disincentive of creditors to participate in the union. But the benefit of the financial aid would accrue exclusively to debtor countries within the payments union as it would be based on balance-of-payments positions in mutual trade rather than the overall balance-of-payments position. Yet, it is the latter rather than the former that provides a rational basis for the granting of outside credits.

These considerations indicate that the establishment of a payments union among Eastern European countries would not be desirable, irrespective of whether outstanding balances would be financed mutually or from the outside. One may envisage, however, clearing arrangements under which mutual credit is provided for a short period (say three months), with repayment at the end of the period.

A clearing arrangement would provide some savings in foreign exchange as countries could hold smaller reserves than would otherwise be the case. But the extent of savings through such an arrangement should not be overestimated as trade among the Eastern European countries (excluding the Soviet Union) amounts to only 15–30 percent of their total trade. At the same time, at the end of the three-months period, payment would need to be made in convertible currencies.

While a clearing arrangement provides some benefit to countries with inconvertible currencies, the goal should be to establish convertibility. This will take some time, given the difficult economic situation in which the Eastern European countries find themselves, but they should take measures to pursue the objective of currency convertibility.

CONCLUSIONS

This chapter has reviewed the activities of the Council for Mutual Economic Assistance since its establishment in 1949. While specialization agreements have permitted exploiting economies of scale, technological progress has been slow. Also, the CMEA countries have not exploited their market potential, due to the centralization of decision-making, the lack of price signals, and bilateral balancing.

The chapter has further considered the issue of subsidization of the partner countries through trade by the Soviet Union. The evidence supports the existence of subsidization that will come to an end, however, as world market prices will be used in intra-CMEA trade. At the same time, the Eastern European countries have suffered dynamic losses in the form of insufficient technological progress in their trade with the Soviet Union and being forced into the straitjacket of the socialist planning system.

As to the future of the CMEA, four alternatives have been considered: the maintenance of the present arrangement, marketization within the CMEA, CMEA reform, and the dissolution of the CMEA. The chapter favors the last alternative and suggests that the more developed CMEA countries seek association with the EC, followed by membership.

The chapter also objects to payments arrangement among the former CMEA countries that would involve providing credit on the basis of their mutual trade rather than total trade. And while clearing arrangements would bring some benefits, the countries in question should take measures to pursue the objective of convertibility.

References

Antaloczy, Katalin, "A KGST egyuttmukodesi rendszere es a magyar illeszkedes problemai (The System of CMEA Cooperation and the Problems of Hungarian Adjustment)," *Kulgandasag* (External Economy), February 1989, pp. 3–13.

Balassa, Bela, "Types of Economic Integration," in (Fritz Machlup, ed.), *Economic Integration, Worldwide, Regional, Sectoral*, New York, John Wiley, 1976, pp. 17–31.

Brabant, Jozef M. van, "Production Specialization in the CMEA – Concepts and Empirical Evidence," *Journal of Common Market Studies*, March 1988, pp. 282–316.

Brabant, Jozef M. van, *Economic Integration in Eastern Europe, A Handbook*, London, Routledge, 1989.

Brada, Josef, C., "Soviet Subsidization of Eastern Europe: The Primacy of Economics over Politics?," *Journal of Comparative Economics*, March 1985, pp. 80–92.

Brada, Josef, C., "Interpreting the Soviet Subsidization of Eastern Europe," *International Organization*, Autumn 1988, pp. 639–58.

Csaba, Laszlo, "Three Studies on the CMEA," *Trends in World Economy*, no. 52, pp. 1–99, 1985.

Ethier, Wilfred J., "Multi-Country Payments in Eastern Europe," Philadelphia, University of Pennsylvania, May 1990 (mimeo).

Hewett, Edward, "A Gravity Model of CMEA Trade," in Josef C. Brada, ed., *Quantitative and Analytical Studies of East–West Economic Relations*, Bloomington, Indiana, International Development Research Center of Indiana University, 1976.

Holzman, Franklyn D., "Comecon: A 'Trade Destroying' Customs Union?," *Journal of Comparative Economics*, December 1985, pp. 410–23.

Kiss, Tibor, "Nemzetkozi tervezesi egyuttmukodes a KGSTben (International Plan Cooperation in the CMEA)," *Kozgazdasagi Szemle* (Economic Review), June 1975, pp. 736–53.

Koves, A., "'Implicit' Subsidies and Some Issues of Economic Relations within the CMEA (Remarks on the Analyses Made by Michael Marrese and Jan Vanous)," *Acta Oeconomica*, 1–2, 1983, pp. 125–36.

Lavigne, Marie, *Le programme du Comecon et l'integration socialiste*, Paris, Editions Cujas, 1973.

Lavigne, Marie, "Chocs et revolutions dans les relations URSS–CAEM, 1975–1995," in Jacques Sapir, ed., *L'URSS en transition, 1975–1995*, Paris, Edition de l'Harmattan, 1990 (cited as 1990a).

Lavigne, Marie, "Economic Relations between Eastern Europe and the USSR; Bilateral Ties vs Multilateral Cooperation," Paris, Institut de Sciences Economiques et Mathematiques Appliquées, April 1990 (mimeo) (cited as 1990b).

Marer, Paul, "The Political Economy of Soviet Relations with Eastern Europe," in Sarah Meiklejohn Terry ed., *Soviet Policy in Eastern Europe*, New Haven, Conn., Yale University Press, 1984.

Marrese, Michael and Jan Vanous, *Soviet Subsidization of Trade with Eastern Europe*, Berkeley, Institute of International Studies of the University of California, 1983.

Marrese, Michael and Lauran Wittenberg, "New Insights into Intra-CMEA Trade Subsidization," Evanston, Ill., Northwestern University, June 1990 (mimeo).

Michalopoulos, Costas, "Payments Arrangements in Eastern Europe in the Post-CMEA Area," Washington, DC, World Bank, June 1990 (mimeo).

Pecsi, Kalman, *The Future of Socialist Economic Integration*, Armonk, NY, M. E. Sharpe, 1981.

Pryor, Frederick, L., "Socialist Industrialization and Trade in Machinery Products: Discussion," in Alan A. Brown and Egon Neuberger, eds, *International Trade and Central Planning*, Berkeley, University of California Press, 1968, pp. 159–64.

Schrenk, Martin, "The CMEA System of Trade and Payments: Today and Tomorrow," Washington, DC, World Bank Strategic Planning and Review, Discussion Paper No. 5, January 1990 (mimeo).

Sobell, Vladimir, *The Red Market, Industrial Co-operation and Specialization in Comecon*, London Aldershot, Gower, 1984.

Part VI

The GATT Negotiations

13 Subsidies and Countervailing Measures: Economic Considerations*

This chapter will examine issues relating to subsidies and countervailing measures and make recommendations for changes in existing rules on the basis of economic considerations. This will be done by analyzing, successively, the concepts of subsidies, countervailing measures and serious prejudice, nullification or impairment, and the special treatment of developing countries.

CONCEPTS OF SUBSIDIES

Economic effects of export subsidies

There is a basic assymetry in GATT. While import tariffs are accepted under GATT rules, export subsidies are prohibited, with exception made for the subsidization of primary exports and subsidies by the developing countries. Yet, import protection and export subsidies are symmetrical in their economic effects: they favor production in the country imposing such measures at the expense of production in other countries for foreign or for domestic markets; in so doing, they introduce distortions in international trade.

A solution to this puzzle may lie in the emphasis on incremental measures, on the assumption that the point of departure is a set of "bound" tariffs and no export subsidies. Now, GATT proscribes increases in tariffs from their bound level as well as the imposition of export subsidies. Under this interpretation, the rules aim at avoiding

---

* Originally published in *Journal of World Trade*, 23, no. 2 April 1989; pp. 63–79.

The author is indebted to Michael Finger, K. Kautzer-Schroder, Paul Meo, Patrick Messerlin, Julio Nogues, Amy Porges, and Richard Snape for helpful comments on an earlier draft.

additional distortions in international trade, whether in the form of increases in import tariffs or the imposition of export subsidies.

An alternative explanation is that countries react differently to measures applied in foreign markets and to measures that affect their domestic markets. They consider foreign trade barriers as reflecting the economic sovereignty of the countries concerned, while they regard foreign export subsidies as interfering with their own economic sovereignty.

An additional consideration is that export subsidies affect third country markets in distorting the conditions of competition among foreign exporters in these markets. In so doing, they interfere with international specialization according to comparative advantage. A case in point is the agricultural subsidies provided by high-cost producers that limit the export possibilities of low-cost producers.

In the following, we will review existing GATT rules on export subsidies on the basis of economic considerations. The scope of the discussion will further be extended to encompass domestic subsidies.

Export subsidies on products other than primary products

According to the General Agreement, "contracting parties shall cease to grant either directly or indirectly any form of subsidy on the export of any product other than a primary product which subsidy results in the sale of such product for export at a price lower than the comparable price charged for the like product to buyers in the domestic market" (XVI:4). This prohibition, applying to developed countries that signed the 1960 Declaration on Article XVI:4, was reaffirmed in the Tokyo Round Code on Subsidies and Countervailing Duties promulgated under the title "Agreement on Interpretation and Application of Articles VI, XVI, and XXIII of the General Agreement on Tariffs and Trade."

But the Code eschews any reference to the dual pricing rule in simply stating that "signatories shall not grant export subsidies on products other than certain primary products" (9:1). This can be considered an improvement since subsidization does not necessarily lead to lower export than domestic prices. Such may be the case, for example, if subsidization takes the form of preferential export credits, guarantees, and insurance, or if exporters take higher profits.

At the same time, the Code refers to the practices listed in the Annex, which "are illustrative of export subsidies" (9:2). Thus, we do not have a definitive list of export subsidies but only an illustrative list. This fact creates uncertainty in the application of the GATT rules.

Uncertainty could be reduced if the Contracting Parties to the General Agreement adopted the illustrative list as definitive, following appropriate revisions. Contracting parties would, then, have the responsibility not to grant the export subsidies listed, with exception made for primary products and for developing countries.

The list includes ten specific items as well as a general category, which covers "any other charge on the public account constituting an export subsidy in the sense of Article XVI of the General Agreement." The last point leads to the question if budgetary cost (a charge on public account) should be considered a necessary condition for there being an export subsidy.

Such is not necessarily the case for item (b), under which "internal transport and freight charges on export shipments, provided or mandated by governments, on terms more favorable than for domestic shipments" is considered an export subsidy. Also, in item (d) reference is made to actions by government agencies, whose budget may not be integrated with that of the government. Finally, export credits may be provided by "special institutions controlled by and/or acting under the authority of governments" (item (k)) without there being a budgetary cost. For example, banks providing export credit may be subject to lower reserve requirements.

It would appear, then, that there being a budgetary cost is not necessarily a condition for an export subsidy. At the same time, several items on the subsidy list may be reconsidered.

Item (d) concerns "the delivery by governments or their agencies of imported or domestic products or services for use in the production of exported goods, on terms or conditions more favorable than for delivery of like or directly competitive products or services for use in the production of goods for domestic consumption, if (in the case of products) such terms or conditions are more favorable than those commercially available on world markets to their exporters." This item permits dual pricing for inputs: charging lower prices for inputs used in production for the export market than for the same inputs used in production for the domestic market is permissible as long as these prices are not below world market prices. Such dual pricing should be considered a subsidy to exports, which are favored over domestic production.

Further questions arise in regard to item (h), which permits exemption, remission, or deferral of indirect taxes on goods and services used in export production if "the prior stage cumulative indirect taxes are levied on goods that are physically incorporated (making normal allowance for waste) in the exported products." The same condition appears in item (i) that relates to the remission or drawback of import charges.

These clauses exclude indirect taxes and import charges on services, such as transportation and communication, as well as on machinery, and on fuels and electricity used to operate machinery, which are not physically incorporated in the product. Such a distinction does not have an economic rationale, and the rules on indirect taxes and import charges should be applicable to all inputs. In the case of machinery, this would involve a pro rata charge of indirect taxes or import charges on the exported products.

The question has been raised, however, if one should accept the rebating of indirect taxes when the rebating of direct taxes is considered an export subsidy. This provision may be rationalized on the grounds that rebating an indirect tax assures the equality of prices received by the producer for domestic and for export sales, when the domestic consumer price will equal the sum of the producer price and the indirect tax. In turn, rebating the income tax would reduce the export price below that for domestic sales.

Export subsidies on primary products

As noted earlier, the General Agreement permits subsidies to exports of primary products. In this connection, the question arises what is meant by a primary product.

In the Note to Article XVI, it is stated that "a 'primary product' is understood to be any product of farm, forest, or fishery, or any mineral, in its natural form or which has undergone only such processing as is customarily required to prepare it for marketing in substantial volume in international trade." This statement clarifies the situation: for example, wheat is a primary product, but pasta is not. The reference to "marketing in substantial volume in international trade" also means that meat (together with livestock) may be regarded as a primary product.

Article XVI:3 states that "contracting parties should seek to avoid the use of subsidies on the export of primary products." There is no obligation, however, to refrain from the use of export subsidies except that the General Agreement seeks to limit subsidization in the following case:

If, however, a contracting party grants directly or indirectly any form of subsidy which operates to increase the export of any primary product from its territory, such subsidy shall not be applied in a manner which results in that contracting party having more than an equitable share of world export trade in that product, account being taken of the shares of the contracting parties in such trade in the product during a previous representative period, and any special factors which may have affected or may be affecting such trade in the product. (XVI:2)

This provision has little practical value as it does not define the meaning of "equitable share" beyond reference to export market shares during a previous representative period, which is subject to diverse interpretation. The introduction of "special factors which may have affected or may be affecting such trade in the product" further adds to uncertainty.

The Code attempted to introduce greater precision in the definition in stating that "'more than equitable share of world export trade' shall include any case in which the effect of an export subsidy granted by a signatory is to displace the exports of another signatory bearing in mind the developments on world markets" and "'a previous representative period' shall normally be the three most recent calendar years in which normal market conditions existed" (10:2).

It is not clear, however, what the reference to the most recent calendar years means in cases of export subsidies for primary products that have been used for some time. Further questions arise in connection with Article 10:3 in the Code, under which "signatories further agree not to grant export subsidies on exports of certain primary products to a particular market in a manner which results in prices materially below those of other suppliers to the same market." This provision covers only the case when there is substantial underpricing, yet export subsidization in primary products generally aims to offset differences in production costs without necessarily undercutting substantially the prices charged by low-cost producers.

Nor can refinements of these provisions suffice. Rather, one should aim at eliminating export subsidies to primary products. There is no economic rationale for the special treatment of such products; the same rules should apply to all. This is not to say that subsidies to primary products could be eliminated immediately. But, the Contracting Parties should take a commitment as to their elimination over time, and establish a timetable for the implementation of this agreement.

Domestic subsidies

While the General Agreement prohibits export subsidies, except for primary exports and for developing countries, there is no such prohibition of domestic subsidies. At the same time, "in any case in which it is determined that serious prejudice to the interest of any contracting party is caused or threatened by any such subsidization, the contracting party granting the subsidy shall, upon request, discuss with the other contracting party or parties concerned, or with the Contracting Parties, the possibility of limiting the subsidization" (GATT, XVI:1). This clause has rarely been used, but domestic subsidies have been countervailed.

While Article XVI of the General Agreement does not define domestic subsidies, the Code states: "Examples of possible forms of such subsidies are: government financing of commercial enterprises, including grants, loans, or guarantees; government provision or government financed provision of utility, supply distribution and other operational or support services or facilities; government financing of research and development programmes; fiscal incentives; and government subscription to, or provision of, equity capital" (11:2).

It is further added: "Signatories note that the above form of subsidies are normally granted either regionally or by sector. The enumeration of forms of subsidies set out above is illustrative and non-exhaustive, and reflects these currently granted by a number of signatories to this Agreement" (11:2).

In fact, the list is far from exhaustive as it does not cover special credit terms provided by banks on the government's behest or preferential transport charges, for example. At the same time, questions have been raised about the specificity of a domestic subsidy.

The Group of Experts on the Calculation of the Amount of a Subsidy has submitted Draft Guidelines for the Application of the Concept of Specificity in the Calculation of the Amount of a Subsidy other than an Export Subsidy (SCM/W/89, 25 April 1985) to the Committee on Subsidies and Countervailing Measures. Under the Guidelines, only measures which are specific to an enterprise or industry or group of enterprises or industries are considered domestic subsidies from the point of view of the application of Article XVI of the Agreement.

This provision may be considered appropriate since generally applicable subsidies do not favor particular enterprises or industries, but apply across the board. For example, a government may introduce incentives to promote investment that are available to any investor regardless of the industry.

At the same time, the Guidelines state that "it remains for the signatories to address the issue of regional specificity." In this connection, it has been argued that regional subsidies to particular enterprises or industries should be admitted as they aim at remedying the cost disabilities of particular regions.

This argument fails to consider that regional subsidies to particular enterprises or industries distort comparative advantage in the industries in question. Thus, on the regional level, too, distinction needs to be made between general and specific subsidies. General subsidies, which aim at offsetting the overall cost disabilities of a region, should not be considered domestic subsidies from the point of view of the application of Article XVI while specific subsidies should be so considered.

Article XVI:1 of the General Agreement refers to indirect as well as to direct subsidies. Indirect subsidies may be provided to inputs that are used in products which enter international trade. In this case the specificity test should apply to the final product; i.e. one should inquire if the subsidized input is specific to the final product. Thus, the existence of subsidization presumes that the input producing enterprise or industry receives a subsidy and that the input is specific to the product concerned.

A related issue is the pricing of natural resources. Governments may set a lower price for natural resources used domestically than sold internationally, thereby bestowing an advantage on domestic industry utilizing the natural resource. And, subsidies to natural resources in general may provide an advantage to industries using these resources in their export as well as domestic sales. Finally, government ownership of natural resources may lead to discriminatory treatment.

These practices should be evaluated on the basis of the described principles on indirect subsidization. This would mean judging them on the basis of subsidization of the input concerned and its specificity to the user industry.

COUNTERVAILING MEASURES, SERIOUS PREJUDICE AND NULLIFICATION OR IMPAIRMENT

According to the General Agreement, "the term 'countervailing duty' shall be understood to mean a special duty levied for the purpose of offsetting any bounty or subsidy bestowed, directly or indirectly, upon the manufacture, production or export of merchandise" (VI:3). At the same time, the condition for levying a countervailing duty is that the subsidy "causes or threatens material injury to an established industry in the territory of a contracting party or materially retards the establishment of a domestic industry" (VI:1). It is further added that "no countervailing duty shall be levied on any product of the territory of any contracting party imported into the territory of another contracting party in excess of an amount equal to the estimated bounty or subsidy determined to have been granted, directly or indirectly, on the manufacture, production, or export of such product in the country of origin or exportation, including any special subsidy to the transportation of a particular product" (VI:3).

It is apparent that export subsidies as well as domestic subsidies can be countervailed. However, the amount of countervailing duty is limited to the subsidy bestowed on products imported into the country taking countervailing action, thus excluding subsidies that benefit exports to third countries or domestic sales although these, too, can cause or threaten material injury to the industry of the country concerned.

Thus, countervailing action is not available in the case when a foreign subsidy adversely affects a country's sales to third markets or to the markets of the country imposing a subsidy. In these cases, Articles XVI or XXIII may apply. The former states that "In any case in which it is determined that serious prejudice to the interest of any other contracting party is caused or threatened by any such subsidization, the contracting party granting the subsidy shall, upon request, discuss with the other contracting party or parties concerned, or with the Contracting Parties, the possibility of limiting the subsidization" (XVI:1). The latter deals with nullification or impairment and states: "If any contracting party should consider that any benefit accruing to it directly or indirectly under this Agreement is being nullified or impaired or that the attainment of any objective of the Agreement is being impeded . . . the contracting party may, with a view to the satisfactory adjustment of the matter, make written representations or proposals to the other contracting party or parties which it considers to be concerned. Any contracting party thus approached shall give sympathetic consideration to the representations or proposals made to it" (XXIII:1).

We will return to the consideration of serious prejudice and nullification or impairment following a review of various aspects of countervailing action. These aspects are the measurement of subsidy, the determination of injury, the definition of domestic industry, cumulative injury assessment, the application of the *de minimis* clause and "nuisance" countervailing actions.

The measurement of subsidy

The General Agreement limits countervailing duties to "the estimated bounty or subsidy determined to have been granted" (VI:3). This provision has been reconfirmed and extended by the Code: "No countervailing duty shall be levied on any imported product in excess of the amount of subsidy found to exist, calculated in terms of subsidization per unit of the subsidized and exported product" (4:2). The General Agreement does not deal with the issue of measurement, however, and the Code is limited to the statement that "an understanding among signatories should be developed setting out the criteria for the calculation of the amount of subsidy" (4:2, footnote 15).

A controversy has arisen as to whether the amount of subsidy should be determined on the basis of the cost to the government or benefit to the recipient. The former position appears to be supported by the fact that, according to the provision just cited, a countervailing duty may not exceed "the estimated bounty or subsidy determined to have been granted" (VI:3). In turn, the Code's provision that "no countervailing duty shall be levied on any imported product in excess of the amount of subsidy found to exist" (4:2) has been interpreted to be consistent with the subsidy being equal to the benefit received by the producer or exporter.

From the economic point of view, the subsidy should be measured in terms of the benefit to the recipient. As a practical matter, this will usually be gauged in terms of the cost to the government. An important exception was noted above: in cases when banks provide a subsidized credit against which there are lower reserve requirements, the interest preference should be calculated relative to generally-applicable interest rates.

Under Article XVI of the General Agreement, it is the responsibility of the country granting the subsidy to indicate the extent of subsidization in notifying GATT of the existence of a subsidy. In taking countervailing action, then, the importing country may consider the estimate made in the notification to GATT as a point of departure in setting countervailing duties.

The proposed procedure would reduce uncertainty as to the measurement of the subsidy for purposes of countervailing action. It would also provide inducement to countries imposing subsidies to notify GATT on the extent of subsidization.

It is further proposed that, in the event countervailing duties are set at a level higher than the subsidy notified to the Contracting Parties, the country granting the subsidy should have the right to ask for consultation, conciliation, and dispute settlement in GATT. This would reduce existing complaints concerning countervailing action.

The determination of injury

The General Agreement speaks of material injury without giving a definition. In turn, the Code provides that "a determination of injury for purposes of Article VI of the General Agreement shall involve an objective examination of both (a) the volume of subsidized imports and their effect on the prices in the domestic market for like products and (b) the consequent impact of these imports on domestic producers of such products" (6:1). It is further stated:

> With regard to volume of subsidized imports the investigating authorities shall consider whether there has been a significant increase in subsidized imports, either in absolute terms or relative to production or consumption in the importing signatory. With regard to the effect of the subsidized imports on prices, the investigating authorities shall consider whether there has been a significant price undercutting by the subsidized imports as compared with the price of a like product of the importing signatory, or whether the effect of such imports is otherwise to depress prices to a significant degree or prevent price increases, which otherwise would have occurred, to a significant degree. No one or several of these factors can necessarily give decisive guidance. (6:2)

> The examination of the impact on the domestic industry concerned shall include an evaluation of all relevant economic factors and indices having bearing on the state of the industry such as actual

and potential decline in output, sales, market share, profits, productivity, return on investments, or utilization of capacity; factors affecting domestic prices; actual and potential negative effects on cash flow, inventories, employment, wages, growth, ability to raise capital or investment and, in the case of agriculture, whether there has been an increased burden on Government support programmes. This list is not exhaustive, nor can one or several of these factors necessarily give decisive guidance. (6:3)

We thus have a series of criteria and while the effect on prices is given pride of place in Article 6:1, in Article 6:3 this is only one of several criteria. At the same time, from the economic point of view, emphasis should be given to profits. Thus, one may examine the extent to which subsidies have led to reductions in profits in the affected industry below what may be considered normal profits. In so doing, adjustment would need to be made for changes in business conditions.

The question remains what is meant by material injury in the General Agreement. While this concept is not elucidated in the Code, material injury should be interpreted to mean substantial injury. Countervailing action would not be appropriate in the event that a subsidy has small and negligible effects. Thus, a substantial decline in profits attributed to the subsidy would be considered an indication of material injury.

The definition of domestic industry

According to the Code, "In determining injury, the term 'domestic industry' shall, except as provided in paragraph 7 below, be interpreted as referring to the domestic producers as a whole of the like products or to those of them whose collective output of the products constitutes a major proportion of the total domestic production of those products" (6:5). The exception refers to the case when "the territory of a signatory may, for the production in question, be divided into two or more competitive markets and the producers within each market may be regarded as a separate industry" (6:7).

It is further stated that "the term 'like product' ('produit similaire') shall be interpreted to mean a product which is identical, i.e. alike in all respects to the product under consideration or in the absence of such a product, another product which although not alike in all respects, has characteristics closely resembling those of the product under consideration" (6:1, note 18). These provisions may be utilized in dealing with the controversies that have arisen in regard to the meaning of like products for raw agricultural products and for parts and components.

While it has been suggested that raw agricultural products be included with processed primary products in respect to countervailing action, this would conflict with the definition of industry in the Code. In fact, rather than being like products, raw agricultural products and processed primary products represent different levels of transformation.

Similar considerations apply to parts and components. Rather than being like products, parts and components materially differ from the assembled product. They should not be included therefore in the same industry as defined by the Code.

A further issue that has arisen in regard to the definition of domestic industry is the representativeness of the petitioners who request countervailing action. The Code refers "to the domestic producers as a whole of the like products or to those of them whose collective output of the products constitutes a major proportion of the total domestic production of those products" (6:5). This may be understood to mean that requests should be acted upon if they are supported by a majority of producers, defined in terms of output value.

Cumulative injury assessment

The term "cumulative injury assessment" refers to the practice of defining material injury with respect to the combined effects of subsidized imports from all countries concerned. The cumulative assessment of injury increases the likelihood of affirmative findings, compared with the situation when injury is determined with respect to each exporting country, taken separately.

Neither the General Agreement nor the Code deals with cumulative injury assessment. And while references to the volume of subsidized imports in the Code (6:1) may be interpreted to refer to the cumulative assessment of injury, the opposite conclusion may be reached on the basis of a passage concerning the imposition of countervailing duty: "When the countervailing duty is imposed in respect of any product, such countervailing duty shall be levied, in the appropriate amounts, on a nondiscriminatory basis on imports of such product from all sources found to be subsidized and to be causing injury" (4:3).

Nevertheless, from the economic point of view, cumulative injury assessment is a sensible procedure since, for the domestic industry, it is the combined effect of foreign subsidies that matters. As long as there is material injury that can be attributed to subsidization by foreign exporting countries, there is justification for countervailing action. The question remains, however, if countervailing action should be taken against all subsidizing countries or only against some of them if they, combined, give rise to material injury. The answer is simple if the exporters are of equal size and provide subsidies of similar magnitude: countervailing action should be taken against all exporters in this case.

The situation is more complicated if exports vary in size and the magnitude of the subsidies differ. Now, it would be inappropriate to levy countervailing duties on the exports of countries that did not contribute to material injury. This, in turn, necessitates examining the possible effects of omitting individual countries from the calculation and taking countervailing action only against those that contributed to the material injury.

De minimis subsidy

Material injury could not be caused if subsidies are "*de minimis*," i.e. they are very small. This is because, if the subsidy is *de minimis*, it can be assumed that no material injury exists. The application of such a procedure conforms to Article 2:12 of the Code, according to which "an investigation will be terminated when the investigating authorities are satisfied that no subsidy exists or that the effects of the alleged subsidy on the industry is not such as to cause injury."

It has been suggested that a general definition of *de minimis* subsidy is not possible because of differences in factors such as the size of exports and their price sensitivity. Nevertheless, one may establish a floor in terms of subsidy rates which involves the presumption that no material injury exists. While the choice is to a considerable extent arbitrary, it may be assumed that a subsidy rate below 1 percent does not cause material injury.

Nuisance countervailing actions

The application of the *de minimis* rule would limit "nuisance" countervailing actions that aim at discouraging exports. The question arises if other measures may also be taken to avoid such actions.

One possibility is to impose a penalty in the case when countervailing action was initiated even though no appropriate basis existed. Another would be to strengthen the preliminary review process before the claim is acted upon by the authorities of the importing country.

Serious prejudice and nullification or impairment

Thus far, the discussion has concerned countervailing action against subsidies that cause material injury in the importing country. As noted earlier, injury may also result when the foreign subsidy adversely affects a country's sales to third markets or to the markets of the country imposing the subsidy. In these cases, Articles XVI and XXIII may apply as noted above.

Articles XVI and XXIII are very weak provisions. Not only is there no obligation to withdraw subsidization but the GATT procedures for dispute settlement do not come into play.

Dispute settlement procedures were introduced in the Code. These would follow consultations concerning the subsidy:

> Whenever a signatory has reason to believe that any subsidy is being granted or maintained by another signatory and that such subsidy either causes injury to its domestic industry, nullification or impairment of benefits accruing to it under the General Agreement, or serious prejudice to its interests, such signatory may request consultations with such other signatory. (12:3).

> If, in the case of consultations under paragraph 3 of Article 12, a mutually acceptable solution has not been reached within sixty days of the request for consultations, any signatory party to such consultations may refer the matter to the Committee for conciliation in accordance with the provisions of Part VI. (13:2)

> If any dispute arising under this Agreement is not resolved as a result of consultations or conciliations, the Committee shall, upon request, review the matter in accordance with the dispute settlement procedures of Part VI. (13:3)

> If, as a result of its review, the Committee concludes that an export subsidy is being granted in a manner inconsistent with the provisions of this Agreement or that a subsidy is being granted or maintained in such a manner as to cause subsidy, nullification or

impairment, or serious prejudice, it shall make such recommendations to the parties as may be appropriate to resolve the issue and,
in the event the recommendations are not followed, it may auth-
orize such countermeasures as may be appropriate, taking into
account the degree and nature of the adverse effects found to exist,
in accordance with the relevant provisions of Part VI. (13:4)

While the provisions of Articles 12 and 13 of the Code introduce
conciliation and dispute settlement procedures in the event of serious
prejudice and nullification or impairment, experience indicates
that these procedures are not always effective. Thus, there have
been cases when the Committee on Subsidies and Countervailing
Measures did not act on a panel report (as in the pasta case) or one of
the parties involved refused to accept the recommendations (as it
occurred in a case where the United States and another where the EC
was found to have violated the General Agreement). Correspondingly, it would be desirable to strengthen the rules on subsidies. This
may be done by taking the EC rules as a point of departure.

The EC severely limits domestic industrial subsidies in order to
avoid distorting competition in the member countries. It would be
appropriate to establish rules limiting domestic subsidies in GATT as
well, so as to minimize distortions in export markets and in domestic
markets. This could be accomplished by prohibiting domestic subsidies that exceed a certain percentage, say 5 percent, of output
value.

It may be added that domestic subsidies can be used as disguised
export subsidies. This will be the case when exports account for a
large proportion of domestic production. One may, then, extend the
prohibition of export subsidies in cases when exports account for,
say, over 50 percent of domestic output to domestic subsidies as well.

Dispute settlement

The proposed extension of the prohibition of export subsidies to
domestic subsidies meeting certain criteria would still leave a broad
range of domestic subsidies. And while specific domestic subsidies
are countervailable, as noted earlier there is no possibility for
countervailing action if the subsidies affect exports to third countries
or to the subsidy-imposing country's own markets.

It follows that there is need to improve GATT mechanisms to deal with cases of serious prejudice and nullification or impairment. This would necessitate improving the existing GATT dispute settlement procedure. Such improvements are also necessary if we consider that other contentious issues may arise in the application of Articles VI and XVI.

Particular importance attaches to timeliness in decision-making and in implementation. A ruling by a panel should be made by a specified date and the party found to have violated the General Agreement should have a specific time to object to the ruling. Once the ruling becomes final, it should be carried out within a short period and it should not be subject to blocking by the party who has been found to have violated the Agreement.

The developed countries have a particular responsibility to abide by panel rulings. In this regard, there are some helpful signs, e.g. Japan accepted the ruling on abolishing restrictions on the imports of 12 foodstuffs. There has also been an increase in the number of trade disputes brought to GATT and dispute settlement panels have speeded up their work.

SPECIAL TREATMENT OF DEVELOPING COUNTRIES

GATT rules on subsidies by developing countries

Developing countries did not subscribe to Article XVI:4 of the General Agreement that prohibits the use of export subsidies on products other than primary products. Article 14 of the Code further notes: "Signatories recognize that subsidies are an integral part of economic development programmes of developing countries" (14:1). "Accordingly, this Agreement shall not prevent developing country signatories from adopting measures and policies to assist their industries, including those in the export sector" (14:2).

At the same time, "developing country signatories agree that export subsidies on their industrial products shall not be used in a manner which causes serious prejudice to the trade or production of another signatory" (14:3). However, "there shall be no presumption that export subsidies granted by developing country signatories result in adverse effects, as defined in this Agreement, to the trade and production of another signatory. Such adverse effects shall be demonstrated by positive evidence, through an economic examination of the impact on trade or production of another signatory" (14:4).

These provisions conform to GATT rules establishing special and differential treatment for developing countries. Thus, Article XVIII added in 1955 recognizes that it may be necessary for developing countries "to take protective or other measures affecting imports" (XVIII:2) and "to grant the governmental assistance required to promote the establishment of particular industries" (XVIII:3). Furthermore, Article XXXVI, added in 1965, takes note of the need "for a rapid and sustained expansion of the export earnings of the less-developed contracting parties" (XXXVI:2), and "for positive efforts designed to ensure that less-developed contracting parties secure a share in the growth in international trade commensurate with the needs of their economic development" (XXXVI:3). Also, it is stated that "the developed contracting parties shall . . . have special regard to the trade interests of less-developed contracting parties when considering the application of other measures permitted under this Agreement to meet particular problems and to explore all possibilities of constructive remedies before applying such measures where they would affect essential interests of those contracting parties" (XXXVII:3).

As noted in a note of the GATT Secretariat ("Incentives to Industrial Exports from Developing Countries," COM/TD/72, 17 March 1970, para. 7), "it is clear from the drafting history of Part IV [of the General Agreement] that countervailing duties are among the measures permitted to meet particular problems" referred to in Article XXXVII:3. It does not appear, however, that the developed countries would have given preferential treatment to developing countries in the application of countervailing duties.

Optimal policies for developing countries

On economic grounds, deviations from free trade can be justified on the grounds of externalities in production. In developing countries, externalities may involve the creation of new skills as well as technological improvements, the benefits of which are not fully captured by the firm. Such externalities exist in the manufacturing sector of the developing countries, although their magnitude should not be overstated. Thus, they warrant preferential treatment of this sector to a limited extent only.

Ideally, preferential treatment to manufacturing activities should be provided by production subsidies that provide the same incentive to sales in domestic and in foreign markets and do not distort the pattern of consumption. By contrast, tariffs discriminate against exports and in favor of import substitution and distort the pattern of consumption by raising the prices of manufactured goods.

Production subsidies are not practicable in most developing countries because of their limited capacity to pay taxes which would finance the subsidies. Rather, developing countries rely largely on import tariffs that constitute government revenue.

The application of import tariffs and export subsidies at equal rates has advantages over reliance on import tariffs alone. Under this alternative, the same increase in domestic production can be attained at lower tariffs and there is no discrimination against exports. And although consumption is distorted, the revenue needs of export subsidies are less than those of production subsidies.

Steps toward the equalization of incentives to import substitution and exports may be taken by a devaluation accompanied by reductions in import duties. The devaluation would provide incentives to exports while import protection would be reduced to the extent that reductions in tariffs exceeded the rate of devaluation. For example, a 10 percent devaluation accompanied by a 20 percent reduction in tariffs would lower import protection by 10 percent and increase incentives to exports by 10 percent. This is because a 10 percent devaluation is equivalent to a 10 percent import tariff cum export subsidy.

The described procedure would reduce but not eliminate the bias of the incentive system against exports. In order to further reduce this bias, developing countries should make use of the rules provided by GATT to rebate import duties on imported inputs and indirect taxes on all inputs used in export production, extending these rebates to indirect inputs.

Rebating duties and indirect taxes, used to good effect by the East Asian NICs, would put the export sector on a free-trade footing. Extending the rebates to indirect inputs is especially important, both to reduce the cost of exports and to ensure the backward integration of the production process through the domestic production of inputs for exports.

Developing countries may also provide preferential credit to exports to the extent allowed by the OECD agreement on official export credits, referred to in the illustrative list of export subsidies, and give preference to exporters in the event credit is rationed. Export insurance schemes can further be set up in the absence of the private provision of such insurance. And, exports can be assisted through investment in infrastructure, from the building of ports complemented by access roads and railway connections to the establishment of a modern telephone system.

Governmental and paragovernmental organizations may further use measures of export promotion. Such promotional measures include the organization of trade fairs and trade missions, the collection of information on market possibilities for export, the establishment of trade centers and of consular services to promote exports, as well as quality control.

Beyond these measures, export subsidies may be provided in cases when countervailing action does not threaten. This will be the case for exporters that do not cause injury to developed country industries, including small countries as well as the exports of large countries that account for a small proportion of developed-country markets.

The graduation clause

As developing countries industrialize, the importance of production externalities, and hence the need for the preferential treatment of the manufacturing sector, will decline. Correspondingly, these countries may reduce reliance on import tariffs and export subsidies. Eventually, developing countries may forego the use of export subsidies and accept GATT rules on the prohibition of these subsidies.

The described situation is foreshadowed in the Code, according to which "a developing country signatory should endeavor to enter into a commitment to reduce or eliminate export subsidies when the use of such export subsidies is inconsistent with its competitive and development needs" (14:5). The Code does not provide, however, for a procedure that would ensure graduation as developing countries industrialize.

Yet, it would be desirable to establish a procedure to deal with the case of advanced developing countries as well as with the case when an industry of a developing country is internationally competitive. This procedure may take the form of the application of the dispute settlement procedure in GATT, involving rulings by a panel on complaints submitted to GATT.

CONCLUSIONS

This chapter has examined issues relating to subsidies and counter-vailing measures and made recommendations for changes in existing rules on the basis of economic considerations. This has been done in regard to subsidies; countervailing measures and serious prejudice, nullification or impairment; and the special treatment of developing countries.

It is suggested that the illustrative list of export subsidies be made definitive, following appropriate revisions. These revisions would eliminate the dual pricing of inputs and remove the requirement of the physical incorporation of inputs for the exemption and remission of indirect taxes and import charges. At the same time, the exception made for primary products in regard to the prohibition of export subsidies should be eliminated over time.

Only measures which are specific to an enterprise or industry or group of enterprises or industries should be considered domestic subsidies from the point of view of the application of Article XVI of the Agreement. This rule should also be applied to regional subsidies and to subsidies provided to inputs.

Both export subsidies and domestic subsidies are countervailable if they cause or threaten material injury to an established industry or materially retard the establishment of a domestic industry of an importing country. In this connection, several issues arise.

First, the subsidy should be measured in terms of the benefit to the recipient and reported to GATT as part of the procedure of notifying the existence of a subsidy, with the estimate used as a point of departure in setting countervailing duties. Second, material injury should be interpreted to mean substantial injury and gauged in terms of changes in profits attendant on the imposition of the subsidy. Third, domestic industry should be defined to exclude raw agricul-tural materials for processed products and parts and components for final products. Fourth, cumulative injury assessment should be ap-plied, with countervailing action foregone in regard to the exports of countries that did not contribute to the material injury. Fifth, mate-rial injury should be assumed not to exist if the subsidy is *de minimis*. Sixth, procedures should be adopted that reduce the chances of initiating nuisance countervailing action.

Countervailing action is not available in cases when a foreign subsidy adversely affects a country's sales to third markets or to the markets of the country imposing the subsidy. In cases when the subsidy causes serious prejudice or nullification or impairment of benefits that would otherwise accrue to a country under the General Agreement, there are only weak provisions for possible rectification.

Correspondingly, it would be desirable to strengthen existing rules on subsidies. This could be accomplished by prohibiting domestic subsidies that exceed a certain percentage of output value as well as domestic subsidies provided in cases where exports account for a large proportion of output. It would also be necessary to improve the existing GATT dispute settlement mechanism.

Developing countries receive preferential treatment in the application of GATT rules on subsidies. They are exhorted, however, to reduce or eliminate export subsidies which are inconsistent with their competitive or development needs. It is suggested that the procedures be established to deal with the case of advanced developing countries and with the case when an industry of a developing country is internationally competitive.

14 Services in the United States*

This chapter focuses on the effects that liberalization of trade in services may have on the United States. It examines US "revealed" comparative advantage in services as indicated by the available trade data, barriers to exports of US services abroad, and restrictions on imports of services into the United States. It concludes with a discussion of the position taken by the US government and private interests with regard to liberalization of trade in services.

THE DETERMINANTS OF COMPARATIVE ADVANTAGE IN SERVICES

The best-known empirical investigation of comparative advantage in trade in services is a nearly decade-old paper by Sapir and Lutz (1981), who sought to explain international trade in services in terms of intercountry differences in factor endowments and country size. Freight, passenger services, and insurance were analyzed, and the sample of countries varied according to the availability of data. The authors hypothesized that comparative advantage in freight services is positively related to an economy's capital–labor ratio (on the assumption that shipping is capital-intensive) and to country size (because of the existence of scale economies in shipping). The results support the first hypothesis – that countries relatively well-endowed with physical capital have a comparative advantage in freight services – but not the second.

Transport of passengers is also considered to be capital-intensive. The hypothesis that comparative advantage in passenger transport is positively related to the country's capital–labor ratio is borne out by the empirical results. It further appears that a positive trade balance

* Originally published in P.A. Messerlin and K.P. Sauvant (eds), *Uruguay Round: Services in the World Economy*, The World Bank, Washington DC, 1990.

The author is indebted to Carol Balassa, Patrick Messerlin, and Karl Sauvant for helpful comments.

in travel contributes to the export of passenger transport services. Carter and Dickinson (1979) have suggested that in international trade in insurance the essential element "is a well-educated labor force, including a whole range of professional expertise in financial, legal, and technical subjects" (pp. 44–5). Here too, a size effect has been postulated. Sapir and Lutz found that human capital and scale are the factors that determine comparative advantage in insurance services. This conclusion applies to total insurance as well as to merchandise and nonmerchandise insurance. Total and nonmerchandise insurance appear to make relatively intensive use of higher education, whereas merchandise insurance appears to be relatively intensive of secondary education.

The implications of these results for the United States depend on the country's relative endowment of physical capital (for freight and passenger transport) and human capital (for insurance). Among the 52 countries studied by Sapir and Lutz, the United States ranks fifth in terms of the ratio of physical capital to labor, behind Israel, Switzerland, Sweden, and Norway. It appears, then, that the United States has a comparative advantage in freight services and in passenger transport. The country ranks seventh – behind New Zealand, Canada, Yugoslavia, Austria, the Republic of Korea, and the Netherlands – in terms of the level of secondary education, measured by the ratio of enrollment to the size of the relevant age cohort. It follows that the United States has a comparative advantage in merchandise insurance. Finally, the United States ranks first in terms of the level of higher education, measured by the ratio of enrollment to the relevant age cohort. This means that it has a comparative advantage in nonmerchandise insurance as well as in total insurance.

"REVEALED" COMPARATIVE ADVANTAGE IN SERVICES

To shed light on the US comparative advantage in a wider array of services, the concept of "revealed" comparative advantage has been used. This concept, originated by Balassa (1965), interprets a country's comparative advantage in terms of its relative trade performance (net exports). It has been widely used in investigations of merchandise trade.

Sapir and Lutz found that passenger transport and freight services are exported by capital-abundant countries and that the United

States is such a country. The United States might therefore be expected to be a net exporter of passenger transport and freight services. But as Table 14.1 shows, the United States has a net import balance in both passenger transport and freight that is not fully offset by its net export balance in port services. Further discussion of these items is not necessary in the present context, however, since regulations on transport services are similar in most countries.

Sapir and Lutz also predicted that the United States would be a net exporter of insurance. This turns out to be the case for primary insurance but not for reinsurance, in which the United Kingdom appears to possess traditional advantages.

The United States' large net import balance in travel largely reflects its comparative disadvantage in this labor-intensive activity. This import balance would be reduced to some extent if foreign exchange restrictions applied by a number of developing countries were eliminated.

The large positive balance in royalties and license fees is not related to the Heckscher–Ohlin explanation of trade flows but is, rather, explained by the United States' technological advantages.

The United States has a large net export balance in business, professional, and technical services and for all items within the category except for accounting, auditing, and bookkeeping and advertising. (It has small import balances in these items.)

US net exports in computer and data processing services are large: sales total $629 million and purchases $61 million. Software services (excluding custom programming) account for two-thirds of the total. This category consists of both prepackaged software and rights to use, reproduce, or distribute such software. Also in the computer and data processing services category are integrated hardware–software systems and system analysis, design, engineering, and custom programming services.

The United States has a net export balance in database and other information services, with sales of $108 million and purchases of $28 million. Business and economic database services and miscellaneous database services fall under this category.

Net export balances are also shown for engineering, architecture, construction, and mining (sales of $936 million and purchases of $368 million); installation, maintenance and repair of equipment ($1023 million and $506 million); legal services ($148 million and $56 million); management, consulting, and public relations ($379 million and $50 million); research and development, commercial testing, and

Table 14.1   US International sales and purchases of services, 1987
(millions of dollars)

Services trade	Sales	Purchases
With unaffiliated foreigners	66 482	66 256
Passenger fares	6 882	7 423
Other transport	16 989	18 164
Freight	4 700	10 999
Port services	11 575	6 360
Other	714	805
Insurance	2 285	3 168
Primary insurance, net	1 596	552
Reinsurance, net	689	2 616
Travel	23 505	29 215
Royalties and license fees	2 171	522
Business, professional, and technical services	4 270	1 425
Accounting, auditing, and bookkeeping	27	37
Advertising	108	140
Computer and data processing	629	61
Database and other information services	138	28
Engineering, architectural, construction, and mining, net	936	368
Installation, maintenance and repair of equipment	1 023	506
Legal services	148	56
Management, consulting, and public relations	379	50
Medical services	516	n.a.
Research and development, commercial testing and laboratory services	182	127
Other	184	52
Telecommunications	2 105	3 701
Financial services	3 731	2 077
Education	3 804	513
Film rentals	740	48
With affiliated foreigners	14 988	6 210
With foreign parents	2 923	3 150
Royalties and license fees	240	1 083
Other services	2 683	2 067
With foreign affiliates	12 065	3 060
Royalties and license fees	7 049	150
Other services	5 016	2 910
Total	81 470	72 466

Source: Ascher and Whichard (1989).

laboratory services ($182 million and $127 million); and other services ($184 million and $52 million). Sales of medical services amount to $516 million; data on purchases are not available but are likely to be small.

A seemingly abnormal case is telecommunications, in which US sales are $2105 million and purchases are $3701 million. The imbalance is entirely attributable to telephone services, in which the United States has a large import balance; it has a net export balance in other telecommunications services. The net import balance for telephone services is a recent phenomenon that is explained by differential rates of increase in the volume of telephone calls and by differential rates of change in the cost of the calls. Between 1985 and 1987 the volume of telephone calls from the United States to other countries, measured in minutes, increased by 47 percent, whereas calls from other countries to the United States increased by only 27 percent (Federal Communications Commission, 1988). In 1987 the volume of outgoing telephone calls totaled 3153 million minutes, as against 1567 million minutes for incoming calls. Moreover, about 75 cents of every dollar collected by US carriers from international telephone calls is owed to the foreign carriers that terminate the telephone calls because the accounting rates used in transfers among the carriers have not been reduced along with the actual rates paid. If it were not for this discrepancy, the United States would not have a net import balance in telephone services (Federal Communications Commission, 1988).

In financial services the United States has exports of $3731 million and imports of $2077 million. A careful study by Hilaire and Whalley (1986) confirms the US export surplus. The authors applied estimates of the spread between deposit and lending rates for US, UK and Canadian banks and for banks in their largest partner countries to corresponding data on the assets and liabilities of domestic banks with nonresidents and of nonresident banks with residents. These yielded an estimate of the value of intermediation services provided by domestic banks to depositors and borrowers abroad, and by nonresident banks to domestic depositors and borrowers. The combined financial intermediation charge was apportioned between the parties to calculate the internationally traded components. The results show US banking exports of $4.03 billion and imports of $3.04 billion, as against UK exports of $2.55 billion and imports of $4.40 billion and Canadian exports of $0.72 billion and imports of $0.42 billion. Thus the United States appears to have a revealed comparative advantage in banking services.

In education US exports were $3804 million and imports were $513 million. Exports in film rentals were $740 million and imports were $48 million.

The information provided so far concerns transactions with unaffiliated foreigners. Transactions within multinational corporations exhibit a large net export balance for the United States, with sales of $14 988 million and purchases of $6210 million (Table 14.1).

BARRIERS TO SERVICES TRADE IN THE UNITED STATES AND ABROAD

The US *Report on Foreign Trade Barriers* (USTR, 1989) reviews perceived foreign barriers to US services exports in various countries. Some of its observations follow.

> Restrictive investment laws, administrative nontransparency, legal and administrative restrictions on remittances and arbitrary application of regulations and laws limit US service exports to Brazil. Service trade possibilities are also affected by limitations on foreign capital participation in many service sectors. (p. 20)

> The Indian government either partially or entirely runs most major service industries. Restrictions on trade in services follow the same pattern and rationale as restrictions on trade in goods and foreign investment. Officials fear allowing more scope to foreigners would diminish control over strategic industries, adversely affect inefficient service monopolies and add a new drain on foreign exchange. (p. 87)

> Korea continues to maintain restrictions on some service sectors through a "negative list." In these sectors foreign investment is prohibited or severely circumscribed through equity participation or other restrictions. Those sectors of greatest interest to US investors and service providers include professional services (such as accounting, legal and financial services) advertising, maritime transport, and telecommunications services. (pp. 120–1)

This section reviews barriers to US services abroad of the kind described above. It interprets services in a broader sense to include patents, trademarks, and copyrights. This is appropriate, since intellectual property involves service transactions.

A variety of products, including foodstuffs, beverages, pharmaceuticals, agrochemicals, chemical compounds, agricultural machinery, and metal alloys, are not patentable in one country or another. Some countries set conditions for patent protection – requiring, for example, that patented pharmaceuticals embody new technology. In several instances, especially for pharmaceuticals, only processes can be protected, and other producers may, consequently, enter the field with competing products that have been manufactured by different processes.

Patent protection is often available for only a short period, thereby limiting the firm's interest in the manufacture of the product. Obtaining patent protection may be a slow process that gives other producers an opportunity to establish themselves.

Continuous use of trademarks may be a requirement for their registration. The process of registering trademarks is often slow, and the enforcement of trademark protection has encountered problems. It may not be possible to register service marks (trademarks pertaining to services).

As for copyright, there have been disputes between the United States and other countries regarding the limitations imposed on the value of broadcasting and video material originating in the United States and regarding taxes on this material. Other disputes have concerned copyright laws. Some countries have no copyright laws for books or audio and video recordings. Others have such laws, but their practical application is deficient, and there is considerable pirating of copyrighted material. Furthermore, the duration of copyright protection is often very short.

Copyright of computer applications has become important in recent years. The Brazilian government has mandated that all data received from unrelated parties be processed in Brazil, and it has limited foreign equity participation in Brazilian information industries. In other countries no copyright protection exists for collective work such as databases and software, and database creators are effectively excluded from protection. Several countries provide no protection, or only weak protection, for computer software and programming.

In accounting and advertising, foreign accounting firms may not be allowed to operate unless they are in partnerships with domestic firms, and majority foreign participation may not be allowed in the advertising industry.

State corporations may have a monopoly position in insurance, and marine insurance for exports and imports may be reserved for domestic firms. Some countries require foreign insurers to cede 30 to 60 percent of all transactions to the state-owned reinsurance company and limit the equity that may be owned by foreign insurance companies. Finally, insurance firms may be prohibited from establishing subsidiaries and joint ventures with noninsurance enterprises.

The offer of what in US terminology is called enhanced telecommunications services (in most other countries the term is value-added telecommunications services) may be limited to a state-owned or state-franchised monopoly. Even where foreign firms are permitted to compete with state-owned telecommunications administrations, restrictive terms and conditions imposed on the use of telephone lines may make competition difficult or impossible. For example, Japan's Ministry of Education uses the TRON (Real Time Operation System Nucleus) system as a technical specification for personal computers, and the NTT (the company that provides basic telecommunications services) has announced that it will require TRON for the next generation of the digital communications network.

Restrictions are also imposed on legal and financial services and on construction, architectural, and engineering services. All of these restrictions are described in USTR (1989), which considers them important obstacles to US exports of services.

There is no comparable compilation on US barriers to imports of services except for the report by the European Community (EC, 1989). That study notes that the United States has entered an exception to Article 11(5) of the Patent Application Treaty, effectively postponing the date by which foreign patents become valid in the United States. It further observes that the application of the cabotage principle effectively denies foreign air carriers access to the internal US market and that, with some limited exceptions, US flag air carriers must be used for international transport of government property and federal employees.

In waterborne transport, access to domestic trade (that is, trade that uses coastal, intercoastal, and inland waterways) is reserved for US flag vessels built in the United States and owned by US citizens. US law prohibits foreign vessels from carrying cargo or passengers from one US port to another if the second US port is the final destination. And at least 50 percent of all international cargoes generated by programs sponsored by the US government is allocated to US-flag vessels unless none are available.

Laws and regulations that affect foreign suppliers of services other than transport are far less significant deterrents. State governments,

however, regulate banking, insurance, transport, and certain communications, and the wide variety of differing requirements compli-
cates the operations of foreign businesses.

DEVELOPING THE US POSITION ON LIBERALIZATION OF TRADE IN SERVICES

US proposals for liberalizing trade in services conform to the general
philosophy of deregulation in the United States, where, over the past
decade, important steps have been taken to deregulate aviation,
truck transport, and banking. Statements by US authorities emphasize the potential gains from the liberalization of services trade for all
participants, not just the United States. According to the official US
statement submitted to the General Agreement on Tariffs and Trade
(GATT) in 1982 by William Brock, then the US Special Trade
Respresentative, "the basic goal of any future negotiations should be
to expand opportunities for trade, making possible the economic
gains that can be obtained from trade based on comparative advantage" (Brock, 1982, p. 238). But the fact that US political and
business groups were in the vanguard in introducing services issues in
the trade negotiations reflects the belief that liberalizing trade in
services would benefit the United States. The extensive barriers
against US exports of services described in the previous section bear
out this perception.

Trade liberalization in services was mandated by the Trade Act of
1974, which for the first time stated that "the term 'international
trade' includes trade in both goods and services" (section 102).
Section 121, which dealt with the reform of the GATT, directed the
administration to seek "the extension of GATT articles to conditions
of trade not presently covered in order to move toward more fair
trade practices." Although the United States was not able to get
more than a few references to services trade in the Tokyo Round
agreements, it subsequently persuaded the other industrial countries
of the Organization for Economic Co-operation and Development
(OECD) to undertake a study on services with a view to identifying
areas for future negotiations. This led to the preparation of a paper
entitled "Elements of a Conceptual Framework for Trade in
Services."

In the meantime the United States pressed for further discussion of
trade in services in the GATT framework and proposed that the work

of the GATT include a study of the topic. After a prolonged debate between the developed countries, which came to support the US position, and the developing countries, which opposed such a study, the trade ministers agreed in November 1982 that countries "that were so inclined could undertake national studies of trade in services."

The United States was the first to circulate a national study, in the spring of 1984. This study was part of a strategy for building support for the negotiations that became part of the Uruguay Round. The strategy has been successful; trade in services is on the Uruguay Round agenda.

The interrelationships between government and business have been important to the development of the US position on trade in services. As Feketekuty (1988, pp. 5, 70) notes:

> International trade in services has become an important issue because international trade in services has become big business, and the enterprises that conduct trade are counted among the largest corporations of the world. . . . A model of the world economy that does not accommodate trade in services has become increasingly unacceptable to enterprises selling services. These enterprises do not see a fundamental distinction between the sale of services and the sale of manufactured goods to customers in other countries.

These statements are supported by a variety of business surveys. Mention may be made, in particular, of Price Waterhouse (1985), which reported on the results of a survey of Fortune's Directory of Service Companies (Price Waterhouse, 1985). It should be added, however, that the interests of large business firms lie not only in their services exports but also in the production of services abroad. Thus, from the point of view of the balance of payments, there may be a divergence between the national interest in promoting exports and the interest of the firm in selling services, no matter where they are produced (Kravis and Lipsey, 1988).

THE UNITED STATES SERVICE PROPOSAL

On 23 October 1989, the United States introduced a comprehensive proposal on services in the Uruguay Round of multilateral trade negotiations. The US proposal seeks to open work services markets. It is a flexible proposal, as it provides for countries to take limited reservations for those existing measures that do not conform to the agreement. Reservations could be entered for a finite period of time and would provide the starting point for future rounds of liberalization of trade in services.

The principal obligations that countries would assume under the US proposal are divided into two parts. Several provisions concern various ways of providing market access (Articles 4 to 7). Others are designed to protect market access (Articles 8 to 15).

Market access includes the following items:

- *Establishment*. Extends the right to establish or expand a business in another country in order to provide a service in that country
- *Cross-border provision of services*. Extends the right to sell a service that is produced by one country in another country
- *Temporary entry for service providers*. States that countries should facilitate the temporary entry of service providers
- *Licensing and certification*. States that such measures should relate principally to competence or ability to provide services and should not discriminate against foreigners.

Other substantive obligations include the following items:

- *National treatment*. States that foreign service providers should receive treatment no less favorable than that accorded to domestic service providers
- *Nondiscrimination*. States that the benefits of the agreement should apply to all signatories, with agreed-on exceptions
- *Exclusive service providers and monopolies*. Requires countries to ensure that an exclusive or monopoly provider of services does not discriminate between domestic and foreign service users
- *Domestic regulation*. Recognizes the right of each country to regulate services and introduce new measures as long as they are consistent with the agreement and are administered in a reasonable manner. Countries must also provide for a prompt hearing and review of complaints.
- *Transparency*. Requires countries to make public all measures relating to services under the agreement. Except in urgent circumstances, countries should publish new measures before they become effective and allow time for prior notification and comment.

- *Government aid.* Prohibits government aid for services if such aid causes injury to another country
- *Payment and transfers relating to provision of a covered service.* States that, subject to IMF regulations, each country should permit free payments and transfers related to services that are provided across the border or by means of a commercial presence located in its territory
- *Short-term restrictions for balance-of-payment reasons.* Allows countries temporarily to apply restrictions, except for exchange controls or restrictions, in the event of a balance-of-payments crisis or under certain other conditions, to be reviewed annually in consultation with the IMF.

Under Article 22 countries may enter reservations to Articles 4–8 and Article 13 with respect to specific services or specific aspects of existing legislation. Article 22 further calls on countries to withdraw these reservations as soon as circumstances permit and makes them subject to periodic negotiations.

This reservation approach, representing a negative list, is superior to the use of a positive list, under which countries indicate the obligations they are willing to assume with regard to various services. The latter alternative would be likely to encompass a limited number of items and cannot extrapolate into the future.

At the same time, the proposed agreement provides the possibility for countries that wish to undertake additional obligations to negotiate separate protocols that would apply only to their signatories. This would permit further deregulation in particular sectors for the participating countries.

One may object, however, to the introduction of special agreements in the US proposal. These agreements would permit the exclusion of selected sectors by individual countries, which would go against the objective of trade liberalization in services.

Under Article 18 it is further proposed to establish a Committee on Trade in Services, composed of representatives from each of the participating countries. The committee should have final decision-making authority with regard to the interpretation and application of the agreement.

All in all, the US approach embodied in the proposed agreement represents an effort to develop a mechanism whereby countries commit themselves to liberalization in services. The United States specifically recognizes the right of countries to regulate services but wants to minimize the trade-distorting effects of regulations.

CONCLUSIONS

The liberalization of trade in services has been a long-standing objective of the United States. This objective conforms to the apparent comparative advantage of the United States in service industries, especially in modern services. It can be expected that freeing trade in services will improve the US balance of payments. The existence of extensive barriers to exports of US services supports this conclusion.

Although US officials have stressed the gains that liberalization of trade in services would bring to the world economy, the benefits that the United States would obtain lie behind the single-minded determination on the part of US authorities to pursue this goal. In fact, the idea of freeing trade in services originated in the United States, and US authorities spearheaded the effort in the OECD as well as in the GATT.

In the United States, public authorities and business have collaborated to support liberalization of trade in services. This cooperation reflects a common view as to the advantages of freer trade for the United States. In the case of business, however, it also reflects the potential benefits from sales of services produced abroad, in addition to the gains to be obtained from exports of services.

The US services proposal to the GATT concerns trade in services as well as investment in service industries. It seeks to open world services markets while allowing countries to take limited reservations for those existing measures that do not conform to the proposed agreement.

References

Ascher, Bernard, and Obie G. Whichard, "Developing a Data System for International Trade in Services: Progress, Problems, and Prospects," paper prepared for the National Bureau of Economic Research Conference on International Economic Transactions: Issues in Measurement and Empirical Research, Cambridge, Mass., 3–4 August 1989.

Balassa, Bela, "Trade Liberalization and 'Revealed' Comparative Advantage," *Manchester School*, May 1965, pp. 99–121.

Brock, William E., "A Simple Plan on Negotiating on Trade in Services," *World Economy*, November 1982, pp. 229–40.

Carter, R.L., and G.M. Dickinson, *Barriers to Trade in Insurance*. Thames Essay 19, London, Trade Policy Research Center, 1979.

EC, *1989 Report on US Trade Barriers*, Brussels, 1989.

Federal Communications Commission, *International Accounting Rates and the Balance of Payments Deficit in Telecommunications Services: Report of the Common Carrier Bureau of the Federal Communications Commission*, Washington, DC, 1988.

Feketekuty, Geza, *International Trade in Services. An Overview and Blueprint for Negotiations*. Cambridge, Mass., Ballinger for the American Enterprise Institute, 1988.

Hilaire, Frances, and John Whalley, "Some Estimates of Trade Flows in Banking Services." Working Paper 8615C, Centre for the Study of International Economic Relations, Department of Economics, University of Western Ontario, London, Canada, 1986.

Kravis, I.B., and R.E. Lipsey, "Production and Trade in Service by US Multinational Firms," NBER Working Paper 2619, Cambridge, Mass., National Bureau of Economic Research, 1988.

Price Waterhouse, *Business Views on Public Policy and International Trade in Services: The Results of a Survey of Fortune's Directory of Service Companies*, Boston, 1985.

Sapir, André, and Ernst Lutz, *Trade in Services: Economic Determinants and Development-Related Issues*. World Bank Staff Working Paper 480. Washington, DC 1981.

USTR, *1988 National Trade Estimate Report on Foreign Trade Barriers*. Washington, DC, 1989.

Whichard, Obie G., "International Services: New Information on US Transactions with Unaffiliated Foreigners," *Survey of Current Business*, October 1988, pp. 27–34.

Part VII

The EEC Enlargement

15 Europe 1992 and its Possible Implications for Nonmember Countries*

A common market has been defined as combining a customs union with free factor movements, where a customs union involves free trade within the union together with common tariffs (Balassa, 1961, p. 2). After noting the extent to which the European Community (EC) has conformed to this definition of a common market, this chapter considers the changes that the implementation of the Europe 1992 program is expected to bring about.

The chapter begins with a discussion of the freeing of all trade in goods within the EC, followed by an analysis of the freeing of trade in services and the freeing of factor movements. Finally, the possible impact of Europe 1992 on nonmember countries is considered.

THE MOVEMENT OF GOODS

The EC has completed a customs union as defined in the GATT. Tariffs on intra-area trade were eliminated between 1 January 1958 and 1 July 1968; a common external tariff was established on 1 July 1968; and quantitative import restrictions on intra-area trade for goods produced in the Common Market countries were also abolished. Nevertheless, intra-area trade still encounters barriers. Border formalities are encountered in transporting goods from one country to another; monetary compensation applies to agricultural products; countries try to limit the transshipment of goods imported under quotas; government procurement tends to favor national sources; and technical barriers limit the shipment of goods across frontiers.

---

* Originally published in Scholt, Jeffery J. (ed), *Free Trade Areas and US Trade Policy*, Institute of International Economics, Washington DC, 1989; pp. 293–312.

BORDER FORMALITIES

Border formalities are maintained within the EC for the following reasons:[1]

- Differences in value-added tax rates and excise duties
- Monetary compensation on agricultural products
- Enforcement on bilateral trade quota regimes with third countries
- Differences in technical and public health standards
- Control of road transport licenses and compliance with national regulations
- Collection of statistical data

These formalities impose an economic cost on the member countries. They include:

- Internal administrative cost borne by exporting and importing firms
- External costs incurred by exporting and importing firms in conjunction with customs clearance
- Costs to exporting and importing firms through delays imposed by customs procedures
- Costs to public authorities of maintaining customs posts and associated administrative services
- Opportunity costs associated with the loss of trade due to the maintenance of border formalities

The internal and external costs of border formalities to firms were estimated on the basis of a firm survey (Commission of the European Communities, 1988a, p. 48). The results showed that internal costs amounted to 5.9 billion ECU and external costs 1.6 billion ECU, for a total of 7.5 billion ECU.

The cost of frontier delays is indicated by the often-cited example that a 1200km truck trip takes 36 hours within the United Kingdom but 58 hours between London and Milan, excluding the time required for Channel crossing. The total cost of delays was estimated at 0.8 billion ECU, of which one-half may be absorbed by compulsory rest periods timed to coincide with delays at customs points.

The budgetary cost of border formalities to the public authorities was estimated at 0.5 to 1.0 billion ECU. The lower figure represents the customs services' estimate and the higher figure an independent estimate. These figures include the staff costs of some 15 000 to 30 000 customs officials.

In total, the cost of border formalities is estimated to be between 8.4 and 9.3 billion ECU, corresponding to 1.7 to 1.9 percent of the value of intra-EC trade and 0.3 percent of community GDP. These figures do not include the opportunity cost of lost trade due to border formalities. The increase in trade resulting from the removal of these formalities was estimated at 1 percent by importers and 3.2 percent by exporters, reflecting a more sanguine view by the latter as to the possibilities for trade expansion.

Nor do the estimates include the cost of border formalities to individuals. On the other side of the coin, it has been suggested that the lack of border formalities may ease the tasks of drug dealers and terrorists in the member countries.

Implications of differences in value-added tax and excise duty rates

As noted above, differences in national value-added tax (VAT) and excise duty rates provide a reason for maintaining border formalities among EC countries. The question arises, then, to what extent VAT and excise duty rates would need to be harmonized once these formalities are abolished.

Standard VAT rates vary from 12 percent (Luxembourg and Spain) to 25 percent (Ireland). Some countries apply increased rates, ranging between 25 percent (Belgium) and 38 percent (Italy), on selected commodities such as cars, jewelry, and electrical equipment. Also, some countries have reduced rates ranging from zero (United Kingdom) to 10 percent (Ireland) on some items. The range of reduced rates is the broadest in the United Kingdom, covering most foods, children's clothing, books and newspapers, water, fuel and power, and public transport and construction, totaling about 30 percent of consumer spending (Davis and Kay, 1985). The EC Commission proposed to reduce the range of standard rates to between 14 and 20 percent, with a band of 4 to 9 percent applicable to a limited range of necessities. The Commission also proposed maintaining the destination principle on the VAT while changing its practical application, with exports subjected to the exporting country's VAT and an adjustment to the VAT of the importing country effected in the latter. This procedure would permit retaining different national VAT rates without the need for harmonization.

The only rationale for the harmonization of VAT rates lies in the desire to avoid cross-border purchases by individuals. For this purpose, however, it would suffice to set minimum tax rates. Since the costs of cross-border shopping are borne by the member country that chooses to set higher tax rates than its neighbors, there is no reason for the Commission to restrict its freedom to do so.[2] In this connection, state sales taxes vary from zero to 9 percent in the United States without an appreciable problem of cross-border purchases. In view of the high cost involved in cross-border shopping, one may also consider maintaining the reduced zero rate in the United Kingdom.

There is considerable variation in excise duties. In the case of cigarettes, specific duties vary from 0.01 ECU (Greece and Spain) to 1.52 ECU (Denmark) per pack, and *ad valorem* duties (inclusive of VAT) between 34 percent (United Kingdom) and 71 percent (France), with the total tax (including VAT) ranging from 0.12 ECU (Spain) to 2.76 ECU (Denmark) per pack for the most popular category of cigarettes. Excise duties on gasoline very from 0.20 ECU (Luxembourg and Spain) to 0.53 ECU (Italy) per liter and on diesel oil from 0.03 ECU (Spain) to 0.29 ECU (Ireland) per liter. Finally, excise duties range from 0.14 ECU (Greece) to 10.50 ECU (Denmark) on a bottle of alcoholic spirits, from zero (Germany, Greece, Italy, Portugal, and Spain) to 2.79 ECU (Ireland) on a liter of wine, and from 0.03 ECU (France and Spain) to 1.13 ECU (Ireland) on a liter of beer.

The Commission proposed equalizing excise duties throughout the EC. The proposed rates are 0.38 ECU per pack (specific duty) and 52 to 54 percent (*ad valorem*, including VAT) for cigarettes; 0.34 ECU per liter of gasoline and 0.18 ECU per liter of diesel oil; and 3.81 ECU per liter of alcoholic spirits, 0.17 ECU per liter of wine, and 0.17 ECU per liter of beer (Lee *et al.*, 1988, ch. 5).

The unification of excise duties would represent substantial changes in national rates that have been established on the basis of the conditions existing in each country. At the same time, one wonders if unification of rates is necessary. In the United States, no particular adverse effects have been observed, although excise rates vary enormously: from 2 to 29 cents on a pack of cigarettes, from 8 to 19 cents on a gallon of gasoline, and from $1.50 to $6.50 on a gallon of alcoholic beverages (Commission of the European Communities, 1988b, p. 541).

Nevertheless, extensive transshipments of excisable goods should be avoided. It could be accomplished by identifying the country of final sale by a stamp or other distinguishing marking on packs of cigarettes, bottles of alcoholic beverages, and shipments of fuels.

At the same time, to the extent that countries wish to discourage their nationals from purchasing excisable goods in other countries, they can do so by lowering excise duty rates. In this way, pressure to reduce differences in excises would be exerted by the market rather than by harmonization imposed by legislative fiat.

Monetary compensation amounts on intra-EC agricultural trade

Intra-EC trade in agricultural products has been liberalized, while EC agriculture is protected under the Common Agricultural Policy. At the same time, monetary compensation has been introduced periodically to ease the effects of changes in the value of member country currencies on the agriculture of individual countries. This means that farmers in a country with a revalued currency do not fully feel the impact of increased competition from the partner countries.

Monetary compensation amounts (MCAs) take the form of border taxes and subsidies that permit the maintaining of different prices for agricultural products within the EC. With the abolition of border formalities, MCAs will also disappear. At the same time, the resulting gains have not been estimated because there have been considerable variations in the amount of MCAs over time.

Third-country quotas

In cases where national quotas are applied on imports from nonmember countries, the transshipment of goods in intra-EC trade can be blocked by the EC Commission at the request of member countries. This can be enforced in the course of the application of border formalities.

Import quotas apply to textiles and clothing and to automobiles throughout the EC; individual member countries may also apply quotas on particular products, such as footwear and bicycles. The textiles and clothing quotas have been established in the course of the renegotiation of the Multi-fiber Arrangement that takes place at regular intervals.

A case of widely disparate import quotas involves Japanese automobiles. Italy admits only 11 000 cars annually from Japan; the French quota equals 3 percent of domestic sales; the quota is 10 percent of domestic sales on the United Kingdom; the other EC countries do not apply quotas.

The abolition of border formalities would not permit the maintenance of national quotas. Thus, EC-wide quotas will have to be established or import quotas abolished. The first alternative has been chosen for textiles and clothing and for automobiles. For other commodities, no decision has been reached as yet.

Public procurement

Public procurement was not included in the Treaty of Rome establishing the European Common Market. In the 1970s, the Commission attempted to induce governments to purchase from other member countries. Its directives called for advertising in the *Official Journal of the European Communities* all public supply contracts worth more than 200 000 ECU and all public works contracts worth more than 5 million ECU.

The rules did not cover water, energy, transportation, telecommunications, or defense. But even in other sectors little cross-country procurement occurred. Thus, only 2 percent of public supply contracts and public works contracts have been awarded to firms from other member countries, out of total contractual procurement of 240 to 340 billion ECU, amounting to 7 to 10 percent of Community GDP and over one-half of intra-EC trade (Cecchini *et al.*, 1988, p. 16).

A variety of factors explain the limited extent of interpenetration as far as public procurement is concerned. There has been abuse of the exceptions from normal tendering and award rules, illegal exclusion of bidders from other member countries, discrimination in scrutinizing bidders' technical capacity and financial standing, and discrimination in the awarding of contracts (Commission of the European Communities, 1988a, p. 56). At the same time, in many countries purchasing is substantially decentralized, making transparency rules hard to enforce. Finally, bids have often been divided into smaller units to avoid exceeding the limits set for the publication of tenders.

The new regulations for Europe 1992 will tighten significantly the enforcement of the current rules and increase the transparency of public procurement. Also, companies will be provided with means of legal redress to avoid discrimination against them. At the same time, the rules will be extended to cover currently excluded markets in water, energy, transportation, and telecommunications.

It has been estimated that the direct effects of liberalizing procurement in the form of purchases from lower-cost sources would bring cost savings of 4.4 billion ECU. There is further said to be a competitive effect of 2.3 billion ECU, with increased competition from the partner countries reducing domestic prices and costs. Finally, gains from economies of scale would amount to 7.2 billion ECU (Commission of the European Communities, 1988a, p. 57).

The total gain from these sources has been estimated at 13.9 billion ECU, or 0.5 percent of Community GDP (ibid.). In addition, the liberalization of defense procurement would bring further gains, estimated at 4.0 billion ECU.

Technical barriers

Although according to customs union theory and GATT rules free trade is established once tariffs and quantitative import restrictions have been abolished, there may be technical barriers that interfere with free trade. These barriers include differences in industry standards, in legal regulations, and in testing and certification procedures.

Industry standards refer to product specifications that may differ from country to country. Legal regulations pertain to health, safety, and environmental protection and may also vary among countries. Finally, there may be differences in testing and certification requirements, often involving an additional certification procedure to that required in the country of origin.

Technical barriers involve a cost because of the need to adapt products to national standards and regulations and because of additional testing and certification requirements. They are thus similar in their effects to trade barriers in limiting the amount traded.

Differences in standards abound in the building materials industry, where the standard used in France differs from the standard employed in Germany, reducing trade in building materials. Different standards are also used in regard to telecommunications equipment, for example, limiting purchases by the national post and telecommunications companies from the partner countries.

Differences in regulations represent an important technical barrier in the case of foodstuffs. Member countries may restrict the use of a generic product name, such as pasta, to products manufactured according to a specific recipe. Also, there may be restrictions on the use of particular ingredients. Finally, packaging and labeling requirements may limit the sales of a product in a given country.

As far as regulations on automobiles are concerned, much harmonization has been achieved, but differences remain in regard to tires, weight and size, and windshields. There are also unique national requirements, such as side repeater headlights in Italy, reclining driver's seats in Germany, dim-dip lighting in the United Kingdom, and yellow headlight bulbs in France.

Certification rules play a particularly important role in the pharmaceutical industry. If a product is to be admitted to a particular national market it must first receive approval by the national registration authority, when criteria vary from country to country. Testing and certification procedures differ also with respect to electrical products and machinery.

Originally, the Common Market aimed at unifying standards, regulations, and certification requirements. While this approach has brought results in some cases, it could not be applied generally. An example is the harmonization process for foodstuffs drawn up in 1973, which listed far in excess of 50 directives to be put in place. By 1985 only 14 directives had been adopted.

In the White Paper from the EC Commission to the Council entitled "Completing the Internal Market" (28–9 June 1985), a new strategy was adopted, involving the mutual recognition of national standards and regulations. The basis for this approach lies in Article 30 of the Treaty of Rome, according to which "quantitative restrictions on imports and all measures having equivalent effect shall be prohibited between member states."

An antecedent of the new approach is found in the 1979 Cassis de Dijon case. The EC Court of Justice decided that Germany cannot keep out French cassis on the grounds that it does not qualify as liquor under German regulations as long as it meets the definition applied in France. Subsequently the court found that, despite the Bavarian requirement that beer contain no additives, the sale of foreign beers containing additives could not be prohibited. Finally, in the recent pasta case, the court overruled the decision of its Italian Advocate General and permitted the importation of pasta containing soft wheat into Italy.

The mutual recognition of national standards and regulations will be complemented by EC directives on the harmonization of health and safety requirements. Furthermore, in the case of high technology products, the development of European standards has been entrusted to private bodies, including the Comité Européen de la Normalisation (CEN) as well as sectoral organizations, such as Conférence

Européenne des Postes et des Télécommunications for telecommunications.

The elimination of technical barriers promises considerable cost savings. According to one study, the savings would amount to 5.7 percent in the case of automobiles, equivalent to more than three-quarters of net profits achieved by the eight leading European car manufacturers in 1987.[3]

TRADE IN SERVICES

Customs union theory deals exclusively with trade in goods. The Treaty of Rome also envisaged the liberalization of trade in services. However, only limited progress has been made in this regard, although trade in services has assumed considerable importance among the EC countries. Also, services have come to account for more than 50 percent of Community GDP.

The following discussion concerns road transportation, air transportation, financial services, business services, and telecommunications services. In each case, existing barriers, proposals for their removal, and the possible effects of removal of the barrier are considered.

Road transportation

Trucks carry about one-half of intra-EC surface transportation by bulk and substantially more in terms of value. Competition is distorted by the need for licenses to undertake cross-border trade. Bilateral permits negotiated between member countries for truck trips, measured in ton-kilometers, regulate much of this trade. Only about one-sixth of the trips are undertaken under EC-wide permits. At the same time, cabotage, involving transportation by out-of-state truckers within a member state, is prohibited.

The present permit system and the prohibition of cabotage are reflected in the cost of empty moves. This cost has been estimated at 1.2 billion ECU, of which 20 percent is said to be related to regulatory restrictions. There is also a black market in EC-wide permits, the cost of which has been estimated at 23 percent of a truck's normal annual costs. According to the EC Commission's estimate, road transport costs would decline by 5 percent in the event of the liberalization of restrictions (Commission of the European Communities, 1988a, p. 97).

In June 1988, an agreement was reached to liberalize regulations on road transport. On 1 July 1988, the number of EC-wide permits was increased by 40 percent, with a further increase of this magnitude taking place a year later. By mid-1991 all national restrictions will be scrapped, and the only requirement will be an EC-wide truck driver's permit, as long as the enterprise is professionally sound. The prohibition of cabotage will also be eliminated.

Air transportation

Airfares in the EC are substantially higher than in the United States, but profits are not, reflecting the fact that costs are considerably higher in Europe. Allowing for differences between American and European airlines in terms of the average length of the trip, the type of aircraft, fuel costs, and landing charges, European costs exceeded American costs in 1980 by 50 percent overall; by 12 percent for maintenance per capacity ton-mile; by 315 percent for ground and passenger service costs, and by 365 percent for administrative overheads.

These cost differences in part reflect inefficiency, in part higher staff costs in Europe. The five leading European airlines average 6.70 hours of flying time per day on narrow-bodied jets, compared with 8.33 hours for American airlines. Also, among the major European airlines, pilots earned 670 percent more than the average annual wage on Air France and 590 percent more on KLM and Alitalia, compared with 370 percent for American airlines; only British Airways pilots' earnings were lower (Pelkmans *et al.*, 1988, p. 49).

The regulatory regime in effect has contributed importantly to the high costs of European airlines. This regime is based on bilateral agreements between individual countries. Rights by an EC carrier based in one country to offer services between two other member states (so-called fifth freedom rights) are effectively prohibited, with only one exception. Entry is restricted and price competition is limited, with revenues on city pair routes often pooled and split 50:50 between the two carriers.

Within the framework of the Europe 1992 program, in December 1987 the Council of Ministers agreed to an initial three-year package covering airfares, capacity control, and market access. There will be greater flexibility in lowering fares and in introducing new discount fares; in regard to bilateral capacity control, the initial 50:50 division will give way to a 45:55 range in the first two years and 40:60 in the third year; greater competition will be achieved by allowing a large number of airlines to operate, especially on dense traffic routes, and certain fifth freedom rights will be exercised by airlines within the EC (Commission of the European Communities, 1988a, pp. 97–8).

Financial services

The financial services sector is of growing importance within the EC, accounting for 6.5 percent of GDP. Financial services include insurance, banking services, and investment services.

There has been freedom of establishment in insurance services throughout the EC, although national regulations differ to a considerable extent from country to country. However, restrictions apply to cross-border insurance. The existence of these restrictions has contributed to the observed large intercountry differences in insurance rates.

For standard services, the results of a survey show that term insurance rates vary from 150 ECU (United Kingdom) to 392 ECU (Italy), home insurance rates from 118 ECU (Belgium) to 266 ECU (United Kingdom), car insurance rates from 316 ECU (United Kingdom) to 942 ECU (Italy); commercial fire and theft insurance rates from 1204 ECU (Luxembourg) to 4896 ECU (Italy); and public liability cover rates from 714 ECU (Netherlands) to 1852 ECU (France).[4]

To liberalize cross-border insurance, the EC Commission took four countries to the European Court of Justice for blocking such business. In a well-known case involving a German broker who had been fined for finding cheap industrial insurance for his clients in London, the court ruled in favor of the transborder selling of insurance; however, it limited this practice to customers that are big enough to form a view as to the soundness of the foreign insurance company, until this was made subject to EC rules.

In June 1988, cross-border insurance was liberalized for so-called "big risks" – nonlife insurance for companies with more than 500 employees or 25 million ECU turnover. The directive, adopted by the Council of Ministers, will go into effect in July 1990. The Commission is also preparing a proposal for the liberalization of car insurance and hopes to have this in force by 1992. It is preparing a draft directive for life insurance, but this raises difficulties because of differences in tax provisions governing the treatment of life insurance among the member countries.

Freedom of establishment for foreign banks exists throughout the EC. However, national banking regulations hinder cross-border banking activities. For example, the active solicitation of deposits on a cross-border basis is generally not permitted. Also, in some member states banks cannot engage in the securities business.

These limitations have contributed to differences in the costs of standard banking services among the member countries. Costs vary from 4375 ECU (France) to 6875 ECU (United Kingdom) for commercial loans, from 12 ECU (Belgium) to 46 ECU (Denmark) for consumer credit, from 37 ECU (France) to 99 ECU (Italy) for credit cards, from 290 ECU (United Kingdom) to 800 ECU (Spain) for mortgage loans, from 22 ECU (Netherlands) to 120 ECU (Spain) for foreign exchange drafts, from 5.0 ECU (Denmark, Luxembourg, and the United Kingdom) to 7.5 ECU (France) for traveler's checks, from nil (Belgium and the Netherlands) to 240 ECU (Italy) for current accounts, and from 425 ECU (Denmark) to 750 ECU (Spain) for letters of credit (Commission of the European Communities, 1988b, p. 280).

In the Second Banking Coordination Directive, proposed in February 1988, the ECU Commission introduced the concept of a "single banking license." This will allow any bank that has been authorized by a member state to market its services in any other state without further authorization. Apart from banking, the freedom to offer financial services extends to the securities business.

The directive aims at establishing the freedom of financial services by the banks by 1992. In the meantime, agreement will need to be reached on harmonizing capital and solvency ratios, deposit guarantees, control rules, qualification of managers, and related issues.

While the single banking license is based on the principle that banks are regulated by their home countries, there are three exceptions to this rule: the conduct of monetary policies, the monitoring of the liquidity position of banks, and the regulation of the securities activities of banks. Furthermore, the European Court of Justice ruled in 1986 that host countries may limit the freedom of financial services on grounds of "general interest," in particular consumer protection.

Several directives have been adopted in regard to securities markets to coordinate investor protection, improve market transparency, and facilitate simultaneous listing on the stock exchanges of different member states. At the same time, there remain considerable differences in regard to the cost of securities services. For standard transactions, costs vary from 9 ECU (France) to 23 ECU (United Kingdom) on private equity transactions, from 21 ECU (Italy) to 180 ECU (Spain) on private gilt transactions, from 719 ECU (United Kingdom) to 3453 ECU (Spain) on institutional equity transactions, and from 3597 ECU (Luxembourg) to 21 583 ECU (Belgium) on international gilt transactions (Commission of the European Communities, 1988b, p. 280).

The first step regarding securities transactions in the framework of the Europe 1992 program was the establishment of an EC-wide regime for the issue of unit trusts (mutual funds). The directive lays down broad rules governing the kinds of investments the unit trusts may make and the characteristics of their managers, leaving the determination of precise rules to the country where the fund is based. The host country controls only the methods of selling the funds to investors.

The EC Commission is in the process of drafting a directive concerning investment services, except for services provided by the banks that are covered by the directive cited earlier. The directive is based on home country control. Once a securities firm has been authorized by its home country regulators, it will be able to do business throughout the EC.

The draft directive further states that each country will designate a competent authority to supervise securities business. This authority will be responsible for monitoring the capital adequacy of the securities firm and the acceptability of its major shareholders, and firms will have to comply with host country rules on advertising and marketing. Each country will also draw up conduct of business rules on internal controls, segregation of client funds, compensation for bankruptcy or default, and conflicts of interest.

The liberalization of financial services would permit the reduction of their costs in the EC. It has been estimated that the cost of financial transactions would decline by an average of 10 percent, amounting to 20.6 billion ECU, or 0.7 percent of GDP in savings. There would be a gain of a similar magnitude in consumer surplus (Commission of the European Communities, 1988a, p. 92).

Business services

Business services represent about 5 percent of the EC's GDP. Sales of professional business services in 1986 were as follows: engineering and related services, 7.5 billion ECU; managerial consultancy, 3.5 billion ECU; advertising and public relations, 57 billion ECU; computing services, 13 billion ECU; research and development, 15 billion ECU; legal services, 13 billion ECU; and financial review (including accounting and audit services), 13 billion ECU (Commission of the European Communities, 1988b, p. 251).

The importance of barriers to trade in professional business services varies. Barriers were reported to have been most significant for engineering and related services, where they pertained to national differences in technical standards, lack of recognition of professional qualifications, and restrictions on government procurement. At the other end of the spectrum, financial review services and managerial consultancy do not encounter barriers. The intermediate category includes advertising and public relations (satellite broadcasting barriers, national differences in advertising laws and allocation of media time, and recognition of qualifications), computing services (government and post and telecommunications procurement), research and development (government procurement), and legal services (licensing of professionals). It has been estimated that the freeing of trade in professional business services in the EC would reduce their cost by 3 percent (Commission of the European Communities, 1988a, pp. 95–6).

Telecommunications services

Telecommunications services play an increasingly important role today. In the EC, sales amounted to 63 billion ECU in 1985, or about one-half of US sales. Telephone services accounted for 85 to 90 percent of the total, with 10 percent derived from data transmission and 5 percent from telex; the latter proportions are much higher in the United States and are expected to grow rapidly in the future in the EC. Even more rapid growth is expected in value-added networks (VANs), such as data banks, electronic mail, and electronic data interchange (Commission of the European Communities, 1988a, pp. 98–9).

The basic objectives of EC policy were set out in the Green Paper on the Development of the Common Market for Telecommunications Services and Equipment (COM (87) 290, June 1987). The Green Paper accepted the role of the national telecommunications administrations to provide basic network infrastructure and basic telephone services (primarily voice telephone services). In turn, the unrestricted provision of so-called competitive telecommunications services, including in particular value-added services, was proposed.

The Commission subsequently made proposals in the telecommunications area in its communication entitled "Towards a Competitive Community-Wide Telecommunications Market in 1992. Implementing the Green Paper on the Development of the Common Market for Telecommunications Services and Equipment" (COM (88) 48, February 1988). The communication called for the full opening of the terminal equipment market to competition by the end of 1989; the progressive opening of the telecommunications services market by the end of 1989, with some exceptions; and the full application of the general principle that telecommunications tariffs should follow overall cost trends by the end of 1991. The Commission further proposed the clear separation of regulatory and operational activities; the EC-wide definition of general requirements on providers of competitive services in the framework of open network provisions; the establishment of a European Telecommunications Standards Institute; the full mutual recognition of type approval to terminal equipment; the creation of transparency in the financial relations between member state governments and the national telecommunication administrations; the assurance of fair conditions of competition; and the independence of procurement decisions and the opening of public procurement.

The implementation of these provisions would bring important cost savings. It has been estimated that open competition for equipment procurement could lead to a reduction in tariff levels and thereby higher demand, permitting the exploitation of economies of scale, with annual cost savings of 0.75 billion ECU. Additional cost savings would be achieved in competitive services through a liberalized equipment certification program (0.5 to 0.7 billion ECU), the liberalization of VANs (0.3 to 0.4 billion ECU), and open network provisions (0.2 billion ECU). There would further be cost savings of 4 billion ECU from moving tariff structures nearer to costs (Commission of the European Communities, 1988a, pp. 100–1).

FACTOR MOVEMENTS

A common market also involves the freeing of factor movements, and the Treaty of Rome contains several provisions to this effect. In the following, the freeing of factor movements is considered under two headings: capital movements and labor movements.

Capital movements

Capital movements were liberalized under EC directives in 1960, 1962, and 1986 and under policies adopted in the individual member states. Capital movements are practically free in the United Kingdom, Germany, Denmark, Luxembourg, and the Netherlands; there remain a few restrictions in Belgium, France, and Italy, while restrictions continue to be in effect in Greece, Ireland, Portugal, and Spain. These restrictions pertain largely to short-term capital transactions and to the establishment of bank accounts abroad.

On 24 June 1988, the Council of Ministers published a directive for the implementation of Article 67 of the Treaty on the freeing of capital movements. According to Article 1 of the directive, "Member States shall abolish restrictions on movements of capital taking place between persons resident in Member States."

Under the directive, all domestic rules and administrative provisions that discriminate between residents and nonresidents in the performance of capital transactions will be eliminated. Also, transactions made for purposes of capital transfer will be implemented at the same exchange rate as current account transactions (this amounts to the abolition of dual exchange markets maintained in Belgium and Luxembourg).

The developed EC countries will liberalize capital movements by July 1990, except that Belgium and Luxembourg can maintain their dual exchange markets until 1992. Greece, Ireland, Portugal, and Spain can delay liberalization for two years, and Greece and Portugal may request an additional two years' extension.

Article 73 of the Treaty of Rome provides a safeguard clause for the liberalization of capital movements in the event of balance-of-payments difficulties. The June 1988 directive adds another safeguard clause, permitting the introduction of restrictions up to six months under authorization by the EC Commission, "where short-term capital movements of exceptional magnitude impose severe strains on foreign exchange markets and lead to serious disturbances in the conduct of a Member State's monetary and exchange rate policies" (Article 3).

At French insistence, the provision was added that "the Commission shall submit to the Council, by 31 December 1988, proposals aimed at eliminating or reducing risks of distortion, tax evasion, and tax avoidance linked to the diversity of national systems for the taxation of savings and for controlling the application of these systems" (Article 6:5). In fact, such measures are desirable in view of differences in national taxation systems.

First of all, distortions in investment decisions may occur in response to differences in business taxation. Other things being equal, countries with lower tax rates will be favored in the establishment of new companies and, in particular, in decisions taken by companies in nonmember countries to invest in the EC.

Furthermore, investments in securities will be favored in countries that do not have withholding taxes. Such is the case for interest income in Denmark, Luxembourg, the Netherlands, and the United Kingdom and for dividends in France and Germany. Also, capital gains generally are not taxed in Belgium, Germany, Italy, Luxembourg, and the Netherlands. Finally, differences in income tax rates may contribute to the flow of capital.

While it has been suggested in EC circles that the liberalization of capital movements would contribute to stability in exchange rates, the opposite may be the case, because small differences in interest rates and speculation about currency values may trigger large movements of funds. Although the EC established a medium-term credit facility in June 1988, it may not suffice in the event of large movements of speculative funds.

Labor movements

The movement of labor has been free within the EC. There remain, however, practical obstacles that discourage migration. The removal of these obstacles would involve the reinforcement of the right of residence (*droit de séjour*) in the event of unemployment or short-term work contracts, the full equality of treatment in public sector jobs, and the portability of social security benefits.

Agreement has recently been reached on the mutual recognition of educational diplomas. The Commission has also made proposals for the mutual recognition of vocational training. This will eventually culminate in the introduction of a European "vocational training card," serving as proof that the holder has been awarded a specific qualification.

The Commission originally sought directives harmonizing the qualifications needed for specific professions. This has in fact been done in regard to doctors, dentists, pharmacists, nurses, midwives, veterinarians, and architects.

In view of the slowness of the process, the Commission has

forsaken this route, and it now aims at the mutual acceptance of professional qualifications. In fact, in June 1988 the EC trade and industry ministers agreed that the holders of professional qualifications should be able to work anywhere in the EC.

In conjunction with labor migration, reference may also be made to efforts toward harmonizing social conditions. The July 1987 Communication of the Commission set out a four-year program for safety, health, and hygiene in the workplace. This has led to various initiatives, including proposals for directives on the exposure of workers to certain carcinogenic agents, on the safety of machinery at the workplace, and on safety standards for machinery.

An earlier proposal for mandatory worker consultation in all large companies operating in the EC (the so-called Vredeling proposal of 1980) was withdrawn, but suggestions have again been made for the consultation of workers in company decisions. This remains a matter of controversy, however.

IMPLICATIONS FOR NONMEMBER COUNTRIES

Jacques Delors, the President of the EC Commission, emphasized that the Europe 1992 program should not lead to a "Fortress Europe." He is also reported to have said, however, that "the external aspect of the internal market will have to be strengthened if we don't want this internal market to be of primary benefit to foreign investors."[5]

It also appears that the member countries differ in their attitudes to external protection following the creation of a single European market. At the time of the French presidential election campaign, President Mitterrand took a position in favor of increased protection: "Let us contemplate as clearly as possible the dangers which menace us. If the large market is not better protected than the present Common Market, the 'extra-Europeans' will rush to the 320 million consumers which we are and which constitute the most important melting pot in the world."[6]

Similar views have been voiced in the new Southern European member states. In turn, the Germans and the British have taken a position against increasing import barriers in the EC. The Benelux countries are also free traders, while Italy generally supports France.

This concluding part of the chapter considers the possible impact of the Europe 1992 program on nonmember countries. Some of the measures to be taken will automatically affect nonmembers; in other cases there are specific provisions concerning these countries.

In regard to the movement of goods, note has been taken of the proposed abolition of border formalities; the elimination of MCAs affecting agricultural products; the removal of national import quotas; the liberalization of government procurement; and the harmonization or mutual recognition of standards. All these measures will have implications for outsiders.

In view of British opposition, it is far from certain that border formalities will be abolished within the EC. But in any case the cost of these formalities will be reduced through simplification of the regulations. This is equivalent to reductions of tariffs on intra-area trade that have trade-diverting effects by favoring partner country producers over nonmember countries.

Similar considerations apply to the elimination of MCAs for agricultural products, which are equivalent to import tariffs and export subsidies on intra-EC trade. At the same time, the export subsidy aspect is of little practical importance, since MCAs aim to safeguard high-cost producers. Thus, MCAs basically amount to import tariffs, the abolition of which involves trade diversion.

The abolition of national quotas in the framework of the Multi-Fiber Arrangement presumably will mean the establishment of EC-wide quotas equal to the sum of national quotas. In this case, imports under the Multi-Fiber Arrangement will not be affected.

In the case of automobiles, there is pressure from France and Italy, which have the smallest import quotas on Japanese cars, to set the EC-wide quota at a low level.[7] At the same time, the Common Agricultural Policy does not augur well for the establishment of EC-wide quotas.

At first glance the liberalization of government procurement legislation would not appear to affect nonmember countries. However, to the extent that purchases have been made from these countries, there may be trade diversion, since under the Europe 1992 program member country producers would be favored over nonmember country producers.

The lack of harmonization and the absence of mutual recognition of standards presently hurt member country as well as nonmember country producers. Complying with the standards of the importing country involves a cost that would disappear as far as member country producers are concerned under the Europe 1992 program. This will, then, result in trade diversion, if national standards are accepted within the EC.

EC-wide standards would, however, benefit nonmember countries because they will have to comply with one set of standards only. On the other hand, nonmember producers will not be involved in their establishment. The standards thus can be expected to favor member country producers, representing another form of discrimination against nonmembers.

It appears, then, that in goods trade the completion of the internal market in the EC will give rise to trade diversion. Trade diversion, in turn, will give incentives to investment by nonmember countries in the Community. The trade creation resulting from the measures taken under the Europe 1992 program will provide similar incentives.

In the case of services, in particular financial services, the EC Commission has proposed the application of the principle of reciprocity that has been incorporated in directives on banking and investment services. Under this principle, nonmember countries could not establish in the EC unless they offer access on similar terms to EC firms in their own country, although existing establishments would continue to operate.

The application of the principle of reciprocity may cause difficulties for nonmember countries. For example, the EC is introducing universal banking, under which banks can engage in the entire range of investment services, which is not the case in the United States. The strict application of the principle of reciprocity may then lead to discrimination against US banks.

Discrimination could be avoided if national treatment is applied, as is the case under friendship, commerce, and navigation treaties. These treaties ensure that foreign firms are treated in the same way as are domestic firms.

Additional issues relate to telecommunications. In this field, the EC is establishing common standards. If these standards are not compatible with those used in the United States and Japan, discrimination against the firms of these countries will ensue. Also, the application of reciprocity provisions may amount to the introduction of "Buy European" preferences.

We have considered here trade diversion in goods and services that may result from the measures to be taken under the Europe 1992 program as well as the opportunities offered for foreign firms in the EC. Nonmember countries will further be affected by the acceleration of economic growth following the completion of the internal market of the EC.

According to an estimate made by the EC Commission, the measures taken under the Europe 1992 program would lead to a 4.5 percent increase in the GDP of the EC countries in the medium term. The gain may reach 7 percent if accompanying macroeconomic policies are applied in regard to government budgets and prices (Cecchini *et al.*, 1988, pp. 101–2).

Higher growth rates in the European Community during the adjustment period will benefit nonmember countries through increased imports. There may also be adverse effects, however, to the extent that productivity increases occur in sectors that compete with imports. Thus, the effects of the acceleration of economic growth in the EC on nonmember countries are ambiguous.

Notes

1. The following discussion is largely based on Commission of the European Communities (1988a and b).
2. This point is made in Lee *et al.* (1988, p. 35).
3. *Financial Times*, 18 May 1988, p. 2.
4. Commission of the European Communities (1988b, p. 280). A list of the standard financial products and services to which these rates and other prices quoted from this survey refer may be found in Commission of the European Communities (1988a, p. 89).
5. *Financial Times*, 27 June 1988, p. 2.
6. *Le Monde*, 8 April 1988.
7. Thus, Raymond Levy, Chairman and Chief Executive Officer of Renault, called for the protection of the European car industry from Japanese imports following the creation of a single European market in 1992. Levy stated, "Europe must defend itself but if Europe does not take measures, I want France alone defending itself" (*Financial Times*, 29 September 1988).

References

Balassa, Bela, *The Theory of Economic Integration*, Homewood, Ill., Richard D. Irwin, 1961.

Cecchini, Paolo *et al.*, *The European Challenge 1992, The Benefits of a Single Market*, Aldershot, Wildwood House, 1988.

Commission of the European Communities, "The Economics of 1992, an Assessment of the Potential Economic Effects of Completing the 'Internal

Market of the European Community'," *European Economy*, no. 35, March 1988a.

Commission of the European Communities, *Research on the "Cost of Non-Europe": Basic Findings*, Vol. 1, Basic Studies: Executive Summaries, Brussels, Commission of the European Communities, 1988b.

Davis, E. M., and J. A. Kay, "Extending the VAT Base: Problems and Possibilities," *Fiscal Studies*, 6, 1985.

Lee, Catherine, Mark Pearson, and Stephen Smith, *Fiscal Harmonization: An Analysis of the European Commission's Proposals*, IFS Report Series no. 28, London, Institute for Fiscal Studies, 1988.

Pelkmans, Jacques, and L. Alan Winters, with Helen Wallace, *Europe's Domestic Market*, Chatham House Papers no. 43, London, Routledge, 1988.

16 EMENA Manufactured Exports and EEC Trade Policy*

This chapter will examine the implications for EMENA manufactured exports of EEC trade policy. The first section of the chapter will analyze EEC trade agreements with EMENA countries and the export performance of these countries in the EEC market for manufactured goods. The next two sections will consider the possible impact on EMENA countries of the enlargement of the EEC and of changes in EEC trade policies in the framework of the Europe 1992 program. The final section will review prospective developments in EMENA exports to the EEC.

EEC TRADE AGREEMENTS WITH EMENA COUNTRIES AND EMENA EXPORTS OF MANUFACTURED GOODS TO THE EEC

The first EEC association agreement with an EMENA country was concluded with Turkey in 1963. This was followed by association agreements with Morocco (1969), Tunisia (1969), Malta (1970), and Cyprus (1972). Preferential trade agreements were signed with Egypt, Lebanon, Jordan, and Syria in 1972. A nonpreferential trade agreement was concluded with Yugoslavia in 1970.

The coverage and conditions of the bilateral agreements varied, thereby introducing discrimination among the Mediterranean countries. Also, apart from the association agreements with Turkey, Malta, and Cyprus, the agreements were of a limited duration.

---

* Originally prepared as a paper for the Europe, Middle East and North Africa Regional Office of the World Bank, and published in *Economia*, January 1990, pp. 89–122.

The author is indebted to Shigeru Akiyama for research assistance.

EMENA refers to the Europe, Middle East and North Africa Regional Office of the World Bank. EMENA countries include the developing countries of the area other than Portugal that has become a member of the EEC.

In 1976, cooperation agreements were signed with Algeria, Morocco, and Tunisia, providing free access to EEC markets for the manufactured exports of these countries for an unlimited period. They were followed by cooperation agreements with Egypt (1976), Jordan (1976), Syria (1976), and Lebanon (1977) under similar conditions. By comparison, the association agreements with Turkey, Malta, and Cyprus provided for the free entry of manufactured goods only at the end of a transitional period.

A preferential trade agreement was concluded with Yugoslavia in 1980. Apart from duty-free tariff ceilings on products representing 16 percent of Yugoslav manufactured exports to the EEC and special rules applying to textiles and clothing, the agreement provides for the free entry of Yugoslav manufactures in the EEC.

As far as EEC imports of textiles and clothing from Yugoslavia are concerned, the Multi-fiber Arrangement applies to some commodities and tariff quotas apply to others. Quotas have also been introduced on selected textiles and clothing items imported by the EEC from Morocco, Tunisia, Egypt, Cyprus, Malta, and Turkey.

Among the other EMENA countries, Afghanistan, Iran, Iraq, Oman, Pakistan, South Yemen, and North Yemen come under the General System of Preferences. The GSP scheme excludes, however, sensitive products, such as textiles and clothing. Imports of textiles and clothing from these countries come under the Multi-fiber Arrangement, if certain limits have been reached.

Finally, the EEC has nonpreferential trade agreements with Hungary, Poland and Romania, among which Romania benefits from GSP. These countries are subject to quotas on textiles and clothing under the Multi-fiber Arrangement. They are also subject to quotas on selected manufactured goods imported by individual EEC countries.

The question arises how have these agreements affected trade in manufactured goods. To examine this issue, data are provided on the geographical composition of the imports of manufactured goods by the EEC as well as by the other industrial countries.

Table 16.1 provides information on EEC imports of manufactured products, with the EEC being defined in its pre-1981 composition. The data show intra-EEC imports as well as EEC imports from the other industrial countries, from the three new entrants (Greece, Portugal, and Spain), from various groups of developing countries, including EMENA, as well as from the European socialist countries that are not Bank–Fund members. EMENA has been defined to exclude Portugal, because Portugal's accession to Common Market membership has affected its trade, as well as the high-income oil exporters (Bahrain, Kuwait, Libya, Qatar, Saudi Arabia, and the United Arab Emirates).

Manufactured products have been defined to include textiles, apparel and leather (ISIC 32), wood products and furniture (ISIC 33), paper and paper products (ISIC 34), chemical products (ISIC 35), nonmetallic mineral products (ISIC 36), iron and steel (ISIC 37), engineering products (ISIC 38), and other industrial products (ISIC 39). For comparison, total imports are also shown.

The table includes data for 1973, 1981, and 1987. 1973 is the first year following the signature of association agreements and preferential trade agreements with countries of North Africa and the Middle East. 1981 is the year preceding the debt crisis, and 1987 is the latest year for which data are available.

Table 16.2 provides details for EMENA countries. It contains information for each of the EMENA countries with which the EEC has association or cooperation agreements as well as for other major exporters of manufactured products. The rest of the EMENA countries are combined in a residual category.

For purposes of comparison, Table 16.3 and 16.4 present data in the same breakdown as Tables 16.1 and 16.2 for the imports of the other industrial countries. These have been defined to include the United States, Canada, Austria, Finland, Norway, Sweden, Switzerland, Japan, Australia, and New Zealand.

The data show the increasing importance of manufactured products in EMENA exports to the EEC in recent years. While these products accounted for 22.1 percent of EMENA's total exports to the EEC in 1973 and 22.3 percent in 1981, their share reached 39.7 percent in 1987.

An increase was also experienced in the share of EMENA countries in the total EEC imports of manufactured products. This share was 2.3 percent in 1973, 2.2 percent in 1981, and 2.7 percent in 1987. However, despite recent increases, the 1973 EMENA share was not again reached in the extra-area imports of the EEC. Thus, EMENA's share in extra-area EEC imports of manufactured goods was 6.9 percent in 1973, 5.5 percent in 1981, and 6.6 percent in 1987.

The decline is even more pronounced if EMENA exports are compared with exports from all developing countries. While EMENA accounted for 42.5 percent of the manufactured exports of the developing countries to the EEC in 1973, this share fell to 29.1

Table 16.1 Manufacturing imports of EEC: geographical composition

(a) Year = 1973

	ISIC 32 textile, apparel, and leather		ISIC 33 wood products and furniture		ISIC 34 paper and paper products		ISIC 35 chemical products		ISIC 36 non-metallic mineral products	
	US$(m)	%	US$(m)	%	US$(m)	%	US$(m)	%	US$(m)	%
World	17 141	100.0	3 037	100.0	5 262	100.0	18 989	100.0	3 234	100.0
EEC	10 850	63.3	1 701	56.0	2 520	47.9	13 377	70.4	2 560	79.1
Industrial countries, excl. EEC	1 597	9.3	660	21.7	2 572	48.9	4 045	21.3	462	14.3
New member of EEC	780	4.5	142	4.7	51	1.0	284	1.5	68	2.1
Developing countries	3 450	20.1	400	13.2	66	1.2	609	3.2	84	2.6
Far eastern NIC	1 285	7.5	111	3.6	16	0.3	145	0.8	15	0.5
Latin American NIC	229	1.3	44	1.5	7	0.1	87	0.5	2	0.1
Israel	51	0.3	11	0.4	1	0.0	46	0.2	1	0.0
Southeast Asia	25	0.1	69	2.3	1	0.0	20	0.1	0	0.0
India	329	1.9	3	0.1	2	0.0	11	0.1	3	0.1
China	136	0.8	12	0.4	1	0.0	52	0.3	6	0.2
EMENA, excl. Portugal	1 397	8.1	150	5.0	37	0.7	248	1.3	57	1.8
Other developing countries	234	1.4	73	2.4	9	0.2	463	2.4	6	0.2
Centrally planned economies	230	1.3	61	2.0	45	0.9	212	1.1	54	1.7

	ISIC 37 iron and steel		ISIC 38 engineering products		ISIC 39 other industries		Manufactures		Total imports	
	US$(m)	%	US$(m)	%	US$(m)	%	US$(m)	%	US$(m)	%
World	10 167	100.0	56 480	100.0	3 560	100.0	117 870	100.0	214 362	100.0
EEC	7 511	73.9	38 007	67.3	1 325	37.2	77 852	66.0	110 368	51.5
Industrial countries, excl. EEC	1 586	15.6	15 589	27.6	609	17.1	27 119	23.0	46 421	21.7
New member of EEC	239	2.4	693	1.2	45	1.3	2 303	2.0	4 773	2.2
Developing countries	319	3.1	1 203	2.1	354	9.9	6 485	5.5	23 765	11.1
Far eastern NIC	35	0.3	464	0.8	154	4.3	2 223	1.9	2 613	1.2
Latin American NIC	22	0.2	70	0.1	19	0.5	481	0.4	4 938	2.3
Israel	0	0.0	37	0.1	61	1.7	209	0.2	539	0.3
Southeast Asia	0	0.0	21	0.0	19	0.5	154	0.1	1 752	0.8
India	2	0.0	31	0.1	41	1.2	423	0.4	807	0.4
China	0	0.0	12	0.0	20	0.6	239	0.2	667	0.3
EMENA, excl. Portugal	260	2.6	569	1.0	39	1.1	2 757	2.3	12 449	5.8
Other developing countries	280	2.8	588	1.0	1 178	33.1	2 830	2.4	25 037	11.7
Centrally planned economies	233	2.3	399	0.7	48	1.4	1 281	1.1	3 998	1.9

(b) Year = 1981

	ISIC 32 textile, apparel, and leather		ISIC 33 wood products and furniture		ISIC 34 paper and paper products		ISIC 35 chemical products		ISIC 36 non-metallic mineral products	
	US$(m)	%	US$(m)	%	US$(m)	%	US$(m)	%	US$(m)	%
World	43 481	100.0	7 715	100.0	14 888	100.0	62 266	100.0	7 880	100.0
EEC	22 879	52.6	4 380	56.8	7 579	50.9	42 845	68.8	5 852	74.3
Industrial countries, excl. EEC	4 592	10.6	1 523	19.7	6 535	43.9	12 864	20.7	1 104	14.0
New member of EEC	2 970	6.8	387	5.0	267	1.8	1 088	1.7	334	4.2
Developing countries	11 674	26.8	1 114	14.4	337	2.3	2 365	3.8	400	5.1
Far eastern NIC	4 822	11.1	373	4.8	140	0.9	654	1.1	190	2.4
Latin American NIC	573	1.3	55	0.7	44	0.3	248	0.4	14	0.2
Israel	319	0.7	16	0.2	6	0.0	267	0.4	6	0.1
Southeast Asia	620	1.4	211	2.7	1	0.0	65	0.1	19	0.2
India	1 024	2.4	10	0.1	3	0.0	31	0.0	9	0.1
China	777	1.8	78	1.0	13	0.1	268	0.4	22	0.3
EMENA, excl. Portugal	3 539	8.1	370	4.8	131	0.9	831	1.3	139	1.8
Other developing countries	936	2.2	144	1.9	46	0.3	1 989	3.2	62	0.8
Centrally planned economies	430	1.0	169	2.2	123	0.8	1 116	1.8	129	1.6

	ISIC 37 iron and steel		ISIC 38 engineering products		ISIC 39 other industries		Manufactures		Total imports	
	US$(m)	%	US$(m)	%	US$(m)	%	US$(m)	%	US$(m)	%
World	18 686	100.0	162 035	100.0	10 030	100.0	326 980	100.0	628 760	100.0
EEC	13 772	73.7	95 149	58.7	3 796	37.8	196 250	60.0	297 544	47.3
Industrial countries, excl. EEC	2 973	15.9	52 895	32.6	3 891	38.8	86 376	26.4	137 932	21.9
New member of EEC	583	3.1	3 679	2.3	112	1.1	9 419	2.9	14 926	2.4
Developing countries	476	2.5	6 732	4.2	1 683	16.8	24 780	7.6	68 011	10.8
Far eastern NIC	33	0.2	3 434	2.1	933	9.3	10 579	3.2	11 499	1.8
Latin American NIC	100	0.5	670	0.4	30	0.3	1 735	0.5	11 608	1.8
Israel	2	0.0	148	0.1	209	2.1	972	0.3	1 966	0.3
Southeast Asia	7	0.0	462	0.3	116	1.2	1 502	0.5	6 003	1.0
India	1	0.0	142	0.1	163	1.6	1 383	0.4	2 079	0.3
China	2	0.0	121	0.1	122	1.2	1 403	0.4	2 543	0.4
EMENA, excl. Portugal	330	1.8	1 755	1.1	110	1.1	7 206	2.2	32 313	5.1
Other developing countries	469	2.5	2 813	1.7	347	3.5	6 806	2.1	92 145	14.7
Centrally planned economies	413	2.2	768	0.5	202	2.0	3 349	1.0	18 202	2.9

(c) Year = 1987

	ISIC 32 textile, apparel, and leather		ISIC 33 wood products and furniture		ISIC 34 paper and paper products		ISIC 35 chemical products		ISIC 36 non-metallic mineral products	
	US$(m)	%	US$(m)	%	US$(m)	%	US$(m)	%	US$(m)	%
World	77 339	100.0	12 521	100.0	27 037	100.0	108 670	100.0	12 777	100.0
EEC	38 322	49.6	7 402	59.1	14 424	53.3	75 065	69.1	9 377	73.4
Industrial countries, excl. EEC	6 694	8.7	2 170	17.3	10 854	40.1	21 753	20.0	1 573	12.3
New member of EEC	6 464	8.4	698	5.6	511	1.9	2 210	2.0	747	5.8
Developing countries	23 154	29.9	1 733	13.8	757	2.8	5 177	4.8	776	6.1
Far eastern NIC	7 641	9.9	323	2.6	256	0.9	1 556	1.4	260	2.0
Latin American NIC	825	1.1	78	0.6	175	0.6	483	0.4	37	0.3
Israel	391	0.5	23	0.2	16	0.1	531	0.5	14	0.1
Southeast Asia	1 546	2.0	471	3.8	4	0.0	232	0.2	28	0.2
India	1 784	2.3	10	0.1	4	0.0	103	0.1	15	0.1
China	2 032	2.6	92	0.7	27	0.1	640	0.6	53	0.4
EMENA, excl. Portugal	8 936	11.6	737	5.9	276	1.0	1 632	1.5	368	2.9
Other developing countries	2 072	2.7	219	1.7	326	1.2	3 360	3.1	115	0.9
Centrally planned economies	631	0.8	300	2.4	165	0.6	1 104	1.0	189	1.5

	ISIC 37 iron and steel		ISIC 38 engineering products		ISIC 39 other industries		Manufactures		Total imports	
	US$(m)	%	US$(m)	%	US$(m)	%	US$(m)	%	US$(m)	%
World	26 758	100.0	312 235	100.0	14 155	100.0	591 492	100.0	874 319	100.0
EEC	18 787	70.2	180 993	58.0	5 254	37.1	349 625	59.1	476 209	54.5
Industrial countries, excl. EEC	4 539	17.0	95 660	30.6	2 928	20.7	146 172	24.7	201 449	23.0
New member of EEC	1 154	4.3	9 525	3.1	191	1.3	21 500	3.6	31 493	3.6
Developing countries	1 074	4.0	17 585	5.6	3 052	21.6	53 308	9.0	97 228	11.1
Far eastern NIC	156	0.6	10 622	3.4	1 721	12.2	22 534	3.8	23 705	2.7
Latin American NIC	259	1.0	1 221	0.4	54	0.4	3 131	0.5	13 221	1.5
Israel	3	0.0	359	0.1	294	2.1	1 630	0.3	3 042	0.3
Southeast Asia	17	0.1	1 404	0.4	236	1.7	3 939	0.7	8 487	1.0
India	10	0.0	179	0.1	240	1.7	2 344	0.4	3 107	0.4
China	14	0.1	581	0.2	350	2.5	3 790	0.6	5 521	0.6
EMENA, excl. Portugal	614	2.3	3 219	1.0	157	1.1	15 939	2.7	40 146	4.6
Other developing countries	612	2.3	7 177	2.3	2 364	16.7	16 245	2.7	49 783	5.7
Centrally planned economies	592	2.2	1 295	0.4	367	2.6	4 643	0.8	18 158	2.1

Table 16.2 Manufacturing imports of EEC: EMENA countries

(a) Year = 1973

	ISIC 32 textile, apparel, and leather		ISIC 33 wood products and furniture		ISIC 34 paper and paper products		ISIC 35 chemical products		ISIC 36 non-metallic mineral products	
	US$(m)	%	US$(m)	%	US$(m)	%	US$(m)	%	US$(m)	%
EMENA, incl. Portugal	1 659	.	209	.	44	.	304	.	73	.
Portugal	262		59		7		56		16	
EMENA, excl. Portugal	1 397	100.0	150	100.0	37	100.0	248	100.0	57	100.0
Cyprus	2	0.1	0	0.0	0	0.1	1	0.3	0	0.6
Malta	30	2.1	0	0.1	0	1.3	7	2.9	0	0.1
Algeria	12	0.9	1	0.5	0	1.0	3	1.2	0	0.0
Morocco	56	4.0	5	3.0	0	0.3	7	2.7	0	0.3
Tunisia	24	1.7	1	0.6	0	1.2	29	11.7	0	0.1
Egypt	25	1.8	1	0.3	0	0.2	4	1.7	0	0.1
Jordan	0	0.0	0	0.0	0	0.0	0	0.0	0	0.0
Lebanon	16	1.1	1	0.4	0	1.2	1	0.2	0	0.1
Syria	3	0.2	0	0.0	0	0.0	0	0.0	0	0.1
Turkey	104	7.5	0	0.1	2	4.5	8	3.0	4	6.9
Pakistan	125	8.9	0	0.1	0	0.1	1	0.2	0	0.3
Iran	242	17.3	0	0.0	0	0.1	3	1.0	0	0.5
Hungary	141	10.1	15	9.7	2	6.4	30	12.0	8	13.5
Poland	115	8.2	21	13.8	9	23.8	56	22.5	16	27.3
Romania	142	10.1	52	34.7	6	15.1	43	17.2	8	14.9
Yugoslavia	343	24.5	55	36.5	17	44.4	58	23.3	20	35.3
Other EMENA	19	1.3	0	0.0	0	0.2	0	0.0	0	0.0

	ISIC 37 iron and steel		ISIC 38 engineering products		ISIC 39 other industries		Manufactures		Total imports	
	US$(m)	%	US$(m)	%	US$(m)	%	US$(m)	%	US$(m)	%
EMENA, incl. Portugal	266	.	683	.	56	.	3 293	.	13 328	.
Portugal	6		114		16		536		879	
EMENA, excl. Portugal	260	100.0	569	100.0	39	100.0	2 757	100.0	12 449	100.0
Cyprus	0	0.0	3	0.5	0	0.0	6	0.2	111	0.9
Malta	0	0.1	13	2.3	1	2.7	52	1.9	62	0.5
Algeria	11	4.1	9	1.6	0	0.8	36	1.3	1 319	10.6
Morocco	0	0.0	6	1.1	2	4.0	75	2.7	716	5.7
Tunisia	5	1.9	1	0.2	0	0.9	60	2.2	236	1.9
Egypt	1	0.5	2	0.4	0	0.1	33	1.2	230	1.8
Jordan	0	0.0	1	0.2	0	0.0	1	0.1	2	0.0
Lebanon	0	0.0	10	1.8	1	2.5	28	1.0	102	0.8
Syria	0	0.0	2	0.3	0	0.1	5	0.2	130	1.0
Turkey	5	1.9	14	2.4	1	1.3	136	5.0	685	5.5
Pakistan	0	0.0	6	1.0	8	21.0	140	5.1	222	1.8
Iran	0	0.0	11	2.0	0	0.4	256	9.3	2 824	22.7
Hungary	56	21.6	64	11.3	8	20.6	324	11.7	789	6.3
Poland	54	20.7	129	22.6	8	19.7	406	14.7	1 384	11.1
Romania	50	19.2	63	11.1	3	8.9	367	13.3	808	6.5
Yugoslavia	78	30.0	229	40.2	5	12.6	804	29.1	1 438	11.6
Other EMENA	0	0.0	6	1.1	2	4.4	27	1.0	1 389	11.2

(b) Year = 1981

	ISIC 32 textile, apparel, and leather		ISIC 33 wood products and furniture		ISIC 34 paper and paper products		ISIC 35 chemical products		ISIC 36 non-metallic mineral products	
	US$(m)	%	US$(m)	%	US$(m)	%	US$(m)	%	US$(m)	%
EMENA, incl. Portugal	4 308	.	531	.	179	.	969	.	209	.
Portugal	769	.	161	.	48	.	137	.	70	.
EMENA, excl. Portugal	3 539	100.0	370	100.0	131	100.0	831	100.0	139	100.0
Cyprus	50	1.4	0	0.1	2	1.8	1	0.1	0	0.0
Malta	194	5.5	3	0.7	11	8.6	18	2.2	0	0.2
Algeria	1	0.0	1	0.4	1	1.1	20	2.4	0	0.0
Morocco	229	6.5	8	2.2	0	0.3	50	6.0	0	0.3
Tunisia	394	11.1	1	0.4	0	0.3	143	17.2	0	0.2
Egypt	93	2.6	0	0.1	2	1.4	7	0.8	0	0.0
Jordan	0	0.0	0	0.0	0	0.1	0	0.0	0	0.0
Lebanon	9	0.3	0	0.0	2	1.2	0	0.0	1	0.5
Syria	4	0.1	0	0.0	0	0.0	1	0.1	0	0.0
Turkey	451	12.7	1	0.3	2	1.6	18	2.1	12	8.9
Pakistan	323	9.1	0	0.1	0	0.1	1	0.2	1	0.6
Iran	250	7.1	0	0.0	0	0.0	0	0.0	0	0.0
Hungary	339	9.6	43	11.7	6	4.8	191	23.0	33	24.0
Poland	245	6.9	60	16.2	19	14.8	106	12.8	32	22.9
Romania	338	9.6	148	40.1	21	16.3	114	13.7	20	14.1
Yugoslavia	576	16.3	102	27.6	62	47.3	160	19.3	39	28.2
Other EMENA	42	1.2	0	0.0	0	0.1	1	0.1	0	0.0

	ISIC 37 iron and steel		ISIC 38 engineering products		ISIC 39 other industries		Manufactures		Total imports	
	US$(m)	%	US$(m)	%	US$(m)	%	US$(m)	%	US$(m)	%
EMENA, incl. Portugal	348	.	2 187	.	123	.	8 853	.	34 660	.
Portugal	17	.	432	.	12	.	1 647	.	2 347	.
EMENA, excl. Portugal	330	100.0	1 755	100.0	110	100.0	7 206	100.0	32 313	100.0
Cyprus	0	0.0	15	0.8	0	0.4	68	1.0	228	0.7
Malta	1	0.2	42	2.4	8	7.0	277	3.8	310	1.0
Algeria	1	0.4	16	0.9	0	0.1	41	0.6	6 741	20.9
Morocco	0	0.0	37	2.1	3	3.1	329	4.6	1 351	4.2
Tunisia	0	0.1	38	2.2	4	3.6	582	8.1	1 320	4.1
Egypt	2	0.5	25	1.4	0	0.2	130	1.8	3 484	10.8
Jordan	0	0.0	32	1.8	0	0.4	33	0.5	49	0.2
Lebanon	1	0.2	12	0.7	4	3.4	28	0.4	45	0.1
Syria	0	0.0	12	0.7	0	0.1	17	0.2	1 277	4.0
Turkey	28	8.5	39	2.2	2	1.5	552	7.7	1 615	5.0
Pakistan	0	0.0	28	1.6	21	19.3	375	5.2	543	1.7
Iran	0	0.0	10	0.6	0	0.2	261	3.6	2 779	8.6
Hungary	71	21.5	202	11.5	24	22.1	909	12.6	1 586	4.9
Poland	99	30.1	342	19.5	13	12.2	917	12.7	2 248	7.0
Romania	77	23.3	147	8.4	10	8.9	875	12.1	2 024	6.3
Yugoslavia	50	15.1	654	37.3	18	16.0	1 661	23.1	2 429	7.5
Other EMENA	0	0.0	104	5.9	2	1.6	149	2.1	4 284	13.3

(c) Year = 1987

	ISIC 32 textile, apparel, and leather		ISIC 33 wood products and furniture		ISIC 34 paper and paper products		ISIC 35 chemical products		ISIC 36 non-metallic mineral products	
	US$(m)	%	US$(m)	%	US$(m)	%	US$(m)	%	US$(m)	%
EMENA, incl. Portugal	11 596	.	1 082	.	353	.	1 972	.	565	.
Portugal	2 660	.	346	.	78	.	340	.	197	.
EMENA, excl. Portugal	8 936	100.0	737	100.0	276	100.0	1 632	100.0	368	100.0
Cyprus	105	1.2	2	0.2	3	1.0	5	0.3	0	0.1
Malta	171	1.9	3	0.4	25	9.1	32	2.0	1	0.1
Algeria	1	0.0	1	0.2	10	3.5	35	2.2	0	0.0
Morocco	817	9.1	10	1.3	4	1.6	150	9.2	3	0.7
Tunisia	793	8.9	3	0.4	2	0.7	172	10.5	3	0.7
Egypt	212	2.4	0	0.0	1	0.5	12	0.7	0	0.1
Jordan	1	0.0	1	0.1	0	0.1	46	2.8	0	0.0
Lebanon	19	0.2	1	0.1	2	0.6	3	0.2	0	0.0
Syria	4	0.0	0	0.0	0	0.0	0	0.0	0	0.0
Turkey	2 380	26.6	5	0.7	7	2.4	148	9.1	82	22.4
Pakistan	828	9.3	0	0.1	1	0.4	3	0.2	1	0.2
Iran	324	3.6	0	0.0	0	0.1	1	0.1	0	0.0
Hungary	477	5.3	68	9.2	22	7.8	244	14.9	47	12.7
Poland	468	5.2	110	14.9	36	13.2	165	10.1	65	17.5
Romania	555	6.2	303	41.2	18	6.4	139	8.5	47	12.7
Yugoslavia	1 743	19.5	229	31.0	144	52.4	459	28.1	120	32.6
Other EMENA	40	0.4	1	0.1	1	0.3	19	1.2	0	0.0

	ISIC 37 iron and steel		ISIC 38 engineering products		ISIC 39 other industries		Manufactures		Total imports	
	US$(m)	%	US$(m)	%	US$(m)	%	US$(m)	%	US$(m)	%
EMENA, incl. Portugal	648	.	4 381	.	186	.	20 785	.	46 172	.
Portugal	34		1 163		29		4 846		6 027	
EMENA, excl. Portugal	614	100.0	3 219	100.0	157	100.0	15 939	100.0	40 146	100.0
Cyprus	0	0.0	35	1.1	0	0.2	150	0.9	337	0.8
Malta	1	0.1	123	3.8	6	3.6	360	2.3	423	1.1
Algeria	41	6.6	27	0.8	0	0.0	114	0.7	5 647	14.1
Morocco	0	0.0	98	3.0	5	3.4	1 086	6.8	1 980	4.9
Tunisia	2	0.3	125	3.9	13	8.3	1 112	7.0	1 586	4.0
Egypt	11	1.8	47	1.4	0	0.1	283	1.8	2 079	5.2
Jordan	0	0.0	60	1.9	0	0.1	109	0.7	136	0.3
Lebanon	0	0.0	12	0.4	7	4.5	43	0.3	94	0.2
Syria	0	0.0	3	0.1	0	0.0	8	0.0	615	1.5
Turkey	30	4.8	126	3.9	7	4.5	2 786	17.5	4 750	11.8
Pakistan	2	0.4	27	0.8	42	27.0	904	5.7	1 169	2.9
Iran	0	0.0	43	1.3	0	0.0	368	2.3	3 849	9.6
Hungary	99	16.1	316	9.8	13	8.3	1 286	8.1	2 254	5.6
Poland	112	18.3	424	13.2	15	9.5	1 394	8.7	3 229	8.0
Romania	62	10.1	265	8.2	16	9.9	1 404	8.8	2 591	6.5
Yugoslavia	254	41.4	1 342	41.7	29	18.6	4 320	27.1	5 775	14.4
Other EMENA	0	0.0	147	4.6	3	2.0	212	1.3	3 631	9.0

Table 16.3 Manufacturing imports of other industrial countries: geographical composition

(a) Year = 1973

	ISIC 32 textile, apparel, and leather		ISIC 33 wood products and furniture		ISIC 34 paper and paper products		ISIC 35 chemical products		ISIC 36 non-metallic mineral products	
	US$(m)	%	US$(m)	%	US$(m)	%	US$(m)	%	US$(m)	%
World	12 680	100.0	2 760	100.0	3 592	100.0	12 343	100.0	2 132	100.0
EEC	4 091	32.3	510	18.5	857	23.9	5 628	45.6	979	45.9
Industrial countries, excl. EEC	2 916	23.0	1 168	42.3	2 586	72.0	5 182	42.0	883	41.4
New member of EEC	556	4.4	67	2.4	15	0.4	142	1.1	38	1.8
Developing countries	4 741	37.4	944	34.2	105	2.9	940	7.6	166	7.8
Far Eastern NIC	2 793	22.0	650	23.6	55	1.5	594	4.8	59	2.8
Latin American NIC	498	3.9	74	2.7	30	0.8	108	0.9	49	2.3
Israel	60	0.5	2	0.1	3	0.1	32	0.3	2	0.1
Southeast Asia	181	1.4	119	4.3	4	0.1	26	0.2	8	0.4
India	377	3.0	5	0.2	1	0.0	13	0.1	4	0.2
China	354	2.8	15	0.5	3	0.1	70	0.6	14	0.6
EMENA, excl. Portugal	477	3.8	79	2.9	10	0.3	97	0.8	31	1.4
Other developing countries	262	2.1	49	1.8	18	0.5	328	2.7	22	1.1
Centrally planned economies	113	0.9	22	0.8	12	0.3	124	1.0	43	2.0

	ISIC 37 iron and steel		ISIC 38 engineering products		ISIC 39 other industries		Manufactures		Total imports	
	US$(m)	%	US$(m)	%	US$(m)	%	US$(m)	%	US$(m)	%
World	6 690	100.0	57 363	100.0	3 388	100.0	100 946	100.0	180 220	100.0
EEC	2 860	42.8	20 087	35.0	1 216	35.9	36 229	35.9	47 104	26.1
Industrial countries, excl. EEC	3 030	45.3	33 492	58.4	986	29.1	50 241	49.8	80 440	44.6
New member of EEC	71	1.1	302	0.5	31	0.9	1 222	1.2	2 060	1.1
Developing countries	381	5.7	3 121	5.4	873	25.8	11 270	11.2	28 669	15.9
Far Eastern NIC	113	1.7	1 997	3.5	523	15.5	6 784	6.7	8 403	4.7
Latin American NIC	122	1.8	711	1.2	59	1.7	1 652	1.6	5 872	3.3
Israel	1	0.0	33	0.1	142	4.2	274	0.3	483	0.3
Southeast Asia	1	0.0	84	0.1	48	1.4	470	0.5	5 532	3.1
India	29	0.4	22	0.0	51	1.5	502	0.5	1 195	0.7
China	0	0.0	10	0.0	25	0.7	491	0.5	1 284	0.7
EMENA, excl. Portugal	115	1.7	264	0.5	24	0.7	1 096	1.1	5 899	3.3
Other developing countries	222	3.3	82	0.1	235	6.9	1 219	1.2	18 619	10.3
Centrally planned economies	126	1.9	278	0.5	47	1.4	765	0.8	3 328	1.8

(b) Year = 1981

	ISIC 32 textile, apparel, and leather		ISIC 33 wood products and furniture		ISIC 34 paper and paper products		ISIC 35 chemical products		ISIC 36 non-metallic mineral products	
	US$(m)	%	US$(m)	%	US$(m)	%	US$(m)	%	US$(m)	%
World	32 669	100.0	6 770	100.0	9 934	100.0	42 101	100.0	5 815	100.0
EEC	8 143	24.9	1 451	21.4	2 162	21.8	15 936	37.9	2 557	44.0
Industrial countries, excl. EEC	5 258	16.1	2 734	40.4	7 205	72.5	19 334	45.9	2 239	38.5
New member of EEC	836	2.6	112	1.7	51	0.5	391	0.9	129	2.2
Developing countries	17 154	52.5	2 266	33.5	471	4.7	4 728	11.2	761	13.1
Far Eastern NIC	11 188	34.2	1 228	18.1	257	2.6	2 724	6.5	409	7.0
Latin American NIC	1 445	4.4	197	2.9	158	1.6	855	2.0	147	2.5
Israel	41	0.1	8	0.1	6	0.1	179	0.4	6	0.1
Southeast Asia	938	2.9	453	6.7	6	0.1	235	0.6	22	0.4
India	798	2.4	12	0.2	4	0.0	48	0.1	11	0.2
China	1 729	5.3	142	2.1	13	0.1	470	1.1	64	1.1
EMENA, excl. Portugal	1 015	3.1	225	3.3	28	0.3	219	0.5	102	1.8
Other developing countries	1 088	3.3	108	1.6	24	0.2	1 205	2.9	47	0.8
Centrally planned economies	190	0.6	99	1.5	22	0.2	508	1.2	81	1.4

	ISIC 37 iron and steel		ISIC 38 engineering products		ISIC 39 other industries		Manufactures		Total imports	
	US$(m)	%	US$(m)	%	US$(m)	%	US$(m)	%	US$(m)	%
World	20 423	100.0	175 841	100.0	10 623	100.0	304 177	100.0	617 977	100.0
EEC	7 129	34.9	46 635	26.5	3 245	30.5	87 258	28.7	120 242	19.5
Industrial countries, excl. EEC	9 210	45.1	109 192	62.1	2 657	25.0	157 830	51.9	229 820	37.2
New member of EEC	574	2.8	720	0.4	80	0.8	2 892	1.0	4 919	0.8
Developing countries	2 474	12.1	18 119	10.3	3 830	36.1	49 803	16.4	128 522	20.8
Far Eastern NIC	1 251	6.1	10 905	6.2	2 340	22.0	30 303	10.0	36 546	5.9
Latin American NIC	568	2.8	3 781	2.2	146	1.4	7 296	2.4	27 292	4.4
Israel	22	0.1	400	0.2	572	5.4	1 233	0.4	1 884	0.3
Southeast Asia	55	0.3	2 077	1.2	282	2.7	4 068	1.3	32 667	5.3
India	23	0.1	164	0.1	274	2.6	1 335	0.4	2 826	0.5
China	172	0.8	172	0.1	130	1.2	2 892	1.0	8 133	1.3
EMENA, excl. Portugal	384	1.9	620	0.4	85	0.8	2 677	0.9	19 174	3.1
Other developing countries	898	4.4	613	0.3	752	7.1	4 734	1.6	123 796	20.0
Centrally planned economies	140	0.7	562	0.3	59	0.6	1 661	0.5	10 678	1.7

(c) Year = 1987

	ISIC 32 textile, apparel, and leather		ISIC 33 wood products and furniture		ISIC 34 paper and paper products		ISIC 35 chemical products		ISIC 36 non-metallic mineral products	
	US$(m)	%	US$(m)	%	US$(m)	%	US$(m)	%	US$(m)	%
World	69 425	100.0	14 864	100.0	18 261	100.0	73 486	100.0	11 560	100.0
EEC	16 739	24.1	3 903	26.3	5 037	27.6	30 541	41.6	4 829	41.8
Industrial countries, excl. EEC	6 637	9.6	4 639	31.2	11 731	64.2	28 119	38.3	3 438	29.7
New member of EEC	2 302	3.3	220	1.5	100	0.5	790	1.1	495	4.3
Developing countries	40 148	57.8	5 801	39.0	1 235	6.8	11 503	15.7	2 508	21.7
Far Eastern NIC	24 389	35.1	2 964	19.9	654	3.6	7 249	9.9	1 483	12.8
Latin American NIC	2 973	4.3	605	4.1	434	2.4	1 478	2.0	571	4.9
Israel	151	0.2	24	0.2	14	0.1	326	0.4	14	0.1
Southeast Asia	2 817	4.1	1 525	10.3	31	0.2	511	0.7	83	0.7
India	1 390	2.0	10	0.1	4	0.0	104	0.1	22	0.2
China	5 888	8.5	287	1.9	57	0.3	1 329	1.8	171	1.5
EMENA, excl. Portugal	2 539	3.7	387	2.6	41	0.2	506	0.7	164	1.4
Other developing countries	3 318	4.8	167	1.1	124	0.7	1 895	2.6	167	1.4
Centrally planned economies	281	0.4	134	0.9	35	0.2	639	0.9	123	1.1

	ISIC 37 iron and steel		ISIC 38 engineering products		ISIC 39 other industries		Manufactures		Total imports	
	US$(m)	%	US$(m)	%	US$(m)	%	US$(m)	%	US$(m)	%
World	20 820	100.0	362 945	100.0	20 868	100.0	592 229	100.0	857 189	100.0
EEC	6 992	33.6	98 360	27.1	5 697	27.3	172 098	29.1	213 776	24.9
Industrial countries, excl. EEC	7 886	37.9	204 953	56.5	4 232	20.3	271 636	45.9	353 069	41.2
New member of EEC	476	2.3	1 466	0.4	139	0.7	5 988	1.0	9 194	1.1
Developing countries	4 281	20.6	56 055	15.4	9 409	45.1	130 940	22.1	204 781	23.9
Far Eastern NIC	1 922	9.2	36 500	10.1	5 617	26.9	80 778	13.6	91 262	10.6
Latin American NIC	1 289	6.2	12 636	3.5	321	1.5	20 308	3.4	39 202	4.6
Israel	19	0.1	986	0.3	1 081	5.2	2 615	0.4	3 732	0.4
Southeast Asia	275	1.3	3 687	1.0	721	3.5	9 650	1.6	30 310	3.5
India	59	0.3	186	0.1	715	3.4	2 490	0.4	4 862	0.6
China	159	0.8	1 044	0.3	806	3.9	9 739	1.6	16 214	1.9
EMENA, excl. Portugal	557	2.7	1 016	0.3	149	0.7	5 360	0.9	19 200	2.2
Other developing countries	842	4.0	1 494	0.4	1 285	6.2	9 291	1.6	66 441	7.8
Centrally planned economies	343	1.6	617	0.2	106	0.5	2 277	0.4	9 927	1.2

Table 16.4 Manufacturing imports of other industrial countries: EMENA countries

(a) Year = 1973

	ISIC 32 textile, apparel, and leather		ISIC 33 wood products and furniture		ISIC 34 paper and paper products		ISIC 35 chemical products		ISIC 36 non-metallic mineral products	
	US$(m)	%	US$(m)	%	US$(m)	%	US$(m)	%	US$(m)	%
EMENA, incl. Portugal	688	·	109	·	12	·	112	·	40	·
Portugal	212	100.0	30	100.0	2	100.0	15	100.0	9	
EMENA, excl. Portugal	477	100.0	79	100.0	10	100.0	97	100.0	31	100.0
Cyprus	0	0.0	0	0.0	0	0.3	0	0.1	0	0.0
Malta	5	1.1	0	0.0	0	0.6	2	1.6	0	0.0
Algeria	1	0.2	0	0.0	0	0.0	4	4.4	0	0.0
Morocco	6	1.3	0	0.1	0	0.2	1	1.2	0	0.1
Tunisia	2	0.4	0	0.0	0	0.3	1	1.0	0	0.0
Egypt	14	2.9	0	0.2	0	0.1	1	0.7	0	0.1
Jordan	0	0.0	0	0.0	0	0.0	0	0.0	0	0.0
Lebanon	15	3.1	0	0.3	0	3.2	7	7.3	0	0.1
Syria	0	0.0	0	0.0	0	0.0	0	0.0	0	0.0
Turkey	22	4.6	0	0.0	1	6.6	1	1.4	1	3.7
Pakistan	141	29.7	0	0.3	0	0.2	1	0.6	0	0.9
Iran	61	12.8	0	0.2	0	0.1	1	0.8	0	0.7
Hungary	39	8.2	5	6.2	2	15.6	28	28.9	6	18.1
Poland	57	11.9	15	18.7	4	45.5	25	25.6	13	41.0
Romania	42	8.8	13	16.3	1	5.9	11	11.0	7	21.8
Yugoslavia	62	13.1	45	57.6	2	21.4	15	15.2	4	13.5
Other EMENA	9	2.0	0	0.0	0	0.0	0	0.1	0	0.0

	ISIC 37 iron and steel		ISIC 38 engineering products		ISIC 39 other industries		Manufactures		Total imports	
	US$(m)	%	US$(m)	%	US$(m)	%	US$(m)	%	US$(m)	%
EMENA, incl. Portugal	118	.	369	.	33	.	1 481	.	6 448	.
Portugal	3	.	105	.	9	.	385	.	549	.
EMENA, excl. Portugal	115	100.0	264	100.0	24	100.0	1 096	100.0	5 899	100.0
Cyprus	0	0.0	1	0.5	0	0.1	2	0.1	14	0.2
Malta	0	0.0	0	0.1	0	0.7	7	0.7	8	0.1
Algeria	3	2.8	0	0.0	0	0.0	8	0.8	301	5.1
Morocco	0	0.0	0	0.0	0	0.4	8	0.7	76	1.3
Tunisia	3	2.9	0	0.0	0	0.0	6	0.6	41	0.7
Egypt	0	0.0	2	0.1	0	0.3	15	1.4	109	1.8
Jordan	0	0.0	0	0.6	0	0.0	2	0.1	6	0.1
Lebanon	0	0.0	0	0.1	2	7.2	25	2.2	51	0.9
Syria	0	0.0	0	0.1	0	0.2	0	0.0	13	0.2
Turkey	1	0.8	1	0.4	1	3.3	28	2.5	267	4.5
Pakistan	0	0.0	3	1.3	4	18.2	150	13.7	227	3.9
Iran	0	0.0	1	0.3	2	6.9	64	5.9	2 765	46.9
Hungary	42	36.7	21	8.0	4	16.3	146	13.3	297	5.0
Poland	40	34.5	98	37.0	5	19.9	255	23.3	626	10.6
Romania	8	7.1	14	5.4	0	2.1	96	8.8	222	3.8
Yugoslavia	17	15.1	122	46.0	5	22.3	273	24.9	432	7.3
Other EMENA	0	0.0	0	0.0	0	1.9	10	0.9	445	7.5

(b) Year = 1981

	ISIC 32 textile, apparel, and leather		ISIC 33 wood products and furniture		ISIC 34 paper and paper products		ISIC 35 chemical products		ISIC 36 non-metallic mineral products	
	US$(m)	%	US$(m)	%	US$(m)	%	US$(m)	%	US$(m)	%
EMENA, incl. Portugal	1 375	.	290	.	34	.	244	.	134	.
Portugal	360		65		6		26		32	
EMENA, excl. Portugal	1 015	100.0	225	100.0	28	100.0	219	100.0	102	100.0
Cyprus	3	0.3	0	0.0	0	0.4	1	0.6	0	0.0
Malta	18	1.8	0	0.0	0	0.8	5	2.2	0	0.0
Algeria	0	0.0	0	0.0	0	0.1	0	0.2	0	0.0
Morocco	10	1.0	0	0.1	0	0.1	1	0.5	0	0.2
Tunisia	9	0.9	0	0.0	0	0.0	0	0.2	0	0.0
Egypt	45	4.4	0	0.1	0	0.6	3	1.2	0	0.0
Jordan	0	0.0	0	0.0	0	0.1	0	0.0	0	0.0
Lebanon	3	0.3	0	0.0	0	1.4	0	0.1	0	0.0
Syria	0	0.0	0	0.0	0	0.0	0	0.0	0	0.0
Turkey	36	3.6	0	0.0	1	3.1	2	0.8	2	2.1
Pakistan	288	28.3	0	0.2	0	0.4	2	1.1	2	2.3
Iran	98	9.7	0	0.0	0	0.0	0	0.1	0	0.0
Hungary	78	7.7	14	6.2	10	34.3	54	24.6	19	18.4
Poland	139	13.7	30	13.4	6	19.9	64	29.2	30	28.9
Romania	147	14.4	51	22.5	7	25.6	28	12.8	27	26.6
Yugoslavia	121	11.9	129	57.3	4	13.1	58	26.4	22	21.3
Other EMENA	19	1.9	0	0.0	0	0.2	0	0.0	0	0.0

	ISIC 37 iron and steel		ISIC 38 engineering products		ISIC 39 other industries		Manufactures		Total imports	
	US$(m)	%	US$(m)	%	US$(m)	%	US$(m)	%	US$(m)	%
EMENA, incl. Portugal	405	.	729	.	101	.	3 313	.	20 082	.
Portugal	21	.	110	.	16	.	636	.	908	.
EMENA, excl. Portugal	384	100.0	620	100.0	85	100.0	2 677	100.0	19 174	100.0
Cyprus	0	0.0	0	0.1	0	0.2	5	0.2	20	0.1
Malta	0	0.0	7	1.2	2	1.9	33	1.2	34	0.2
Algeria	0	0.1	0	0.0	0	0.0	1	0.0	6 691	34.9
Morocco	0	0.0	1	0.1	0	0.2	13	0.5	244	1.3
Tunisia	0	0.0	1	0.1	0	0.0	10	0.4	90	0.5
Egypt	0	0.0	1	0.1	0	0.3	48	1.8	710	3.7
Jordan	0	0.0	1	0.1	0	0.0	1	0.0	20	0.1
Lebanon	0	0.0	1	0.2	28	32.8	32	1.2	49	0.3
Syria	0	0.0	1	0.1	0	0.2	1	0.0	114	0.6
Turkey	5	1.4	6	0.9	3	3.4	55	2.0	518	2.7
Pakistan	0	0.0	21	3.3	10	11.7	324	12.1	521	2.7
Iran	0	0.0	1	0.2	0	0.4	100	3.7	2 291	12.0
Hungary	31	8.1	119	19.2	8	8.9	332	12.4	797	4.2
Poland	97	25.4	210	33.8	6	7.4	581	21.7	1 179	6.1
Romania	185	48.3	132	21.3	2	2.7	579	21.6	1 000	5.2
Yugoslavia	65	16.8	119	19.2	14	17.0	531	19.8	857	4.5
Other EMENA	0	0.0	1	0.2	11	13.0	31	1.2	4 040	21.1

(c) Year = 1987

	ISIC 32 textile, apparel, and leather		ISIC 33 wood products and furniture		ISIC 34 paper and paper products		ISIC 35 chemical products		ISIC 36 non-metallic mineral products	
	US$(m)	%	US$(m)	%	US$(m)	%	US$(m)	%	US$(m)	%
EMENA, incl. Portugal	3 693	.	500	.	51	.	587	.	258	.
Portugal	1 154	.	112	.	10	.	81	.	94	.
EMENA, excl. Portugal	2 539	100.0	387	100.0	41	100.0	506	100.0	164	100.0
Cyprus	14	0.6	0	0.0	0	0.2	2	0.3	1	0.5
Malta	15	0.6	0	0.0	0	0.1	6	1.3	0	0.3
Algeria	0	0.0	0	0.0	0	0.0	4	0.9	0	0.0
Morocco	29	1.1	1	0.2	0	0.1	24	4.7	1	0.4
Tunisia	22	0.9	0	0.1	0	0.1	9	1.8	0	0.2
Egypt	131	5.2	1	0.4	0	1.0	3	0.5	0	0.1
Jordan	2	0.1	0	0.0	0	0.2	10	1.9	0	0.0
Lebanon	5	0.2	1	0.3	0	0.9	2	0.4	0	0.2
Syria	1	0.1	0	0.0	0	0.0	0	0.0	0	0.0
Turkey	508	20.0	1	0.2	1	3.2	33	6.4	25	15.4
Pakistan	834	32.8	1	0.2	0	0.3	3	0.6	8	4.8
Iran	204	8.0	0	0.0	0	0.9	2	0.3	1	0.4
Hungary	159	6.3	30	7.6	7	17.7	152	30.1	23	14.1
Poland	132	5.2	46	11.9	9	22.1	93	18.4	36	22.1
Romania	222	8.7	75	19.4	6	15.6	41	8.0	27	16.2
Yugoslavia	246	9.7	231	59.7	16	37.6	123	24.3	42	25.3
Other EMENA	16	0.6	0	0.0	0	0.1	0	0.1	0	0.1

411

	ISIC 37 iron and steel		ISIC 38 engineering products		ISIC 39 other industries		Manufactures		Total imports	
	US$(m)	%	US$(m)	%	US$(m)	%	US$(m)	%	US$(m)	%
EMENA, incl. Portugal	586	.	1 268	.	167	.	7 110	.	21 346	.
Portugal	29	.	252	.	19	.	1 750	.	2 147	.
EMENA, excl. Portugal	557	100.0	1 016	100.0	149	100.0	5 360	100.0	19 200	100.0
Cyprus	2	0.3	7	0.7	0	0.1	26	0.5	57	0.3
Malta	0	0.0	38	3.7	6	3.9	66	1.2	75	0.4
Algeria	10	1.7	0	0.0	0	0.0	15	0.3	2 548	13.3
Morocco	0	0.0	7	0.7	1	0.4	61	1.1	377	2.0
Tunisia	4	0.7	7	0.7	2	1.6	45	0.8	127	0.7
Egypt	0	0.0	4	0.4	1	0.8	141	2.6	816	4.2
Jordan	0	0.0	4	0.4	4	2.5	19	0.4	50	0.3
Lebanon	0	0.0	9	0.9	54	36.0	71	1.3	94	0.5
Syria	0	0.0	1	0.1	0	0.0	2	0.0	80	0.4
Turkey	211	37.9	39	3.8	12	8.1	830	15.5	1 540	8.0
Pakistan	9	1.7	44	4.3	17	11.5	915	17.1	1 161	6.0
Iran	0	0.0	5	0.5	1	0.5	213	4.0	3 619	18.9
Hungary	65	11.6	163	16.1	6	4.3	606	11.3	1 304	6.8
Poland	54	9.6	221	21.7	6	4.3	597	11.1	1 444	7.5
Romania	131	23.6	65	6.4	3	2.2	570	10.6	1 168	6.1
Yugoslavia	72	12.8	400	39.3	35	23.8	1 164	21.7	1 604	8.4
Other EMENA	0	0.0	3	0.3	0	0.0	19	0.4	3 136	16.3

percent in 1981 and increased only to 29.9 percent by 1987.

But the data for EMENA cover considerable differences among countries and country groups. This is shown in Table 16.5 that separates market economies having association or cooperation agreements with the EEC (Algeria, Morocco, Tunisia, Egypt, Jordan, Syria, Lebanon, Turkey, Cyprus, and Malta); Yugoslavia; other socialist countries (Hungary, Poland, and Romania); and other EMENA countries (South Yemen, North Yemen, Oman, Iraq, Iran, Afghanistan, and Pakistan).

It appears that market economies having association or cooperation agreements with the EEC have gained substantially within EMENA at the expense of socialist countries other than Yugoslavia and other EMENA countries while Yugoslavia's share underwent little change. Thus, the share of these market economies in EMENA manufactured exports to the EEC rose from 15.7 percent in 1973 to 38.0 percent in 1987 while the share of Yugoslavia declined from 29.1 percent to 27.1 percent, that of other socialist countries fell from 39.8 percent to 25.6 percent, and that of other EMENA countries decreased from 15.3 percent to 9.3 percent.

The observed changes in the composition of EMENA manufactured exports reflect the fact that the share of market economies with association or cooperation agreements with the EEC in EEC imports of manufactured products increased from 0.4 percent in 1973 to 1.0 percent in 1987, surpassing by a considerable margin increases in the share of all developing countries from 5.5 percent to 9.0 percent. Thus, whereas these market economies accounted for only 7 percent of the developing countries' manufactured exports to the EEC in 1973, they came to provide 11 percent of their exports in 1987.

Much of the increase occurred between 1981 and 1987, with Turkey and, to a lesser extent, Morocco being responsible for the observed changes. While Turkey accounted for only 0.2 percent of EEC manufactured imports in 1981, its share reached 0.5 percent in 1987; the corresponding figures for Morocco are 0.1 percent and 0.2 percent.

After earlier declines, Yugoslavia recaptured its 1963 share in the EEC imports of manufactured goods in 1987 while the erosion of the share of other socialist countries continued. This pattern was observed in Poland and Romania whereas in Hungary increases in market shares between 1973 and 1981 were followed by a decline between 1981 and 1987.

The decline in the share of the other EMENA country group was entirely due to Iran whose share in EMENA exports of manufactured

Table 16.5   Shares of EMENA countries in manufactured exports
(percent)

	Shares in EMENA exports to EEC			Shares in total imports of EEC		
	1973	*1981*	*1987*	*1973*	*1981*	*1987*
Market economies, association or cooperation agreements with EEC	15.7	28.6	38.0	0.4	0.6	1.0
Yugoslavia	29.1	23.1	27.1	0.7	0.5	0.7
Other socialist countries	39.8	37.5	25.6	0.9	0.8	0.7
Other EMENA countries	15.3	10.9	9.3	0.4	0.2	0.3
EMENA total, excl. Portugal	100.0	100.0	100.0	2.3	2.2	2.7
Developing countries	.	.	.	5.5	7.6	9.0

	Shares in EMENA exports to other industrial countries			Shares in total imports of other industrial countries		
	1973	*1981*	*1987*	*1973*	*1981*	*1987*
Market economies, association or cooperation agreements with EEC	9.2	7.4	23.8	0.1	0.1	0.2
Yugoslavia	24.9	19.8	21.7	0.3	0.2	0.2
Other socialist countries	45.4	55.7	33.1	0.5	0.5	0.3
Other EMENA countries	20.5	17.0	21.4	0.2	0.1	0.2
EMENA total, excl. Portugal	100.0	100.0	100.0	1.1	0.9	0.9
Developing countries	.	.	.	11.2	16.4	22.1

products to the EEC fell from 9.3 percent in 1973 to 3.6 percent in 1981 and to 2.3 percent in 1987. In turn, Pakistan experienced a slight increase in its share from 5.1 percent in 1973 to 5.2 percent in 1981 and to 5.7 percent in 1987.

The results indicate the importance of economic policies for export expansion. Thus, among countries having association or cooperation agreements with the EEC, the increases were concentrated in Turkey and Morocco which reformed their economic policies in the second part of the period. The reforms, oriented towards export expansion, were particularly far-reaching in Turkey where much of the increase in exports occurred.

Economic reform also seemed to have some effect in Hungary between 1973 and 1981 but these effects were more than undone after 1981, when decision-making was increasingly centralized and the exchange rate appreciated in real terms. Economic reforms were of limited scope in Poland and they were not undertaken in Romania while excessively expansionary policies before 1981 were followed by adjustment afterwards in Yugoslavia. Finally, in the case of Iran, the war with Iraq may explain the outcome.

The conclusions reached in regard to the importance of economic policies are supported by data on EMENA manufactured exports to industrial countries outside the EEC. Table 16.5 shows that the share in these exports of market economies having association or cooperation agreements with the EEC increased from 7.4 percent in 1981 to 23.8 percent in 1987. Within this total, the share of Turkey rose from 2.0 percent to 15.5 percent and that of Morocco from 0.5 percent to 1.1 percent. The counterpart of these increases lies in the decline of the share of socialist countries other than Yugoslavia while the share of Yugoslavia and that of the other EMENA country group underwent little change. (Iran never had an important share in the imports of manufactured goods by the other industrial countries.)

The findings show the importance of economic policies in their effects on export market shares in the EEC as well as in the other industrial countries. Nevertheless, preferences do matter. Thus, while market economies having association or cooperation agreements with the EEC had a 38.0 percent share, and Yugoslavia a 27.1 percent share, in EMENA manufactured exports to the EEC in 1987, their share was 23.8 percent and 21.7 percent, respectively, in EMENA manufactured exports to the other industrial countries. In turn, other socialist countries and other EMENA countries had a smaller share in EMENA manufactured exports to the EEC than in exports to the other industrial countries.

Note finally that manufactured exports are importantly affected by geographical factors. Thus, while they had relatively low shares in EMENA exports to the EEC, the other socialist countries and the other EMENA country group had a much higher share in the EEC imports of manufactured goods (0.7 percent and 0.3 percent) than in the imports of the other industrial countries (0.3 percent and 0.2 percent). The differences are even larger for market economies having association or cooperation agreements with the EEC, whose 1987 shares were 1.0 percent in the EEC and 0.2 percent in the other industrial countries, and for Yugoslavia, whose shares were 0.7 percent and 0.2 percent, respectively. For all of EMENA, the relevant shares were 2.7 percent in the EEC and 0.9 percent in other industrial countries (Table 16.5).

Further interest attaches to the commodity composition of EMENA manufactured exports to the EEC. Table 16.1 shows the high and increasing share of these countries in textiles, apparel, and leather products, with EMENA providing 8.1 percent of EEC imports in 1973 and in 1981 and 11.6 percent in 1987. Increases were also experienced in wood products and furniture (from 5.0 percent in 1973 to 5.9 percent in 1987), paper and paper products (from 0.7 percent to 1.0 percent), chemical products (from 1.3 percent to 1.5 percent), and nonmetallic minerals (from 1.8 percent to 2.9 percent). In turn, the share of engineering products remained unchanged at 1.0 percent and that of other industries at 1.1 percent while the share of iron and steel fell from 2.6 percent to 2.3 percent between 1973 and 1987.

Textiles, apparel, and leather products are by far the most important manufactured exports of EMENA sold in EEC markets. In 1982, they accounted for 56.1 percent of these exports, followed by engineering products (20.2 percent), chemical products (10.2 percent), wood products and furniture (4.6 percent), iron and steel (3.9 percent), nonmetallic mineral products (2.3 percent), paper and paper products (1.7 percent), and other industries (1.0 percent).

In textiles, apparel, and leather products, Turkey leads with a 26.6 percent share in EMENA exports to the EEC countries in 1987, followed by Yugoslavia (15.5 percent), Pakistan (9.3 percent), Morocco (9.1 percent), and Tunisia (8.9 percent). Romania has the highest share (41.2 percent) in EMENA exports of wood products and furniture to the EEC. It is followed by Yugoslavia (31.0 percent), Poland (14.9 percent), and Hungary (9.2 percent).

Yugoslavia dominates EMENA exports of paper and paper products to the EEC, with a share of 52.4 percent; Poland's share is 13.2 percent and Malta's 9.1 percent. Yugoslavia is also in the lead in chemical products (28.1 percent), followed by Hungary (14.9 percent), Tunisia (10.5 percent), Poland (10.1 percent) and Romania (8.5 percent).

Yugoslavia is ahead in nonmetallic mineral products as well, with a share of 32.6 percent in EMENA exports to the EEC. In turn, Turkey has a share of 22.4 percent, Poland, 17.5 percent, and Hungary and Romania 12.7 percent each. Furthermore, Yugoslavia has a leading position, with a share of 41.4 percent, in iron and steel. It is followed by Poland (18.3 percent), Hungary (16.1 percent), Romania (10.1 percent) and Algeria (6.6 percent).

A similar situation is observed in engineering products, where Yugoslavia has a share of 41.7 percent; among the other socialist countries, Poland's share is 13.2 percent, Hungary's 9.8 percent, and Romania's 8.2 percent. Finally, Pakistan leads in the other industry group, with a share of 27.0 percent, followed by Yugoslavia (18.6 percent), Romania (9.9 percent), Poland (9.5 percent), and Hungary and Tunisia (8.3 percent).

THE ENLARGEMENT OF THE EEC AND ITS POTENTIAL EFFECTS ON EMENA COUNTRIES

The second enlargement of the EEC involves the membership of Greece, Portugal, and Spain. All three countries had trade agreements with the EEC beforehand. Greece signed an association agreement in 1962, Spain concluded a preferential trade agreement in 1970, and Portugal participated in the EEC–EFTA free trade area in manufactured products, established in 1973.

The association agreement provided free entry for Greek manufactured products into the EEC, except that tariffs continued to be levied on iron and steel products and quantitative limitations applied to some textiles and clothing. In acceding to full membership, trade between the EEC and Greece was freed, and Greece adopted the common external tariff in steps over the 1981–6 period.

The EEC reduced tariffs on manufactured imports from Spain by 60 percent as of 1 January 1973, except that tariff reductions were postponed to 1977 on some sensitive items. Also, tariff reductions did not apply to iron and steel products while some textiles and clothing remained subject to quantitative limitations. Similar exceptions were made in regard to the imports of manufactured goods from Portugal. In acceding to membership, the remaining barriers to imports from both Portugal and Spain will be eliminated between 1986 and 1993, during which time these countries will adopt the common external tariff.

In the period under consideration, EEC imports of manufactured goods increased much more rapidly from Greece, Portugal, and Spain than from the EMENA countries. Thus, the share of the manufactured exports of the three countries in the EEC rose from 2.0 percent in 1973 to 3.6 percent in 1987 while the corresponding figures for EMENA were 2.3 percent and 2.7 percent. But, the increases fell behind those of EMENA market economies having association or cooperation agreements with the EEC, whose shares were 0.4 percent in 1973 and 1.0 percent in 1987.

It is noteworthy that among the three countries the increases were the most pronounced in Spain (from 1.2 percent in 1973 to 2.4

percent in 1987), followed by Portugal (from 0.5 percent to 0.8 percent) and by Greece (from 0.3 percent to 0.4 percent). In Greece, there was even a decline from 0.5 percent in 1981 to 0.4 percent in 1987, i.e. after acceding to full membership.

These results again indicate the importance of economic policies. Adjustment policies were the most vigorous in Spain that opened its economy during the period under consideration. Adjustment policies were also pursued in Portugal while a clear policy line was not established in Greece after the socialist government came to power (by contrast, adjustment was carried out under the socialist government in Spain).

It follows that the effects of enlargement will also depend on the policies applied. The continuation of past policies is observed in Spain that is attracting a considerable amount of capital from the other EEC countries. Also, adjustment effects have accelerated under the social democratic government in Portugal. In Greece, however, political conflicts have slowed economic change.

In any case, Spain's accession to EEC membership will have the greatest effects on the EMENA countries. For one thing, Spain is by far the largest country of the three, with its GDP exceeding the combined GDP of Portugal and Greece more than three times. For another thing, Spain has only a 60 percent tariff preference in the EEC while, with some exceptions, Greek and Portuguese manufactured products have long entered the Common Market duty-free.

The duty-free treatment of Spanish manufactured products will create discrimination against EMENA countries that do not enjoy preferential treatment in the EEC. They will also unfavorably affect other EMENA countries since their preferential margin *vis-à-vis* Spain in the EEC market will disappear.

Among product categories, special considerations apply to textiles, apparel, and leather products. As we have seen, these products account for 56 percent of EMENA manufactured exports to the EEC. At the same time, there is considerable competition with the three new member countries which had 72 percent of EMENA exports of textiles, apparel, and leather products to the EEC in 1987.

While imports of textiles and clothing from the three new member countries were subject to some limitations in the EEC, the limitations are eliminated in conjunction with their membership status. This will, then, disfavor EMENA countries whose textiles and clothing exports to the EEC remain subject to various limitations.

There is further the danger that increased imports of textiles and

clothing from the three new member countries would increase protectionist pressures in the EEC. But even if such pressures do not lead to
protectionist action, the risk of such action may discourage textiles
and clothing imports from the EMENA countries. This may affect, in
particular, outward processing that involves the reimportation of
material processed in these countries. Some such processing may
conceivably shift to the three new member countries.

More generally, membership offers advantages over preferences as
the former but not the latter is immutable. These considerations,
then, again favor imports from the three new member countries over
imports from the EMENA countries.

On the other side of the coin, the membership of Greece, Portugal,
and Spain in the EEC also means extending preferences to the
EMENA market economies having association or cooperation agreements with the EEC. In terms of GDP, this will add about 10 percent
to the size of the preferential market.

In the case of EMENA market economies having association or
cooperation agreements with the EEC, then, there are negative as
well as positive factors. The balance of these factors is not clear
although the negative factors may predominate, given the much
larger economic size of the old EEC than that of the new member
countries.

At the same time, EMENA countries not having such preferential
ties will unambiguously lose as a result of the membership of Greece,
Portugal, and Spain in the EEC, since increased discrimination
against them will not be offset by preferential entry into the markets
of the three new member countries. Nevertheless, these losses will be
mitigated by reason of the fact that the adoption of the common
external tariff of the EEC represents a reduction in the tariffs of the
three new member countries.

THE EUROPE 1992 PROGRAM AND ITS POTENTIAL
EFFECTS ON EMENA COUNTRIES

The EEC set out to complete the internal market by 1992. The
measures envisaged to be taken would increase intra-area trade in the
Common Market, but may also have an impact on imports from
nonmember countries. The proposed measures on trade in goods and
services will be briefly described in the following, with further consideration given to their possible effects on EMENA countries.

While the EEC has eliminated tariff and nontariff barriers to intra-area trade, some barriers to this trade remain. They include border formalities in transporting goods from one country to another; monetary compensation amounts applying to agricultural products; the prohibition of the transshipment of goods imported under national quotas; government procurement favoring national suppliers; and technical barriers limiting the shipment of goods across frontiers.

Border formalities impose economic costs on the member countries mainly in the form of the cost of administration and border delays for exporting and importing firms, thereby limiting the amount of intra-area trade. The abolition of these formalities among the member countries is equivalent to reductions in tariffs that will lead to trade creation. But it will also involve trade diversion by favoring partner-country producers over nonmembers, including EMENA countries.

Monetary compensation amounts, introduced to ease the effects of changes in the value of member-country currencies on the agriculture of the revaluing countries, are equivalent to import tariffs. Their abolition will lead to trade creation among EEC countries. It will not affect imports from nonmember countries, however, as these imports are limited by variable levies imposed in the framework of the common agricultural policy of the EEC.

In cases when national import quotas are applied on imports from EMENA and other nonmember countries, the transshipment of goods in intra-EC trade is prohibited. For EMENA countries, the principal restrictions apply to textiles and clothing. With the abolition of border formalities, Community-wide quotas will be established, presumably equal to the sum of national quotas. There may still be a slight gain to EMENA countries through the globalizational quotas as, under present conditions, some national quotas are underfulfilled while other quotas represent an effective constraint.

Public procurement was not included in the Treaty of Rome establishing the European Economic Community. And while in the 1970s the EEC Commission attempted to induce governments to purchase from the partner countries, the rules did not cover water, energy, transportation, telecommunications, and defense and, even in the other sectors, little cross-country procurement has occurred. The liberalization of government procurement, in turn, will result in trade creation without however affecting EMENA countries that have not supplied goods to EEC countries under government procurement.

Technical barriers to trade include differences in industry standards, in legal regulations, and in testing and certification procedures. Industry standards refer to product specifications that tend to differ from country to country in the EEC. Legal regulations pertain to health, safety, and environmental protection that again vary among countries. Finally, there are intercountry differences in testing and certification requirements, often involving an additional certification procedure to that required in the country of origin.

Under the Europe 1992 program, there will be mutual recognition of national standards for some products and Community-wide standards for others. This will involve trade creation as well as trade diversion, since products from partner countries will have advantageous treatment over products from the outside, including EMENA countries. Trade diversion may be further enhanced if Community-wide standards are formulated so as to favor EEC products.

Similar considerations apply to the unification of legal regulations and to testing and certification requirements. The recognition of national rules, or the establishment of common rules, will favor imports from partner countries over imports from the outside.

While the Treaty of Rome also envisaged the liberalization of trade in services, little progress has been achieved in this regard. The principal tradeable services are road transportation, air transportation, financial services, business services, and telecommunications services.

Competition in trucking is distorted by the need for licenses to undertake cross-border trade; also, cabotage, involving transportation by out-of-state truckers within a member state, is prohibited. Scrapping national restrictions and the prohibition of cabotage under the Europe 1992 program will increase competition among truckers of the member countries without affecting nonmember countries.

The regulatory regime in effect for airlines also limits the extent of competition. Competition will increase under the Europe 1992 program but nonmember countries will not be affected either favorably or unfavorably.

Financial services include insurance, banking services, and investment services. Under the Europe 1992 program these services will be freely provided by firms established in any member state in other member states. At the same time, the EEC will apply the principle of reciprocity, under which nonmember countries could not establish in the Common Market unless they offer national treatment to EEC firms in their country.

The discussion on reciprocity has thus far concerned banking. In this case, it has been decided that the requirement of reciprocity will not apply to subsidiaries of foreign banks that are already established in an EEC country. This is hardly the case for EMENA banks, so the exception does not apply to them. But, given the undeveloped stage of banking in EMENA countries, the requirement of reciprocity will have little effect for some time to come. Similar considerations apply to insurance and investment services.

Professional business services include engineering services, managerial consultancy, advertising and public relations, computing services, research and development, legal services, and financial services. Existing barriers to trade in professional business services among EEC countries will be eliminated by 1992. As a result, competition in these services among member countries will increase without, however, affecting nonmember countries.

The EEC will open the telecommunications market for trade among the member countries and will establish standards in the telecommunications field. These measures will favor member-country over nonmember-country producers but EMENA countries are not generally competing in this area. The principal exception is Hungary whose telecommunications exports may be adversely affected.

While the freeing of service trade in the framework of the Europe 1992 program will have little direct effect on EMENA countries, there will be indirect effects. This is because the cheapening of services will reduce production costs in the EEC, thereby favoring domestic production over imports from the outside, including EMENA.

We have considered so far the static effects of the Europe 1992 program for the EMENA countries. These countries will also be affected by the dynamic effects of the Europe 1992 program. To the extent that the establishment of this program leads to more rapid economic growth, there will be increased demand for EMENA products.

It has been officially estimated that the application of the Europe 1992 program will add 5.5 percent to the gross domestic product of the EEC. While the methodology used in arriving at this estimate is open to question, indications are that the promise of a fully-integrated market is having a beneficial effect on the economic climate of the EEC. This is apparent in increased investment activity as well as in cross-border mergers and concentration.

The acceleration of economic growth in the EEC may also have unfavorable effects on the EMENA countries, however. This is because increases in productivity will improve the competitiveness of EEC firms, adversely affecting imports. But, it may be surmised that productivity gains will be concentrated in high-technology industries that are of little importance for EMENA countries.

PROSPECTIVE DEVELOPMENTS IN EMENA MANUFACTURED EXPORTS TO THE EEC

We have reviewed the potential impact on EMENA manufactured exports to the Common Market of the EEC's enlargement and of the Europe 1992 program. A brief summary of these effects may be helpful as a starting-point in examining future prospects for EMENA manufactured exports in the EEC.

Duty-free treatment of Spanish exports will disfavor imports from EMENA countries. The elimination of restrictions on textiles and clothing imports from the three new member countries will have a similar effect. There is also the danger that protectionist pressures will increase in the EEC, especially in textiles and clothing.

EMENA countries having association or cooperation agreements with the EEC will however benefit from extending their preferences to the markets of the three new member countries, although these gains may not offset the potential losses. And, the negative effects will not be compensated in the case of EMENA countries which are not party to such agreements, even so their losses will be mitigated by the lowering of tariffs by the three new EEC members.

The Europe 1992 program will give rise to trade diversion due to the abolition of border formalities and the establishment of new regulations on technical barriers to trade. But, EMENA countries may obtain some gains due to greater flexibility in textiles and clothing quotas.

At the same time, given their relative underdevelopment, EMENA countries are not likely to experience trade diversion in services. However, the cheapening of services will reduce production costs in the EEC, thereby favoring domestic production over imports from the outside, including imports from EMENA.

There will further be dynamic effects of the Europe 1992 program. Indications are that the promise of a fully-integrated market favorably affects economic growth in the EEC countries, which will lead to increased imports from EMENA. And while more rapid increases in productivity will improve the competitive position of EEC firms, this is likely to be concentrated in high-technology industries that are of little importance in EMENA countries.

It appears, then, that the net effects on EMENA countries of the EEC's enlargement and the Europe 1992 program are far from unambiguous. At the same time, one should emphasize the existence of a large and growing market in Western Europe, where the EMENA countries have the advantage of geographical proximity.

The question arises which industries would offer the best export prospects for EMENA countries. As a general proposition, it can be said that these are industries where EMENA countries can exploit the advantages of their low labor costs. According to data published in the ILO, *Yearbook of Labor Statistics*, hourly wages in manufacturing are $0.46 in Turkey, $0.48 in Egypt, $0.73 in Poland, $0.87 in Romania, $0.89 in Hungary, and $1.28 in Yugoslavia. This compares with manufacturing wages of $1.59 in Portugal, $3.97 in Greece, and $5.49 in Spain.

It appears, then, that EMENA countries have a considerable labor cost advantage *vis-à-vis* the new member countries of the EEC, especially as far as Greece and Spain are concerned. EMENA countries also have a labor cost advantage *vis-à-vis* the East Asian newly-industrializing economies. While these economies had traditionally been regarded as having low wages, the situation has changed as their wages have been rising at a rapid rate over the past quarter of a century. Thus, hourly wages in manufacturing are $1.70 in Korea, $1.72 in Singapore, $1.91 in Hong Kong, and $2.29 in Taiwan.

This is not to say that all EMENA countries would have a comparative advantage in the same industries. While the advantages of the Maghreb (Algeria, Morocco, and Tunisia) and Mashreg (Egypt, Jordan, Lebanon and Syria) countries and Pakistan lie in unskilled labor-intensive industries, the socialist EMENA countries have a comparative advantage in skill-intensive industries, due to their low-cost skilled labor. Turkey may be considered to fall between the two groups.

A recent study by Alexander Yeats, "Developing Countries' Exports of Manufactures: Past and Future Implications of Shifting Pattern of Comparative Advantage" (World Bank, January 1989), presents estimates of labor intensity for the year 1982. The data show value added per worker in individual industries, expressed as a proportion of the average for the entire manufacturing sector; the lower this ratio, the more labor-intensive the industry in question.

According to the results, the ratio is 59.9 for textiles, 50.8 for apparel, 55.3 for leather products, 61.8 for wood products, 68.2 for furniture, and 85.1 for miscellaneous manufactures. These are all products, then, where the Maghreb and Mashreg countries, Turkey and Pakistan possess considerable cost advantages.

Particular interest attaches to textiles, apparel, and leather products that accounted for 56.1 percent of EMENA manufactured exports to the EEC in 1987. But EMENA provided only 11.6 percent of EEC imports of these products, and one-third of this amount came from the socialist EMENA countries.

We have noted above the dangers inherent in the accession of Greece, Portugal, and Spain to EEC membership for the imports of textiles and clothing from EMENA. To cope with the situation, and to ensure increases in the future, the Maghreb and Mashreg countries should negotiate with the EEC that the free entry provisions of their agreements apply, without exception, to the exports of textiles, apparel, and leather products. Turkey may do the same with reference to its future membership in the EEC and Pakistan may request increases in its MFA quota with reference to its least-developed status.

The labor-cost advantages of the low-wage EMENA countries in wood products and furniture are circumscribed by limitations on the availability of wood. They could nevertheless import wood for the making of wood products and furniture.

In the other industries category, EMENA had only a 1.1 percent share in EEC imports in 1987, compared with 12.2 percent for the Far Eastern NICs. This category includes a variety of unskilled labor-intensive products, such as toys, sport goods, and travel articles. The possibilities for expanding the exports of these products are very considerable and they do not generally face barriers in the EEC.

The EMENA countries have an even lower share, 0.2 percent, in Common Market imports of engineering products. Yet, after recent increases, these products have come to account for over one-half of EEC total manufactured imports and are expected to continue increasing their share in the future.

Subcontracting offers possibilities for export expansion in engineering products in the low-wage EMENA countries. This conclusion applies, *a fortiori*, to the socialist EMENA countries whose comparative advantage lies in skill-intensive engineering products. These countries should also be able to offer finished products for export in the engineering industries.

In turn, while EMENA countries account for 2.3 percent of EEC imports of iron and steel, they do not possess cost advantages in these industries. This is because of the lack of availability of high-quality iron ore and the high costs of transportation. In turn, there are possibilities in the exportation of nonmetallic mineral products, several of which are highly labor-intensive.

These considerations indicate the possibilities for expanding EMENA manufactured exports to the Common Market. The main limitation to this expansion does not appear to lie in market constraints in the EEC or competition from the outside but rather in the economic policies applied by the EMENA countries themselves. This is apparent in the export success of Turkey and Morocco once they carried out economic reforms.

While the policies applied would have to depend on the conditions existing in particular countries, in the nonsocialist EMENA countries they would generally include the establishment of competitive exchange rates; the liberalization of imports, investment regimes, and prices; the streamlining and privatizing of public enterprises; financial sector reform; and reductions in budget deficits. These policies would have to be fitted into a package of structural adjustment.

In the socialist EMENA countries, enterprise reforms would be needed. These would involve setting rational prices, ensuring competition, and providing appropriate incentives to managers. The enterprise reforms would have to be accompanied by capital market and labor market reforms, so as to assure the availability of capital and labor to efficient firms.

CONCLUSIONS

This chapter has examined the implications for EMENA of EEC trade policy. Following an analysis of EEC trade agreements with EMENA countries, the chapter has shown that EMENA's trade performance in the EEC has been far from uniform. While Turkey and Morocco, countries that carried out economic reforms, increased their market share to a considerable extent, the European socialist countries and Iran lost market shares.

As to the future, it has been suggested that the enlargement of the Common Market may have a slightly negative effect on EMENA countries having association or cooperation agreements with the EEC and a more pronounced negative effect on countries that do not have such agreements. In turn, the completion of the internal market of the EEC by 1992 would favor products from the member countries over products from the outside, including EMENA countries. However, EMENA countries would benefit from the acceleration of economic growth in the EEC upon completion of the Europe 1992 program.

The chapter has further indicated that the comparative advantage of the EMENA countries lies in labor-intensive products, with the low-wage countries having good prospects in unskilled labor-intensive products and the socialist EMENA countries in skill-intensive products. At the same time, the investigation of export prospects would have to be carried further by providing greater product and country detail.

Part VIII

Trends in Economic Policies

17 France before Europe 1992*

The deadline of Europe 1992 is approaching. By this date, it is planned to eliminate border formalities and to liberalize to a considerable extent goods and services transactions as well as capital and labor movements in the Common Market. The question arises how well France is prepared for this eventuality. The present chapter aims at contributing some clarifications to answering this question. This will be done by reviewing French economic performance in the 1980–8 period and examining some issues relevant for the future.

ECONOMIC GROWTH

France experienced approximately average economic growth rates compared with the other three major EEC countries, Germany, Italy, and the United Kingdom, in the 1980–4 period (Table 17.1). This was the result of the expansionary policies applied by the newly-elected socialist government after May 1981 and the deflationary measures subsequently taken in response to the adverse balance-of-payments effects of these policies.

Economic growth accelerated in the Common Market after 1984. However, France places last among the major EEC countries in terms of economic growth rates, with an average of 2.4 percent a year between 1984 and 1988. The corresponding figures are 3.8 percent for the United Kingdom, 3.3 percent for Italy, and 2.5 percent for Germany.

Relatively slow economic growth in France was associated with small increases in gross domestic investment. While the decline of 1980–4 gave place to an increase in 1984–8, for the entire period France shares the last place with Germany; the two countries exhibited a 6 percent rise in gross domestic investment between 1980 and 1988 (Table 17.2). Investments rose at more than double this rate in

* Originally published in the *Tocqueville Review*, 1988/89.

Table 17.1   Economic growth rates

	1980–4	1984–8	1980–8
France	1.4	2.4	1.9
Germany	1.0	2.5	1.8
Italy	1.4	3.2	2.3
United Kingdom	1.6	3.8	2.7

Source: OECD, *Economic Outlook*, December 1988, Table R1 and Country Tables.

Table 17.2   Growth rates of gross domestic investment

	1980–4	1984–8	1980–8
France	–2.4	3.9	0.7
Germany	–1.5	3.0	0.7
Italy	–0.7	3.7	1.5
United Kingdom	2.3	5.2	3.6

Source: OECD, *Economic Outlook*, December 1988, Table R6 and Country Tables.

Italy and five times more rapidly in the United Kingdom.

The rate of economic growth was not sufficient in France to absorb the increment of the labor force in France. Correspondingly, unemployment rates increased from 6.4 percent in 1980 to 9.9 percent in 1984 and, again, to 10.2 percent in 1988[1] (Table 17.3). By contrast, after increases in earlier years, unemployment rates declined between 1984 and 1988 in Germany as well as in the United Kingdom. Only Italy shares with France the distinction of continuing increases in unemployment rates.

At the same time, French economic growth in recent years was achieved at the expense of growing current accounts deficits. While France had a current account surplus of $3 billion in 1986, this gave place to a deficit of $5 billion in 1987 which increased further to $6 billion in 1988 (Table 17.4). By contrast, Germany had a surplus of $39 billion in 1986 which grew to $45 billion in 1987 and remained at this level in 1988.

The main contributing factor to the French current account deficit has been the loss in export market shares. Apart from a small gain in 1988, France lost market shares in recent years much exceeding the

Table 17.3   Unemployment rates

	1980	1984	1988
France	6.4	9.9	10.2
Germany	3.3	8.2	7.7
Italy	7.1	9.3	11.25
United Kingdom	6.1	11.4	8.5

Source: OECD, *Economic Outlook*, Table R18 and Country Tables.

Table 17.4   Current account balance of EEC countries ($ billion)

	1986	1987	1988	1989
Germany	39	45	45	51
France	3	–5	–6	–6
Belgium and Netherlands	7	6	8	10
Other EEC	2	–8	–33	–42

Source: OECD, *Economic Outlook*, December 1988, Table 24.

losses experienced in the other major Common Market countries (Table 17.5). And, in 1988, relatively rapid economic growth in France added to imports.

The appreciation of the real exchange rate (the trade-weighted exchange rate adjusted for changes in wholesale prices at home and abroad) contributed to the loss in French market shares. As shown in Table 17.6, the extent of appreciation has been greater in France than in the other major Common Market countries.

Vis-à-vis Germany, France also suffered the effects of the unfavorable commodity composition of exports. Thus, while German exports are concentrated in machinery and equipment where income elasticities are high and prices elasticities low, France has a higher share of traditional export products with low income and high price elasticities where increased competition comes from the newly-industrializing countries.

PROSPECTS FOR THE FUTURE

The OECD Secretariat projects a slowdown of French economic growth in the next two years, with the gross national product increasing by 3.0 percent in 1989 (after 3.5 percent in 1988) and 2.5 percent

Table 17.5 Trade in manufactured goods: export market growth and relative export performance

	(1) Export volume growth				(2) Export market growth				(3) Relative export performance (1)–(2)			
	1985	1986	1987	1988	1985	1986	1987	1988	1985	1986	1987	1988
France	0.5	–0.7	6.9	8.7	5.9	3.3	1.8	9.2	–5.1	–3.8	–4.8	0.5
Germany	8.7	2.7	6.9	9.5	6.2	4.8	3.0	6.5	2.4	–2.0	–3.7	–2.7
Italy	5.2	1.8	5.7	9.0	4.3	3.5	4.1	6.7	0.9	–1.5	–1.5	–2.0
UK	8.8	2.5	5.9	8.5	4.9	3.3	8.0	4.2	3.7	–0.9	2.0	–3.7

Source: OECD, *Economic Outlook*, various issues.

Table 17.6 Real effective exchange rates (1982 = 100)

	France	Germany	Italy	United Kingdom
1982	100	100	100	100
1983	100	99	98	106
1984	96	103	98	109
1985	94	103	98	105
1986	92	95	96	106
1987	92	93	93	104
1988	92	94	94	95

Source: International Monetary Fund, *International Financial Statistics*, various issues.

in 1990. This would not permit absorbing the increment of the labor force, so that the unemployment rate would rise from 10.25 percent in 1988 to 10.5 percent in 1989 and 10.75 percent in 1990.[2]

Looking further ahead, the Commissariat du Plan notes that the French economy would have to grow more rapidly than the EEC average because its labor force is increasing at a higher rate than that of the other Common Market countries. In fact, it is estimated that the French labor force would grow by 2 million from now to the year 2000.

The arguments for rapid economic growth are strengthened if we consider the high rate of unemployment in France. It would be necessary to provide increased employment for French labor that could be done productively by accelerating the rate of economic growth.

But how can France grow more rapidly than the other Common Market countries? First of all, France would have to ease the balance-of-payments constraint under which it operates. This constraint is apparent in the maintenance of high interest rates to safeguard the franc. Thus, the intervention rate of the Banque de France was raised from 6.75 percent to 7.00 percent in the summer of 1988 to 7.25 percent in October 1988 and to 7.75 percent two months later.

The latter increase was said to be made in anticipation of next day's rise of interest rates by the German central bank. But, there continues to be a considerable difference between French and German interest rates. In mid-December 1988, three months' money market rates were 8.7 percent and 6.2 percent. [In February 1990, France's rates were 10.13 percent and Germany's 8.05 percent (*The Economist*, 17–23 February 1990).]

Nor are interest rate differentials offset by differences in inflation rates. Thus, as a result of successful efforts at disinflation, the inflation differential *vis-à-vis* Germany – as measured by the consumer price index – declined from 8.1 percent in 1980 to 5.0 percent in 1984 and to 0.8 percent in 1988. Thus, differences in nominal interest rates in large part represent differences in real (inflation-adjusted) interest rates.

At any rate, at given exchange rates, nominal interest rate differentials are relevant since they represent the cost of doing business *vis-à-vis* other countries. Furthermore, high long-term corporate bond rates discourage domestic investment in France. Thus, at present interest rates, French business enterprises are disadvantaged relative to their German counterparts.

Attaining higher growth rates would further require increased investment. Increased investment is also necessary in order to expand exports and substitute for imports that would permit easing the balance-of-payments constraint. We now turn to the policies that may be used to increase domestic savings and investment in France.

INCREASING DOMESTIC SAVINGS

The share of gross domestic investment in GNP is lower today in France than it was in 1980. And the differences are much larger if comparisons are made with the pre-1973 period. At that time, the investment share was between 25 and 30 percent; it is now slightly below 20 percent. Declines in personal saving, in government saving, and in business saving have all contributed to this outcome.

Household saving was 19 percent of disposable income in France in the early 1970s; it declined slightly to 18 percent in 1980; and it has fallen precipitously since. Thus, in 1987 household saving amounted to only 12 percent of disposable income.

In order to increase investment, it would be desirable to reverse the tendency of declining personal saving. This may be accomplished by providing tax incentives to savings. In order to channel private savings to business investments, the incentives should be linked to security purchases. Such incentives, associated with the name of Monory, have had favorable effects on private savings and business investments under the Barre Government of 1976–81.

At the same time, in order to avoid an outflow of savings, differences among the EEC countries in regard to withholding taxes on dividend and interest income would need to be reduced. Such taxes are the highest in France, raising the danger of an outflow of funds, in particular to Luxembourg, once all barriers to capital movements are eliminated within the EEC.

To avoid this eventuality, the French government has suggested equalizing withholding taxes at their highest level. This is, however, objected to by other EEC member countries. In fact, the danger exists that high withholding taxes in the Community would lead to the outflow of funds to non-EEC countries, especially Switzerland.

There would further be need to reduce the dissaving of the French government. While the government budget had a surplus in the early 1970s, small deficits in the second half of the 1970s were followed by equilibrium in 1980, but then the budget deficit rapidly grew under the socialist government. It reached 3.1 percent of the gross national product in 1983 and, while it declined afterwards, it is still 2.3 percent of GNP.

The financing of the government deficit leads to crowding out as less financing is available for private uses. And, with deficit financing representing a demand for funds, it also raises interest rates, thereby adding to the burden of private business.

One way to eliminate the budget deficit is to raise taxes. But the tax burden is greater in France than in the other major Common Market countries. Thus, the ratio of government revenues to the gross national product was 47.1 percent in France in 1986, compared with 44.7 percent in Germany, 41.9 percent in the United Kingdom, and 38.9 percent in Italy. This represents considerable increases over 1980 when the ratio was 44.5 percent in France; it was 44.7 in

Germany, 40.1 percent in the United Kingdom, and 32.9 percent in Italy.

Similar conclusions are reached if individual taxes are compared. The standard rate of the value-added tax is the highest in France, 18.6 percent, compared with 14 percent in Germany, 18 percent in Italy, and 15 percent in the United Kingdom. While France has no obligation to reduce its standard TVA rate under the Europe 1992 program, the existing large differences *vis-à-vis* Germany and another neighboring country, Belgium, whose standard rate is 15 percent, will create incentives for cross-border purchases by individuals once border formalities are eliminated. Thus, in no case should France raise its standard TVA rate; it may rather contemplate reducing it to limit cross-border purchases by its nationals.

Nor can France consider increasing income tax rates as its marginal rate, 57 percent, is higher than in Germany (53 percent), Italy (56 percent), and the United Kingdom (40 percent). High marginal income tax rates discourage savings, work, and risk-taking. They also favor setting up firms in countries where their principal employees pay lower taxes.

Finally, rather than increasing, France should reduce the taxation of business enterprises. According to the November 1987 rapport du Conseil des impôts, in 1984 taxes and social charges paid by business enterprises amounted to 17.9 percent of the gross national product in France, followed by 13.9 percent in Italy, 11.0 percent in the United Kingdom, and 10.9 percent in Germany. And while some reductions occurred in subsequent years in France, this was also the case in the other countries so that the differences hardly changed.

It appears, then, that one could not rely on increases in taxation to reduce the budget deficit in France. Rather, at the least, the taxation of business enterprises would have to be reduced. Correspondingly, there is need to lower budgetary expenditures as a percentage of the gross national product. This would represent a reversal of the tendency observed since 1980.

Apart from Italy, public consumption increased much more rapidly in France than in the other major Common Market countries. Between 1980 and 1987, the increase was 19.3 percent in real terms in France, compared with 10.3 percent in Germany and 7.0 percent in the United Kingdom. The corresponding figure was 23.1 percent in Italy.

The growth of government consumption shows no sign of abating in France. While increases of 3.1 percent in 1981 and 3.7 percent in

1982 have not again been reached, after a slowdown in 1983 (2.1 percent) and 1984 (1.1 percent), the growth of public consumption has accelerated again. Thus, increases of 2.3 percent were observed in 1985, 2.6 percent in 1986, and 3.0 percent in 1987. Also, unexpected increases in revenues have been used to raise government expenditures in 1988 and further increases in expenditures are planned for 1989.

It is curious that the growth of public consumption has received little attention in France. Yet, this lies behind the continued deficit of the government budget, which reduces the amount available for investment. It has also contributed to the deficit in the balance of payments. France would have to accept a substantial deceleration in the growth of public consumption, leading to a decline in the share of public expenditure in GNP, in order to increase the rate of savings and investment and to improve its economic performance in general.

INCREASING COMPETITIVENESS

Raising private and government savings would contribute to higher investments in France. This objective would further be served by providing increased incentives for business enterprises to save and to invest. While business savings increased in recent years, they still remain below the level reached before 1981.

Reducing corporate income taxes would add to business savings, although part of the increment in profits would be paid out in dividends. Investment could be furthered more directly by abolishing the *taxe professionelle* that is imposed by the localities on new equipment and construction. At the same time, the localities would have to be compensated for the loss of revenue, amounting to 2.5 percent of value added by nonfinancial enterprises in 1984, by receiving a portion of taxes collected by the government.

Increased investment would improve the competitiveness of French business in various ways. It would reduce costs in existing industries and increase capacity in present as well as in new activities. Higher capacity, in turn, would permit expanding exports and replacing imports.

Competitiveness can further be improved by lowering social charges and changing existing currency relationships. Social charges amount to 50 percent of wages in France, representing a substantial wedge between the renumeration of the worker and the cost of labor.

This wedge discourages employment and encourages the use of capital-intensive methods.

Lowering social charges, then, would have a double effect by improving competitiveness and increasing employment. For one thing, the cost of doing business would fall; for another thing, the cost of labor would decline relative to that of capital.

It will be objected that reducing social charges would increase the deficit of the social security system in France. As suggested in a previous article (Bela Balassa, "The French Economy at the Outset of the New Septennat"), this would require applying the procedure proposed in the report of the "sages" on social security to levy a proportional tax on all incomes.

The competitiveness of French industry would also be improved by changing existing currency relationships. But, this should not be looked upon as exclusively a French problem. Rather, as shown in Table 17.4, there is considerable imbalance within the European Common Market. This imbalance exists between Germany and two countries closely linked to it, Belgium and the Netherlands, on the one hand, and the rest of the Common Market, on the other.

Thus, Germany, Belgium, and the Netherlands had a current account surplus of $46 billion in 1986 that grew to $51 billion in 1987 and $53 billion in 1988; it is estimated to reach $61 billion in 1989. By contrast, the rest of the EEC (inclusive of France) had a surplus of $5 billion in 1986 that gave place to a deficit of $13 billion in 1987 and $39 billion in 1988. The deficit is expected to reach $48 billion in 1989.

These imbalances are not tenable and would have to be reduced, requiring changes in currency relationships. Stephen Marris of the Institute for International Economics estimates that a 15 percent change in relative currency values would be necessary to reduce the imbalance to manageable proportions.

From the economic point of view, it makes no difference whether currency relationships are changed through a devaluation in the deficit countries or a revaluation in the surplus countries. For adjustments of equal magnitude, the effects on the balance of payments will be the same.

At the same time, from the political and psychological point of view, it would be desirable that changes in currency values occurred through revaluation in the surplus countries. This is because a devaluation is looked upon as a penalty for the policies applied by the government in power and it creates an atmosphere of inflation. Yet, in particular in France, it is important to maintain the achievements of anti-inflationary policies that reduced the rate of increase of consumer prices from 13.6 percent in 1980 to 7.4 percent in 1984 and 2.5 percent in 1988 [3.6 in 1989].

Thus, France should make common cause with other deficit countries in the Common Market to induce Germany to revalue the mark, the Netherlands the Dutch guilder, and Belgium the Belgian franc.

Changes in currency values would not only improve the competitiveness of French industry but also lead to increased investment. This is because differences in interest rates in excess of inflation rate differentials, which result from anticipation of changes in currency values, would be eliminated.

CONCLUSIONS

France will confront a new situation in 1992 when border formalities among EEC countries will be eliminated and goods and service transactions as well as capital and labor movements will be liberalized. Also the French economy will need to grow more rapidly than the other EEC countries, in part because the French labor force is increasing at a higher rate and in part because of the need to reduce unemployment from present levels.

To pursue these objectives would require easing the balance-of-payments constraint under which the French economy operates. This, in turn, would necessitate increasing investment and improving the competitiveness of French industry.

To reach higher investment levels one would need to reverse the decline in personal savings that occurred in recent years and to reduce the deficit in the government budget. But reductions in the budget deficit cannot be accomplished through higher taxes.

To begin with, France has the highest standard value-added tax rate that will create incentives for cross-border purchases by individuals once border formalities among EEC countries are eliminated. Furthermore, France has the highest marginal income tax rate that tends to discourage savings, work, and risk-taking, and it favors setting up firms in other EEC countries. Finally, taxes and social charges paid by business are the highest in France, with adverse effects on competitiveness.

In order to reduce the budget deficit, then, recent increases in the ratio of government expenditures to GNP would have to be reversed.

Apart from adverse effects on savings, the rapid rise of public spending contributed to the deficit in the balance of payments.

At the same time, increased incentives would need to be provided to business enterprises to save and to invest. These objectives would be served by lowering corporate income tax rates, eliminating the *taxe professionnelle* that bears on investment activity, and reducing social charges.

Lower social charges would also improve the competitiveness of French business and increase employment. At the same time, the revenue loss of the social security system may be replaced by a proportional tax on all incomes.

Improving competitiveness would further require changing currency relationships. Under the present exchange rates, there is a large imbalance between Germany and the two small countries linked to it, on the one hand, and the rest of the EEC, on the other, which is not tenable. Reducing this imbalance, in turn, would ease the balance-of-payments constraint on the French economy and permit France to reach economic growth rates that are above the average for the EEC.

Notes

1. This article was written in February–March of 1989. The French unemployment figure was down to 9.5 in November 1989. German unemployment remained stationary. The surplus of the German balance of payments had increased in 1989 to $71.5 billion. France's deficit has increased to $7.5 billion (*The Economist*, 17–23 February 1990).
2. Unless otherwise noted, the data originate in French official sources and OECD statistics.

18 Economic Policies of the Rocard Government*

This chapter will examine the economic policies of the Rocard Government in the 1988–90 period. The first section will consider economic growth rates and the factors contributing to growth. The second section will examine the factors affecting investment activity. The third section will analyze French foreign trade and the current account. The fourth section will deal with the question if the current account deficit and, more generally, foreign capital needs represent a constraint for French economic growth. The fifth section will review recent changes in employment and unemployment. The sixth section will examine monetary and fiscal policies. The final section will analyze the prospects for the French economy and make recommendations for the future.

THE RECORD OF ECONOMIC GROWTH IN FRANCE[1]

As Table 18.1 indicates, France is in a middle position among the major Common Market countries as far as economic growth rates are concerned. Thus, in the years 1989–90, it has been ahead of the United Kingdom, *ex aequo* with Italy, and behind Germany.

The situation is more favorable if changes over time are considered. French economic growth rates averaged 2.2 percent in 1985–7 and have risen to 3.3 percent in 1988–90, an increase of 1.1 percentage points. The OECD *Economic Survey* of 1989/90 for France attributes the acceleration of growth rates to the following factors:

First, there were favorable movements in the terms of trade, primarily because of the weakness of oil prices. Second, the rest of the world also began to grow more rapidly, stimulating French exports, especially of manufactures. Third, interest rates declined

---

* Originally published as a paper in *Commentaire*, Summer 1991, no. 54; pp. 307–314.

  The author alone is responsible for the contents of the chapter, which should not be interpreted to represent the views of the World Bank.

Table 18.1   Economic growth rates

	1985	1986	1987	1988	1989	1990
France	1.9	2.5	2.2	3.8	3.6	2.5
Germany	1.9	2.3	1.6	3.7	3.9	4.2
Italy	2.6	2.5	3.0	4.2	3.2	2.6
United Kingdom	3.6	3.9	4.7	4.6	2.2	1.6

Source: OECD, *Economic Outlook*, December 1990, Tables 24 and R1.

in nominal terms and, through most of the period, in real terms as well, once expected inflation is taken into account. Fourth, the franc depreciated slightly on a trade-weighted basis in the years 1987–1989, providing a small impetus to net foreign demand at the end of the period. Finally, fiscal policy, while remaining tight, would appear to have become less restrictive by 1988, primarily due to tax cuts. (p. 11)

Another way to approach the problem is to inquire into the contribution of elements of aggregate demand to economic growth. Here the major change has occurred in regard to investment. As shown in Table 18.2, the growth rate of gross domestic investment (GDI) has increased from an average of 3.9 percent in 1985–7 to an average of 6.0 percent in 1988–90. As a result, the growth of GDI has contributed 1.0 percentage points to the rate of economic growth.

Improvements in France's trade position have been another contributing factor to economic growth. While foreign trade made a negative contribution to growth in 1985–7, inasmuch as increases in the volume of imports exceeded increases in the volume of exports, it had a neutral effect on GDP growth in 1988–90.

Among individual sectors, growth rates were the highest in services, 6.8 percent a year between 1987 and 1990. It was followed by construction (5.1 percent) and manufacturing (4.2 percent). Within manufacturing, investment goods showed above average performance (4.7 percent), indicating the importance of investment activity. Automobiles also did well, with an increase of 5.6 percent, followed by intermediate goods (4.3 percent) and consumer goods (3.2 percent). The laggards were energy (1.5 percent) and agriculture and food processing (1.3 percent).

Table 18.2   Growth rates of gross domestic investment

	1985	1986	1987	1988	1989	1990
France	3.2	4.5	4.1	8.6	5.9	3.4
Germany	0.1	3.3	2.2	5.1	7.1	8.2
Italy	1.4	1.6	5.8	6.7	5.1	3.4
United Kingdom	4.0	1.9	9.5	14.8	4.8	1.3

Source: OECD, *Economic Outlook*, December 1990, Table R5 and Country Tables.

FACTORS AFFECTING INVESTMENT ACTIVITY

The growth of French investment is particularly favorable if comparisons are made with the early 1980s when investment declined in absolute terms. As a result of these changes, the ratio of investment to value added increased from 14 percent in 1984 to 17 percent in 1989. Nevertheless, it has not reached the 20 percent ratio observed in the early 1970s.

The rise in investment has responded to increases in the rate of return to capital. The rate of return has reached 14.2 percent in 1990, compared with 10 percent in the first half of the 1980s. Higher rates of return reflect in part the rise in the share of capital in value added. This share was below 36 percent in the first half of the 1980s; it has surpassed 37 percent in recent years.

The slowdown in increases in unit labor costs has contributed to the rise of capital's share in value added. While in the first half of the 1980s unit labor costs rose 8 percent a year, increases have averaged 2 percent in 1987–90. Nevertheless, there has been an acceleration in the rise of unit labor costs in recent years, reflecting increases in wages. Wages rose at an annual rate of 3.4 percent in 1988, 4.0 percent in 1989, and 4.9 percent in 1990.

Another factor boosting the rate of return to capital has been the decrease in corporate income tax rates. The rate of corporate income tax has been reduced from 45 percent in 1986 to 37 percent on undistributed profits and 42 percent on distributed profits in 1990.

Investment activity has also been favorably affected by the decline in long-term interest rates. Long-term rates were in the 14–15 percent range in the first half of the 1980s; they declined to below 10 percent in 1989, although again surpassing 10 percent in 1990.

Increases in capital incomes have not sufficed however to fully finance the growth of investment. As a result, the rate of self-financing that reached 90 percent in 1987 and 1988 fell to 85 percent in 1989 and it is estimated at 75 percent in the fourth quarter of 1990.

Above-average increases in investment occurred in the manufacturing sector. Between 1987 and 1990, manufacturing investment grew by 10 percent a year. Within the manufacturing sector, the largest increases occurred in automobiles, with investment rising by 22 percent a year. Substantial increases were experienced also in intermediate products, where higher investment permitted to surmount capacity limitations in iron and steel and in basic chemicals. However, capacity limitations continue to be observed in non-ferrous metals, glass, and paper. At the same time, excess capacity limited investment in professional equipment.

While most industrial investment prior to 1986 was devoted to efficiency improvements, since 1987 there has been a noticeable increase in the share devoted to increasing capacity (from 10 percent to 22 percent). This is reflected in the share of industrial investment in construction, which fell by 25 percent from 1980 to 1986 but grew by 30 percent in the two years following.

In the other sectors, investments increased by 8 percent a year in trade and services, 8 percent in construction, and 8 percent in agriculture. Finally, the increases did not exceed 2 percent in the large public enterprises where higher investments in aircraft barely offset the decline in investment in nuclear energy.

FOREIGN TRADE AND THE CURRENT ACCOUNT
BALANCE

It has been noted above that the contribution of foreign trade to economic growth has improved over time in France. Nevertheless, the trade deficit has increased, from $9 billion in 1987 to $13 billion in 1990, reflecting a deterioration of the terms of trade. At the same time, interest attaches to changes in regard to various product groups.

For the ninth consecutive year (except for 1986) the agriculture and food processing product group has seen its trade surplus increase, most recently from $6.6 billion in 1988 to $7.8 billion in 1990; the corresponding figure was $2.8 billion in 1984. This result is explained by increases in the exports of cereals as well as of processed food.

In turn, the trade deficit in energy rose from $11.2 billion in 1988 to $12.5 billion in 1990, due to increases in oil prices followed by earlier declines. In 1984, the deficit of the energy sector was $21.4 billion. The most preoccupying changes have been the shift from surplus to deficit, and the subsequent increase in the deficit, of trade in manufactured goods. While France had a trade surplus of $11.8 billion in this product group in 1984, this gave place to a deficit of $6.4 billion in 1988 and $9.2 billion in 1990. This deficit is composed of a military surplus of $4.2 billion and a civilian deficit of $13.4 billion.

Within the manufacturing sector, the largest increase in the trade deficit occurred in intermediate products, from $3.7 billion in 1989 to $6.1 billion in 1989. Also, the trade surplus in automobiles declined from $4.0 billion to $2.8 billion as against an increase in the surplus in professional equipment from nil to $1.3 billion. Little change occurred in the other commodity categories; their 1983 trade balances were consumer durables, $-2.8 billion; consumer nondurables $-4.3 billion; and other products, $1.6 billion.

Taking manufactured exports and imports separately, we find that France has continued to lose export market shares. While some declines in these losses occurred in 1988 and 1989, they accelerated in 1990.

At the same time, France has a relatively high income elasticity of import demand (the ratio of the import growth rate to the rate of economic growth). This elasticity has averaged 2.9 in recent years, exceeding the average of 2.5 for the Common Market countries. Thus, for every 1 percent increase in the gross domestic product, France's imports rise by nearly 3 percent.

Import increases have occurred across the board, including investment goods, intermediate products, consumer durables and nondurables and, more recently, automobiles. Thus, one cannot explain the rapid growth of imports by the demand for investment goods brought about by the rise in investment alone. At the same time, despite the expansion of investment, domestic capacity could not keep pace with demand. As a result the rate of capacity utilization reached 88 percent in 1990, surpassing the very high level of 85 percent attained in 1978.

France's trade deficit is more than compensated by the surplus in services that has amounted to $18 billion in 1990. Two-thirds of this total is represented by tourism, one-third by technology-related services, such as major infrastructural projects and technical cooperation. Nevertheless, with official and private transfers of $13 billion, France had a current account deficit of $8 billion in 1990.

France's foreign capital needs have increased further as a result of growing foreign direct investment. In 1988, outflows amounted to $12.8 billion as against inflows of $7.2 billion. In the first half of 1989, outflows reached $8.2 billion, nearly three times the amount of inflows of $3.2 billion.

While foreign direct investment brings benefits to France, it adds to its needs for foreign capital. These needs are supplied by the inflow of portfolio capital. The question arises, then, if these inflows may continue. More generally, the question is if France's foreign capital needs represent a constraint to economic growth.

A FOREIGN CONSTRAINT TO ECONOMIC GROWTH IN FRANCE?

In the 1970s, France had inflation rates of about 10 percent. Inflation reached 13 percent a year in 1982 as a result of the expansionary policies followed by the first socialist government. Inflation rates began to decline in 1983 when deflationary monetary and fiscal policies were adopted and wage indexation was brought to an end. Nevertheless, the decline in inflation proceeded at a slow rate and the exchange rate had to be repeatedly devalued because of inflation differentials between France and Germany.

The last devaluation occurred in September 1987 when inflation came down to 3 percent a year. In that year German inflation was 0.2 percent. Inflation differentials declined to 1.4 percent in 1988 and 0.8 percent in 1989. Still, there were runs on the franc as French current account deficits contrasted with German current account surpluses that rose from $15 billion in 1985 to $49 billion in 1986, and $55 billion in 1989.

The franc was defended by a high interest rate policy. Short-term French–German interest rate differentials were 4.3 percent in 1987 and 3.6 percent in 1988. These differentials were considered necessary in order to avoid a devaluation of the franc. Still, the French situation was considered precarious and it was suggested that France would have to accept lower growth rates it if wanted to maintain the parity of the franc.

The situation changed with reform measures taken in East Germany.

It soon became apparent that the eventual result would be the absorption of East Germany by West Germany. This, in turn, led to rising interest rates in West Germany (for short, Germany). Short-term interest rates rose from 4.3 percent in 1988 to 7.1 percent in 1989 and increased further to 9.3 percent in December 1990. Correspondingly, the interest differential between France and Germany declined to 2.3 percent in 1989 and to 0.8 percent in December 1990.

Also, the absorption of East Germany has favorably affected Germany's economic growth rates that reached 4.2 percent in 1990. High German growth rates, in turn, promote French economic growth by creating demand for French products. This is apparent in the decline of the German current account surplus to $49 billion in 1990, estimated to decrease further to $30 billion in 1991.

Thus, while the policies applied by the Rocard Government improved the French economic situation, the position of the franc remained precarious until the East German events. It is, then, the *deus ex machina* of political liberalization in East Germany that strengthens the French economic position and eases the balance-of-payments constraint.

But not everything is favorable for France. The rising interest rates in Germany, associated with a budget deficit amounting to 5 percent of GDP, keep French interest rates high. This, in turn, limits French investment and growth.

Also, along with other industrial countries, France has been unfavorably affected by increases in oil prices associated with the Middle East crisis. The rise in oil prices from $17 a barrel to $27 a barrel adds $10 billion to the French annual import bill.

Increases in oil prices have also created uncertainty for French business decisions, leading to cutbacks in production and investment plans. Thus, while in July 1990 it was estimated that gross domestic investment in France would rise by 4.2 percent in 1990, the revised figure is 3.4 percent. Also, the estimated growth of GDP has been revised from 3.1 percent to 2.5 percent.

These uncertainties will disappear once the Middle East situation is resolved. In that event, the dominant factor will be the absorption of East Germany by West Germany, with its favorable effects on the French balance of payments.

Table 18.3 Unemployment rates

	1985	1986	1987	1988	1989	1990
France	9.7	10.2	10.4	10.5	10.0	9.4
Germany	7.1	7.2	6.4	6.2	6.2	5.6
Italy	9.4	9.6	10.5	10.9	11.0	10.9
United Kingdom	11.7	11.2	11.2	10.3	8.5	6.9

Source: OECD, *Economic Outlook*, December 1990, Table R18.

CHANGES IN EMPLOYMENT AND UNEMPLOYMENT

The deflationary policies followed in France after 1983 contributed to higher unemployment. As shown in Table 18.3, unemployment rates increased from 9.7 percent in 1985 to 10.5 percent in 1988. Even larger increases are shown if comparisons are made with 1981 when the unemployment rate was 7.4 percent.

These results compare unfavorably with Germany and the United Kingdom where unemployment rates declined from 7.1 percent to 6.2 percent from 11.7 percent to 10.3 percent, respectively, between 1984 and 1988. Only Italy matched France's poor performance.

Unemployment increased in France as sufficient employment opportunities were not created. Employment declined in absolute terms between 1981 and 1985 and increased slowly afterwards. And increases in employment between 1985 and 1987, averaging 0.2 percent a year, did not match the growth of the labor force.

Increases in employment accelerated after 1987. Employment grew by 0.8 percent in 1988 and by 1.0 percent in 1989. Employment growth was particularly strong in the services sector. But employment increased also in manufacturing after a 15-year decline. Nevertheless, increases in employment were smaller than in Germany and in the United Kingdom.

Also, the growth of employment was not accompanied by a similar decline in the number of unemployed. While 240 000 new jobs were created in 1989, the number of registered unemployed fell by only 60 000. The principal reason for the discrepancy was the increase in the labor force that is estimated to have grown by 160 000 in 1989.

As a result of these changes, unemployment rates declined from 10.5 percent in 1988 to 10.0 percent in 1989 and, again, to 9.4 percent in 1990. These decreases have not matched the decline experienced in the United Kingdom, where the rate of unemployment fell from 10.3 percent in 1988 to 6.9 percent in 1990. It compares favorably, however, with the decrease from 6.2 percent to 5.6 percent in Germany and the maintenance of unemployment at 10.9 percent in Italy, between 1987 and 1989.

Future decreases of unemployment in France will be mitigated, however, by the continued growth of the labor force. Assuming nil migration, the labor force would rise by 160 000 in 1990 and by 150 000 in subsequent years. At the same time, France has experienced immigration in recent years that may well continue in the future.

In view of the increases in the labor force, France needs rapid economic growth in order to further reduce unemployment. This, in turn, requires a high rate of investment. But investment can increase only if profits are adequate.

At the same time, a solution must be found to the "mismatch" problem. While unemployment remains high, there is unfulfilled demand for technical and skilled labor. This is apparent in the number of unfilled vacancies that increased by 14 percent in 1988 and by 20 percent in 1989.

MONETARY AND FISCAL POLICIES

For 1988 and 1989, the Banque de France set a target range of 4 to 6 percent for the broadly defined money supply (M2). In fact, the money supply increased by 4.0 percent in 1988 and 4.3 percent in 1989, compared with 4.2 percent in 1987. For 1990, the target range has been set at 3.5 to 5.5 percent. Actual increases were 2.1 percent between September 1989 and September 1990.

It should be added, however, that the narrowly defined money supply (M1) has shown a relatively steady upward trend since March 1988, and between September 1989 and September 1990 it increased by 4.1 percent. The opposite pattern was exhibited by savings that are part of M2 but not of M1. This can be attributed to the moderate returns on savings as well as to the attractiveness of financial markets.

More rapid increases have been experienced in the overall liquidity of the economy, although a deceleration is shown if comparisons are made with 1987. Thus, liquidity increased by 11.8 percent in 1987, 8.7 percent in 1988, 8.8 percent in 1989, and 5.7 percent between

September 1989 and September 1990. At the same time, the growth of domestic credit was maintained at 12 percent a year.

The budget deficit in France was nil in 1980, but increased rapidly as the first socialist government followed expansionary policies. It was 1.9 percent of the gross domestic product in 1981, 2.8 percent in 1982, and 3.1 percent in 1983. With changes in policies, the deficit declined in subsequent years, reaching 1.9 percent in 1987, 1.8 percent in 1988, 1.7 percent in 1989, and 1.2 percent in 1990.

Recent decreases in the budget deficit corresponded to government forecasts. This outcome conceals, however, the fact that increases in revenues were above expectations and financed unbudgeted increases in expenditure, especially the rise in public sector remunerations. This has halted the reduction in the share of budgetary expenditures that fell from 52.2 percent of GDP in 1985 to 50.3 percent in 1988.

The share of budgetary expenditures is relatively high in France. The 50.3 percent figure for 1988 compares with 46.6 percent in Germany and 40.7 percent in the United Kingdom. Among the major EC countries, it is only exceeded by 50.8 percent in Italy.

The high share of budgetary expenditures necessitated high taxes in France. In 1988, the ratio of tax revenue to GNP was 47.1 percent in France compared with 43.7 percent in Germany, 40.7 percent in the United Kingdom and 39.9 percent in Italy. This represents considerable increases over 1980, when the ratio was 44.5 percent in France; it was 44.7 percent in Germany, 40.5 percent in the United Kingdom, and 32.9 percent in Italy.

POLICY RECOMMENDATIONS

France needs a rapid growth of production capacity to increase exports and to limit the rise of imports while providing employment for its expanding labor force. The high rate of capacity utilization (88 percent) increases the urgency of raising investment.

In fact, while the trough of 19.3 percent has been surpassed as the share of gross domestic investment in GDP reached 20.3 percent in 1988, this is much below the 23.0 percent figure for 1980. The comparisons with the early 1970s are even more unfavorable, since the share of investment was between 25 and 30 percent of GDP at that time.

Part of the problem lies in the relatively low profitability of French enterprises that is about one-third lower than in the early 1970s. Another constraining factor has been household savings. While savings accounted for 20 percent of disposable income in the early 1970s, the ratio was 12.2 percent in 1989.

Household savings may be increased by providing tax incentives to savings. In order to channel private savings to business investments, the incentive should be linked to stock and bond purchases. Such incentives, associated with the name of Monory, had favorable effects on private savings and business investment under the Barre Government of 1976–81.

At the same time, in order to avoid an outflow of savings, differences among EEC countries in regard to tax withholdings on interest on government bonds and in regard to interest on deposits would need to be reduced. These taxes are 16 percent and 35 percent, respectively, in France or the marginal income tax rates, whichever is higher. By comparison, there are no taxes on interest or government bonds in Germany and Luxembourg and on interest on deposits in Luxembourg while in Germany a 25 percent tax is levied on interest on deposits.

There would further be need to reduce the dissaving of the French government. Rather than the existing deficit, it would be desirable to aim at the surpluses of the early 1970s. The financing of the budgetary deficit leads to crowding out as less financing is available for private uses. And, with deficit financing representing a demand for funds, it also raises interest rates, thereby adding to the burden of private business. In turn, a surplus can be re-lent to business investors.

One way to eliminate the budgetary deficit is to raise taxes. But as we have seen, the tax burden is higher in France than in the other major Common Market countries. Thus, one could not rely on increases in taxation to reduce the budget deficit in France. Rather, at the least, the taxation of business enterprises would need to be reduced. Correspondingly, there is need to lower budgetary expenditures as a percentage of the gross domestic product. More generally, the share of public consumption, financed in part by taxes and in part by bond issues, would need to be reduced.

Apart from Italy, public consumption increased much more rapidly in France than in the other major Common Market countries. Between 1980 and 1989, the increase was 25.3 percent in real terms in France, compared with 10.7 percent in Germany and 9.1 percent in the United Kingdom. The corresponding figure was 24.1 percent in Italy.

The growth of public consumption shows no sign of abating in France. While average increases declined from 3.0 percent in 1981–3 to 1.7 percent in 1984–6, they increased again to 2.4 percent in 1987–9. Similar increases are estimated for 1990.

The growth of public consumption has received little attention in France. Yet this lies behind the continued deficit in the government budget, which reduces the amount available for investment. It has also contributed to the deficit in the balance of payments. France would have to accept a substantial deceleration in the growth of public consumption, leading to a decline in the share of public expenditure in GDP, in order to increase the rate of savings and investment.

Raising private and government savings would contribute to higher investment in France. This objective would further be served by providing increased incentives for business enterprises to save and to invest. While business savings increased in recent years they still remain below the level reached before 1981.

Measures may further be taken to increase the competitiveness of business enterprises. Public sector firms should be given a greater degree of independence and be exposed more fully to competitive pressures. The enforcement of competition policy in the private sector should also be strengthened. Competition policy should extend to the nonmanufacturing sector, including the removal of entry barriers in certain service sectors, deregulation in housing and in the airline industry, the ending of enforced cross-subsidization in banking, and increasingly determining the allocation of funds by market forces in the financial sector.

Finally, reference may be made to the "mismatch" problem existing in the labor market. This would necessitate taking measures to encourage the formation of technical and skilled labor. The establishment of technical schools and tax benefits to training may serve this objective.

CONCLUSIONS

On the whole, the Rocard Government deserves a favorable judgment on the economic front. Aided by the expansion of investment, economic growth has accelerated while inflation has remained at a low level. Also, employment growth has accelerated and unemployment rates have declined.

The fly in the ointment has been the continued balance-of-payments deficit. This deficit has been due to losses in export market shares and the lack of sufficient domestic capacity to limit import growth. But, in the next few years, France will be helped by a *deus ex machina*, the absorption of East Germany by West Germany. Thus, one may not have to fear unfavorable developments in the balance of payments once the Middle East crisis is settled.

Looking beyond the next several years, however, France would need to carry out policy reforms to strengthen its economy. There is need in particular to promote household savings, to reduce public dissavings, and to increase business savings. This would require to reduce taxes on savings, to constrain the growth of public expenditures, to reduce business taxes, and to lower social charges. Also, competitive pressures would have to be increased throughout the economy. Finally, it would be desirable to promote the formation of technical and skilled labor.

Note

1. All data in this paper have been taken from the following sources: *Note de Conjoncture de l'INSEE*, December 1990; OECD, *Economic Outlook*, December 1990; and OECD, *Economic Surveys: France*, 1989/90. Figures for 1990 are estimates.

My Life Philosophy*

Bela Balassa

My life philosophy can be described at three levels. At one level it means that I try to make the best of any situation, whatever the circumstances. This goes from writing my first paper on economics in English while I was deported in Hungary between 1951 and 1953 to rebuilding my professional life after a serious cancer operation in August 1987.

At another level, my life philosophy refers to the importance I attach to personal freedoms, including the freedom of economic opportunity. In fact, I was exhilarated to find on arriving in the United States in April 1957 that as a foreigner I had no handicap in competing at the university and later for jobs.

Finally, my attachment to economic freedoms has led me to espouse a liberal economic philosophy, in the European sense. This philosophy has influenced my views on economic policies in developed, socialist and developing countries alike. But more about this later.

A BRIEF LIFE HISTORY

I was born on 6 April 1928 in Budapest. My father was an officer in the Hungarian army that meant high social standing on a very small income. Nonetheless, I was sent to the best schools and the education I received at the Cistercian Gymnasium remained a major asset in all my professional life.

Having finished high school in 1946. I simultaneously enrolled at the Law and Political Science Faculty of the University of Budapest and at the Foreign Trade Academy, completing both with honors. At the University, my interest soon turned to economics. I was much influenced in this by my mentor. Professor István Varga, with whom I worked at the University as well as at an Institute he directed. This

* Originally published in *American Economist*, Summer, 1989, pp. 16–23.

work, but not our relationship, ended in 1949 when Varga was pensioned under the Stalinist regime. In view of the changes at the University, it appeared safer for me to write my doctoral dissertation on sampling theory rather than on economics.

With my newly-minted doctorate, I went to the Construction Trust in Miskolc, the third largest Hungarian city, as a planner in May 1951. I soon became known to the director, József Bondor, who wanted to appoint me as head of planning. Then came, however, deportation from Budapest (that remained my domicile) for people of a particular social or political background, of which I was considered to be one. While I was not in Budapest on the night the deportation was to take place, when next day I appeared at Police Headquarters armed with a laudatory letter from Bondor, this was rejected and I was summarily taken to the train just before it departed for the eastern part of Hungary.

There followed three months of working in the cotton fields, a crop that represented a misuse of land in Hungary's climatic conditions. Fortunately, my parents were living and working on our land in the western part of Hungary, hence they escaped deportation, and I was allowed to join them while being confined to their village. I soon got a job as head of finances in an alcohol factory and stayed there until it was discovered that as a deportee I was not to do intellectual work.

The next year-and-a-half was a period that greatly strengthened my physique through work in the fields, in the forest, and in construction. It also brought a deepening of my intellectual interests. István Varga provided me with books on economics (Keynes was prescribed at the time in Hungary). I tried my hand in writing papers on economics, including comparisons of Karl Marx and John Stuart Mill as well as Marx and Keynes; the former subsequently saw the light of day in a revised form.[1] My first published paper in English was also on John Stuart Mill.[2]

During the deportation, I learned Italian (to read Pirandello and to listen to the Italian radio), in which I was helped by eight years of Latin in the Gymnasium. I also acquired a life-long taste in music, in particular opera (I still remember chancing unto Pelléas et Mélisande on the radio and recognizing it immediately for what it was).

Deportation came to a sudden end in June 1953 under the first Nagy government. By that time, József Bondor was heading a large construction trust in Sztalinváros (subsequently renamed Dunaujváros) and he hired me to be organizer of the Trust, later to become what might be called business manager. This was a unique opportunity since few former deportees were able to return to their old, or equivalent, jobs.

There followed a very pleasant period of three years. Interesting work, including considerable travel to the enterprises supervised by the Trust and weekends in Budapest, on a relatively high income. I also wrote two books, both of them on the construction industry. There was a fly in the ointment, however. I had nowhere to go, in terms of advancement, because of my social background. Thus, at 28 years of age, I had an excellent job without any possibility for further advancement.

On 23 October 1956 the Revolution broke out. With four engineers, I became a member of a committee that took over the Ministry of Construction and I was also to teach economics at the University with my mentor, István Varga.

At the Ministry, we started to think how to proceed. On 2 November, we called the Prime Minister's office and asked for a meeting over the weekend. We were told that the Prime Minister wanted to rest for the first time in weeks and we should see him on Monday. It was too late. On Sunday, 4 November, Russian troops regained Budapest. The rest is history.

On 18 November I left Budapest for Austria, where I arrived by travelling successively on truck, bicycle, and boat. It was the last night before the lake froze and I spent it under some cornstalks on the Austrian side of the border.

Armed with a letter of introduction from István Varga I went to Vienna, where I visited the Institute for Economic Research. I met there Professor Gottfried Haberler, spending his sabbatical in Vienna, who helped me to write an application to the Rockefeller Foundation. Haberler became a fatherly friend who cheered me on in my subsequent career.

I received one of the Foundation's postgraduate grants for Hungarian refugees and applied to Yale for graduate studies in economics. Haberler advised me to go to the United States and to choose Yale over the Institute for Graduate Studies in Geneva from where I received an invitation. My reason for selecting Yale among American universities was that Willy Fellner, a friend of István Varga, taught there. It turned out to be a good choice and Fellner became a guiding light in my studies and, subsequently, my daughter's godfather.

From Vienna I went to Salzburg and to Frankfurt, where I wrote and lectured on the Hungarian economy in German, a language that has since been largely pushed out by English and French. However, I had little chance to shore up my knowledge of economics although I would have badly needed it.

I had a curious background in economics, having been taught successively by a member of the German historical school, a follower of Veblen and Commons (István Varga), and a Marxist. I had no access to books published after the war and never read Chamberlin or Joan Robinson. I knew practically no microeconomics and Keynes was my only source for macroeconomics.

It should not be surprising that on reading Samuelson's introductory textbook, I found it very advanced. I consoled myself that since my interest was in international economics, I did not have to know the theoretical chapters. . . .

Life in the United States

It was with such naiveté that I arrived at Yale on 1 April 1957. Then came the cold shower and an understanding of what was required of me. Fortunately Keynes helped in the macro course and in May I successfully passed the examinations for the second semester.

In the summer, I took courses in microeconomics and in statistics at the Harvard summer school. As luck would have it, I had as my professor of microeconomics Franco Modigliani, the later Nobel Prize winner, whose rapid-fire Italian-accented English I understood better than my American fellow students. Statistics was taught by a young professor with a French-sounding name, Louis Lefeber. One day, however, I read on his lips that he was counting the number of students in Hungarian. Thus, I found at Harvard also the Hungarian connection.

Returning to Yale I completed a full year of studies and passed the comprehensives with distinction, an honor I shared with Sidney Winter who is now professor at Yale. At Yale, I specialized in international economics. I learned the subject by myself as I had an impossible teacher, a visitor for the year, in whose class I took only half a page of notes. But, going through the readings, I developed lecture notes myself that I used two years later when I began teaching.

But first the dissertation had to be written. My original intention was to write the thesis on economic integration. But, I wanted to write what became my first book in English on the *Hungarian Experience in Economic Planning* (1959). Having finished the book in about six months and having it accepted for publication by the Yale University Press, the idea occurred to me to use it as a dissertation. This was agreed to, and a committee was set up with the membership of Willy Fellner, Lloyd Reynolds, and Robert Triffin who accepted the finished product. It received the Addison Porter prize of Yale University.

This meant that I completed the requirements for the PhD in economics in less than two years and in June 1959 I received the degree. My children would like to have this certified as a world record but they have yet to contact the Guinness outfit to receive confirmation.

I stayed on at Yale as assistant professor to teach international trade and microeconomics, where my notes from Modigliani's course were of great help. I continued at Yale the following year, although I received an invitation from MIT, in the hope that I could teach the PhD course in international economics (at the time I was teaching the course in the master's program in international economic administration). This occurred soon afterwards when I returned from a year's leave at Berkeley. I was accompanied there by my wife, the former Carol Levy, a graduate student in international relations, whom I married in June 1960. She received her PhD at Johns Hopkins and has become an international economist with the Office of the US Trade Representative.

Before going to Berkeley, I finished my book on *The Theory of Economic Integration* (1961), which was translated into Spanish, Portuguese, Japanese, and Czech, and seems to have remained the standard book in the field. At Berkeley, I embarked on a large research project that became my *Trade Prospects for Developing Countries* (1964), also published in Spanish and Portuguese.

I edited *Changing Patterns in Foreign Trade and Payments* (1964), with two subsequent editions (1970 and 1978). I also gave a series of lectures at the Centro de Estudios Monetarios Latinoamericanos that were published under the title *Economic Development and Integration* (1965) simultaneously in English and Spanish.

After my return to Yale as associate professor, I wrote chiefly on international economics. Then came, in rapid succession, a paper on purchasing power parity;[3] the introduction of the concept of "revealed" comparative advantage;[4] a paper on effective protection,[5] simultaneously with Max Corden and Harry Johnson; the introduction of the concepts of intra-industry vs inter-industry trade and horizontal vs vertical specialization; and a new method for measuring trade creation and trade diversion.[6]

My next large research project was at the Council on Foreign Relations where I directed a group of studies on international trade policy. They were published under the title *Studies in Trade Liberalization* (1967) while my own book on the subject appeared under the title *Trade Liberalization among Industrial Countries: Objectives and Alternatives* (1967). When these books were published, I was already at Johns Hopkins where I was appointed Professor of Political Economy in 1966.

There came a period of dual existence as professor at Johns Hopkins and consultant to the World Bank over the next 21 years. I found this arrangement, combining teaching at Hopkins with research and policy advising at the World Bank, a happy one. Each of the two institutions may have benefited as my experience at the World Bank helped my teaching of international trade, development policy, and comparative systems at Hopkins, while keeping up with the economic literature for my teaching helped my work at the Bank.

THE DEVELOPMENT EXPERIENCE

At the World Bank I divided my time between my own research, research and policy advising, and advising developing countries. I particularly enjoyed the latter as it meant applying economic principles to practical situations. My first experience was in the Dominican Republic, followed by advising in Argentina, Chile, Mexico, Venezuela, Portugal, Turkey, Egypt, Morocco, Tunisia, Korea, and Taiwan.

My advice to developing countries was impregnated by my liberal economic philosophy. I advocated liberalizing trade and reducing state interventions in economic life. This came at a time when a dirigiste philosophy still held sway. Acclaimed writers like Gunnar Myrdal, Raul Prebisch, and Hans Singer called for import protection and state intervention.

In the older generation, Gottfried Haberler alone espoused a liberal economic philosophy in the development field. In 1966, when I wrote my first paper on development, I was practically alone with such a philosophy among economists of my generation. At the World Bank also, protection and state intervention were the order of the day.

Things changed slowly in subsequent years as more and more economists recognized the need for import liberalization and for reducing the extent of state interventions. Changes occurred also at the World Bank, which came to be regarded as one of the mainstays of a liberal economic philosophy in development.

In 1969 I was first asked to head a Bank economic mission. This led to the preparation of a report under the title *Policies for Economic Growth in Portugal* (1970). There followed a hiatus of nearly a decade but afterwards I led a Bank mission every two years. The reports of three of my missions, *Industrial Development Strategy in Thailand* (1980), *Turkey: Industrialization and Trade Strategy* (1982), and, originally written in French, *Morocco: Industrial Incentives and Export Promotion* (1984), were published by the Bank; two, *Tunisia: Industrial Sector Report* (1986) and *Development Strategy in Venezuela* (1988) remained confidential.

At the World Bank, I also directed several research projects. The findings of the first of these projects appeared under the title *The Structure of Protection in Developing Countries* (1971), also published in Spanish; those of the second were published under the title *Development Strategies in Semi-Industrial Economies* (1982). Other research projects on Western Africa and on Export Incentives resulted in articles and short monographs.[7]

Over the years, my country advisory reports and comparative papers were published successively in several volumes. They include *Policy Reform in Developing Countries* (1977), translated into Chinese and Spanish; *The Newly Industrializing Countries in the World Economy* (1981), translated into French and Spanish; and *Change and Challenge in the World Economy* (1985).

"The Process of Industrial Development and Alternative Development Strategies" was the subject of my Frank D. Graham Memorial Lecture at Princeton,[8] while the topic of my V.K. Ramaswami Memorial Lecture in New Delhi was "Policy Making for Economic Development."[9] International trade and economic development married in my work on the "stages approach" to comparative advantage[10] and, again, on policy responses to external shocks.[11]

My teaching also increasingly moved in the direction of development economics. On the graduate level, I continued with my international economics course but added a new course on development policies and programming. Subsequently, I also taught a graduate course on the theory of development.

My interests in development again came to the fore when I joined the Institute for International Economics as a visiting fellow while on sabbatical from Johns Hopkins. My first project there, carried out with three outstanding Latin American economists, was to write a book entitled *Toward Renewed Economic Growth in Latin American* (1986), simultaneously published in English, Spanish and Portuguese, in which the adoption of an outward-oriented development strategy with less government intervention was recommended. I stayed on at the Institute on a part-time basis afterwards, leading to the publication of *Adjusting to Success: Balance of Payments Policy in the East Asian NICs* with John Williamson (1987), translated into Chinese.

THE FRENCH CONNECTION

For centuries, Hungarians looked to Paris as the center of the universe. Apart from French culture, they were attracted to the French political philosophy, and they regarded France as a counterweight to Germany (after the Second World War it was said in newspapers that Hungarians now look to Moscow but this was not taken seriously).

My own interest in France goes back to reading French literature while in high school. It was followed by the preparation of an anthology of French poetry – in the original and in Hungarian translation – during my first year at the University. From François Villon onwards all major French poets were represented in the anthology.

Not surprisingly, after arriving in the United States, I soon explored possibilities to visit France. The opportunity presented itself in 1959 when I obtained travel documents to go to France in the summer. While I did some travelling, I spent most of my time in Paris that has become my favored city. I had an office at the Institut d'Economie Appliquée that published one of my first papers in its journal.[12]

In 1960, I spent my honeymoon in France, with a side trip to Italy. We visited friends of my wife whom she met under the Experiment in International Living Program a few years earlier. At 18 years of age, she wrote on the application form that she liked to play tennis and was chosen by a family that had a tennis court – a rare case in France. They became her French family who subsequently also acquired a swimming pool.

I was well-received by Carol's French family and we went back there every year; first by ourselves and later with our children, Mara born in 1970 and Gabor born in 1972. We stayed with the family that originally welcomed Carol, Aymé Bernard, now 94, an amazingly intelligent and knowledgeable man and his charming wife. We also developed lifelong friendships with people of our age who had summer homes on the same property. And, we bought a house there ourselves in 1985, helped by a dollar worth 9.50 French francs at the time, as one of our friends moved to the château of his deceased parents.

But France was not all vacation for me. In 1963 I spent a sabbatical semester in Paris at CEPREL, a research institute, where I studied French planning. This led to the publication of a paper entitled "Whither French Planning?"[13] where I correctly predicted its demise following entry into the Common Market. In another paper, "Planning in an Open Economy,"[14] I emphasized the incompatibility of planning and full participation in international trade.

Paris was not only a place of intellectual pursuits for me. It was also a culinary delight. After exploring many bistros with my wife and discussing their merits with my friends, it was suggested that I write a culinary guide. This I did under the title "A Primer in Culinary Economics or How to Maximize the Culinary Utility of the Dollar in Paris." The first edition, prepared in 1969, covered 20 restaurants with one page each; in the subsequent seven editions figured 25 restaurants with two pages each. The eighth edition of the guide also appeared in print.[15]

In 1970 I returned to Paris on sabbatical to teach at the Université de Paris IX (Dauphine). I also started writing on the French economy and in 1979 the French translation of my paper "The French Economy under the Fifth Republic, 1958–1978"[16] received the Prix Rossi of the Académie des Sciences Morales et Politiques, which gave me the title Lauréat de l'Institut. In subsequent years, I wrote annually a paper for the French review *Commentaire*, the English versions of which were published in *The Tocqueville Review*.

In my papers, I emphasized the need to liberalize the French economy which has been the direction taken in subsequent years. I also called for improving competitiveness, using the exchange rate and incentives to investment activity, as well as to research and development, as instruments.

At the same time, I started teaching mini courses in France. I began at the Institut d'Etudes Politiques (customarily called Sciences-Po) and continued at the Université de Paris I (Sorbonne–Panthéon) and at the Université de Clermont-Ferrand. My subjects were international trade and development economics.

In 1984, I travelled to Kiel in Germany to receive the Bernhard Harms Prize in International Economics at the Institute for World

Economics of the University of Kiel. My prize lecture was entitled "The Economic Consequences of Social Policies in the Industrial Countries,"[17] a subject that is of particular importance for France. In fact, my paper was translated into French.

MY HUNGARIAN RELATIONS

I did not return to Hungary between 1956 and 1968. During this period my mother died in an automobile accident but my father was still alive; he died in 1988.

In 1968, I was invited officially to Budapest. I gave a public lecture at the Karl Marx University of Economics that was chaired by two former ministers. The lecture was announced in the Communist Party newspaper and was well-attended.

In subsequent years, I returned to Hungary at least once a year to lecture and to participate in conferences. On these occasions I usually met with the Ministers of Planning and of Finance and had discussions with leading academic and governmental economists. I published several papers in Hungarian economic journals, which also appeared in English.[18]

In my discussions and papers I emphasized the need for continuing with the reform effort and for carrying out adjustment measures to reduce Hungary's large external debt. The taking of such measures was unfortunately postponed until a much larger adjustment effort has become necessary.

My trips to Hungary provided opportunities to meet with relatives and friends. Apart from seeing my father, I particularly cherished the meetings with my economist friends and with my former co-workers in Dunaujváros for whom my visit provided an occasion to get together.

Every two years I took my children to Hungary to visit Budapest and to spend a few days at Lake Balaton where my father joined us. My wife also came with us when her work permitted.

My children very much enjoyed these trips. While they had no common language with my father (the children speak English and French and my father Hungarian, German, and Italian), they were linked by strong feelings that obviate the need for verbal communication. In fact, just like the yearly stays in France, the trips to Hungary became part of my children's life.

EPILOGUE AND PROLOGUE

This is an epilogue as my 30-year career in economics described here came to an end with my cancer operation of 3 August 1987. It is also a prologue because it describes my activities as they have developed after the operation.

On 30 July 1987 I was diagnosed to have had neck and head cancer. This came as a complete surprise. Not only did I not have any warning signs but I had a complete physical check-up in June. Also, I gave up the sporadical smoking of my youth a long time ago and was a moderate consumer of alcohol.

The cancer was very far advanced. I overheard an intern saying that I was on the very limit where an operation was still possible. In fact, because of the advanced stage of the cancer, I was admitted to the Johns Hopkins University Hospital on an emergency basis and was operated on two days later. It involved removing part of my jaw, my palate and part of my tongue. It necessitated putting a piece of steel in my jaw and transplanting a flap from my left breast. My neck was also operated on and I often have the feeling of having a collar inside of it.

The operation, which took 13 hours, was performed by Dr John Price, an outstanding surgeon at the Johns Hopkins Hospital, who considers it his masterwork. I spent five weeks at the hospital, partly because of pneumonia I contracted there. During my stay I had the daily visits of my wife and children whose support has been of immense benefit since the operation.

My wife and daughter also often accompanied me on daily visits for radiotherapy to the Johns Hopkins Hospital over a seven-week period. On other visits friends and students drove me there. The radiotherapy necessitated removing one-third of my teeth, fortunately from the back of my mouth. It also gave me dryness of the mouth that requires using artificial saliva on a regular basis.

I cannot swallow and have to take nourishment through a gastro-ostomy tube. I was also given a tracheostomy tube that was removed in December 1987 but reinstated a few days afterwards as I developed a life-threatening breathing problem. It is scheduled to be removed by the first anniversary of my operation.

My inability to swallow brings to an end my writing of the culinary guide and removes one of the pleasures of life. Because of the danger of infection around the tube I cannot swim either, thus ending another of my pleasures: daily swimming of a kilometer which I rarely ever missed. Also, movement in my left arm is impaired so that I have some difficulty in putting on a coat.

More importantly for my professional career, my speech is impaired. This brings to an end leading Bank missions to developing countries, creates difficulties in day-to-day contacts, and does not permit me to lecture. I have continued directing a dissertation seminar at Johns Hopkins and next year I am to give a graduate seminar on development policies, relying on notes distributed to the students and having students make presentations.

Nevertheless, following the operation I started anew my professional life. At the World Bank I completed the report on Venezuela that was referred to above. I also finished a book, written with Luc Bauwens, on *Changing Patterns of Trade in Manufactured Goods: An Econometric Investigation* (1988) and collected comparative papers and country advisory reports written between 1985 and 1987 in a volume entitled *New Directions in the World Economy* (1989). Furthermore, I wrote several papers on varied subjects in development.

My work at the World Bank involves writing papers and commenting on papers written by others as well as reports by the economics staff. Also, I was given responsibility for reviewing submissions to the new Working Paper series at the Bank.

I continue part-time at the Institute for International Economics. Following my operation I completed, with Marcus Noland, a book on *Japan in the World Economy* (1988). I also started work on a Pacific project that deals with the developing countries of the area. And, I am organizing a conference on *Europe 1992* to examine the measures to be taken to complete the internal market of the European Community.

I am also resuming travel although this is made difficult by having to carry cans of liquid food and a variety of paraphernalia necessary for mouth care that requires about an hour a day. Consultations at the OECD and OECD Development Centre in June will be followed by trips to Middlebury, Geneva, and New York to deliver papers. In fact, the papers will be read by my wife while I will intervene in the discussion stage.

The continuation of these activities will depend on future developments regarding my health. At the time of the operation, I was told that the probability of recurrence of the cancer was 80 percent. This probability however declines rapidly as time progresses. It is 50 percent one year after the operation and 35 percent two years later. I sometimes feel as if I am living on borrowed time.

My Life Philosophy   465

Notes

1. "Karl Marx and John Stuart Mill," *Weltwirtschaftliches Archiv*, Band 83, Heft 2, 1959, pp. 147–55 (This and all papers cited below have been written by the author).
2. "John Stuart Mill and the Law of Markets," *Quarterly Journal of Economics*, May 1959, pp. 263–74.
3. "The Purchasing Power Parity Doctrine: A Reappraisal," *Journal of Political Economy*, December 1964, pp. 384–96.
4. "Trade Liberalization and 'Revealed' Comparative Advantage," *Manchester School*, May 1965, pp. 99–121.
5. "Tariff Protection in Industrial Countries: An Evaluation," *Journal of Political Economy*, December 1965, pp. 573–94.
6. "Trade Creation and Trade Diversion in the European Common Market," *Economic Journal*, March 1967, pp. 1–21.
7. Cf. e.g. "The 'Effects Method' of Project Evaluation," *Oxford Bulletin of Economics and Statistics*, November 1976, pp. 219–32 and "Export Incentives and Export Growth in Developing Countries: An Econometric Investigation" (with E. Voloudakis, P. Pylaktos, and S.T. Suh), Washington, DC, World Bank Development Research Department Discussion Paper No. 159, February 1986.
8. *Essay in International Finance*, No. 141, December 1980.
9. *Indian Economic Review*, vol 23, no. 1, January–June 1988, pp. 27–43.
10. "A 'Stages Approach' to Comparative Advantage," in Irma Adelman, ed., *Economic Growth and Resources*, Vol. 4, National and International Issues, London, Macmillan, 1971, pp. 121–56.
11. "The Newly-Industrializing Developing Countries After the Oil Crisis," *Weltwirtschaftliches Archiv*, Band 117, Heft 1, 1981, pp. 142–94.
12. "La théorie de la firme socialiste," *Economie Appliquée*, July–December 1959, pp. 535–70.
13. *Quarterly Journal of Economics*, November 1965, pp. 537–54.
14. *Kyklos*, 1966(3), pp. 383–410.
15. *The Tocqueville Review*, 1986/87, pp. 377–415.
16. *Revue Economique*, November 1979, pp. 939–71.
17. Institute for World Economics at the University of Kiel, June 1984.
18. Cf. e.g. "The Economic Reform in Hungary," *Economica*, February 1970, pp. 1–22; "The Economic Reform in Hungary Ten Years After," *European Economic Review*, December 1978, pp. 245–68; and "The 'New Growth Path' in Hungary," *Banca Nazionale del Lavoro, Quarterly Review*, December 1985, pp. 347–77.

Name and Author Index

Subject Index